STRE

Maidstone

Chatham, Gillingham, Rochester

First published 2007 by

Philip's, a division of
Octopus Publishing Group Ltd
2–4 Heron Quays
London E14 4JP

First edition 2007
First impression 2007

ISBN-10 0-540-09146-4
ISBN-13 978-0-540-09146-1

hotographic acknowledgements:
'III and IX Stewart Cocking

rinted by Toppan, China

Contents

II **Key to map symbols**

III **Key to map pages**

IV **Route planning**

VIII **Visitor Attractions**

2 **Street maps** at 4½ inches to 1 mile

108 **Index**

127 **List of numbered locations**

Key to map symbols

Roads

12 **Motorway** with junction number

A42 **Primary route** – dual/single carriageway

A42 **A road** – dual/single carriageway

B1289 **B road** – dual/single carriageway

Through-route – dual/single carriageway

Minor road – dual/single carriageway

Rural track, private road or narrow road in urban area

Path, bridleway, byway open to all traffic, road used as a public path

Road under construction

Pedestrianised area

Gate or obstruction to traffic restrictions may not apply at all times or to all vehicles

P P&R **Parking, Park and Ride**

Railways

Railway

Miniature railway

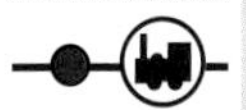

Metro station, private railway station

Emergency services

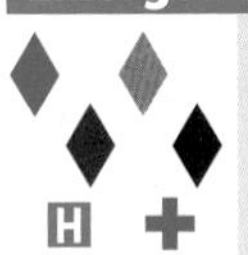

Ambulance station, coastguard station

Fire station, police station

H **Hospital, Accident and Emergency entrance to hospital**

General features

PO **Place of worship, Post Office**

Information centre (open all year)

Bus, coach station

Important buildings, schools, colleges, universities and hospitals

Woods, built-up area

Tumulus FORT **Non-Roman antiquity, Roman antiquity**

Leisure facilities

Camping site, caravan site

Golf course, picnic site

Boundaries

Postcode boundaries

County and unitary authority boundaries

Water features

Tidal water, water name

Non-tidal water – lake, river, canal or stream

Lock, weir

Scales

4½ inches to 1 mile 1:14 080

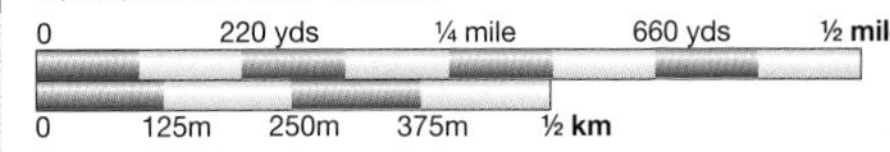

Adjoining page indicators The mapping continues on the page indicated by the arrow

Abbreviations

Acad	Academy	Mkt	Market
Allot Gdns	Allotments	Meml	Memorial
Cemy	Cemetery	Mon	Monument
C Ctr	Civic Centre	Mus	Museum
CH	Club House	Obsy	Observatory
Coll	College	Pal	Royal Palace
Crem	Crematorium	PH	Public House
Ent	Enterprise	Recn Gd	Recreation Ground
Ex H	Exhibition Hall	Resr	Reservoir
Ind Est	Industrial Estate	Ret Pk	Retail Park
IRB Sta	Inshore Rescue Boat Station	Sch	School
		Sh Ctr	Shopping Centre
Inst	Institute	TH	Town Hall/House
Ct	Law Court	Trad Est	Trading Estate
L Ctr	Leisure Centre	Univ	University
LC	Level Crossing	Wks	Works
Liby	Library	YH	Youth Hostel

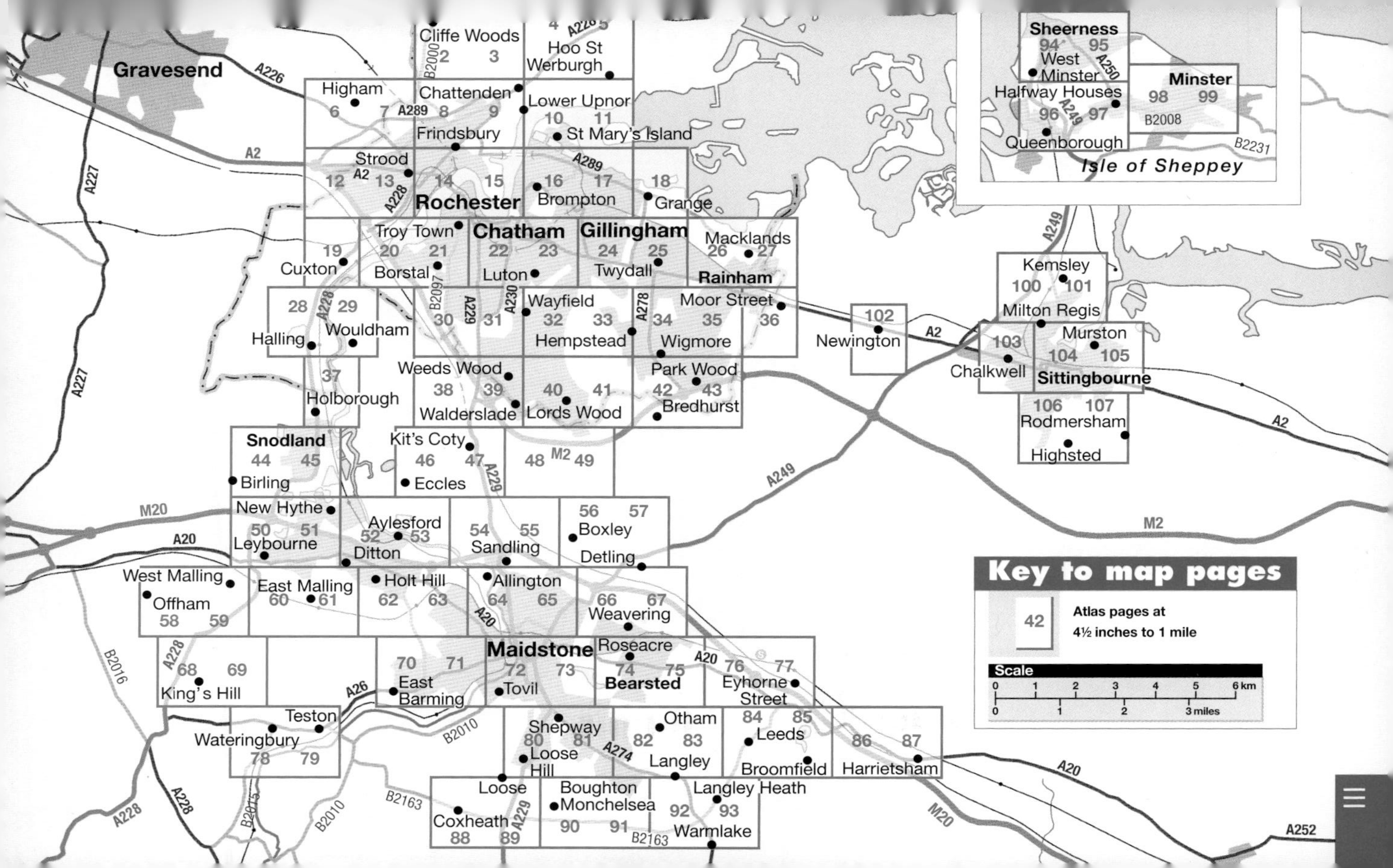

Key to map pages
42
Atlas pages at
4½ inches to 1 mile
Scale
0 1 2 3 4 5 6 km
0 1 2 3 miles
Gravesend
Cliffe Woods
Hoo St Werburgh
Higham
Chattenden
Lower Upnor
Frindsbury
St Mary's Island
Strood
Rochester
Brompton
Grange
Troy Town
Chatham
Gillingham
Macklands
Cuxton
Borstal
Luton
Twydall
Rainham
Wayfield
Hempstead
Moor Street
Wigmore
Halling
Wouldham
Holborough
Weeds Wood
Walderslade
Lords Wood
Park Wood
Bredhurst
Snodland
Birling
Kit's Coty
Eccles
New Hythe
Leybourne
Aylesford
Ditton
Sandling
Boxley
Detling
West Malling
Offham
East Malling
Holt Hill
Allington
Weavering
Maidstone
Roseacre
Bearsted
Eyhorne Street
King's Hill
East Barming
Tovil
Teston
Wateringbury
Shepway
Loose Hill
Otham
Langley
Leeds
Broomfield
Harrietsham
Loose
Coxheath
Boughton Monchelsea
Langley Heath
Warmlake
Newington
Kemsley
Milton Regis
Murston
Chalkwell
Sittingbourne
Rodmersham
Highsted
Sheerness
West Minster
Minster
Halfway Houses
Queenborough
Isle of Sheppey
A2
A20
A26
A226
A227
A228
A229
A230
A249
A250
A252
A274
A278
A289
M2
M20
B2000
B2008
B2010
B2015
B2016
B2097
B2163
B2231

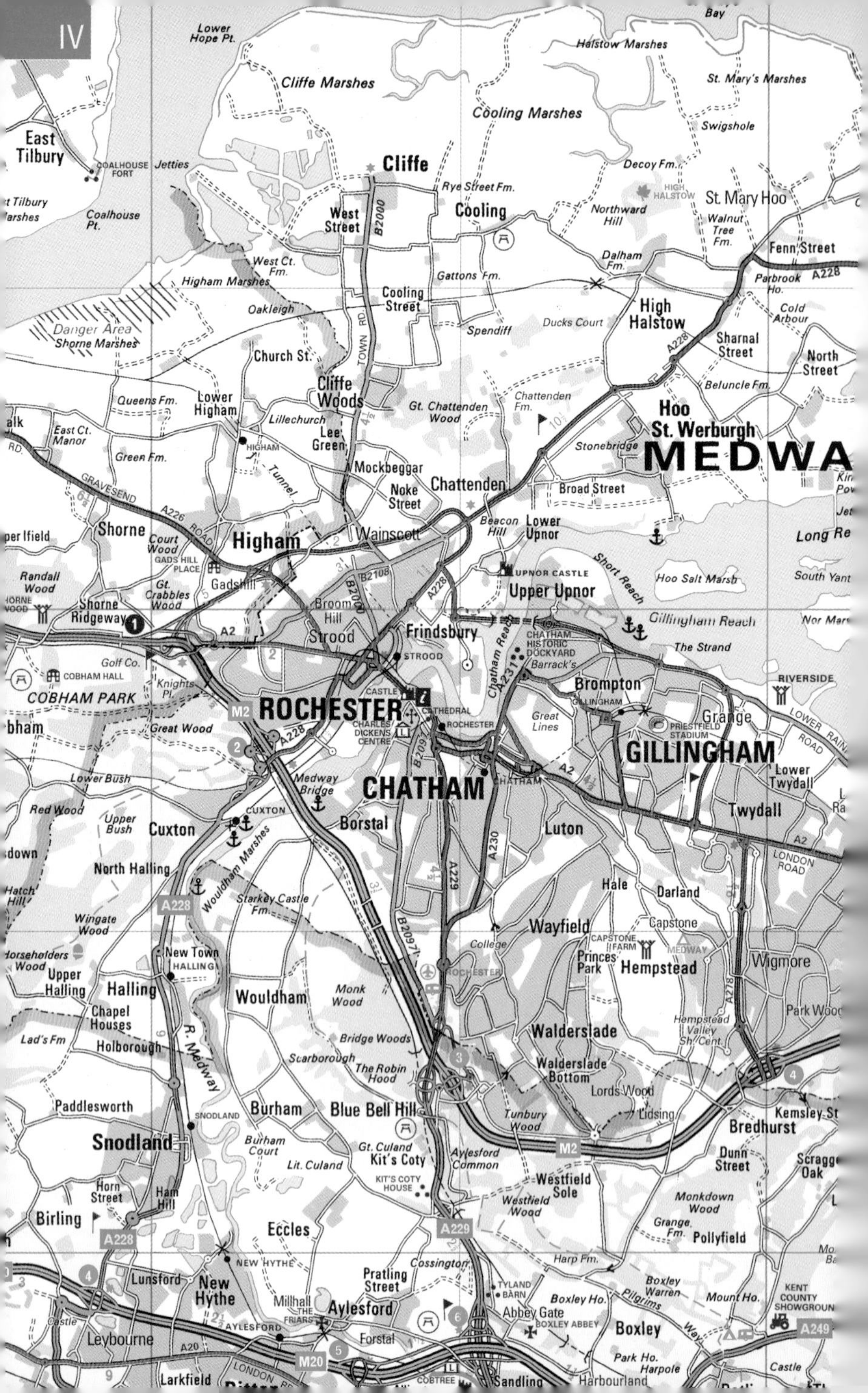
Lower Hope Pt.
Cliffe Marshes
Halstow Marshes
St. Mary's Marshes
Cooling Marshes
Swigshole
East Tilbury
COALHOUSE FORT
Jetties
Cliffe
Decoy Fm.
Rye Street Fm.
HIGH HALSTOW
St Mary Hoo
West Street
B2000
Cooling
Northward Hill
Walnut Tree Fm.
Coalhouse Pt.
Dalham Fm.
Fenn Street
West Ct. Fm.
Gattons Fm.
A228
Parbrook Ho.
Higham Marshes
Cooling Street
High Halstow
Cold Arbour
Oakleigh
Danger Area
Shorne Marshes
Spendiff
Ducks Court
Sharnal Street
North Street
Church St.
TOWN RD.
Chattenden Fm.
Belunce Fm.
Queens Fm.
Lower Higham
Cliffe Woods
Gt. Chattenden Wood
Hoo St. Werburgh
East Ct. Manor
Lillechurch
Lee Green
MEDWA
HIGHAM
Stonebridge
Green Fm.
Tunnel
Mockbeggar
GRAVESEND
Noke Street
Chattenden
Broad Street
A226
ROAD
Shorne
Court Wood
Higham
Wainscott
Beacon Hill
Lower Upnor
Long Re
GADS HILL PLACE
Gadshill
B2108
Hoo Salt Marsh
South Yant
Randall Wood
Gt. Crabbles Wood
Short Reach
UPNOR CASTLE
Upper Upnor
Shorne Ridgeway
Broom Hill
Gillingham Reach
Nor Mars
A2
Strood
Frindsbury
CHATHAM HISTORIC DOCKYARD
The Strand
Golf Co.
STROOD
Chatham Reach
Barrack's
COBHAM HALL
Knights Pl.
A231
Brompton
RIVERSIDE
COBHAM PARK
CASTLE
M2
ROCHESTER
CATHEDRAL
GILLINGHAM
Grange
CHARLES DICKENS CENTRE
ROCHESTER
Great Lines
PRIESTFIELD STADIUM
LOWER RAINHAM ROAD
Great Wood
A228
B2097
GILLINGHAM
Lower Bush
Medway Bridge
CHATHAM
CHATHAM
Lower Twydall
Red Wood
Upper Bush
CUXTON
Cuxton
Borstal
Luton
Twydall
A230
LONDON ROAD
North Halling
Wouldham Marshes
A229
Hale
Darland
Starkey Castle Fm.
A228
Capstone
Wingate Wood
Wayfield
College
CAPSTONE FARM
MEDWAY
B2097
Princes Park
Hempstead
Wigmore
New Town
HALLING
ROCHESTER
Upper Halling
Halling
Wouldham
Monk Wood
A278
Chapel Houses
Walderslade
Hempstead Valley Sh. Cent.
Park Wood
Lad's Fm
Holborough
R. Medway
Bridge Woods
Scarborough
The Robin Hood
Walderslade Bottom
Lords Wood
Paddlesworth
Burham
Blue Bell Hill
Tunbury Wood
Lidsing
Kemsley St
SNODLAND
Bredhurst
Snodland
Burham Court
Gt. Culand
Kit's Coty
Aylesford Common
M2
Dunn Street
Scragg Oak
Lit. Culand
KIT'S COTY HOUSE
Westfield Sole
Horn Street
Ham Hill
Westfield Wood
Monkdown Wood
Birling
Eccles
A229
Grange Fm.
Pollyfield
A228
Harp Fm.
NEW HYTHE
Cossington
Lunsford
New Hythe
Pratling Street
TYLAND BARN
Boxley Warren
Mount Ho.
KENT COUNTY SHOWGROUN
Boxley Ho.
Millhall
THE FRIARS
Aylesford
Abbey Gate
Pilgrims Way
Castle
AYLESFORD
BOXLEY ABBEY
Boxley
A249
Leybourne
Forstal
A20
M20
Park Ho.
Harpole
LONDON
Castle
COBTREE
Larkfield
Sandling
Harbourland

V
Route planning
Scale
0 1 2 3 4 km
Allhallows-on-Sea
Allhallows Marshes
Roas Bank
Binney Fm.
Yantlet Creek
Rose Court Fm.
The Flats
Allhallows
Isle of Grain
Grain
B2001
Lower Stoke
Stoke
A228
Power Sta.
OIL REFINERY
Stoke Saltings
Elphinstone Pt.
Medway
River
Bee Ness Jetty
E. Hoo Creek
Sharp Ness
Burntwick Island
Deadmans I.
Oakham Ness Jetty
Kethole Reach
Half Acre
Ham Ooze
Greenborough Marshes
Chetney Marshes
Long Reach
Millfordhope Marsh
Bayford
Ham Green
Barksore Marshes
Chetney Cotts.
Wetham Green
Horsham Marsh
Windmill Hill
Funton
Iwade
Tiptree Fm.
Culnells
Upchurch
Holywell
Otterham Quay
Lower Halstow
Callum Hill
Gore Fm.
Boxted
Gt. Norwood
Cambray Fm.
Howt Green
Hawes Wood
Lit. Norwood
Breach
Oak Hill
Bobbing
Newington
NEWINGTON
A2
Hartlip Hill
Hartlip
Newington Manor
Keycol
Lower Hartlip
Chestnut Street
Wormdale
Key Street
Chalkwell
Chesley
Services
Queen Down Warren
Danaway
Oad Street
Hill Green
Stockbury
Borden
SITTINGBOURNE
Harman's Corner
Sutton Baron
Hearts Delight
Parsonage Fm.
M2
Wrens Fm.
Tunstall
A249
Stiff Street
Norton Green
Deans Hill
Bredgar
Grove End
South Green
Silver Street
Woodstock
Deans Bottom
Broadoak
Squirrel Wood
Rumstead Ct.
Hazel Street
Old Forge
Manor Ho.
Swanton Ct.
Swanton Street
BREDGAR & WORMSHILL LT. RLY.
Bicknor
Milstead
Hucking
Admiral Wood
Bedmonton Ho.
Sheerness
Garrison Pt.
Blue Town
Pier
SHEERNESS ON SEA
Cheyney Rock
Barton's Pt.
Mile Town
Marine Town
Scrapsgate
A250
West Minster
Halfway Houses
Minster
ABBEY
QUEENSB'H RD.
B2008
QUEENBOROUGH
Queenborough
B2007
Furze Hill
Neats Ct.
LOWER ROAD
B2231
Brambledown
Rushenden
Wallend
Neatscourt Marshes
South Lees
Isle of Sheppey
Minster Marshes
Old Ho.
The Sheppey Crossing
Kingsferry Bridge
SWALE
Ridham Dock
ELMLEY
Elmley Island
Kings Hill Fm.
Elmley Marshes
Paper Mill
STA.
SITTINGBOURNE & KEMSLEY LIGHT RLY.
Kemsley
KEMSLEY
B2005
Milton Creek
Lit. Murston
Tonge Corner
Blacketts
Milton Regis
Mere Ct.
Murston
Cheke's Ct.
SITTINGBOURNE
Snipeshill
Teynham
Barrow Green
Frognal
Radfield
TEYNHAM
LONDON ROAD
Bapchild
Morris Ct.
Rodmersham
Sunderland
Nouds
Highsted
Highsted Forstal
Rodmersham Green
Dully Ho.
Bogle
Lynsted
Ludgate
Pitstock Fm.
Newbury
Lynsted Park
Dungate
Erriottwood
Mintching Wood
Bistock
Bluetown

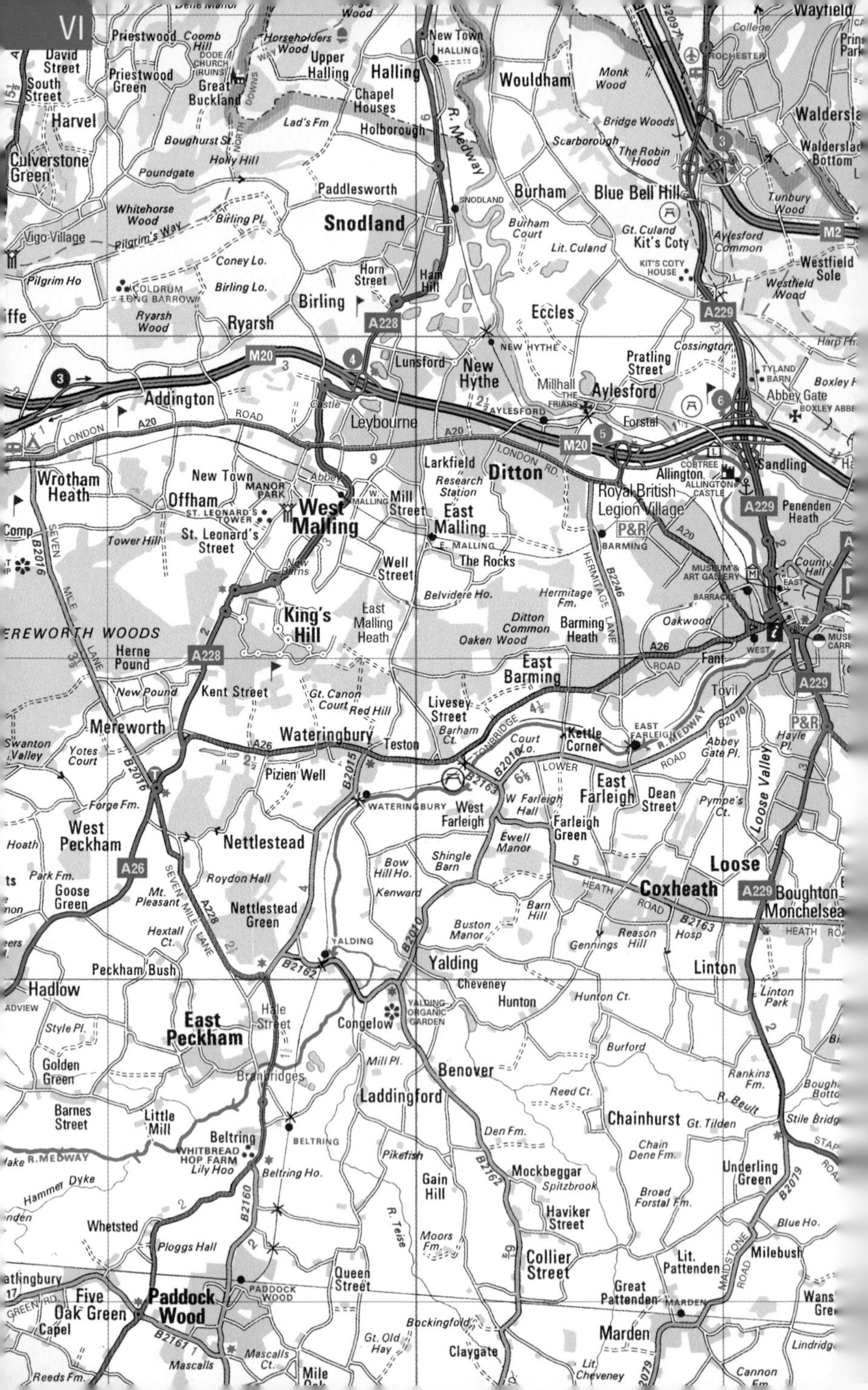
Priestwood
Coomb Hill
Horseholders Wood
Wood
New Town
HALLING
Wayfield
College
Prin Park
David Street
DODE CHURCH (RUINS)
Upper Halling
Halling
Wouldham
Monk Wood
ROCHESTER
South Street
Priestwood Green
Great Buckland
Chapel Houses
NORTH DOWNS
WAY
R. Medway
Harvel
Lad's Fm
Holborough
Bridge Woods
Walderslade
Boughurst St.
Scarborough
The Robin Hood
Walderslade Bottom
Culverstone Green
Holly Hill
Poundgate
Paddlesworth
Burham
Blue Bell Hill
Tunbury Wood
SNODLAND
M2
Whitehorse Wood
Birling Pl.
Snodland
Burham Court
Gt. Culand
Kit's Coty
Aylesford Common
Vigo Village
Pilgrim's Way
Lit. Culand
Westfield Sole
Coney Lo.
KIT'S COTY HOUSE
Pilgrim Ho
COLDRUM LONG BARROW
Birling Lo.
Horn Street
Ham Hill
Westfield Wood
Birling
Eccles
A229
Ryarsh Wood
Ryarsh
A228
NEW HYTHE
Cossington
Harp Fm
M20
Lunsford
New Hythe
Pratling Street
TYLAND BARN
Boxley
Addington
Castle
Millhall
THE FRIARS
Aylesford
Abbey Gate
AYLESFORD
BOXLEY ABBEY
LONDON
A20
ROAD
Leybourne
Forstal
Sandling
Wrotham Heath
New Town
Abbey
Larkfield
Ditton
LONDON RD.
COBTREE
Allington
ALLINGTON CASTLE
MANOR PARK
W. MALLING
Mill Street
Research Station
Royal British Legion Village
Penenden Heath
Offham
West Malling
East Malling
ST. LEONARD'S TOWER
P&R
BARMING
Comp
St. Leonard's Street
Tower Hill
E. MALLING
The Rocks
HERMITAGE LANE
B2246
SEVEN MILE LANE
B2016
New Barns
Well Street
MUSEUM & ART GALLERY
County Hall
Belvidere Ho.
Hermitage Fm.
BARRACKS
King's Hill
East Malling Heath
Ditton Common
Barming Heath
Oakwood
EREWORTH WOODS
Oaken Wood
Herne Pound
A26
WEST
Fant
East Barming
ROAD
Tovil
New Pound
Kent Street
Gt. Canon Court
Red Hill
Livesey Street
Mereworth
Wateringbury
Barham Ct.
Kettle Corner
EAST FARLEIGH
R. MEDWAY
Abbey Gate Pl.
Hayle Pl.
Swanton Valley
Yotes Court
Teston
TONBRIDGE
Court Lo.
B2010
Pizien Well
B2015
B2163
LOWER
ROAD
Loose Valley
East Farleigh
Dean Street
Pympe's Ct.
Forge Fm.
WATERINGBURY
W Farleigh Hall
West Farleigh
Farleigh Green
Hoath
West Peckham
Nettlestead
Ewell Manor
Park Fm.
Shingle Barn
Loose
Bow Hill Ho.
HEATH
ROAD
Coxheath
Boughton Monchelsea
Goose Green
Mt. Pleasant
Roydon Hall
Kenward
Barn Hill
HEATH
Nettlestead Green
Buston Manor
Reason Hill
B2163
Hosp
Hextall Ct.
SEVEN MILE LANE
A228
YALDING
Gennings
Linton
Yalding
Linton Park
Peckham Bush
B2162
Cheveney
Hadlow
ADVIEW
Hale Street
YALDING ORGANIC GARDEN
Hunton
Hunton Ct.
East Peckham
Style Pl.
Congelow
Burford
Golden Green
Mill Pl.
Benover
Bramridges
Rankins Fm.
Laddingford
Reed Ct.
R. Beult
Barnes Street
Little Mill
Chainhurst
Gt. Tilden
Stile Bridge
Beltring
Den Fm.
BELTRING
R. MEDWAY
WHITBREAD HOP FARM
Lily Hoo
Pikefish
Chain Dene Fm.
Underling Green
Hammer Dyke
Beltring Ho.
Mockbeggar
Spitzbrook
B2162
Gain Hill
Broad Forstal Fm.
B2160
B2079
R. Teise
Whetsted
Haviker Street
Blue Ho.
Moors Fm.
MAIDSTONE ROAD
Ploggs Hall
Milebush
Collier Street
Lit. Pattenden
Queen Street
Great Pattenden
Five Oak Green
Paddock Wood
PADDOCK WOOD
MARDEN
GREEN RD.
Capel
Bockingfold
B2167
Gt. Old Hay
Marden
Claygate
Mascalls Ct.
Lindridge
Mascalls
Reeds Fm.
Mile Oak
Lit. Cheveney
Cannon Fm.

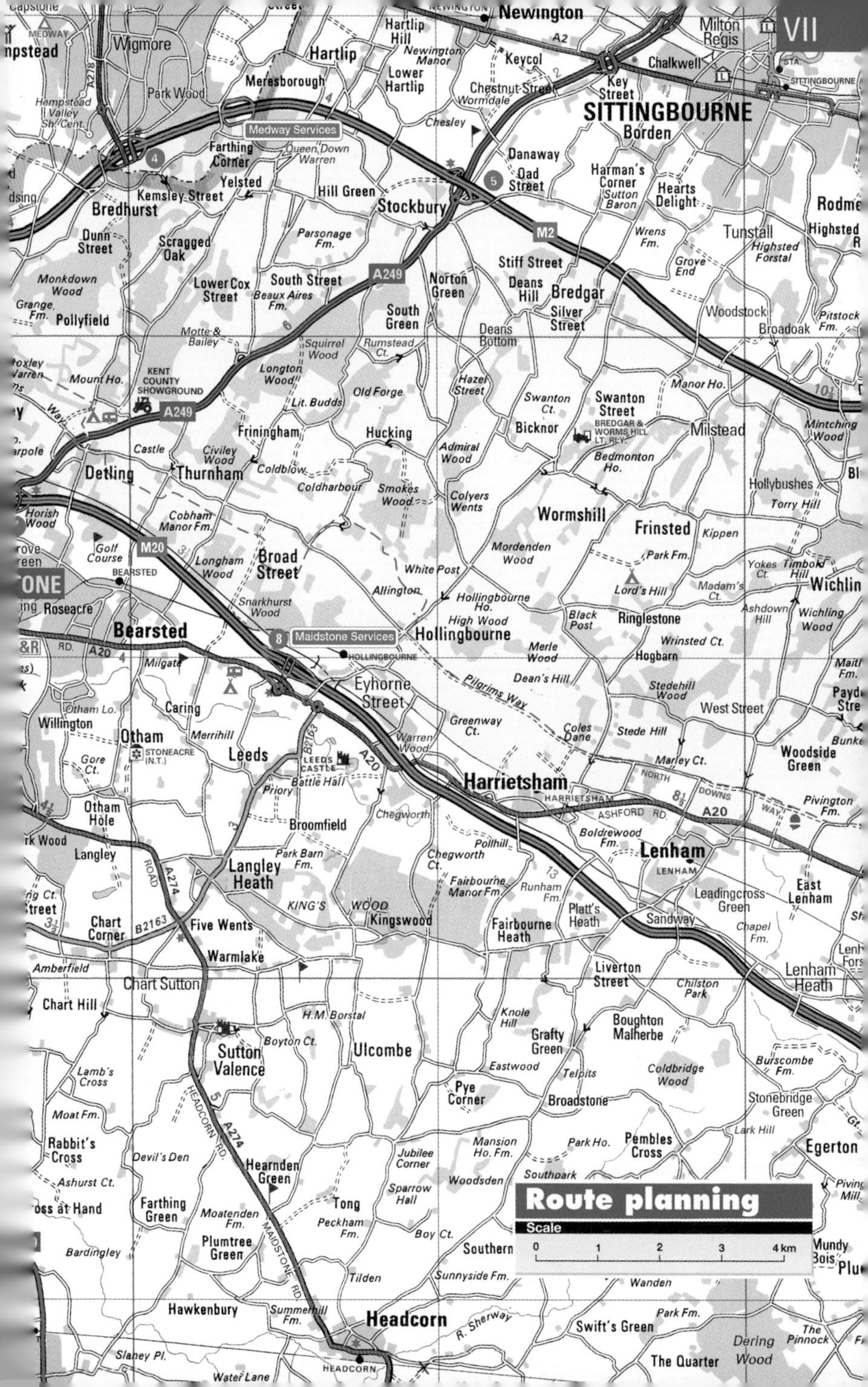
Newington
Hartlip Hill
Hartlip
Newington Manor
Keycol
A2
Milton Regis
Chalkwell
Key Street
SITTINGBOURNE
Wigmore
Meresborough
Lower Hartlip
Chestnut Street
Wormdale
Borden
Park Wood
Hempstead Valley Sh. Cent.
Medway Services
Chesley
Farthing Corner
Queen Down Warren
Danaway
Oad Street
Harman's Corner
Sutton Baron
Hearts Delight
Kemsley Street
Yelsted
Hill Green
Stockbury
Bredhurst
Rodmersham
M2
Highsted
Tunstall
Highsted Forstal
Dunn Street
Scragged Oak
Parsonage Fm.
Wrens Fm.
Grove End
Stiff Street
A249
Norton Green
Deans Hill
Bredgar
Monkdown Wood
Lower Cox Street
South Street
Beaux Aires Fm.
Grange Fm.
Pollyfield
South Green
Silver Street
Woodstock
Pitstock Fm.
Broadoak
Deans Bottom
Motte & Bailey
Squirrel Wood
Rumstead Ct.
Longton Wood
Hazel Street
Manor Ho.
Mount Ho.
KENT COUNTY SHOWGROUND
Old Forge
Swanton Ct.
Swanton Street
Lit. Budds
A249
Bicknor
BREDGAR & WORMS HILL LT. RLY.
Milstead
Mintching Wood
Frinningham
Hucking
Admiral Wood
Castle
Civiley Wood
Bedmonton Ho.
Detling
Thurnham
Coldblow
Coldharbour
Smokes Wood
Colyers Wents
Hollybushes
Torry Hill
Horish Wood
Cobham Manor Fm.
Wormshill
Frinsted
Kippen
Golf Course
M20
Longham Wood
Broad Street
Mordenden Wood
Park Fm.
BEARSTED
White Post
Yokes Ct.
Timbold Hill
Wichling
Lord's Hill
Madam's Ct.
Roseacre
Snarkhurst Wood
Allington
Hollingbourne Ho.
High Wood
Black Post
Ringlestone
Ashdown Hill
Wichling Wood
Bearsted
Maidstone Services
Hollingbourne
Merle Wood
Wrinsted Ct.
A20
HOLLINGBOURNE
Hogbarn
Milgate
Dean's Hill
Maiti Fm.
Eyhorne Street
Pilgrims Way
Stedehill Wood
Payden Street
Otham Lo.
Caring
Greenway Ct.
West Street
Willington
Coles Dane
Stede Hill
Otham
Merrihill
Warren Wood
Bunce
STONEACRE (N.T.)
Leeds
B2163
LEEDS CASTLE
Woodside Green
Gore Ct.
A20
Marley Ct.
Battle Hall
Harrietsham
NORTH DOWNS WAY
Priory
HARRIETSHAM
Otham Hole
Pivington Fm.
ASHFORD RD.
A20
Chegworth
Broomfield
Boldrewood Fm.
Pollhill
Lenham
Langley
Park Barn Fm.
Chegworth Ct.
LENHAM
ROAD
A274
Langley Heath
Fairbourne Manor Fm.
Runham Fm.
East Lenham
Platt's Heath
Leadingcross Green
KING'S WOOD
Kingswood
Chart Corner
B2163
Five Wents
Fairbourne Heath
Sandway
Chapel Fm.
Warmlake
Liverton Street
Lenham Heath
Amberfield
Chart Sutton
Chilston Park
Chart Hill
Knole Hill
H.M. Borstal
Boughton Malherbe
Grafty Green
Boyton Ct.
Sutton Valence
Ulcombe
Burscombe Fm.
Lamb's Cross
Eastwood
Telpits
Coldbridge Wood
Pye Corner
Broadstone
Stonebridge Green
Moat Fm.
HEADCORN RD.
A274
Mansion Ho. Fm.
Lark Hill
Rabbit's Cross
Devil's Den
Park Ho.
Pembles Cross
Egerton
Hearnden Green
Jubilee Corner
Southpark
Ashurst Ct.
Woodsden
Sparrow Hall
Pivington Mill
Farthing Green
Tong
Moatenden Fm.
Peckham Fm.
Route planning
Scale
0
1
2
3
4 km
Boy Ct.
Mundy Bois
Bardingley
Plumtree Green
MAIDSTONE RD.
Southern
Sunnyside Fm.
Wanden
Tilden
Hawkenbury
Summerhill Fm.
Headcorn
R. Sherway
Park Fm.
Swift's Green
Dering Wood
The Pinnock
Slaney Pl.
HEADCORN
The Quarter
Water Lane

Visitor Attractions

Museums and Galleries

Maidstone Carriage Museum *Mill Street, Maidstone* A unique collection of horse-drawn vehicles including Royal and state carriages, housed in the medieval stables of the Archbishops' Palace. 01622 602838 www.tour-maidstone.com 72 C3

Maidstone Museum & Bentlif Art Gallery★★ *St Faith Street, Maidstone* Housed in Chillington Manor. Rich in fine, applied and oriental art, ethnography, archaeology, natural, local and social history. Earth Heritage Gallery and Egyptian Mummy. 01622 602838 www.museum.maidstone.gov.uk 64 C1

Museum of Kent Life★ *Cobtree, Lock Lane, Sandling* Award-winning open air museum with exhibitions on life in Kent over the past 150 years. Herb, hop and kitchen gardens, farm animals, adventure playground and Britain's last traditional working oast house. Tea room. www.museum-kentlife.co.uk 01622 763936 54 B1

Rochester's Guildhall Museum★ *High Street, Rochester* Founded in 1897 in honour of Queen Victoria's diamond jubilee. The collections are a timeline of Medway's history. Two new rooms dedicated to Charles Dickens. www.medway.gov.uk 01634 848717 14 C2

Royal Engineers Museum *Prince Arthur Road, Gillingham* Tells the story of the Corps of Royal Engineers and military engineering. The Library holds 1860s photographs of Canada and World War I war diaries. www.remuseum.org.uk 01634 822839 16 B2

Sheerness Heritage Centre *Rose Street, Sheerness* Charting the history of the dockyard in Bluetown from the 17th century. www.sheernessheritagecentre.com 01795 663317 94 C3

Sittingbourne Heritage Museum *East Street, Sittingbourne* Local history museum, illustrating the past 3000 years of Sittingbourne. www.sittingbourne-museum.co.uk 104 C2

Six Poor Travellers' House *High Street, Rochester* Early Tudor almhouse museum with Dickens association. Served travellers for over 400 years. Dining room, sleeping quarters and herb garden. 01634 845609 14 C2

Historic Sites

Fort Amherst★ *Dock Road, Chatham* Constructed in 1756 to defend against a French invasion. Contains a maze of tunnels. 01634 847747 www.fortamherst.com 15 C1

The Friars★ *off High Street, Aylesford* England's first Carmelite priory in 1242, restored in 1949 by Carmelite monks. Tranquil gardens and medieval buildings. Now a pilgrimage centre, with pottery and upholstery workshops. www.thefriars.org.uk 01622 717272 52 C2

Gads Hill Place *Gravesend Road, Higham* Purchased by Charles Dickens in 1857. Where he wrote 'A Tale of Two Cities' and 'Great Expectations'. He died here in 1870. www.kentattractions.co.uk 01474 822366 6 C2

Kit's Coty House & Little Kit's Coty House *Blue Bell Hill, off A229, nr Maidstone* The ruins of two prehistoric burial chambers. Thought to be older than Stonehenge. www.tour-maidstone.com 47 A2 & A1

Leeds Castle★★ *off A20 Ashford Road, Leeds* Built on two islands in the middle of a lake. Surrounded by 500 acres of parkland and gardens. Duckery, aviary, maze, grotto and vineyard. www.leeds-castle.com 01622 765400 85 B3

Maidstone Town Hall *High Street, Maidstone* Georgian building dating from 1762. Now includes the Visitor Information Centre. Council chamber and prison cell, with guided tours available. 01622 602169 www.digitalmaidstone.co.uk 72 C4

Old Brook Pumping Station *Solomons Road, Chatham* Listed as an ancient monument, it houses original equipment and engines. www.oldbrookpumping.co.uk 01634 842059 22 C4

Rochester Castle★★ *Castle Hill, Rochester* A fine Norman castle with one of the tallest keeps in the country. It has a chequered history of destruction and rebellion. Guided tours available. 01634 402276 www.english-heritage.org.uk 14 C2

St Leonard's Tower *St Leonard's Street, West Malling* Remains of a free-standing Norman tower keep, built c.1080 by the Bishop of Rochester. www.english-heritage.org.uk 01732 870872 59 A3

Stoneacre House & Garden★ *Otham Street, Otham* A 15th century half-timbered Yeoman's house, restored by the National Trust. Cottage gardens and wildflower meadows. www.nationaltrust.org.uk 01622 862157 82 C3

Temple Manor *Knight Road, Strood, Rochester* Manor house of the Knights Templar, constructed during the 13th century. www.english-heritage.org.uk 14 A2 01634 827980

Upnor Castle★ *High Street, Upper Upnor, Rochester* An Elizabethan fort built in 1559, contains displays of ammunition and the battle against the Dutch in 1667. 01634 402276 www.medway.gov.uk 9 C2

▼ ***Rochester Castle***

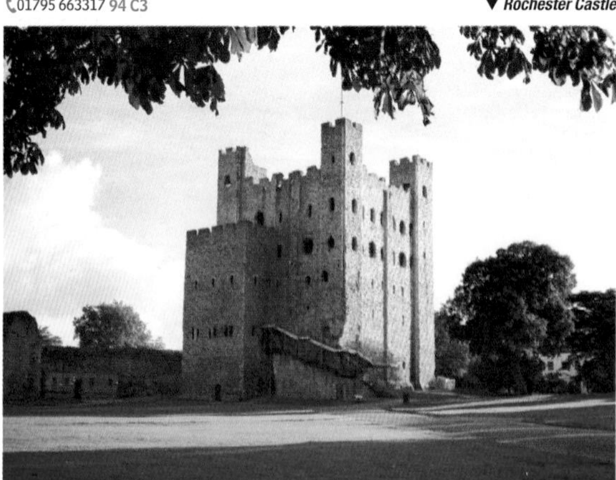

Places of Worship

All Saints Church *Mill Street, Maidstone* Rebuilt in the 14th century, becoming what has been called 'the grandest perpendicular church in England'. Medieval choir stalls and the Washington family memorial. 01622 843298 www.tour-maidstone.com 72 C3

Rochester Cathedral★★ *High Street, Rochester* The second oldest Cathedral in England, founded in 604AD by Bishop Justus. Gothic and Norman styles. Contains the magnificent 14th century Chapter Library door and crypt. www.rochestercathedral.org 01634 843366 14 C2

St Michael's Church *High Street, Sittingbourne* This attractive church is thought to have been constructed between 1100 and 1130. www.saintsinsittingbourne.org.uk 104 B2

Other Sights

Archbishop's Palace★ *Palace Gardens, Mill Street, Maidstone* Formerly part of the Manor of Maidstone. Built in the late 14th century for the Archbishops of Canterbury. Apothecary herb garden in the grounds of the Palace. www.tour-maidstone.com 01622 602169 72 C3

Bank Street *leading from Week Street to River Medway, Maidstone* Most buildings on this street are listed for architectural or historic interest. Quality wine bars and speciality shops. www.tour-maidstone.com 72 C4
Chatham Historic Dockyard★★ *Main Great Road, Rochester* With 400 years of naval history. The birthplace of many of Britain's finest sailing shops, including Nelson's flagship at the Battle of Trafalgar HMS Victory. Museums, exhibitions and conducted tours. 01634 823807 www.chdt.org.uk 16 A4
The Corn Exchange *Earl Street, Maidstone* Variety of independent specialist shops from clothing to cake decorating and art. www.tour-maidstone.com 72 B4
Restoration House & Garden★ *Crow Lane, Rochester* City mansion famed for a visit from Charles II. Antique furniture and English portraits. Walled garden. 01634 848520 www.restorationhouse.co.uk 14 C1
Teston Bridge *Teston, Maidstone* Riverside walks and large picnic site near the historic medieval bridge. www.kent.gov.uk 79 C3

Green Spaces

Brenchley Gardens *St Faith's Street, Maidstone* An oasis of calm in the town centre. Victorian bandstand hosting Sunday afternoon concerts in the summer months. www.tour-maidstone.com 72 B4
Burham Down Nature Reserve *Common Road, Blue Bell Hill* A 104 acre reserve of woodland. Beautiful views of the Weald of Kent. www.tour-maidstone.com 38 B2
Capstone Farm Country Park *Capstone Road, Gillingham* Covers over 280 acres of former farmland on the North Downs. Ancient woodland, old orchards and a freshwater lake. Visitor centre and picnic facilities. 01634 812196 www.medway.gov.uk 33 A2
Maidstone Millennium River Park On the banks of the River Medway, 10km in length from Teston to Allington. Boat trips through the park depart from Archbishops' Palace and Allington. www.digitalmaidstone.co.uk/mmrp 79 C3 to 64 B4
Manor Park Country Park *St Leonard's Street, West Malling* A Site of Nature Conservation Interest. Large green open space with a lake and children's play equipment. 01622 817623 www.kent.gov.uk 59 B3
Mote Park *Mote Avenue, Maidstone* Set in 450 acres of mature parkland with a 30 acre lake. Miniature railway, cycling path, pitch and putt and children's play area. 01622 602188 www.tour-maidstone.com 73 A3
Riverside Country Park *Lower Rainham Road, Rainham, Gillingham* Haven for wildlife with meadows, marshes, ponds, grassland and mudflats. Visitor centre and cafe. 01634 378987 www.medway.gov.uk 18 C2
Vinters Valley Nature Reserve *via New Cut Road and Lodge Road, Maidstone* A 90 acre park managed as a nature reserve, with woodlands, wetlands and grasslands. www.tour-maidstone.com 66 A1

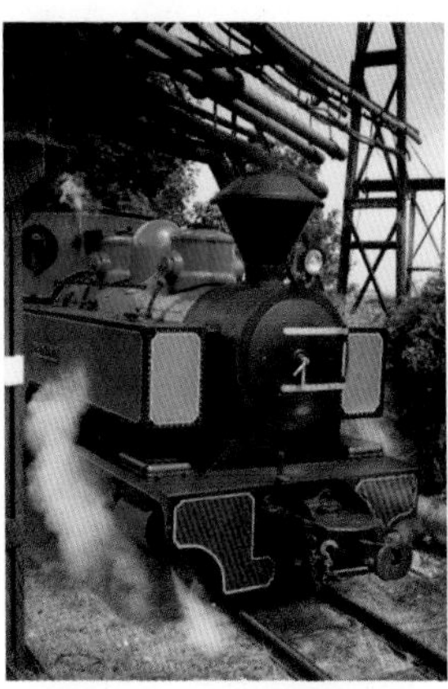

▲ *Sittingbourne and Kemsley Light Railway*

Activities

Broadway Shopping Centre *Tonbridge Road, Maidstone* Variety of clothing outlets and large supermarket. www.digitalmaidstone.co.uk 72 B4
The Brook Theatre *Old Town Hall, The Brook, Chatham* A professional theatre, with community productions, jazz and folk evenings and home to the Medway Comedy Club. www.medway.gov.uk/theatres 01634 338338 15 C1
Central Theatre *High Street, Chatham* Live entertainment, including music, comedy, drama and panto. 01634 338338 www.medway.gov.uk/theatres 22 C4
Chequers Shopping Centre (The Mall) *Pads Hill, Maidstone* Popular shopping centre, full of high street shops. Multi-storey car park. www.themall.co.uk/chequers 01622 691130 72 C4
Cobham Manor Riding Centre *Water Lane, Thurnham, Maidstone* Area of Outstanding Natural Beauty located in the Kent Downs. Contains 3 all-weather horse riding arenas offering lessons from beginners to advanced. www.cobham-manor.co.uk 01622 738497 67 C4
Cobtree Manor Park Golf Club *Chatham Road, Sandling* Public pay and play golf course. Golf tuition, shop and restaurant. 01622 753276 www.medwaygolf.co.uk 54 B2
Dickens World★★ *Leviathan Way, Chatham Maritime, Chatham* New themed attraction based on the life and works of Charles Dickens. Period architecture, rides, shopping mall, restaurants and cinema. 01622 356580 www.dickensworld.co.uk 16 A4
Fremlin Walk *Earl Street, Maidstone* New shopping centre containing 50 shops, restaurants and large car park. 01622 356580 www.fremlinwalk.co.uk 72 B4
Gillingham Football Club *Priestfield Stadium, Redfern Avenue, Gillingham* Formed in 1893, currently in League One. A well supported club, nicknamed 'The Gills'. 01634 300000 www.gillinghamfootballclub.co.uk 17 B1
Hazlitt Theatre *Earl Street, Maidstone* Varied programme including contemporary drama, ballet, opera and comedy. 01622 758611 www.hazlitttheatre.co.uk 72 B4
Lockmeadow Entertainment Centre *Barker Road, Maidstone* Bars, restaurants, nightclubs, multiplex cinema and healthclub. Also hosts Lockmeadow market, with up to 100 stalls held every day of the week. www.lockmeadowcentre.co.uk 01622 764410 72 B3
Maidstone Rugby Football Club *The Mote, Willow Way, Maidstone* Home to Maidstone's premier rugby club. 01622 754159 www.maidstonerugby.org.uk 73 A3
Maidstone Symphony Orchestra *Maidstone Leisure Centre, Mote Park, Maidstone* Impressive orchestra with 5 performances each season. www.mso.org.uk 01622 761111 73 B2
Royal Star Arcade *High Street, Maidstone* Shopping centre with a variety of fashion outlets and gift shops under one roof. www.tour-maidstone.com 72 B4
Sittingbourne and Kemsley Light Railway★ *The Wall, Sittingbourne* Preserved industrial steam railway, two miles long. Museum and miniature railways. 0871 222 1568 www.skir.net 104 A3
Tyland Barn Wildlife Conservation Centre *Chatham Road, Sandling* A 17th century barn, now headquarters to the Kent Wildlife Trust. With wildlife displays, an educational centre and nature park with trails. 01622 662012 www.kentwildlifetrust.org.uk 54 C3
Week Street *Maidstone* Follows the route of the old Roman road from Rochester to the Weald. It is now pedestrianised and has a number of independent stores. www.maidstoneonline.com/week.htm 72 C4

Information

Tourist Information
Maidstone: Town Hall, Middle Row, High Street 01622 602169 72 C4
Rochester: High Street 01634 843666 14 C2
Maidstone Borough Council
London Road, Maidstone 01622 602000 72 A4 01622 751457 (car parking) www.digitalmaidstone.co.uk
Medway Council
Civic Centre, Strood, Rochester 01634 306000 01622 332266 (car parking) www.medway.gov.uk 14 B2
NCP Car Parking
0870 606 7050 www.ncp.co.uk
National Rail Enquiries
0845 748 4950 www.nationalrail.co.uk
Local Bus and Rail
0870 608 2608 www.traveline.org.uk

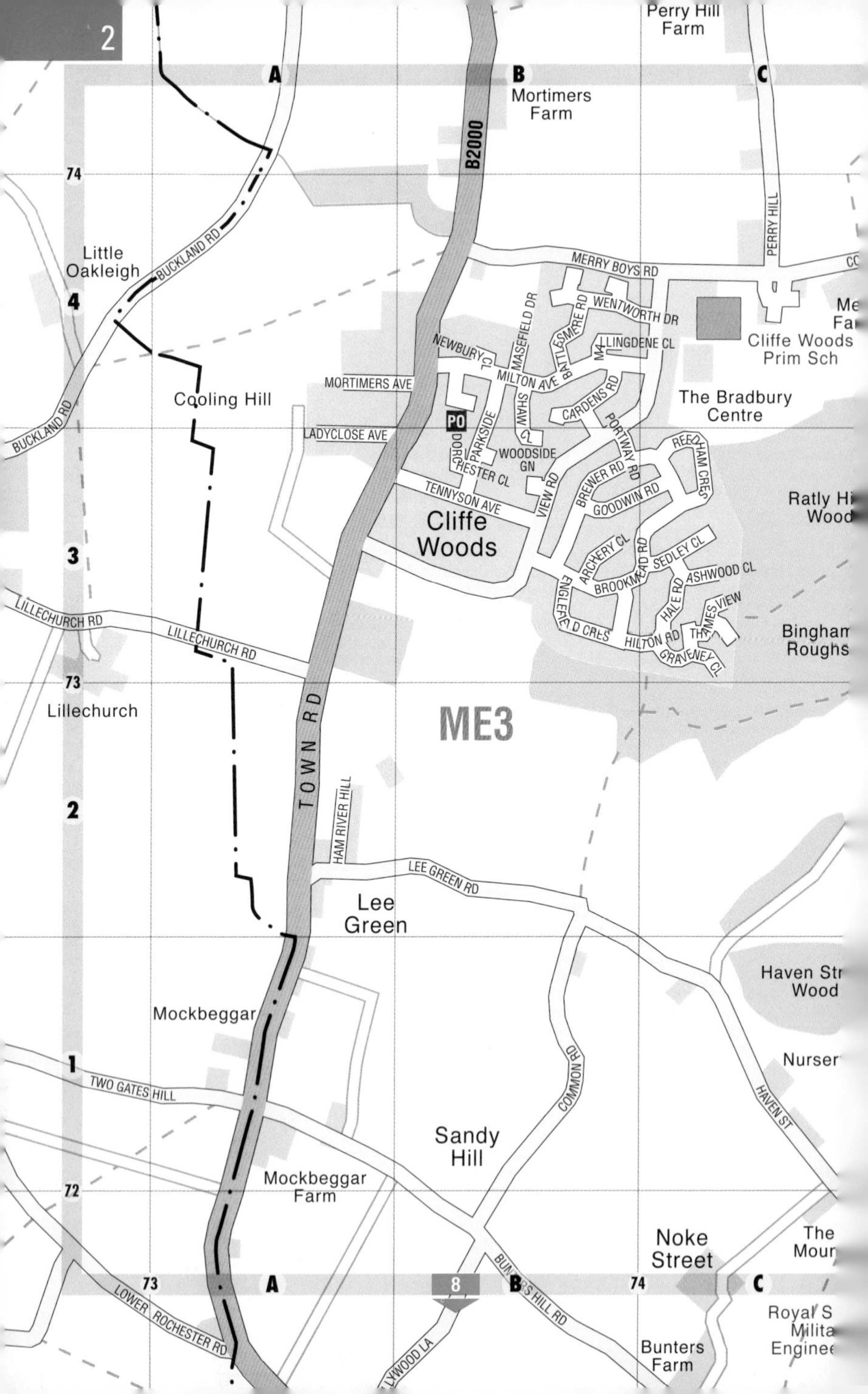
2
Perry Hill Farm
A
B
C
Mortimers Farm
B2000
74
PERRY HILL
Little Oakleigh
BUCKLAND RD
MERRY BOYS RD
4
MASEFIELD DR
WENTWORTH DR
BATTLESMERE RD
LLINGDENE CL
Cliffe Woods Prim Sch
NEWBURY CL
MILTON AVE
MORTIMERS AVE
Cooling Hill
CARDENS RD
The Bradbury Centre
SHAW CL
PARKSIDE
PORTWAY RD
PO
LADYCLOSE AVE
BUCKLAND RD
REEDHAM CRES
DORCHESTER CL
WOODSIDE GN
BREWER RD
GOODWIN RD
VIEW RD
TENNYSON AVE
Ratly Hi Wood
Cliffe Woods
3
ARCHERY CL
SEDLEY CL
BROOKMEAD RD
ASHWOOD CL
ENGLEFIELD CRES
HALE RD
THAMES VIEW
LILLECHURCH RD
LILLECHURCH RD
HILTON RD
GRAVENEY CL
Bingham Roughs
73
Lillechurch
ME3
TOWN RD
2
HAM RIVER HILL
LEE GREEN RD
Lee Green
Haven Str Wood
Mockbeggar
1
Nurser
TWO GATES HILL
COMMON RD
HAVEN ST
Sandy Hill
Mockbeggar Farm
72
Noke Street
The Moun
73
A
8
B
74
C
BUNTERS HILL RD
LOWER ROCHESTER RD
Royal S Milita Enginee
Bunters Farm
LYWOOD LA

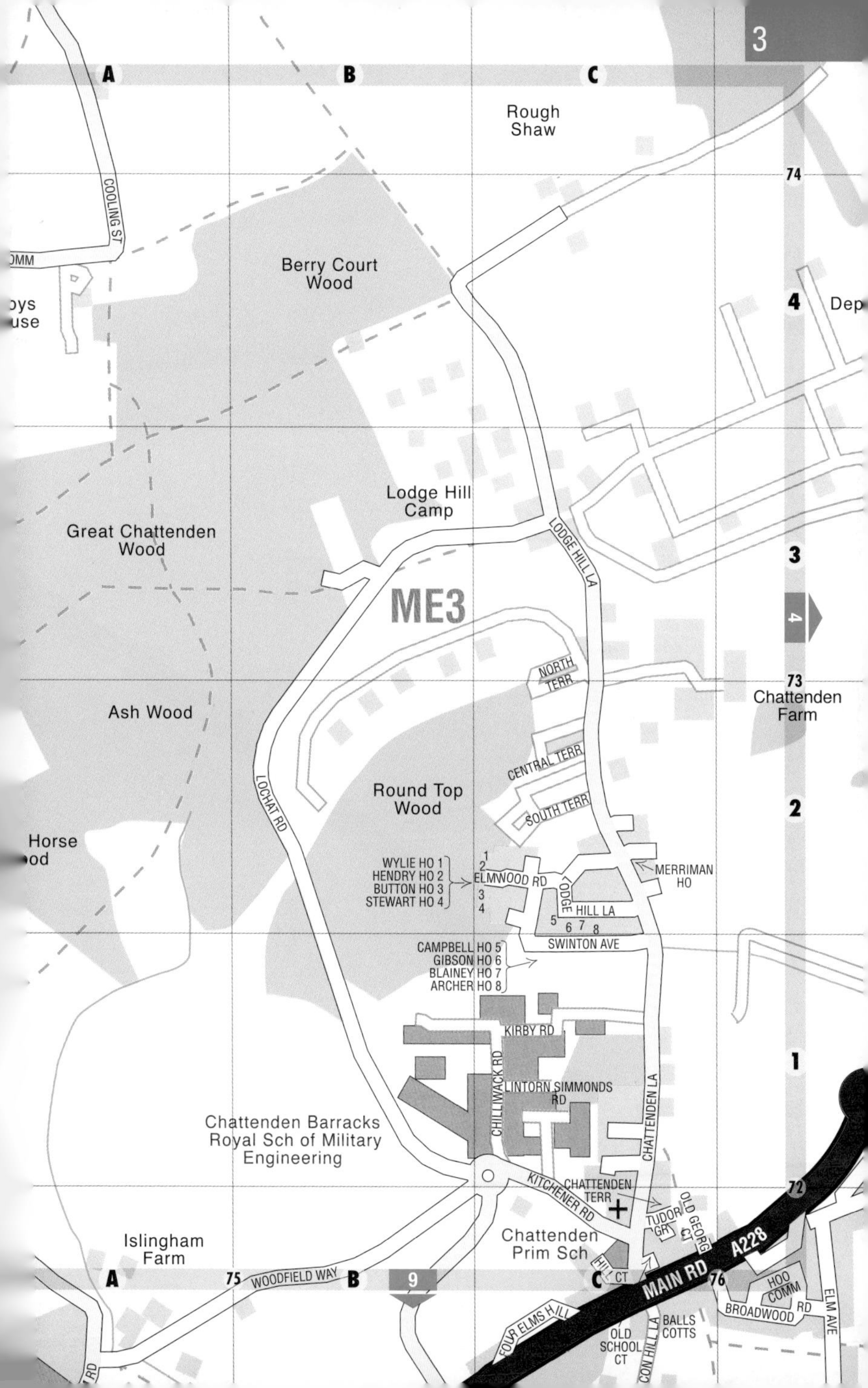
A
B
C
Rough Shaw
74
COOLING ST
Berry Court Wood
4
Lodge Hill Camp
Great Chattenden Wood
LODGE HILL LA
3
ME3
4
NORTH TERR
73
Chattenden Farm
Ash Wood
CENTRAL TERR
Round Top Wood
LOCHAT RD
SOUTH TERR
2
Horse
WYLIE HO 1
HENDRY HO 2
BUTTON HO 3
STEWART HO 4
ELMWOOD RD
MERRIMAN HO
LODGE HILL LA
SWINTON AVE
CAMPBELL HO 5
GIBSON HO 6
BLAINEY HO 7
ARCHER HO 8
KIRBY RD
CHILLIWACK RD
1
LINTORN SIMMONDS RD
CHATTENDEN LA
Chattenden Barracks Royal Sch of Military Engineering
KITCHENER RD
CHATTENDEN TERR
72
TUDOR GR
OLD GEORG CT
Chattenden Prim Sch
Islingham Farm
HILL CT
A228
MAIN RD
A
75
WOODFIELD WAY
B
9
C
76
HOO COMM RD
BROADWOOD
ELM AVE
FOUR ELMS HILL
BALLS COTTS
OLD SCHOOL CT
CON HILL LA

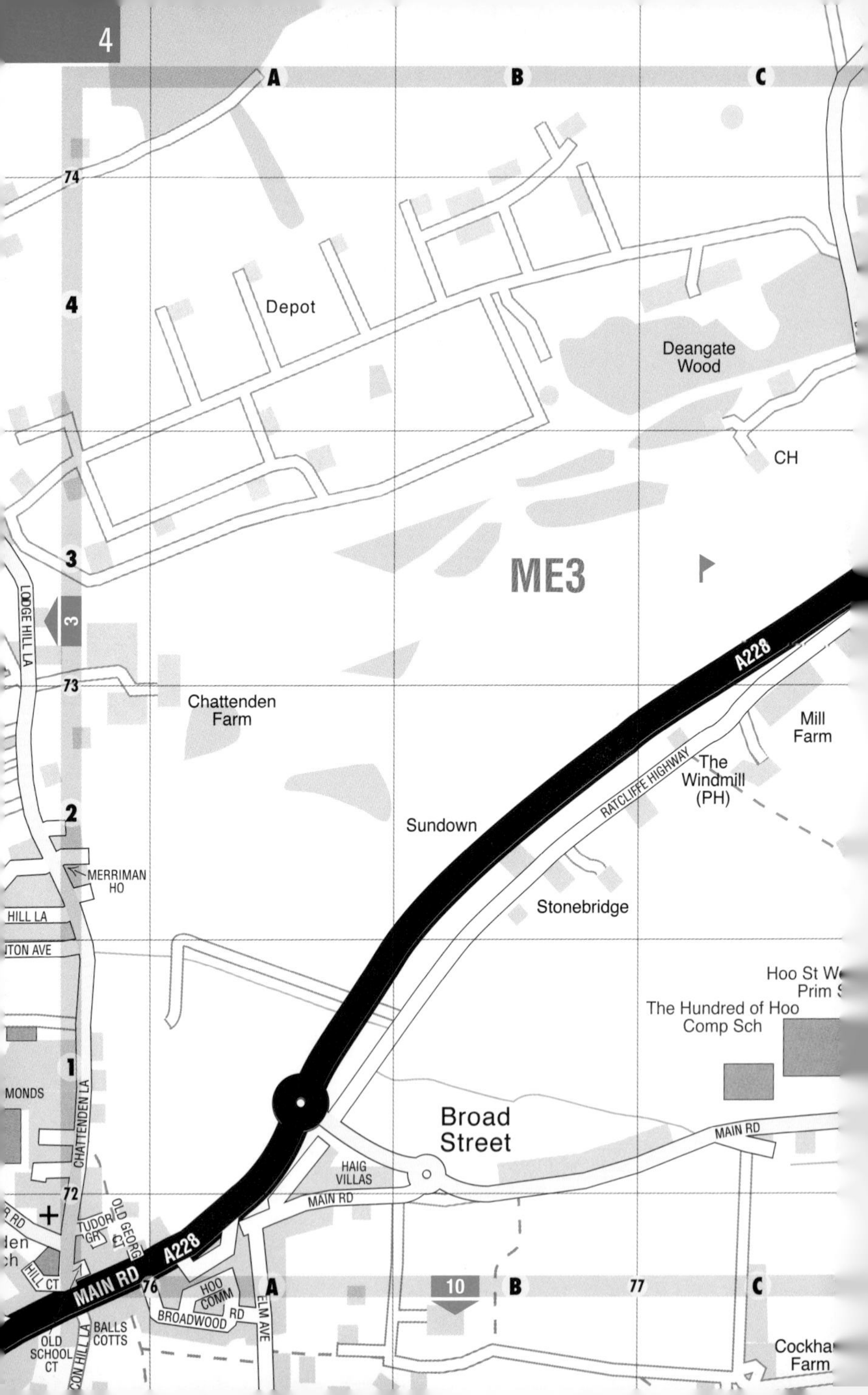
A
B
C
74
4
Depot
Deangate Wood
CH
3
ME3
LODGE HILL LA
3
73
A228
Chattenden Farm
Mill Farm
The Windmill (PH)
RATCLIFFE HIGHWAY
2
Sundown
MERRIMAN HO
HILL LA
TON AVE
Stonebridge
Hoo St W
Prim S
The Hundred of Hoo Comp Sch
1
MONDS
CHATTENDEN LA
Broad Street
MAIN RD
HAIG VILLAS
MAIN RD
72
TUDOR GR
OLD GEORG CT
A228
MAIN RD
HILL CT
76
HOO COMM RD
BROADWOOD
ELM AVE
A
10
B
77
C
BALLS COTTS
OLD SCHOOL CT
CON HILL LA
Cockha Farm

A228 Grain (B2001)
A
B
C
74
Roper's Farm
4
Deangate Ridge Sports Gd
Deangate
RATCLIFFE HIGHWAY
ROPER'S LA
ROPER'S GREEN LA
Saxon Shore Way
Angel Farm
ME3
3
BLACKMAN CL
WALL CL
FOURWENTS RD
ROPER'S LA
73
STURDEE COTTS
ROCHESTER CRES
KINGSHILL DR
GRANDSIRE GDNS
BELL'S LA
WEBB CL
PANKHURST RD
MOREMENT RD
MARLEY RD
KINGSHILL DR
WALTERS RD
Caravan Site
Mast
STREET FARM COTTS
2
ST JOHNS RD
KINGSNORTH CL
ROBSON DR
WYLIE RD
STOKE RD
KNIGHTS CL
PO
MISKIN RD
PEAL CL
Hoo St Werburgh
POTTERY RD
ST WERBURGH CT
GORDON RD
TRUBRIDGE RD
KILLICK RD
JENNIFER CT
1
NEWITT RD
COOMBE RD
FLACK GDNS
PH
P
1 NURSERY GDNS
2 BUTT HAW CL
ST WERBURGH CRES
TILLEY CL
PO
BROOKSIDE
CHURCH ST
Sewag Works
Mast
ABBOTS COURT RD
72
ARMYTAGE CL 1
EVEREST MEWS 2
EVEREST DR
WHITE HOUSE CL
Liby
A
78
B
11
C
79
VICARAGE LA
Shore Way

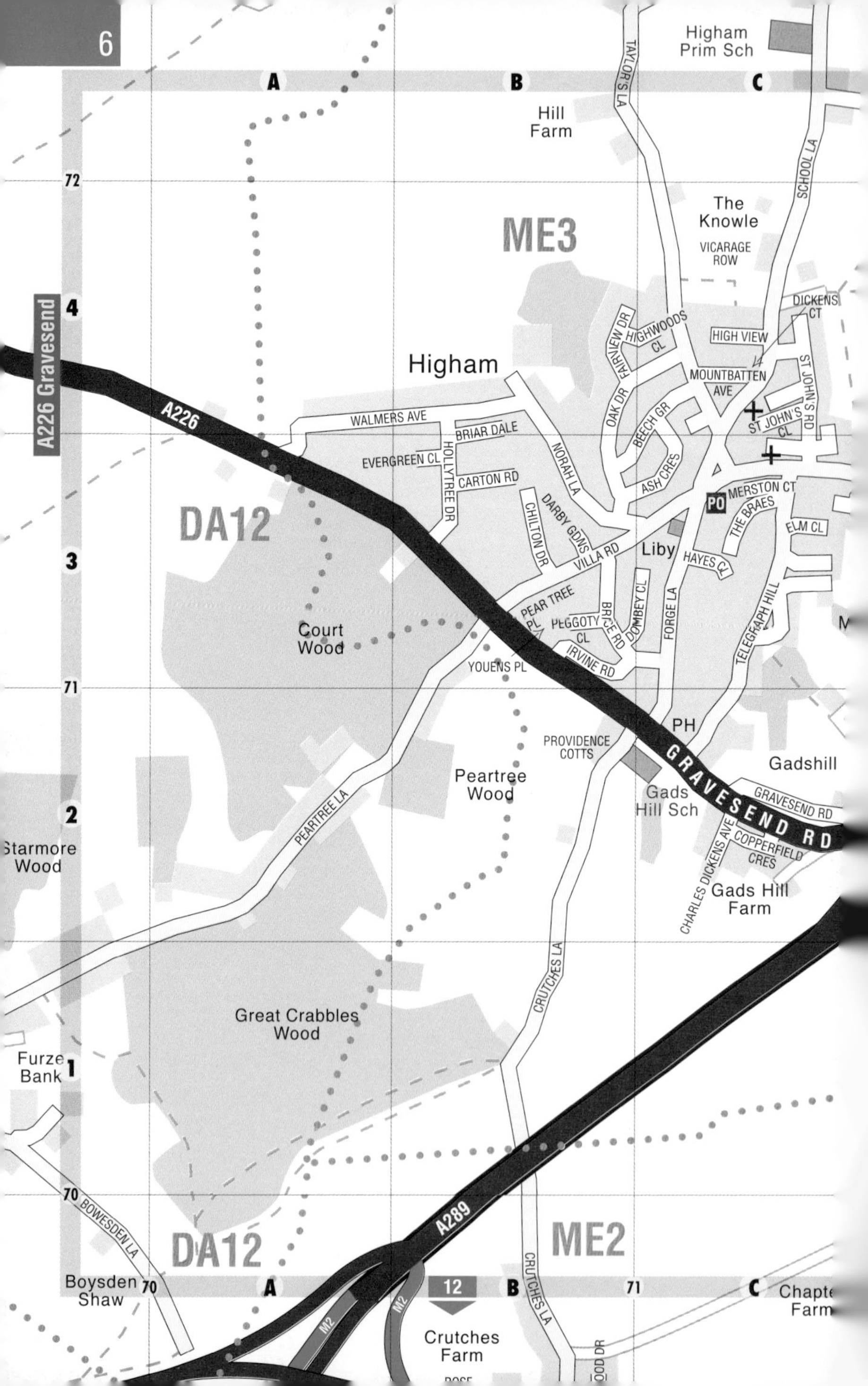
A
B
C
Higham Prim Sch
Hill Farm
TAYLOR'S LA
SCHOOL LA
72
The Knowle
VICARAGE ROW
ME3
A226 Gravesend
4
DICKENS CT
HIGHWOODS CL
HIGH VIEW
FAIRVIEW DR
MOUNTBATTEN AVE
ST JOHN'S RD
Higham
OAK DR
A226
WALMERS AVE
BEECH GR
ST JOHN'S CL
BRIAR DALE
NORAH LA
EVERGREEN CL
HOLLYTREE DR
CARTON RD
ASH CRES
MERSTON CT
PO
THE BRAES
DA12
DARBY GDNS
CHILTON DR
ELM CL
Liby
3
VILLA RD
HAYES CL
DOMBEY CL
FORGE LA
PEAR TREE PL
PEGGOTY CL
TELEGRAPH HILL
Court Wood
IRVINE RD
YOUENS PL
71
PH
PROVIDENCE COTTS
GRAVESEND RD
Gadshill
Peartree Wood
Gads Hill Sch
GRAVESEND RD
2
PEARTREE LA
Starmore Wood
CHARLES DICKENS AVE
COPPERFIELD CRES
Gads Hill Farm
CRUTCHES LA
Great Crabbles Wood
Furze Bank
1
70
BOWESDEN LA
A289
DA12
ME2
Boysden Shaw
70
A
12
B
CRUTCHES LA
71
C
M2
Crutches Farm

Two Gates Farm
TWO GATES HILL
TWOGATES HILL
White House Farm
LAND WAY
Dusty Hill
LOWER ROCHESTER RD
B2000
HERMITAGE RD
MES VIEW COTTS
Hillyfield
ME3
The Stone Horse (PH)
DILLYWOOD LA
Stone House Farm
STONEHORSE LA
Garden Centre
Gouge Farm
egraph Hill
rove arm
A289
A226
DILLYWOOD COTTS
Little Hermitage
Mast
ME2
GODFREY CL
HYPERION DR 1
HILLYFIELD CL 2
BROMPTON FARM RD
HYPERION DR
KING ARTHUR
LYNETTE AVE
SAXON CL
CHEQUERS CT
ROSEMOUNT CT
LYCHFIELD DR
HARLECH CL
SANDYCROFT RD
WOODVIEW RISE
FARM HILL AVE
WESTERGATE RD
ORCHARD AVE
CARISBROOKE RD
FOUNTAIN RD
CONWAY CL
BEAUFORT RD
B2108
WHITE GATE
Abbey Court Specl Sch
A226 GRAVESEND RD
GORSE RD
Broom Hill
BURLEIGH CL
ROMSEY CL
CLINTON AVE
COBB CL
REDE COURT RD
CRISPIN RD
RUSSET CT
DUCHESS CL
BRAMLEY
WORCESTER CL
ABBEY RD
BROOM HILL RD
DRAKE'S AVE
PEPY'S WAY
MINERVA RD
CAMBRIDGE

8
13

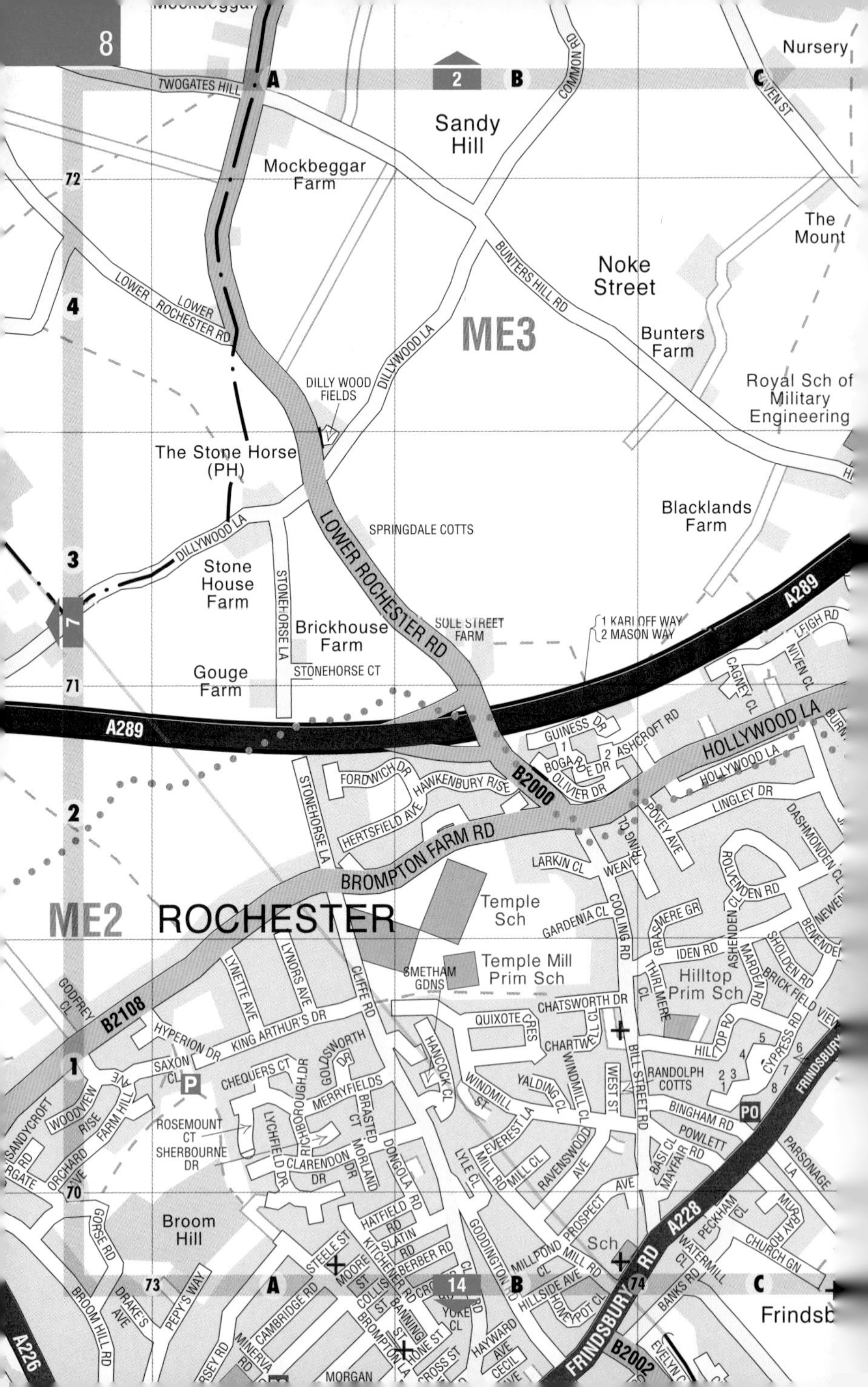
Sandy Hill
Mockbeggar Farm
Noke Street
ME3
Bunters Farm
Royal Sch of Military Engineering
The Mount
Nursery
The Stone Horse (PH)
Blacklands Farm
Stone House Farm
Brickhouse Farm
Gouge Farm
SPRINGDALE COTTS
SOLE STREET FARM
1 KARLOFF WAY
2 MASON WAY
DILLY WOOD FIELDS
TWOGATES HILL
COMMON RD
BUNTERS HILL RD
LOWER ROCHESTER RD
DILLYWOOD LA
STONEHORSE LA
STONEHORSE CT
A289
B2000
HOLLYWOOD LA
BROMPTON FARM RD
ME2
ROCHESTER
Temple Sch
Temple Mill Prim Sch
Hilltop Prim Sch
B2108
A228
FRINDSBURY RD
B2002
A226
Broom Hill
Sch
Frindsb

Chattenden Barracks
Royal Sch of Military Engineering
ME3
Islingham Farm
WOODFIELD WAY
KIRBY RD
CHILLIWACK RD
LINTORN SIMMONDS RD
CHATTENDEN LA
KITCHENER RD
CHATTENDEN TERR
Chattenden Prim Sch
TUDOR GR
OLD GEORGE CT
HILL CT
MAIN RD
A228
BROADWOOD RD
HOO COMM
ELM AVE
BALLS COTTS
OLD SCHOOL CT
BEACON HILL LA
FOUR ELMS HILL
ISLINGHAM FARM RD
Chattenden
UPCHAT RD
Beacon
Beacon Hill
FOUR ELMS RDBT
A289
HOO RD B2108
CHAPLIN CL
Wainscott
GREENFIELDS CL
WAINSCOTT WLK
GILL AVE
Wainscott Prim Sch
WINSTON DR
HOLLY RD
WAINSCOTT RD
FRITTENDEN RD
PO
ME2
MARGETTS PL
ALBION PL
UPNOR RD
BRISSENDEN CL
PIER PL
GALLEON WAY
SCHOONER WLK
CUTTER CL
Lower Upnor
Upnor Reach
Pier
PH
Upnor Castle
River Medway
CASTLE ST
HIGH ST
ADMIRALTY RD
ADMIRALTY TERR
RICHMOND CL
Upper Upnor
Sewage Works
Tower Hill
ANTHONYS WAY
PARSONAGE LA
Medway Tunnel
VANGUARD WAY
Maritime Est
Loaland Bsns Ctr
Kenyon Bsns Pk
MARITIME CL
Berglar Pk
TERANCE BUTLER AVE
Sheldon Bsns Ctr
Northpoint Bsns Est
Medway Ent Ctr
ENTERPRISE CL
KEEL
ANTHONYS
ROCHESTER CT
GEORGE SUMMERS CL
Whitewall Creek
LEVIATHAN WAY
Dickens World
The Historic Dockyard
WESTERN

The Hundred of Hoo Comp Sch
Broad Street
MAIN RD
HAIG VILLAS
CHATTENDEN LA
TUDOR GR
OLD GEORG CT
A228
MAIN RD
HILL CT
HOO COMM RD
BROADWOOD
ELM AVE
BALLS COTTS
OLD SCHOOL CT
BEACON HILL LA
ME3
Cockham Farm
Hoo Lodge
Beacon
ME2
Saxon Shore Way
Cockham Wood
MARGETTS PL
ALBION PL
UPNOR RD
BRISSENDEN CL
PIER PL
UPNOR RD
CUTTER CL
Lower Upnor
GALLEON WAY
Upnor Reach
Pier
Upnor Castle
HIGH ST
ADMIRALTY RD
ADMIRALTY TERR
RICHMOND CL
Upper Upnor
ME4
STILLWATER MEWS
MAIN ST
WESTVIEW
TAPPAN DR
ISLAND WAY W
DEERING CL
GOLDCREST DR
BRADFORDS CL
CHELDOC RISE
EGRET CL 1
PARTRIDGE DR 2
EDGEWAY
St Mary's Island CE Prim Sch
RINGLET RD
THE AVENUE
APOLLO WAY
DUNLIN DR
RIVERMEAD
PHALAROPE WAY
SAMPHIRE WAY
ISLAND WAY W
MEADOWSWEET VIEW
FOXTAIL CL
WOODRUSH PL
THE PINNACLES
ISLAND WAY E
WOODLARK RD
REDSHANK RD
THE CRESCENT
PINTAILS
THE POCHARD CL
MARINE VIEW
SANDLING WAY
RESTHARROW WAY
SALLOW CL
St Mary's Island
STONES RDBT
STONECROP CL
WINTERGREEN
HAVEN WAY 1
THE WHIMBRELS 2
WILLOWHERB CL 3
DEWBERRY CL 4
Marina
MARITIME WAY
LEVIATHAN WAY
DOCK HEAD RD
Dickens World
Dockside Outlet Ctr
QUAYSIDE
NORTH SIDE THREE R
Chatham Docks
Medway Tunnel
76
77
16
A289
BARRACK RD
SOUTH SIDE THREE RD
ME4
LEVIATHAN WAY
The Historic Dockyard
WESTERN A
MARITIME WAY
Compass Ctr
PEMBROKE
NORTH RD
72
71
70
A
B
C
4
3
2
1
9

Hoo
St Werburgh
A
B
5
C
RUBRIDGE RD
KILLICK RD
NEWITT RD
COOMBE RD
FLACK GDNS
GORDON RD
ST WERBURGH CT
ST WERBURGH CRES
TILLEY CL
BROOKSIDE
CHURCH ST
PO
P
ARMYTAGE CL 1
EVEREST MEWS 2
EVEREST DR
WHITE HOUSE CL
ABBOTS COURT RD
Liby
ME3
CHURCH FARM CL
VICARAGE LA
Saxon Shore Way
Mast
Sewage Works
72
4
Hoo Marina Park
THE COPSE
ELM RD
OAK CL
DAMSON DR
BERRY RD
BAY CL
MARINE DR
POPLAR CL
WILLOW AVE
OAK RD
HAZEL AVE
DAMSON DR
MAPLE RD
BIRCH RD
LARCH CRES
CHERRY RD
CEDAR RD
ASTER RD
YEW RD
BEECH RD
CYPRESS AVE 1
CLOVER RD 2
Hoo Marina
VICARAGE LA
Works
Gull Down Plantation
3
71
River Medway
2
Middle Creek
ME3
Hoo Salt Marsh
Short Reach
ME7
Hoo Ness
1
70
Gillingham Reach
Bull Nose
BROOKSIDE
A
78
B
17
C
79
Gillingham Pier
ME7

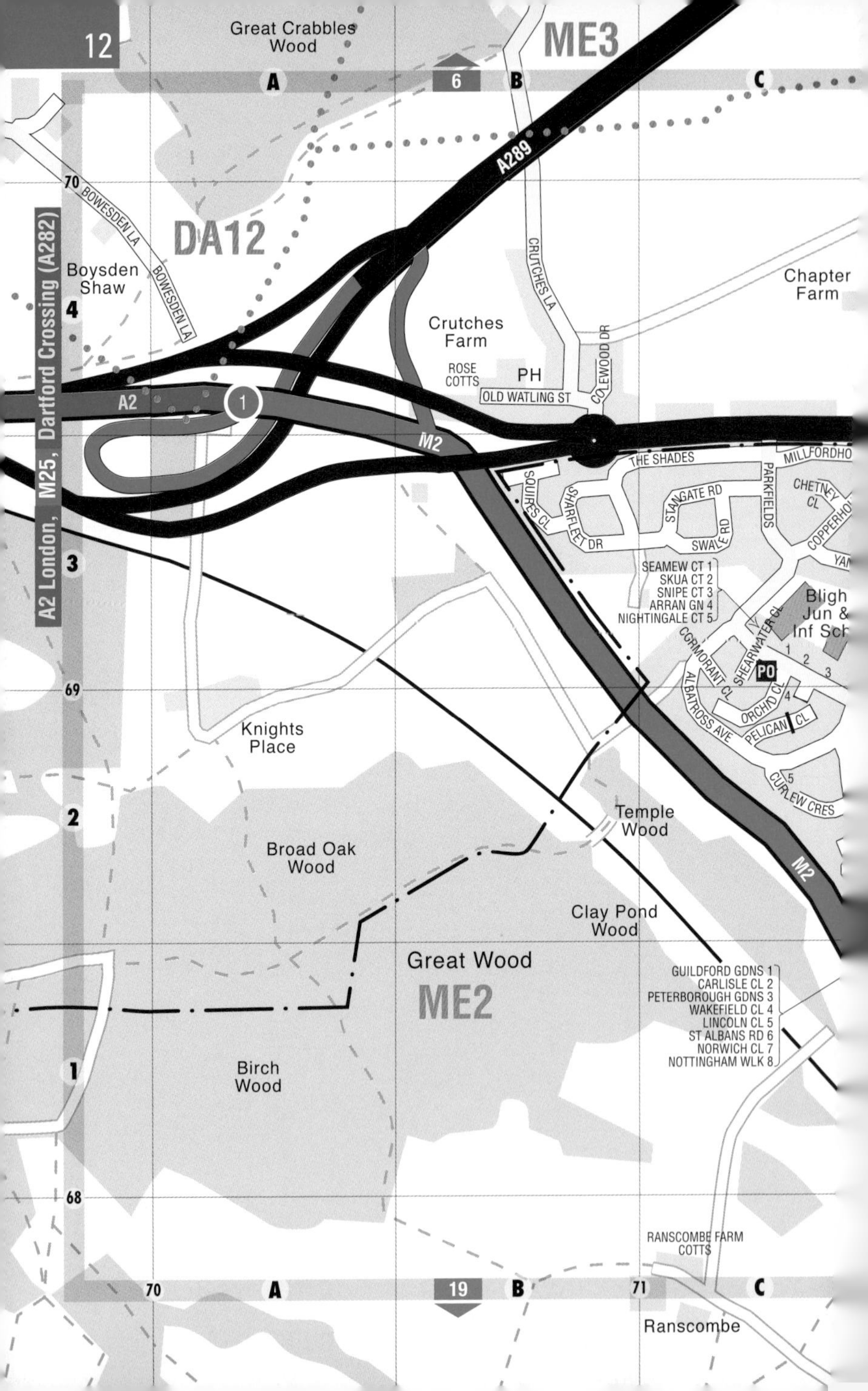
Great Crabbles Wood
ME3
A
6
B
C
A289
70
BOWESDEN LA
A2 London, M25, Dartford Crossing (A282)
DA12
Boysden Shaw
4
CRUTCHES LA
Chapter Farm
Crutches Farm
COLEWOOD DR
ROSE COTTS
PH
OLD WATLING ST
A2
1
M2
THE SHADES
MILLFORDHO
SQUIRES CL
SHARFLEET DR
STANGATE RD
SWALE RD
PARKFIELDS
CHETNEY CL
COPPERHO
3
SEAMEW CT 1
SKUA CT 2
SNIPE CT 3
ARRAN GN 4
NIGHTINGALE CT 5
Bligh Jun & Inf Sch
CORMORANT CL
SHEARWATER CL
PO
69
ALBATROSS AVE
ORCHID CL
PELICAN CL
Knights Place
CURLEW CRES
2
Temple Wood
Broad Oak Wood
M2
Clay Pond Wood
Great Wood
ME2
GUILDFORD GDNS 1
CARLISLE CL 2
PETERBOROUGH GDNS 3
WAKEFIELD CL 4
LINCOLN CL 5
ST ALBANS RD 6
NORWICH CL 7
NOTTINGHAM WLK 8
1
Birch Wood
68
RANSCOMBE FARM COTTS
70
A
19
B
71
C
Ranscombe

ME3
A
B
7
C
A226
B2108
BROMPTON FARM RD
SAXON CL
HARLECH CL
SANDYCROFT RD
WOODVIEW RISE
FARM HILL AVE
ROSEMOUNT CT
LYCHFIELD DR
CARISBROOKE RD
FOUNTAIN RD
CONWAY CL
WESTERGATE RD
ORCHARD AVE
70
BEAUFORT RD
BURLEIGH CL
WHITE GATE
GORSE RD
Broom Hill
Abbey Court Specl Sch
ROMSEY CL
REDE COURT RD
RUSSET CL
THE PARADE
BRAMLEY RISE
WORCESTER CL
ABBEY RD
BROOM HILL RD
DRAKE'S AVE
PEPY'S WAY
CLINTON AVE
CRISPIN RD
COBB CL
DUCHESS CL
ALLINGTON DR
DEACON CL
LEYBOURNE RD
GRAVESEND RD
4
JERSEY RD
MINERVA RD
CAMBRIDGE
PO
Schs
GORDON RD
LINWOOD AVE
CADNAM CL
ROAN CT
SWAN CL
CHAPTER RD
DEAN RD
ST NICHOLAS GDNS
PEPY'S WAY
A2
WATLING ST
Chapter Sch
THURSTON DR
CENTRAL RD
CASTLE VIEW RD
Sch
COLUMBINE CL
DAFFODIL RD
COBHAM CL
RIVER DR
HARVEL AVE
Strood
Sports Ctr
A2 LONDON RD
DOWNSIDE
3
STOUR CL
P
HUMBER CRES
WYATT PL
Recn Gd
NORTHCOTE RD
14
CUXTON RD
CARNATION RD
LANCELOT AVE
ELAINE AVE
ME2
CLIFTON CL
WITHAM WAY
THE MEWS
WOODSTOCK RD
COLUMBINE RD
TAMAR DR
TINTAGEL GDNS
DART CL
69
HYACINTH RD
Elaine Prim Sch
GALAHAD AVE
ST FRANCIS CL
ELAINE CT
A228
PRIORY
DARNLEY CL
LANCELOT CL
DARNLEY RD
PO
PENGUIN CL
MAPLE RD
PINE RD
TEMPLE GDNS
Strood
2
Knights Pk
WIDGEON RD
PORTSMOUTH CL
FULMAR RD
UPLANDS
HAWTHORN RD
WOTTON RD
BEECH RD
ASH RD
SEAGULL RD
SOUTHWARK RD
OAK RD
CHESTNUT RD
CEDAR RD
Sheridale Bsns Ctr
Temple Manor
CHELMSFORD RD
CHESTER CL
COVENTRY CL
LILAC CRES
Cemy
HIGHLANDS CL
LILAC RD
HOLLY RD
Conquest Ind Est
BRISTOL CL
WINSTON RD
GLAMFORD RD
NORTH BANK CL
Sherwin Knight Jun & Inf Schs
WELLS CT
WELLS RD
HEVER CROFT
THE SPIRES
MERRALS WOOD RD
LABURNUM RD
POPLAR CL
1
HILLSHAW CRES
POPLAR RD
ELGIN GDNS
RANSCOMBE CL
SYCAMORE RD
RUSHDEAN RD
CUXTON RD
SAXON PL
BOOTHAM CL
Ballard Bsns Pk
VIKING CL
NORMAN CL
68
M2
Pit (dis)
ROMAN WAY
2
Temple Marsh
A
72
B
20
Diggerland
C
73
A228
Merrals Shaw

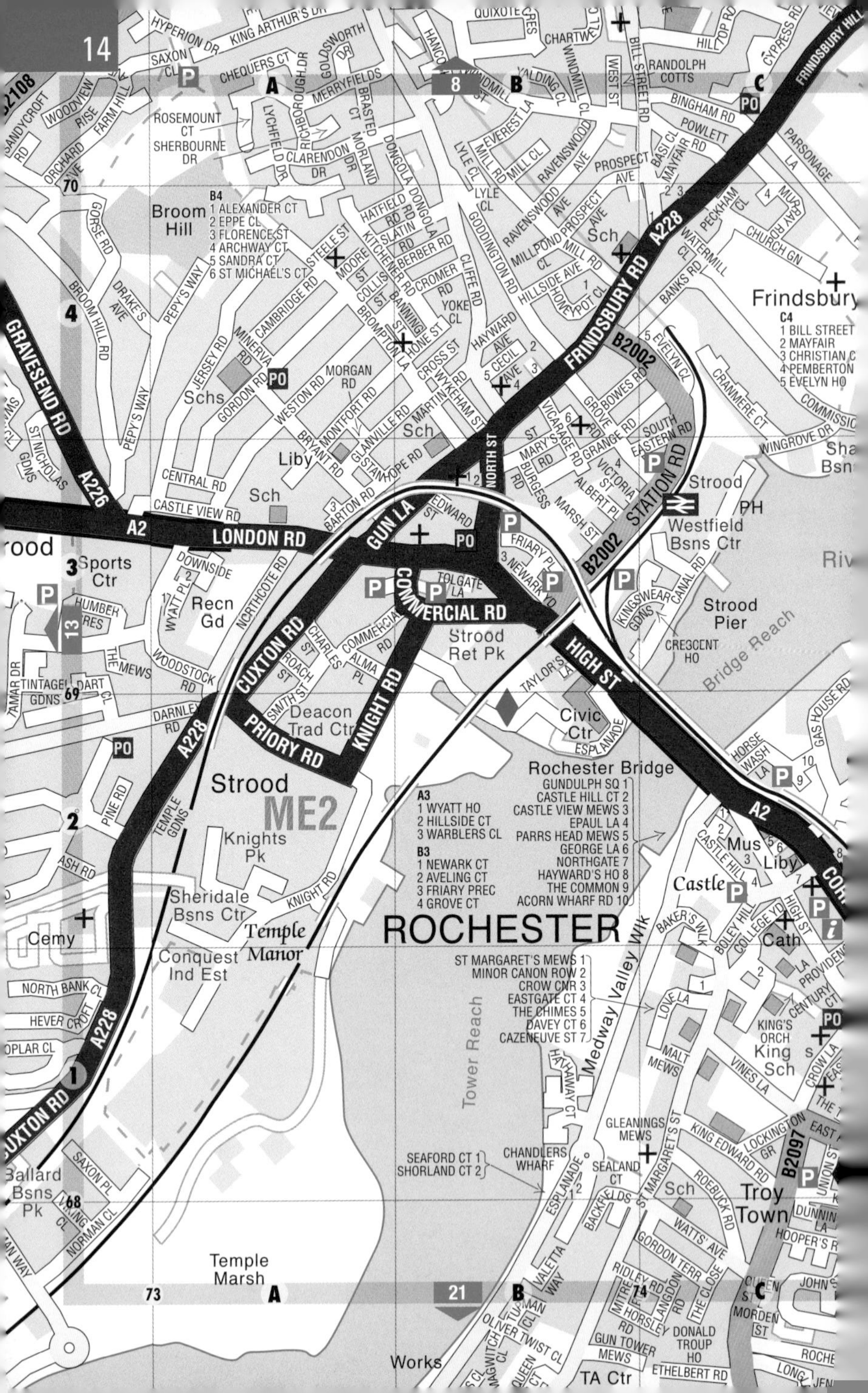

HYPERION DR
KING ARTHUR'S DR
QUIXOTE CRES
CHARTWELL CL
HILLTOP RD
CYPRESS RD
FRINDSBURY HILL
SAXON CL
CHEQUERS CT
GOLDSWORTH DR
RANDOLPH COTTS
A
8
B
C
B2108
WOODVIEW RISE
FARM HILL AVE
SANDYCROFT RD
ORCHARD AVE
MERRYFIELDS
ROSEMOUNT CT
SHERBOURNE DR
LYCHFIELD DR
RICHBOROUGH DR
BRASTED CT
MORLAND DR
CLARENDON DR
DONGOLA RD
YALDING CL
EVEREST LA
WINDMILL CL
WEST ST
BILL STREET RD
BINGHAM RD
POWLETT RD
PARSONAGE LA
MAYFAIR
BASI CL
PROSPECT AVE
RAVENSWOOD AVE
LYLE CL
MILL RD
MILL CL
70
Broom Hill
B4
1 ALEXANDER CT
2 EPPE CL
3 FLORENCE ST
4 ARCHWAY CT
5 SANDRA CT
6 ST MICHAEL'S CT
GORSE RD
HATFIELD RD
SLATIN RD
BERBER RD
KITCHENER RD
STEELE ST
MOORE ST
COLLIS ST
CROMER RD
CLIFFE RD
GODDINGTON RD
MILLPOND CL
HILLSIDE AVE
HONEYPOT CL
PECKHAM CL
MURRAY RD
CHURCH GN
WATERMILL CL
BANKS RD
Frindsbury
C4
1 BILL STREET RD
2 MAYFAIR
3 CHRISTIAN CT
4 PEMBERTON
5 EVELYN HO
A228
FRINDSBURY RD
Sch
BROOM HILL RD
DRAKE'S AVE
PEPY'S WAY
CAMBRIDGE RD
MINERVA RD
BANNING ST
BROMPTON LA
RHONE ST
YOKE CL
HAYWARD AVE
CECIL AVE
GRAVESEND RD
JERSEY RD
GORDON RD
Schs
PO
WESTON RD
MORGAN RD
MONTFORT RD
GLANVILLE RD
MARTIN RD
CROSS ST
WYKEHAM ST
B2002
EVELYN CL
BOWES RD
CRANMERE CT
COMMISSIONERS
WINGROVE DR
ST NICHOLAS GDNS
A226
Liby
BRYANT RD
HOPE RD
Sch
NORTH ST
ST MARY'S RD
VICARAGE RD
GROVE RD
GRANGE RD
SOUTH EASTERN RD
STATION RD
Strood
Sha Bsns
CENTRAL RD
CASTLE VIEW RD
BARTON RD
GUN LA
EDWARD ST
BURGESS RD
VICTORIA ST
ALBERT PL
MARSH ST
PH
Westfield Bsns Ctr
Sch
A2
LONDON RD
FRIARY PL
NEWARK YD
Strood
Sports Ctr
DOWNSIDE
TOLGATE LA
COMMERCIAL RD
CANAL RD
KINGSWEAR GDNS
Strood Pier
Riv
HUMBER CRES
13
WYATT PL
Recn Gd
NORTHCOTE RD
CUXTON RD
CHARLES ST
COMMERCIAL RD
ALMA PL
Strood Ret Pk
CRESCENT HO
Bridge Reach
THE MEWS
ROACH ST
TAYLOR'S LA
HIGH ST
WOODSTOCK RD
TAMAR DR
TINTAGEL GDNS
DART CL
69
SMITH ST
KNIGHT RD
Deacon Trad Ctr
Civic Ctr
ESPLANADE
GAS HOUSE RD
DARNLEY RD
PO
A228
PRIORY RD
HORSE WASH LA
Rochester Bridge
GUNDULPH SQ 1
CASTLE HILL CT 2
CASTLE VIEW MEWS 3
EPAUL LA 4
PARRS HEAD MEWS 5
GEORGE LA 6
NORTHGATE 7
HAYWARD'S HO 8
THE COMMON 9
ACORN WHARF RD 10
Strood
ME2
PINE RD
TEMPLE GDNS
A3
1 WYATT HO
2 HILLSIDE CT
3 WARBLERS CL
B3
1 NEWARK CT
2 AVELING CT
3 FRIARY PREC
4 GROVE CT
Knights Pk
ASH RD
2
Mus
Liby
CASTLE HILL
Castle
COR
Sheridale Bsns Ctr
KNIGHT RD
Temple Manor
Conquest Ind Est
ROCHESTER
Medway Valley Wlk
BAKER'S WLK
BOLEY HILL
COLLEGE YD
HIGH ST
Cath
Cemy
ST MARGARET'S MEWS 1
MINOR CANON ROW 2
CROW CNR 3
EASTGATE CT 4
THE CHIMES 5
DAVEY CT 6
CAZENEUVE ST 7
LA PROVIDENCE
CENTURY CT
NORTH BANK CL
HEVER CROFT
POPLAR CL
A228
Tower Reach
HATHAWAY CT
LOVE LA
MALT MEWS
KING'S ORCH
King Sch
VINES LA
CROW LA
THE T
1
CUXTON RD
GLEANINGS MEWS
ST MARGARET'S ST
KING EDWARD RD
LOCKINGTON GR
EAST
B2097
SEAFORD CT 1
SHORLAND CT 2
CHANDLERS WHARF
SEALAND CT
ESPLANADE
Sch
ROEBUCK RD
UNION ST
Ballard Bsns Pk
SAXON PL
VIKING CL
NORMAN CL
68
BACKFIELDS
WATTS' AVE
Troy Town
DUNNING LA
HOOPER'S R
GORDON TERR
THE CLOSE
VALETTA WAY
Temple Marsh
73
A
21
B
TURMAN CL
RIDLEY RD
MITRE RD
HORSLEY RD
LANGDON RD
74
C
QUEEN ST
MORDEN ST
JOHN ST
OLIVER TWIST CL
MAGWITCH CL
QUEEN CT
GUN TOWER MEWS
DONALD TROUP HO
ROCHE
Works
TA Ctr
ETHELBERT RD
LONG

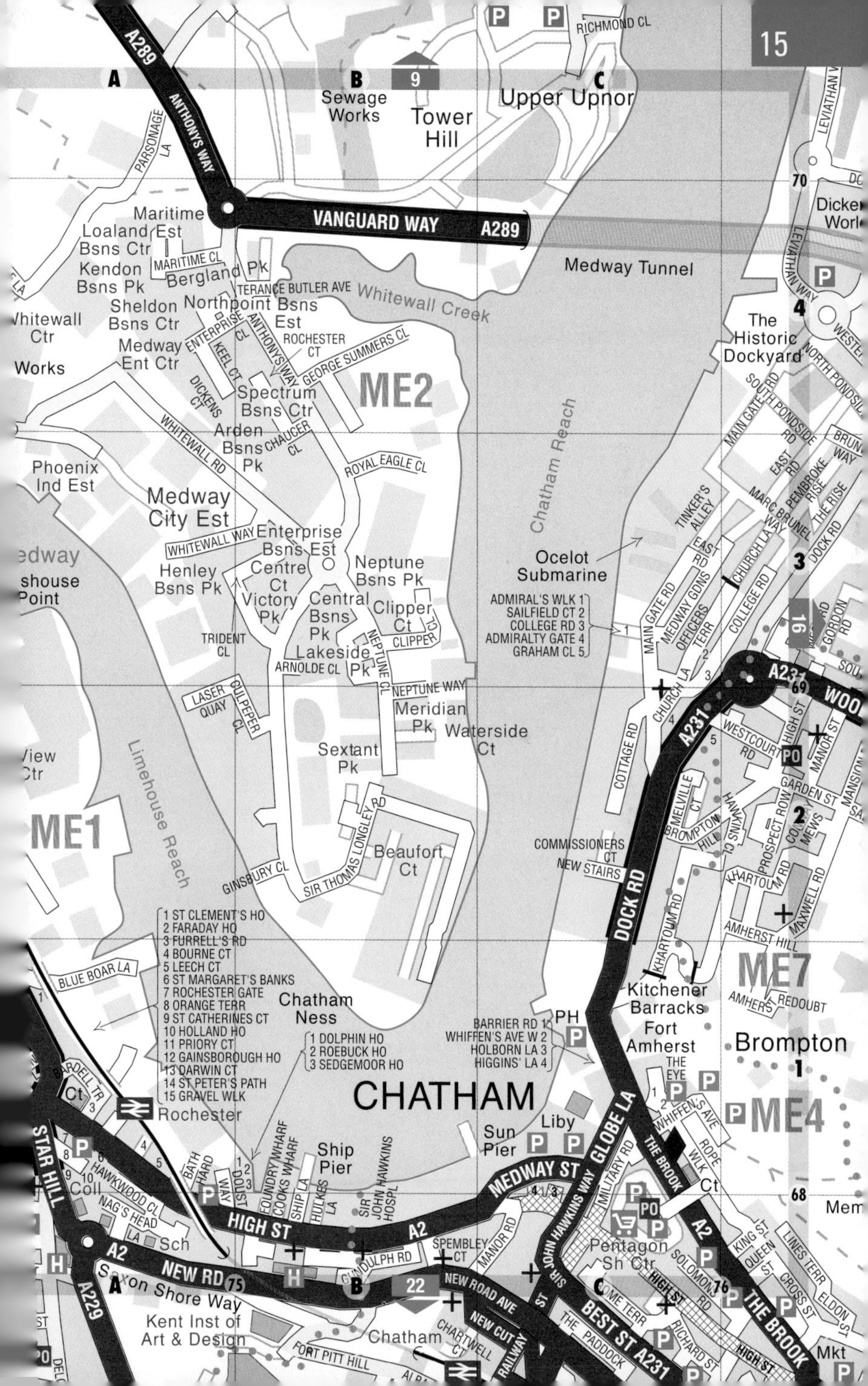
15
A
B
9
C
Sewage Works
Tower Hill
Upper Upnor
RICHMOND CL
A289
ANTHONYS WAY
PARSONAGE LA
Maritime Est
Loaland Bsns Ctr
Kendon Bsns Pk
Sheldon Bsns Ctr
Whitewall Ctr
Works
Medway Ent Ctr
MARITIME CL
Bergland Pk
VANGUARD WAY
A289
Medway Tunnel
TERANCE BUTLER AVE
Whitewall Creek
Northpoint Bsns Est
ENTERPRISE CL
KEEL CT
ROCHESTER CT
GEORGE SUMMERS CL
ME2
DICKENS CT
Spectrum Bsns Ctr
Arden Bsns Pk
CHAUCER CL
WHITEWALL RD
ROYAL EAGLE CL
Phoenix Ind Est
Medway City Est
WHITEWALL WAY
Enterprise Bsns Est
Centre Ct
Neptune Bsns Pk
Henley Bsns Pk
Victory Pk
Central Bsns Pk
Clipper Ct
CLIPPER CL
TRIDENT CL
Lakeside Pk
ARNOLDE CL
NEPTUNE CL
NEPTUNE WAY
Meridian Pk
Waterside Ct
LASER QUAY
CULPEPER CL
Sextant Pk
Medway
shouse Point
View Ctr
Limehouse Reach
ME1
SIR THOMAS LONGLEY RD
Beaufort Ct
GINSBURY CL
Chatham Reach
Ocelot Submarine
ADMIRAL'S WLK 1
SAILFIELD CT 2
COLLEGE RD 3
ADMIRALTY GATE 4
GRAHAM CL 5
COMMISSIONERS CT
NEW STAIRS
1 ST CLEMENT'S HO
2 FARADAY HO
3 FURRELL'S RD
4 BOURNE CT
5 LEECH CT
6 ST MARGARET'S BANKS
7 ROCHESTER GATE
8 ORANGE TERR
9 ST CATHERINES CT
10 HOLLAND HO
11 PRIORY CT
12 GAINSBOROUGH HO
13 DARWIN CT
14 ST PETER'S PATH
15 GRAVEL WLK
BLUE BOAR LA
Chatham Ness
1 DOLPHIN HO
2 ROEBUCK HO
3 SEDGEMOOR HO
CHATHAM
Rochester
BARDELL TR
Ct
STAR HILL
Coll
HAWKWOOD CL
NAG'S HEAD LA
Sch
BATH HARD
DOUST WAY
FOUNDRY WHARF
COOKS WHARF
SHIP LA
HULKES LA
SIR JOHN HAWKINS HOSPL
Ship Pier
Sun Pier
Liby
MEDWAY ST
GLOBE LA
HIGH ST
A2
NEW RD
Saxon Shore Way
A229
Kent Inst of Art & Design
SPEMBLEY CT
GUNDULPH RD
MANOR RD
22
NEW ROAD AVE
NEW CUT
RAILWAY ST
CHARTWELL CT
FORT PITT HILL
Chatham
BEST ST A231
THE PADDOCK
SIR JOHN HAWKINS WAY
MILITARY RD
Pentagon Sh Ctr
COME TERR
RICHARD ST
HIGH ST
SOLOMON RD
THE BROOK
A2
KING ST
QUEEN ST
LINES TERR
CROSS ST
ELDON ST
Mkt
68
Mem
76
LEVIATHAN WAY
70
Dickens World
4
The Historic Dockyard
WESTERN
NORTH PONDSIDE
SOUTH PONDSIDE RD
MAIN GATE RD
EAST RD
BRUNEL WAY
MARC BRUNEL WAY
PEMBROKE RISE
THE RISE
TINKER'S ALLEY
EAST RD
CHURCH LA
DOCK RD
3
MEDWAY GDNS
OFFICERS TERR
COLLEGE RD
16
GORDON RD
A231
69
WOOD
HIGH ST
MANOR ST
WESTCOURT RD
PO
COTTAGE RD
MELVILLE CT
HAWKINS CL
BROMPTON HILL
GARDEN ST
PROSPECT ROW
MANSION
2
KHARTOUM RD
MAXWELL RD
AMHERST HILL
DOCK RD
ME7
AMHERST REDOUBT
Kitchener Barracks
Fort Amherst
BARRIER RD 1
WHIFFEN'S AVE W 2
HOLBORN LA 3
HIGGINS' LA 4
PH
Brompton
1
THE EYE
WHIFFEN'S AVE
ROPE WLK
ME4

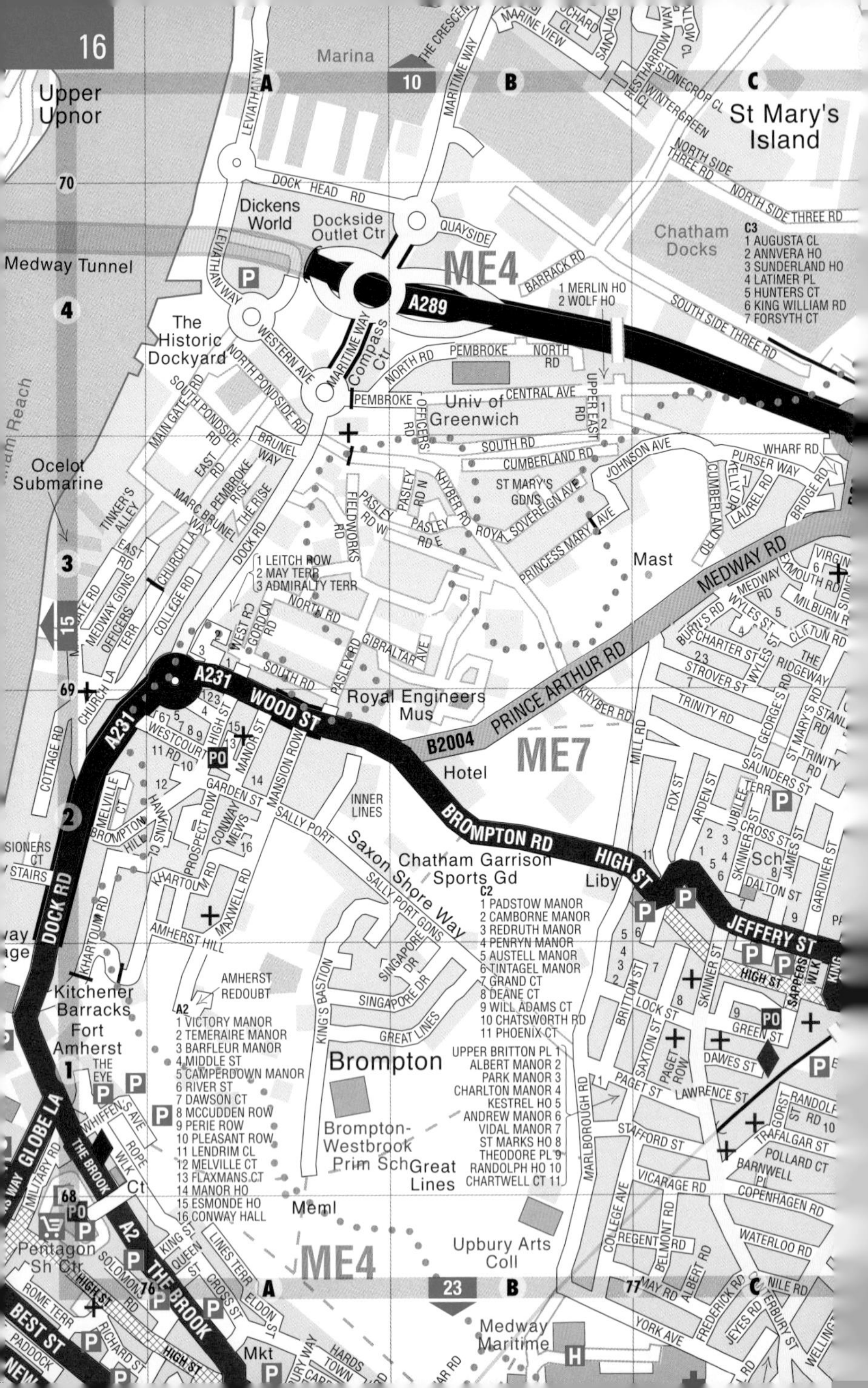

16
Marina
Upper Upnor
St Mary's Island
Dickens World
Dockside Outlet Ctr
Medway Tunnel
The Historic Dockyard
Ocelot Submarine
Compass Ctr
Univ of Greenwich
Chatham Docks
ME4
A289
C3
1 AUGUSTA CL
2 ANNVERA HO
3 SUNDERLAND HO
4 LATIMER PL
5 HUNTERS CT
6 KING WILLIAM RD
7 FORSYTH CT
1 MERLIN HO
2 WOLF HO
1 LEITCH ROW
2 MAY TERR
3 ADMIRALTY TERR
Mast
A231
WOOD ST
B2004
PRINCE ARTHUR RD
MEDWAY RD
Royal Engineers Mus
Hotel
ME7
BROMPTON RD
HIGH ST
JEFFERY ST
Chatham Garrison Sports Gd
Liby
Sch
C2
1 PADSTOW MANOR
2 CAMBORNE MANOR
3 REDRUTH MANOR
4 PENRYN MANOR
5 AUSTELL MANOR
6 TINTAGEL MANOR
7 GRAND CT
8 DEANE CT
9 WILL ADAMS CT
10 CHATSWORTH RD
11 PHOENIX CT
Saxon Shore Way
INNER LINES
AMHERST REDOUBT
A2
1 VICTORY MANOR
2 TEMERAIRE MANOR
3 BARFLEUR MANOR
4 MIDDLE ST
5 CAMPERDOWN MANOR
6 RIVER ST
7 DAWSON CT
8 MCCUDDEN ROW
9 PERIE ROW
10 PLEASANT ROW
11 LENDRIM CL
12 MELVILLE CT
13 FLAXMANS CT
14 MANOR HO
15 ESMONDE HO
16 CONWAY HALL
Kitchener Barracks
Fort Amherst
Brompton
Brompton-Westbrook Prim Sch
Great Lines
UPPER BRITTON PL 1
ALBERT MANOR 2
PARK MANOR 3
CHARLTON MANOR 4
KESTREL HO 5
ANDREW MANOR 6
VIDAL MANOR 7
ST MARKS HO 8
THEODORE PL 9
RANDOLPH HO 10
CHARTWELL CT 11
Meml
Upbury Arts Coll
ME4
Pentagon Sh Ctr
DOCK RD
GLOBE LA
THE BROOK
A2
Medway Maritime
Mkt
10
23
15

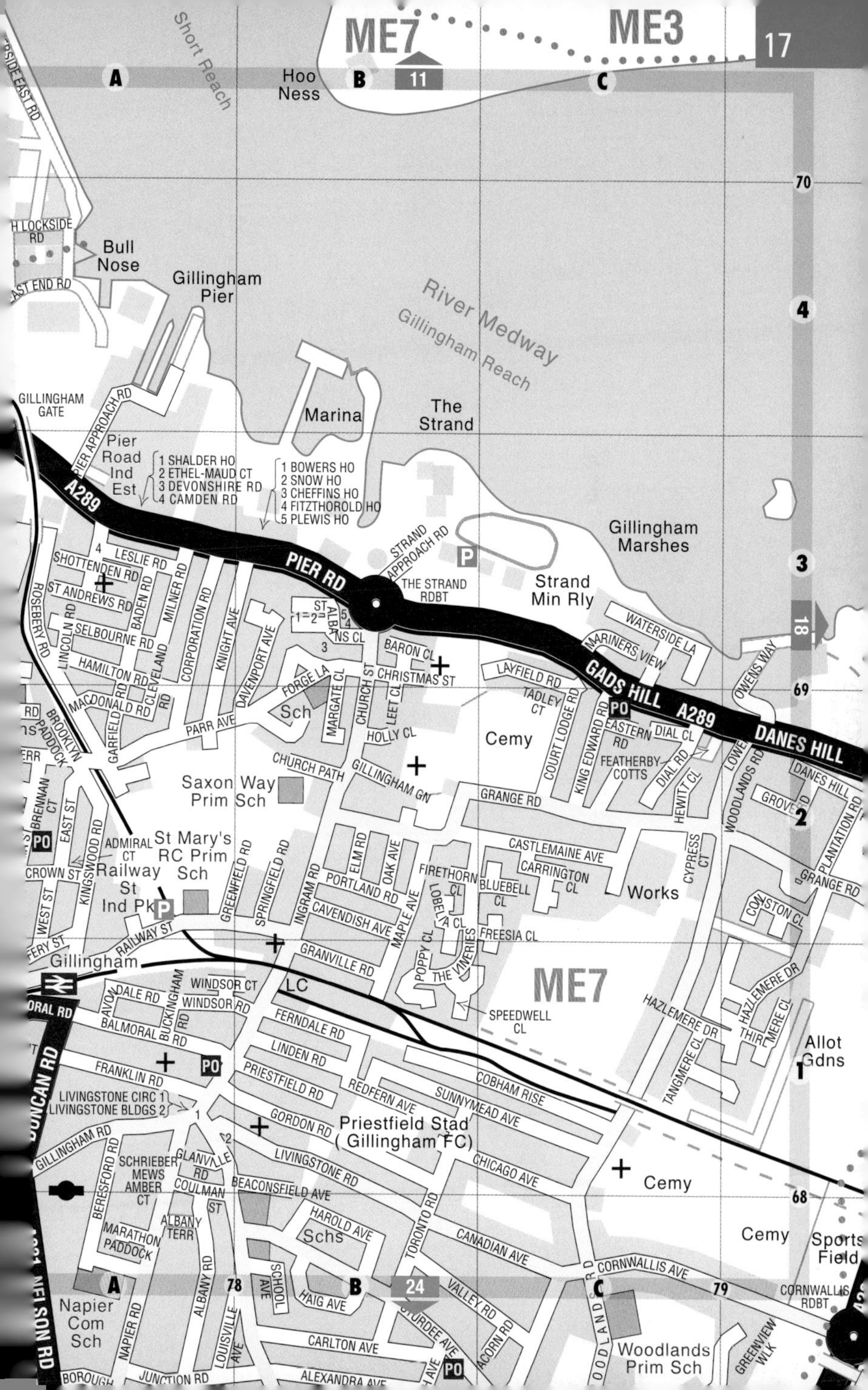
ME7
ME3
11
Hoo Ness
Short Reach
Bull Nose
Gillingham Pier
River Medway
Gillingham Reach
Marina
The Strand
GILLINGHAM GATE
PIER APPROACH RD
Pier Road Ind Est
1 SHALDER HO
2 ETHEL-MAUD CT
3 DEVONSHIRE RD
4 CAMDEN RD
1 BOWERS HO
2 SNOW HO
3 CHEFFINS HO
4 FITZTHOROLD HO
5 PLEWIS HO
A289
PIER RD
STRAND APPROACH RD
THE STRAND RDBT
Strand Min Rly
Gillingham Marshes
WATERSIDE LA
MARINERS VIEW
GADS HILL
DANES HILL
OWENS WAY
LESLIE RD
SHOTTENDEN RD
ST ANDREWS RD
SELBOURNE RD
HAMILTON RD
MACDONALD RD
ROSEBERY RD
LINCOLN RD
BADEN RD
MILNER RD
CLEVELAND RD
GARFIELD RD
CORPORATION RD
KNIGHT AVE
DAVENPORT AVE
PARR AVE
FORGE LA
Sch
MARGATE CL
CHURCH ST
BARON CL
CHRISTMAS ST
LEET CL
HOLLY CL
LAYFIELD RD
TADLEY CT
COURT LODGE RD
KING EDWARD RD
EASTERN RD
DIAL CL
DIAL RD
FEATHERBY COTTS
HEWITT CL
Cemy
CHURCH PATH
GILLINGHAM GN
Saxon Way Prim Sch
GRANGE RD
BROOKLYN PADDOCK
BRENNAN CT
EAST ST
KINGSWOOD RD
ADMIRAL CT
St Mary's RC Prim Sch
Railway St Ind Pk
CROWN ST
WEST ST
RAILWAY ST
GREENFIELD RD
SPRINGFIELD RD
INGRAM RD
ELM RD
OAK AVE
PORTLAND RD
CAVENDISH AVE
MAPLE AVE
FIRETHORN CL
LOBELIA CL
BLUEBELL CL
CASTLEMAINE AVE
CARRINGTON CL
Works
FREESIA CL
POPPY CL
THE VINERIES
SPEEDWELL CL
GRANVILLE RD
Gillingham
LC
WINDSOR CT
WINDSOR RD
DALE RD
AVON CL
BUCKINGHAM RD
BALMORAL RD
FERNDALE RD
LINDEN RD
PRIESTFIELD RD
REDFERN AVE
SUNNYMEAD AVE
COBHAM RISE
FRANKLIN RD
LIVINGSTONE CIRC 1
LIVINGSTONE BLDGS 2
GORDON RD
Priestfield Stad (Gillingham FC)
GILLINGHAM RD
BERESFORD RD
SCHRIEBER MEWS
AMBER CT
GLANVILLE RD
COULMAN ST
ALBANY TERR
MARATHON PADDOCK
BEACONSFIELD AVE
LIVINGSTONE RD
CHICAGO AVE
HAROLD AVE
Schs
TORONTO RD
CANADIAN AVE
CORNWALLIS AVE
CYPRESS CT
WOODLANDS RD
LOWER WOODLANDS RD
GROVE RD
PLANTATION RD
GRANGE RD
CONISTON CL
HAZLEMERE DR
THIRLMERE CL
TANGMERE CL
Allot Gdns
Sports Field
CORNWALLIS RDBT
DUNCAN RD
NELSON RD
Napier Com Sch
NAPIER RD
ALBANY RD
LOUISVILLE AVE
SCHOOL AVE
HAIG AVE
STURDEE AVE
VALLEY RD
ACORN RD
CARLTON AVE
ALEXANDRA AVE
JUNCTION RD
BOROUGH
WOODLANDS RD
Woodlands Prim Sch
GREENVIEW WLK
24
18
A B C
70 69 68
78 79
4 3 2 1

ME3
Hoo Fort
A
B
C
ME7
Folly Point
70
River Medway
Gillingham Reach
4
Copperhouse Marshes
Gillingham Marshes
3
17
Cinque Port Marshes
MARINERS VIEW
GADS HILL
69
PO
A289
OWENS WAY
DANES HILL
EASTERN RD
DIAL CL
FEATHERBY COTTS
DIAL RD
HEWITT CL
WOODLANDS RD
DANES HILL
GROVE RD
PLANTATION RD
LOWER RAINHAM RD
COPPERHOUSE LA
Walnut Tree Farm
Saxon Shore Way
2
B2004
PH
GRANGE RDBT
A289
Grange
Works
CYPRESS CT
GRANGE RD
CONISTON CL
Mill Hill
Sharp Green
THE SPIERS
LOWER RAINHAM RD
Grace Manor
HAZLEMERE DR
THIRLMERE CL
ME7
Lower Twydall
Allot Gdns
YOKOSUKA WAY
1
TANGMERE CL
1 BUTTERMERE CL
2 PENRITH CT
3 KESWICK CT
4 BRAITHWAITE CT
FEATHERBY RD
GRANGE RD
LADDS CNR
EASTCOURT LA
Cemy
68
ME8
Little London Farm
Cemy
Sports Field
EASTCOURT LA
LOWER TWYDALL LA
MANOR CT
CORNWALLIS AVE
BREDGAR RD
25
79
CORNWALLIS AVE
CORNWALLIS RDBT
A
B
80
C
LITTLE YORK MDWS
GODDEN WAY
CHALMERS WAY
Beechings Way Ind Ctr
NORTHBOURNE RD
Twydall Ent Ctr
Woodlands Prim Sch
GREENVIEW WLK
WOODLANDS RD

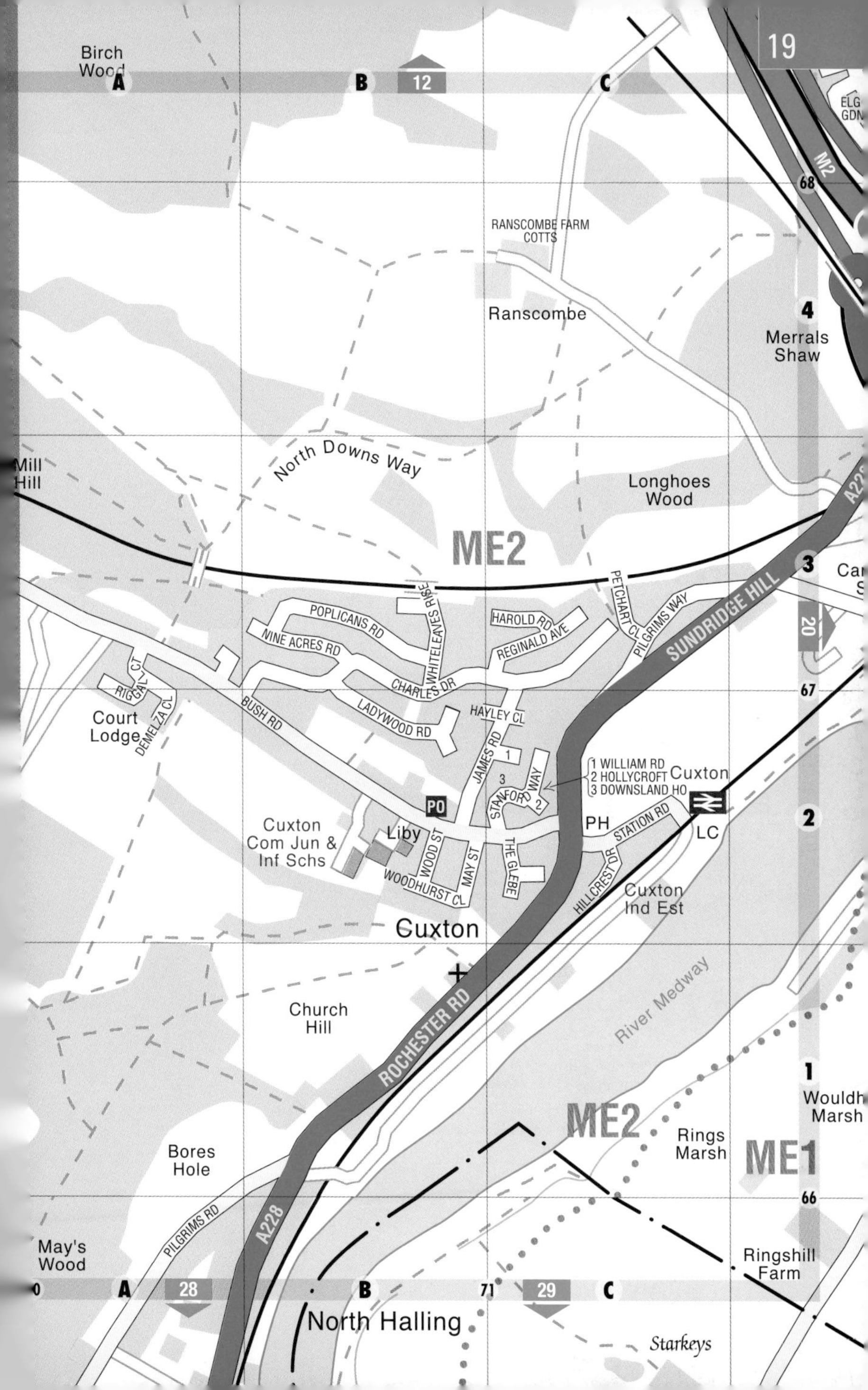
Birch Wood
A
B
12
C
ELG GDN
M2
68
RANSCOMBE FARM COTTS
Ranscombe
4
Merrals Shaw
Mill Hill
North Downs Way
Longhoes Wood
A228
ME2
3
20
POPLICANS RD
NINE ACRES RD
WHITELEAVES RISE
HAROLD RD
REGINALD AVE
PETCHART CL
PILGRIMS WAY
SUNDRIDGE HILL
CHARLES DR
RIGGAL CT
DEMELZA CL
Court Lodge
BUSH RD
LADYWOOD RD
HAYLEY CL
JAMES RD
67
1 WILLIAM RD
2 HOLLYCROFT
3 DOWNSLAND HO
Cuxton
STANFORD WAY
PO
PH
STATION RD
LC
2
Cuxton Com Jun & Inf Schs
Liby
WOOD ST
MAY ST
THE GLEBE
WOODHURST CL
HILLCREST DR
Cuxton Ind Est
Cuxton
River Medway
ROCHESTER RD
Church Hill
1
Wouldh Marsh
ME2
Rings Marsh
ME1
Bores Hole
66
PILGRIMS RD
A228
May's Wood
Ringshill Farm
A
28
B
71
29
C
North Halling
Starkeys

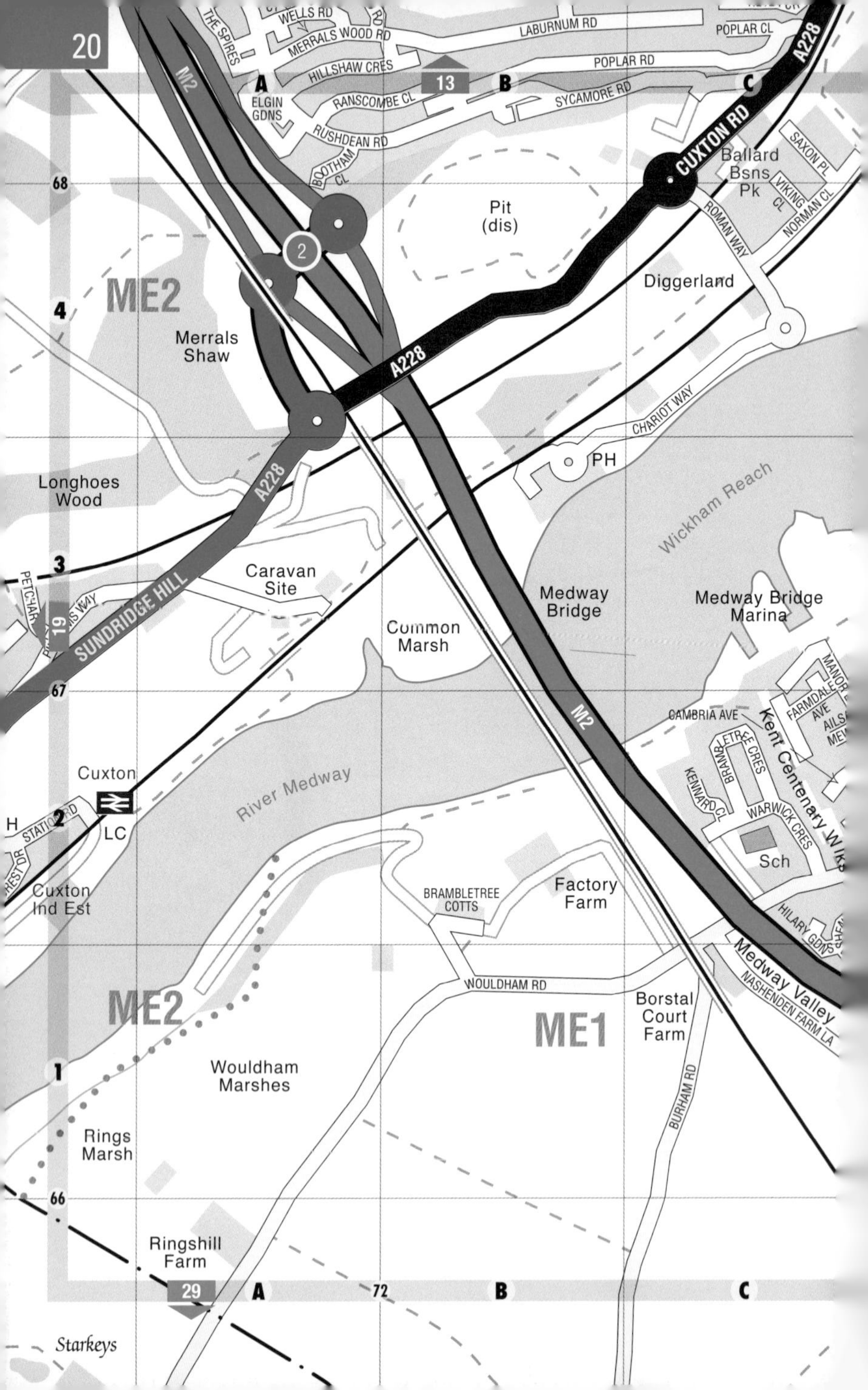
WELLS RD
THE SPIRES
MERRALS WOOD RD
LABURNUM RD
POPLAR CL
HILLSHAW CRES
POPLAR RD
A
13
B
C
A228
M2
ELGIN GDNS
RANSCOMBE CL
SYCAMORE RD
RUSHDEAN RD
CUXTON RD
BOOTHAM CL
Ballard Bsns Pk
SAXON PL
VIKING CL
NORMAN CL
ROMAN WAY
68
Pit (dis)
2
Diggerland
ME2
4
Merrals Shaw
A228
CHARIOT WAY
PH
Longhoes Wood
A228
Wickham Reach
3
Caravan Site
Medway Bridge
Medway Bridge Marina
SUNDRIDGE HILL
19
Common Marsh
67
MANOR
FARMDALE AVE
AILSA MEWS
CAMBRIA AVE
Kent Centenary Wlk
M2
Cuxton
River Medway
BRAMBLETREE CRES
KENNARD CL
WARWICK CRES
2
STATION RD
LC
Sch
Cuxton Ind Est
BRAMBLETREE COTTS
Factory Farm
HILARY GDNS
WOULDHAM RD
Medway Valley
NASHENDEN FARM LA
ME2
Borstal Court Farm
ME1
1
Wouldham Marshes
BURHAM RD
Rings Marsh
66
Ringshill Farm
29
A
72
B
C
Starkeys

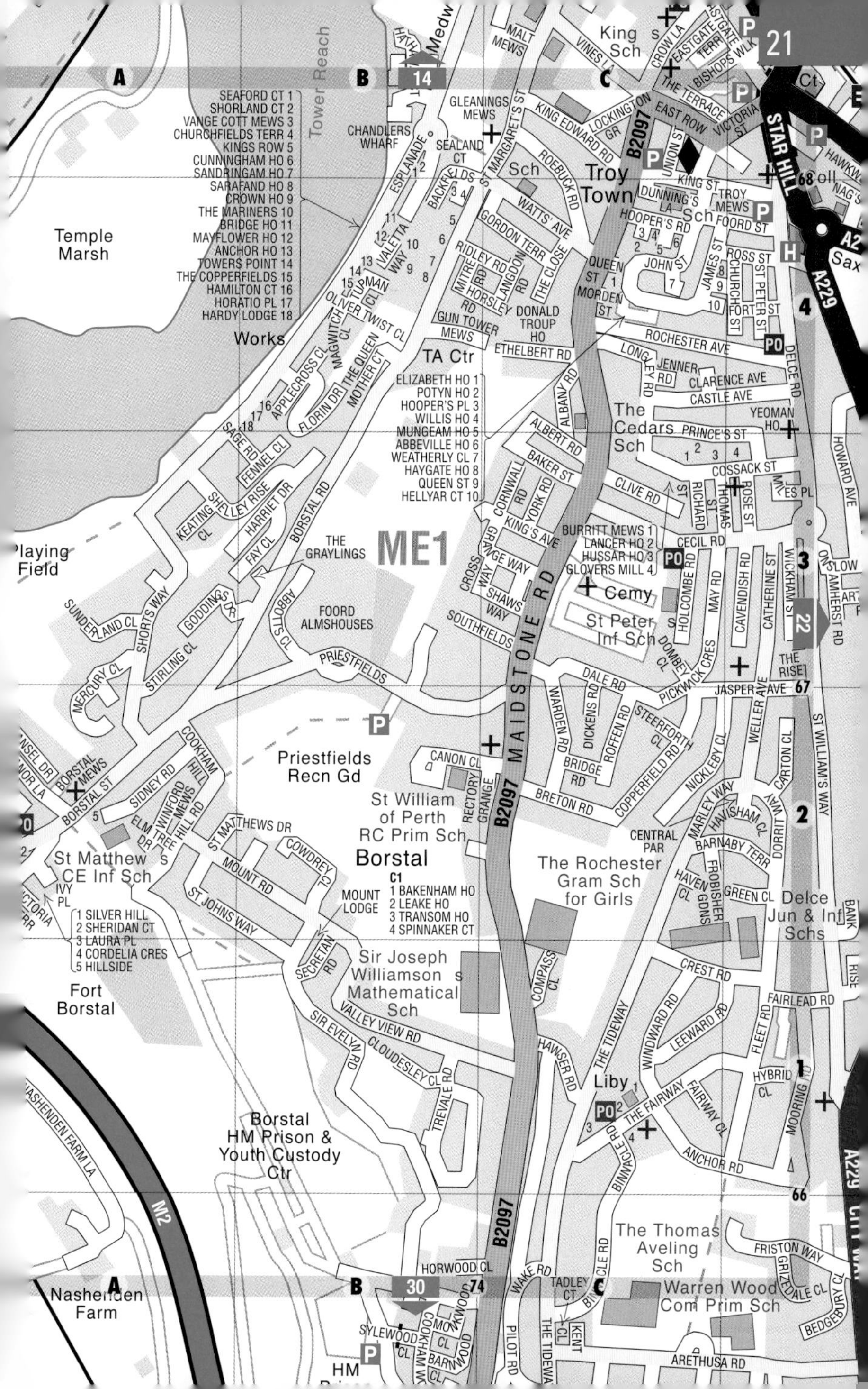
A
B
C
14
Tower Reach
Temple
Marsh
SEAFORD CT 1
SHORLAND CT 2
VANGE COTT MEWS 3
CHURCHFIELDS TERR 4
KINGS ROW 5
CUNNINGHAM HO 6
SANDRINGAM HO 7
SARAFAND HO 8
CROWN HO 9
THE MARINERS 10
BRIDGE HO 11
MAYFLOWER HO 12
ANCHOR HO 13
TOWERS POINT 14
THE COPPERFIELDS 15
HAMILTON CT 16
HORATIO PL 17
HARDY LODGE 18
Works
CHANDLERS
WHARF
GLEANINGS
MEWS
MALT
MEWS
King's
Sch
VINES LA
CROW LA
EASTGATE
TERR
BISHOPS WLK
THE TERRACE
EAST ROW
VICTORIA
ST
STAR HILL
LOCKINGTON
GR
KING EDWARD RD
B2097
SEALAND
CT
ESPLANADE
BACKFIELDS
ST MARGARET'S ST
Sch
ROEBUCK RD
Troy
Town
UNION ST
KING ST
TROY
MEWS
DUNNING'S
LA
HOOPER'S RD
FOORD ST
Sch
Coll
NAG'S
HAWKWOOD
A229
Sax
WATTS' AVE
GORDON TERR
RIDLEY RD
MITRE
RD
LANGDON
RD
THE CLOSE
HORSLEY
RD
QUEEN
ST
MORDEN
ST
JOHN ST
JAMES ST
ROSS ST
CHURCH ST
ST PETER ST
FORT ST
VALETTA
WAY
TUPMAN
CL
OLIVER TWIST CL
MAGWITCH
CL
GUN TOWER
MEWS
DONALD
TROUP
HO
ROCHESTER AVE
PO
DELCE RD
TA Ctr
ETHELBERT RD
LONGLEY RD
JENNER
RD
CLARENCE AVE
CASTLE AVE
APPLECROSS CL
FLORIN DR
THE QUEEN
MOTHER CT
ELIZABETH HO 1
POTYN HO 2
HOOPER'S PL 3
WILLIS HO 4
MUNGEAM HO 5
ABBEVILLE HO 6
WEATHERLY CL 7
HAYGATE HO 8
QUEEN ST 9
HELLYAR CT 10
ALBANY RD
ALBERT RD
The
Cedars
Sch
PRINCE'S ST
YEOMAN
HO
HOWARD AVE
SAGE RD
FENNEL CL
BAKER ST
CLIVE RD
COSSACK ST
RICHARD ST
THOMAS ST
ROSE ST
ES PL
KEATING
CL
SHELLEY RISE
HARRIET DR
BORSTAL RD
CORNWALL
RD
YORK RD
KING'S AVE
Playing
Field
FAY CL
THE
GRAYLINGS
ME1
BURRITT MEWS 1
LANCER HO 2
HUSSAR HO 3
GLOVERS MILL 4
CECIL RD
PO
HOLCOMBE RD
MAY RD
CAVENDISH RD
CATHERINE ST
WICKHAM ST
ONSLOW
AMHERST RD
GRANGE WAY
CROSS
WAY
SHAWS
WAY
Cemy
St Peter's
Inf Sch
GODDINGS
DR
SHORTS WAY
SUNDERLAND CL
ABBOTTS CL
FOORD
ALMSHOUSES
SOUTHFIELDS
MAIDSTONE RD
DOMBEY
CL
PICKWICK CRES
22
STIRLING CL
MERCURY CL
PRIESTFIELDS
DALE RD
THE
RISE
JASPER AVE
67
WELLER AVE
ST WILLIAM'S WAY
WARDEN RD
DICKENS RD
ROFFEN RD
STEERFORTH
CL
P
COOKHAM
HILL
BORSTAL
MEWS
BORSTAL ST
SIDNEY RD
Priestfields
Recn Gd
CANON CL
RECTORY
GRANGE
BRIDGE
RD
COPPERFIELD RD
NICKLEBY CL
CARTON CL
BRETON RD
MARLEY WAY
HAVISHAM CL
DORRIT WAY
WINFORD
MEWS
HILL RD
ELM TREE
DR
ST MATTHEWS DR
St William
of Perth
RC Prim Sch
CENTRAL
PAR
BARNABY TERR
St Matthew's
CE Inf Sch
COWDREY
CL
MOUNT RD
Borstal
C1
1 BAKENHAM HO
2 LEAKE HO
3 TRANSOM HO
4 SPINNAKER CT
The Rochester
Gram Sch
for Girls
HAVEN
CL
FROBISHER
GDNS
GREEN CL
Delce
Jun & Inf
Schs
IVY
PL
VICTORIA
TERR
1 SILVER HILL
2 SHERIDAN CT
3 LAURA PL
4 CORDELIA CRES
5 HILLSIDE
ST JOHNS WAY
MOUNT
LODGE
SECRETAN
RD
Sir Joseph
Williamson's
Mathematical
Sch
COMPASS
CL
CREST RD
Fort
Borstal
VALLEY VIEW RD
SIR EVELYN RD
CLOUDESLEY CL
THE TIDEWAY
WINDWARD RD
LEEWARD RD
FLEET RD
FAIRLEAD RD
HAWSER RD
Liby
PO
THE FAIRWAY
FAIRWAY CL
HYBRID
CL
MOORING RD
TREVALE RD
NASHENDEN FARM LA
Borstal
HM Prison &
Youth Custody
Ctr
BINNACLE RD
ANCHOR RD
66
A229 CITY WAY
M2
The Thomas
Aveling
Sch
FRISTON WAY
GRIZEDALE CL
BEDGEBURY CL
Nashenden
Farm
HORWOOD CL
74
30
WAKE RD
TADLEY
CT
Warren Wood
Com Prim Sch
SYLEWOOD CL
COOKHAM WOOD
MONKWOOD
CL
BARNWOOD
PILOT RD
THE TIDEWAY
KENT CL
ARETHUSA RD
HM
Prison

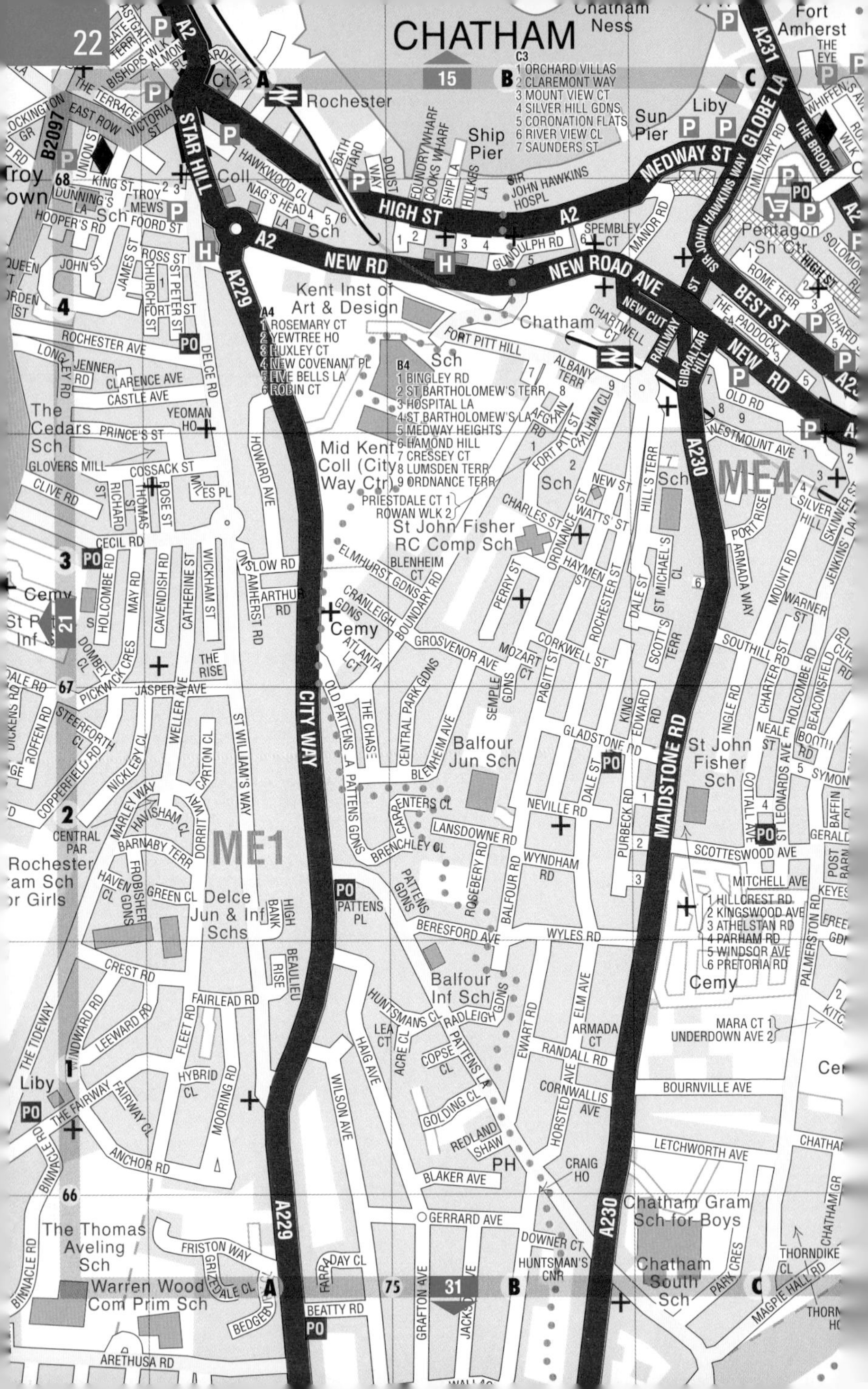
CHATHAM
Chatham Ness
Fort Amherst
15
31
21
C3
1 ORCHARD VILLAS
2 CLAREMONT WAY
3 MOUNT VIEW CT
4 SILVER HILL GDNS
5 CORONATION FLATS
6 RIVER VIEW CL
7 SAUNDERS ST
A4
1 ROSEMARY CT
2 YEWTREE HO
3 HUXLEY CT
4 NEW COVENANT PL
5 FIVE BELLS LA
6 ROBIN CT
B4
1 BINGLEY RD
2 ST BARTHOLOMEW'S TERR
3 HOSPITAL LA
4 ST BARTHOLOMEW'S LA
5 MEDWAY HEIGHTS
6 HAMOND HILL
7 CRESSEY CT
8 LUMSDEN TERR
9 ORDNANCE TERR
PRIESTDALE CT 1
ROWAN WLK 2
1 HILLCREST RD
2 KINGSWOOD AVE
3 ATHELSTAN RD
4 PARHAM RD
5 WINDSOR AVE
6 PRETORIA RD
MARA CT 1
UNDERDOWN AVE 2
Rochester
Sun Pier
Ship Pier
Liby
Coll
Sch
Kent Inst of Art & Design
Mid Kent Coll (City Way Ctr)
St John Fisher RC Comp Sch
St John Fisher Sch
Pentagon Sh Ctr
The Cedars Sch
Cemy
Balfour Jun Sch
Balfour Inf Sch
Delce Jun & Inf Schs
Rochester Gram Sch for Girls
Chatham Gram Sch for Boys
Chatham South Sch
The Thomas Aveling Sch
Warren Wood Com Prim Sch
Troy Town
ME1
ME4
A2
A229
A230
A231
B2097
STAR HILL
HIGH ST
NEW RD
NEW ROAD AVE
MEDWAY ST
GLOBE LA
BEST ST
CITY WAY
MAIDSTONE RD
SIR JOHN HAWKINS WAY
SIR JOHN HAWKINS HOSPL
FORT PITT HILL
GIBRALTAR HILL
RAILWAY ST
NEW CUT
CHARTWELL CT
ROCHESTER AVE
CLARENCE AVE
CASTLE AVE
PRINCE'S ST
CLIVE RD
CECIL RD
HOLCOMBE RD
MAY RD
CAVENDISH RD
CATHERINE ST
WICKHAM ST
JASPER AVE
WELLER AVE
ST WILLIAM'S WAY
HOWARD AVE
ONSLOW RD
ARTHUR RD
ELMHURST GDNS
BOUNDARY RD
GROSVENOR AVE
CENTRAL PARK GDNS
BLENHEIM AVE
OLD PATTENS LA
PATTENS GDNS
CARPENTERS CL
LANSDOWNE RD
BRENCHLEY CL
ROSEBERY RD
BALFOUR RD
WYNDHAM RD
NEVILLE RD
GLADSTONE RD
CORKWELL ST
ROCHESTER ST
PERRY ST
HAYMEN ST
ORDNANCE ST
WATTS' ST
NEW ST
CHARLES ST
HILL'S TERR
DALE ST
ST MICHAEL'S CL
SCOTT'S TERR
KING EDWARD RD
PURBECK RD
WESTMOUNT AVE
OLD RD
SILVER HILL
PORT RISE
ARMADA WAY
MOUNT RD
SOUTHILL RD
INGLE RD
CHARTER ST
HOLCOMBE RD
BEACONSFIELD AVE
ST LEONARDS AVE
COTTALL AVE
SCOTTESWOOD AVE
MITCHELL AVE
PALMERSTON RD
WYLES RD
BERESFORD AVE
HUNTSMANS CL
RADLEIGH GDNS
PATTENS LA
EWART RD
ELM AVE
ARMADA CT
RANDALL RD
CORNWALLIS AVE
HORSTED AVE
BOURNVILLE AVE
LETCHWORTH AVE
BLAKER AVE
GERRARD AVE
DOWNER CT
HUNTSMAN'S CNR
CRAIG HO
REDLAND SHAW
GOLDING CL
COPSE CL
ACRE CL
LEA CT
HAIG AVE
WILSON AVE
GRAFTON AVE
JACKSON AVE
BEATTY RD
FARADAY CL
FRISTON WAY
GRIZEDALE CL
BEDGEBURY CL
ARETHUSA RD
ANCHOR RD
MOORING RD
HYBRID CL
FLEET RD
FAIRLEAD RD
LEEWARD RD
WINDWARD RD
CREST RD
THE TIDEWAY
THE FAIRWAY
FAIRWAY CL
BINNACLE RD
HIGH BANK
BEAULIEU RISE
HAVEN GDNS
FROBISHER GDNS
GREEN CL
BARNABY TERR
HAVISHAM CL
MARLEY WAY
DORRIT WAY
CARTON CL
NICKLEBY CL
COPPERFIELD RD
STEERFORTH CL
PICKWICK CRES
DOMBEY CL
ROFFEN RD
CENTRAL PAR
MAGPIE HALL RD
PARK CRES
THORNDIKE CL
CHATHAM GR
KING ST
HOOPER'S RD
JOHN ST
JAMES ST
ROSS ST
ST PETER ST
FORT ST
CHURCH ST
FOORD ST
TROY MEWS
NAG'S HEAD LA
HAWKWOOD CL
EAST ROW
VICTORIA ST
THE TERRACE
BISHOPS WLK
UNION ST
GUNDULPH RD
SPEMBLEY CT
MANOR RD
ROME TERR
THE PADDOCK
MILITARY RD
THE BROOK
SOLOMON RD
HIGH ST
RICHARD ST
WHIFFEN'S AVE
HULKES LA
SHIP LA
COOKS WHARF
FOUNDRY WHARF
DOUST WAY
BATH HARD
ALBANY TERR
AFGHAN RD
FORT PITT ST
CHATHAM CL
CRANLEIGH GDNS
ATLANTA CT
BLENHEIM CT
THE CHASE
SEMPLE GDNS
MOZART CT
PAGITT ST
DELCE RD
YEOMAN HO
COSSACK ST
GLOVERS MILL
ROSE ST
THOMAS ST
RICHARD ST
ST ALBANS RD
AMHERST RD
THE RISE
PATTENS PL
WARNER ST
NEALE ST
BOOTH RD
SYMONS AVE
BAFFIN CL
JENKINS' DALE
SKINNER ST

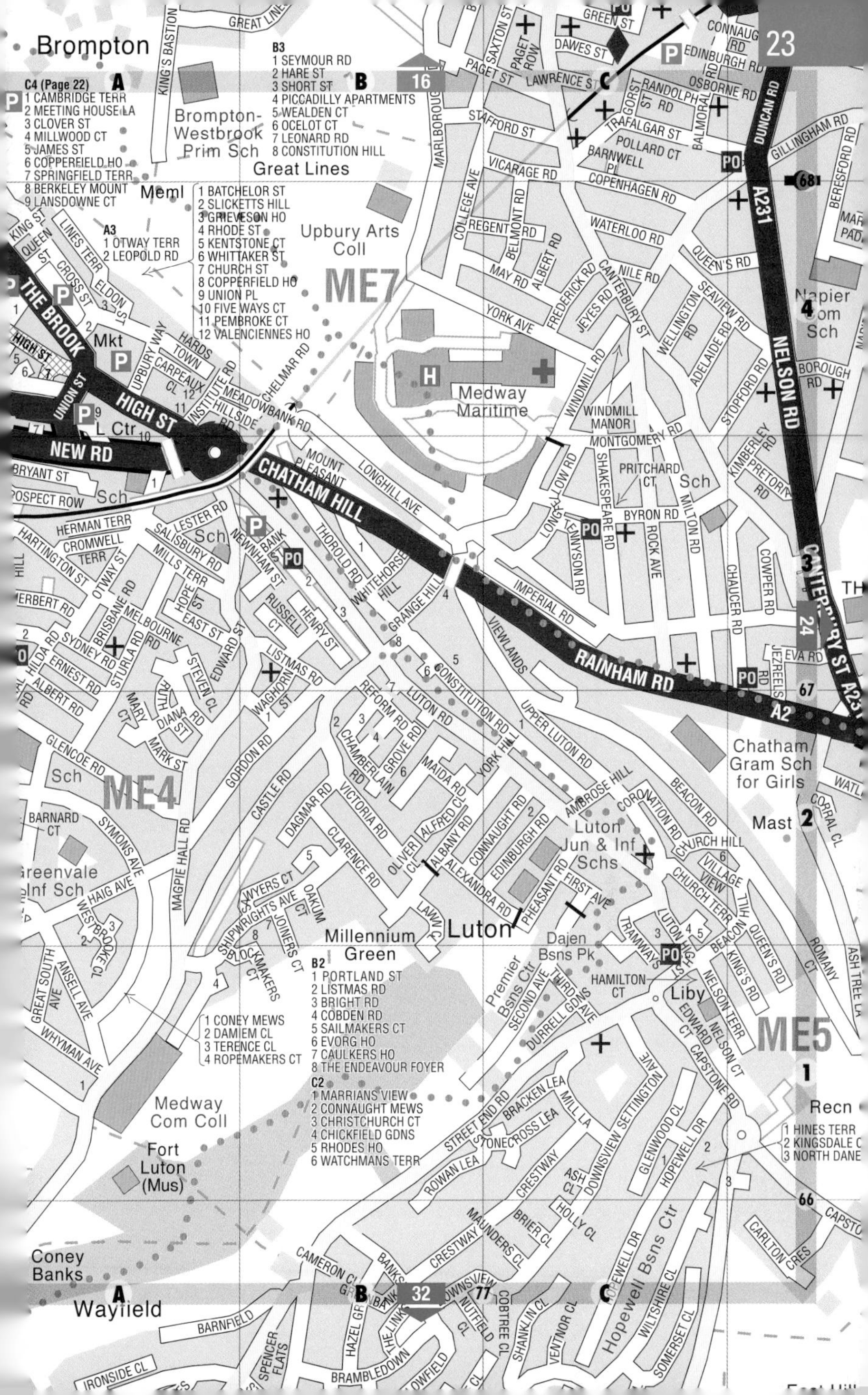

23
Brompton
C4 (Page 22)
1 CAMBRIDGE TERR
2 MEETING HOUSE LA
3 CLOVER ST
4 MILLWOOD CT
5 JAMES ST
6 COPPERFIELD HO
7 SPRINGFIELD TERR
8 BERKELEY MOUNT
9 LANSDOWNE CT
A3
1 OTWAY TERR
2 LEOPOLD RD
B3
1 SEYMOUR RD
2 HARE ST
3 SHORT ST
4 PICCADILLY APARTMENTS
5 WEALDEN CT
6 OCELOT CT
7 LEONARD RD
8 CONSTITUTION HILL
1 BATCHELOR ST
2 SLICKETTS HILL
3 GRIEVESON HO
4 RHODE ST
5 KENTSTONE CT
6 WHITTAKER ST
7 CHURCH ST
8 COPPERFIELD HO
9 UNION PL
10 FIVE WAYS CT
11 PEMBROKE CT
12 VALENCIENNES HO
Brompton-Westbrook Prim Sch
Great Lines
Meml
Upbury Arts Coll
ME7
Medway Maritime
Windmill Manor
Napier Com Sch
THE BROOK
HIGH ST
NEW RD
CHATHAM HILL
RAINHAM RD
NELSON RD
DUNCAN RD
A231
A2
Mkt
L Ctr
Sch
ME4
Greenvale Inf Sch
Luton Jun & Inf Schs
Luton
Millennium Green
Dajen Bsns Pk
Premier Bsns Ctr
Liby
Chatham Gram Sch for Girls
Mast
ME5
Recn
1 HINES TERR
2 KINGSDALE C
3 NORTH DANE
B2
1 PORTLAND ST
2 LISTMAS RD
3 BRIGHT RD
4 COBDEN RD
5 SAILMAKERS CT
6 EVORG HO
7 CAULKERS HO
8 THE ENDEAVOUR FOYER
C2
1 MARRIANS VIEW
2 CONNAUGHT MEWS
3 CHRISTCHURCH CT
4 CHICKFIELD GDNS
5 RHODES HO
6 WATCHMANS TERR
1 CONEY MEWS
2 DAMIEM CL
3 TERENCE CL
4 ROPEMAKERS CT
Medway Com Coll
Fort Luton (Mus)
Coney Banks
Wayfield
Hopewell Bsns Ctr
16
24
32

17
33
23
A
B
C
1
2
3
4
ME7
ME5
GILLINGHAM
A231 DUNCAN RD
NELSON RD
CANTERBURY ST A231
WATLING ST
SOVEREIGN BVD
A2
ITO WAY
Priestfield Stad (Gillingham FC)
Cemy
Napier Com Sch
Gillingham Park
TH
Woodlands Prim Sch
The Robert Napier Sch
1 ASHBURN MEWS
2 KEETREE MEWS
3 PORTREE MEWS
Chatham Gram Sch for Girls
Mast
CH
WILL ADAMS RDBT
Sports Gd
Liby
Recn Gd
Wagon at Hale (PH)
Hale
Hopewell Bsns Ctr
BALMORAL RD
FRANKLIN RD
LINDEN RD
COBHAM RISE
SUNNYMEAD AVE
REDFERN AVE
GORDON RD
LIVINGSTONE RD
CHICAGO AVE
BEACONSFIELD AVE
HAROLD AVE
CANADIAN AVE
CORNWALLIS AVE
TORONTO RD
VALLEY RD
ACORN RD
STURDEE AVE
HAIG AVE
SCHOOL AVE
CARLTON AVE
ALEXANDRA AVE
LARKFIELD AVE
FOURTH AVE
THIRD AVE
SECOND AVE
FIRST AVE
BEATTY AVE
WOODLANDS RD
WOODLANDS TERR
JUNCTION RD
BOROUGH RD
NAPIER RD
ALBANY RD
ALBANY TERR
LOUISVILLE AVE
COULMAN ST
GLANVILLE RD
SCHRIEBER MEWS
AMBER CT
MARATHON PADDOCK
BERESFORD RD
GILLINGHAM RD
CONNAUGHT RD
OSBORNE RD
RANDOLPH RD
GORST ST
TRAFALGAR ST
POLLARD CT
COPENHAGEN RD
WATERLOO RD
QUEEN'S RD
NILE RD
CANTERBURY ST
WELLINGTON RD
SEAVIEW RD
ADELAIDE RD
STOPFORD RD
KIMBERLEY RD
PRETORIA RD
MONTGOMERY RD
PRITCHARD CT
SHAKESPEARE RD
BYRON RD
MILTON RD
ROCK AVE
CHAUCER RD
COWPER RD
BRASENOSE RD
BARNSOLE RD
ST BARNABAS CL
OXFORD RD
CHADA AVE
SEATON RD
PARK AVE
CLEAVE RD
MALVERN RD
HOLMSIDE
GLEBE RD
CROSLEY RD
STUART RD
CHESTER RD
EVA RD
JEZREELS RD
PALACE CT
WATLING AVE
STAR MILL LA
MAYNARD PL
STAR MILL CT
CORRAL CL
BEECHWOOD AVE
MONTROSE AVE
OSPREY AVE
DERBY RD
AUSTIN CL
ZETLAND AVE
ROWLAND AVE
ROWLAND CL
NORE CL
LEYTON AVE
PRESTON AVE
ALLISON AVE
DARLAND AVE
HUNTERS WAY
HUNTERS WAY W
KINGSWAY
WINDYRIDGE
AUDLEY AVE
YEOMAN DR
HIGHRIDGE
HERITAGE DR
EMBASSY CL
ACADEMY DR
CENTURION
STONEY BANK
HAMELIN RD
STAR LA
WILL ADAMS WAY
BEACON RD
CORONATION RD
CHURCH HILL
VILLAGE VIEW
CHURCH TERR
BEACON HILL
QUEEN'S RD
KING'S RD
NELSON TERR
NELSON CT
EDWARD CT
LUTON HIGH ST
TRAMWAYS
HAMILTON CT
CAPSTONE RD
ROMANY CT
ASH TREE LA
GLENWOOD CL
HOPEWELL DR
SETTINGTON
CARLTON CRES
NORTH DANE WAY
WILTSHIRE CL
SOMERSET CL
PO
P

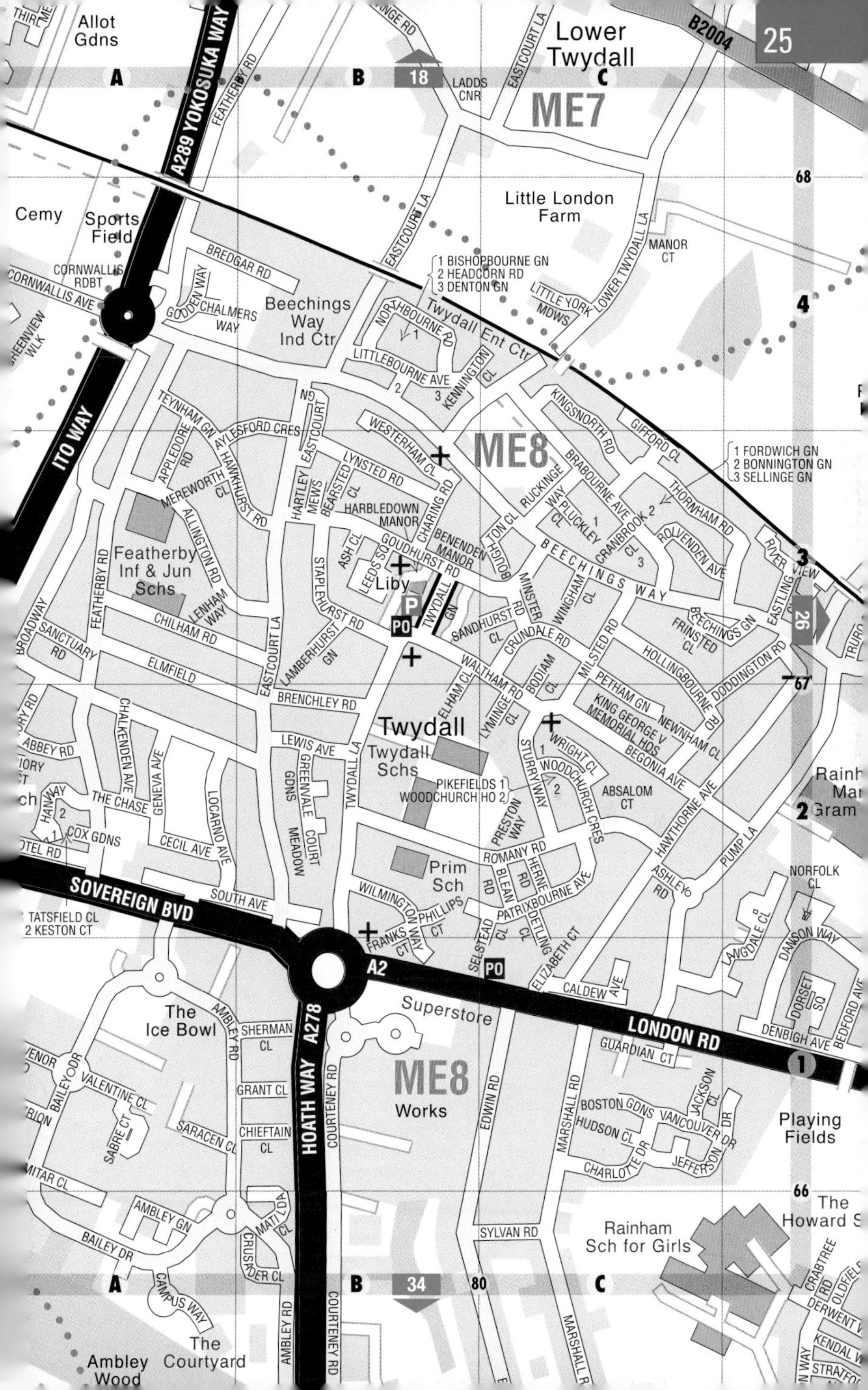
Lower Twydall
ME7
Little London Farm
Beechings Way Ind Ctr
Twydall Ent Ctr
ME8
Featherby Inf & Jun Schs
Twydall
Twydall Schs
Prim Sch
Superstore
ME8
Works
The Ice Bowl
Rainham Sch for Girls
Playing Fields
The Courtyard
Ambley Wood
SOVEREIGN BVD
LONDON RD
HOATH WAY A278
A289 YOKOSUKA WAY
ITO WAY
B2004
A2
1 BISHOPBOURNE GN
2 HEADCORN RD
3 DENTON GN
1 FORDWICH GN
2 BONNINGTON GN
3 SELLINGE GN
PIKEFIELDS 1
WOODCHURCH HO 2
1 TATSFIELD CL
2 KESTON CT

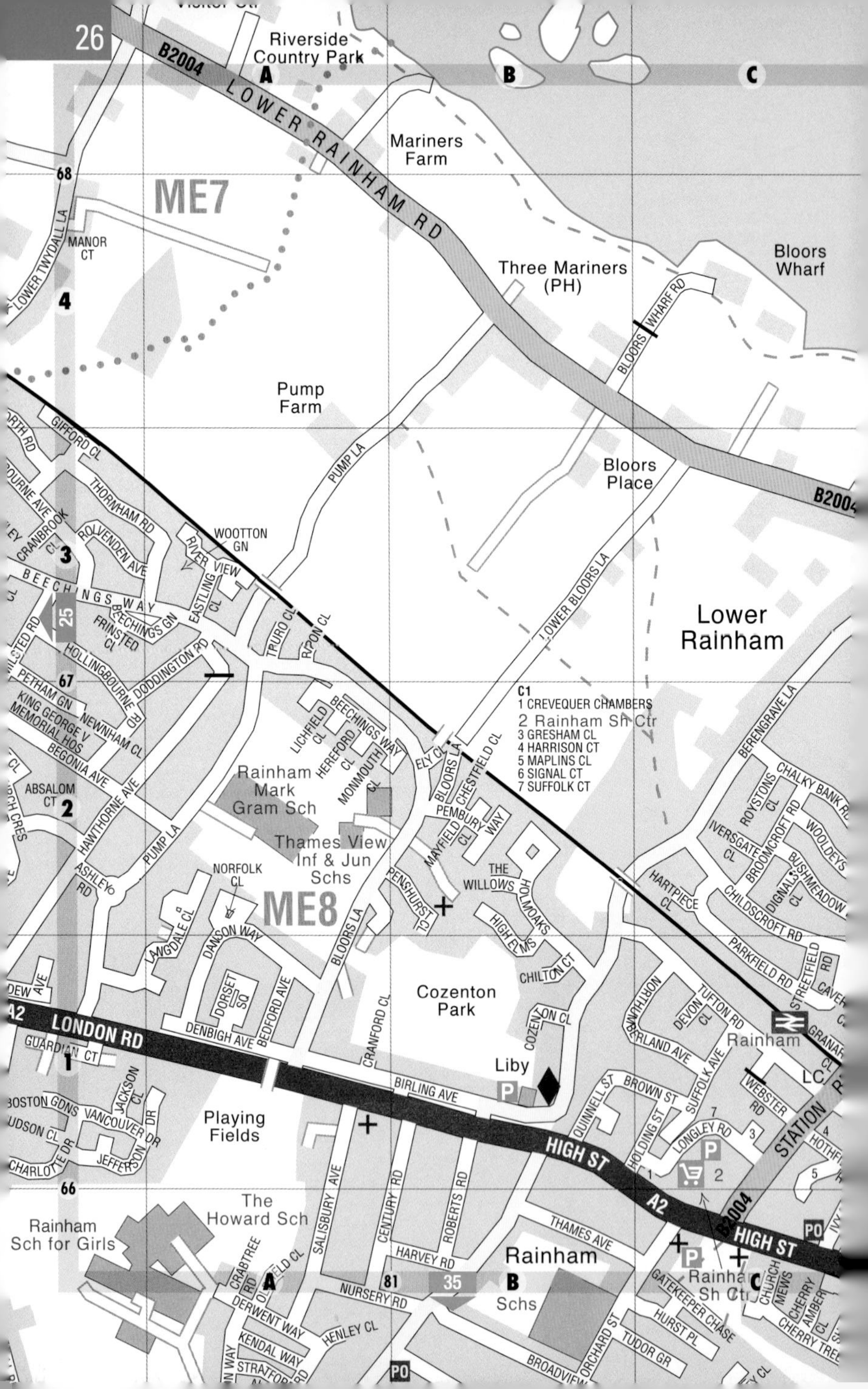
Riverside Country Park
A
B
C
B2004
LOWER RAINHAM RD
Mariners Farm
ME7
68
LOWER TWYDALL LA
MANOR CT
4
Three Mariners (PH)
Bloors Wharf
BLOORS WHARF RD
Pump Farm
GIFFORD CL
THORNHAM RD
PUMP LA
Bloors Place
B2004
CRANBROOK CL
ROLVENDEN AVE
WOOTTON GN
RIVER VIEW
3
BEECHINGS WAY
BEECHINGS GN
EASTLING CL
25
FRINSTED CL
TRURO CL
RIPON CL
LOWER BLOORS LA
Lower Rainham
HOLLINGBOURNE RD
DODDINGTON RD
67
PETHAM GN
NEWNHAM CL
KING GEORGE V MEMORIAL HOS
BEGONIA AVE
LICHFIELD CL
BEECHINGS WAY
HEREFORD CL
MONMOUTH CL
ELY CL
BLOORS LA
CHESTFIELD CL
C1
1 CREVEQUER CHAMBERS
2 Rainham Sh Ctr
3 GRESHAM CL
4 HARRISON CT
5 MAPLINS CL
6 SIGNAL CT
7 SUFFOLK CT
BERENGRAVE LA
CHALKY BANK RD
ABSALOM CT
2
HAWTHORNE AVE
Rainham Mark Gram Sch
PEMBURY WAY
MAYFIELD CL
ROYSTONS CL
BROOMCROFT RD
WOOLDEYS
IVERSGATE CL
Thames View Inf & Jun Schs
PUMP LA
ASHLEY RD
NORFOLK CL
THE WILLOWS
HOLMOAKS
HARTPIECE CL
DIGNALS CL
BUSHMEADOW
CHILDSCROFT RD
PENSHURST CL
ME8
HIGH ELMS
LANGDALE CL
DANSON WAY
BLOORS LA
CHILTON CT
PARKFIELD RD
STREETFIELD RD
DEW AVE
DORSET SQ
BEDFORD AVE
Cozenton Park
CRANFORD CL
COZENTON CL
NORTHUMBERLAND AVE
DEVON CL
TUFTON RD
A2
LONDON RD
DENBIGH AVE
Rainham
GRANARY CL
GUARDIAN CT
1
Liby
P
BIRLING AVE
QUINNELL ST
BROWN ST
SUFFOLK AVE
WEBSTER RD
LC
JACKSON CL
BOSTON GDNS
VANCOUVER DR
Playing Fields
HIGH ST
HOLDING ST
LONGLEY RD
7
3
STATION RD
4
HUDSON CL
JEFFERSON DR
CHARLOTTE DR
P
1
2
5
66
A2
B2004
The Howard Sch
SALISBURY AVE
CENTURY RD
ROBERTS RD
THAMES AVE
PO
Rainham Sch for Girls
CRABTREE RD
HARVEY RD
Rainham
P
HIGH ST
A
81
35
B
Rainham Sh Ctr
C
CHURCH MEWS
CHERRY AMBER CL
NURSERY RD
Schs
GATEKEEPER CHASE
CHERRY TREE
DERWENT WAY
HENLEY CL
HURST PL
KENDAL WAY
ORCHARD ST
TUDOR GR
STRATFORD
PO
BROADVIEW

27
A
B
C
Saxon Shore Way
Otterham Creek
68
MOTNEY HILL RD
Wharf
Horsham Marsh
4
Horsh
Farr
WOODRUFF CL
HORSHAM LA
WEST MOTNEY WAY
Wharf
Caravan Park
ME
PH
Mill Farm
3
Berengrave Nature Reserve
LOWER RAINHAM RD
PH
GILLS TERR
Windmill Hill
WALLBRIDGE LA
Macklands
LAMBOURNE PL
Otterham Quay
67
ANGEL COTTS
HUBBARDS COTTS
MACKLANDS WAY
COBDOWN GR
ELLISON WAY
MACKLANDS HO
ME8
The Three Sisters (PH)
2
GRENADIER CL
WIVENHOE CL
FINWELL RD
CLOVER LAY
HOMEFIELD DR
WILKS CL
COODEN CL
TWYFORD CL
B2004 STATION RD
OTTERHAM QUAY LA
LITTLEFIELD RD
WOOLBROOK CL
KENT TERR
Natal Farm
TILBURY RD
SHOREFIELDS
WARLINGHAM CL
TEN ACRE WAY
BURRSTOCK WAY
CALDECOTE CL
Cloverlay Ind Pk
WILLIAM ST
BYTHORNE CT
ME9
CANTERBURY LA
HENRY ST
TASWELL RD
SKENE CL
BANKY FIELDS CL
2
1
Riverside Prim Sch
PEARMAN CL
BEDSON WLK
1 ST EDMUNDS WAY
2 HARWOOD RD
1
DURLING CT
SEYMOUR RD
WAKELEY RD
Meredale Sch
SCOTT AVE
MARDALE CL
VINEYARD CRES
SMARDEN WLK
SCOTT AVE
FARNHAM CL
FARNHAM CL
66
WINCHESTER WAY
THOMPSON CL
SOLOMON RD
RUSSELLS AVE
BRAMLEY CL
OTTERHAM QUAY LA
SUNDERLAND DR
HIGH DEWAR RD
GLOUCESTER CL
CHICHESTER CL
P
A
B
36
83
C
SEYMOUR RD
OAK LA
HIGH ST A2
QUEENS CT
PEARTREE COTTS
MIERSCOURT CL
Culver

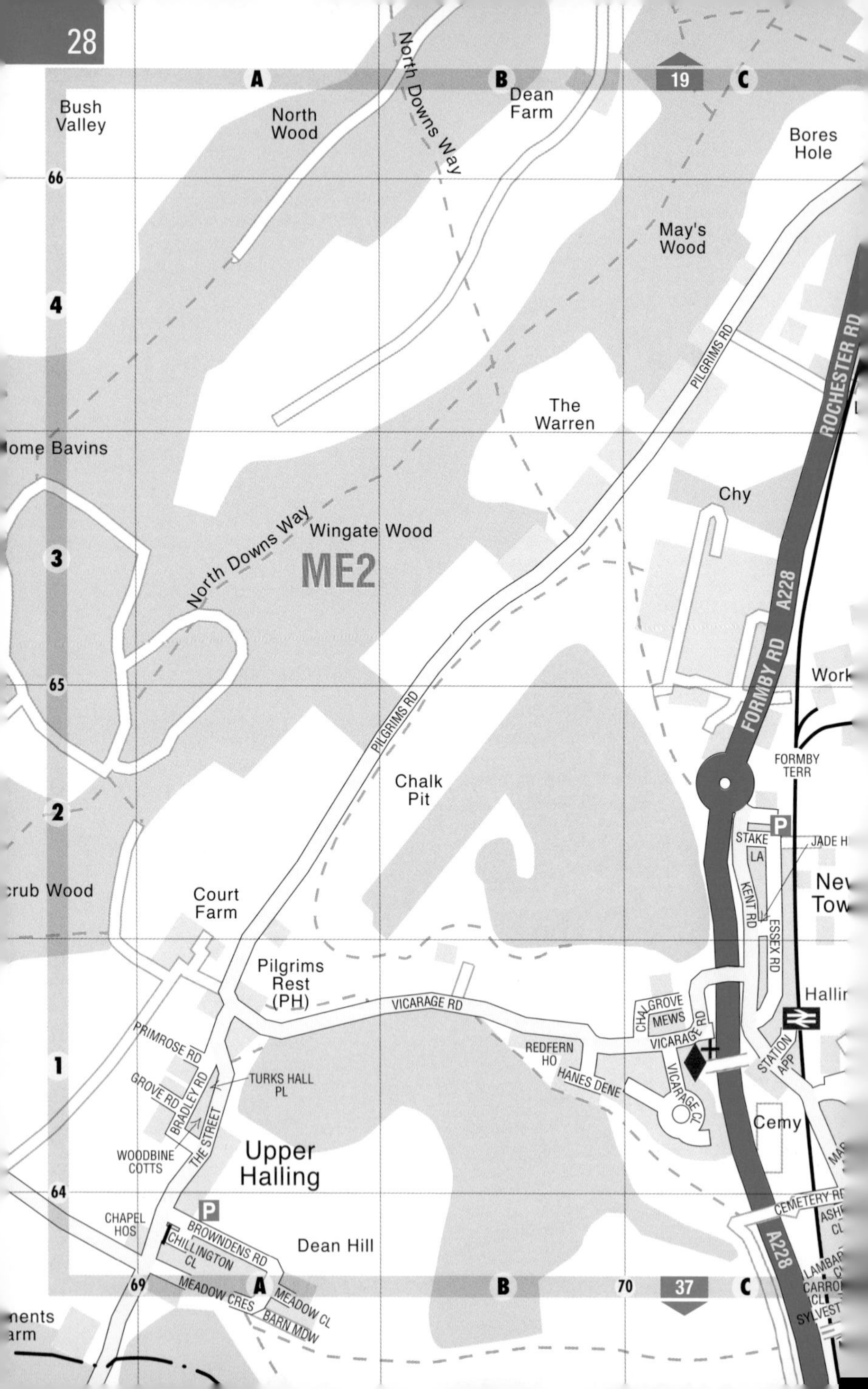

A
B
C
19
Dean Farm
Bush Valley
North Wood
North Downs Way
Bores Hole
66
May's Wood
4
PILGRIMS RD
ROCHESTER RD
The Warren
ome Bavins
Chy
North Downs Way
Wingate Wood
3
ME2
A228
FORMBY RD
Work
65
PILGRIMS RD
FORMBY TERR
Chalk Pit
2
STAKE LA
JADE H
KENT RD
ESSEX RD
crub Wood
Court Farm
Pilgrims Rest (PH)
VICARAGE RD
CHALGROVE MEWS
VICARAGE RD
Hallin
PRIMROSE RD
REDFERN HO
STATION APP
1
TURKS HALL PL
HANES DENE
GROVE RD
BRADLEY RD
VICARAGE CL
THE STREET
Cemy
WOODBINE COTTS
Upper Halling
64
CEMETERY RD
CHAPEL HOS
BROWNDENS RD
CHILLINGTON CL
Dean Hill
69
MEADOW CRES
MEADOW CL
BARN MDW
70
37
A
B
C
A228

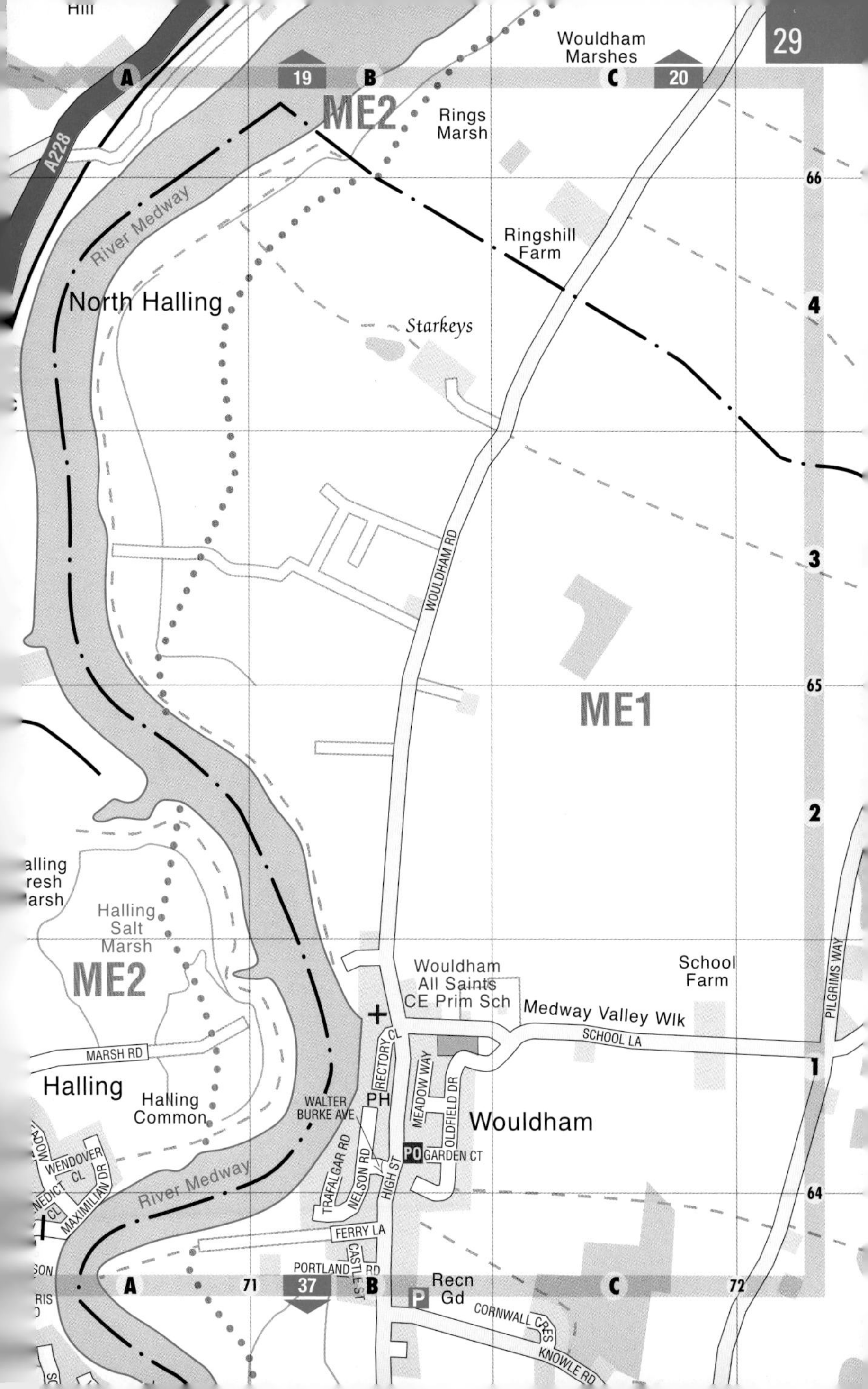

Wouldham Marshes
A
19
B
C
20
ME2
Rings Marsh
A228
66
River Medway
Ringshill Farm
North Halling
4
Starkeys
WOULDHAM RD
3
65
ME1
2
Halling Fresh Marsh
Halling Salt Marsh
ME2
Wouldham All Saints CE Prim Sch
School Farm
PILGRIMS WAY
Medway Valley Wlk
SCHOOL LA
MARSH RD
RECTORY CL
1
Halling
Halling Common
WALTER BURKE AVE
PH
MEADOW WAY
OLDFIELD DR
Wouldham
PO
GARDEN CT
WENDOVER CL
MAXIMILIAN DR
TRAFALGAR RD
NELSON RD
HIGH ST
River Medway
64
FERRY LA
CASTLE ST
PORTLAND RD
A
71
37
B
Recn Gd
P
C
72
CORNWALL CRES
KNOWLE RD

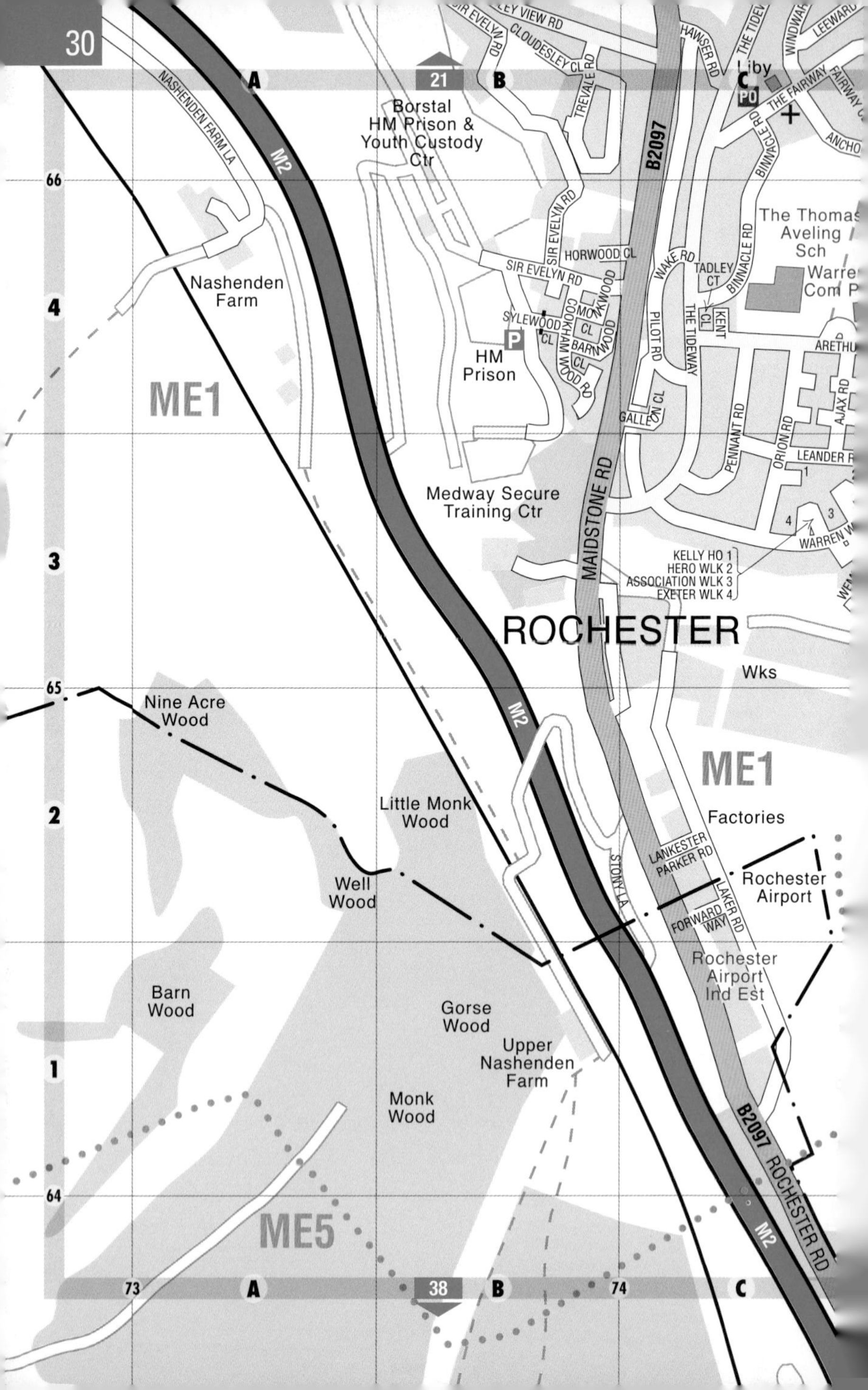

21
A
B
C
Borstal
HM Prison &
Youth Custody
Ctr
NASHENDEN FARM LA
M2
SIR EVELYN RD
CLOUDESLEY CL
TREVALE RD
HAWSER RD
THE TIDEWAY
B2097
Liby
PO
THE FAIRWAY
BINNACLE RD
66
The Thomas
Aveling
Sch
Warre
Com P
HORWOOD CL
SIR EVELYN RD
WAKE RD
TADLEY CT
Nashenden
Farm
4
SYLEWOOD CL
COOKHAM WOOD RD
BARNWOOD CL
PILOT RD
THE TIDEWAY
KENT CL
HM
Prison
ME1
GALLEON CL
PENNANT RD
ORION RD
AJAX RD
LEANDER RD
Medway Secure
Training Ctr
MAIDSTONE RD
WARREN W
3
KELLY HO 1
HERO WLK 2
ASSOCIATION WLK 3
EXETER WLK 4
ROCHESTER
Wks
65
Nine Acre
Wood
M2
ME1
2
Little Monk
Wood
Factories
STONY LA
LANKESTER PARKER RD
Rochester
Airport
Well
Wood
LAKER RD
FORWARD WAY
Rochester
Airport
Ind Est
Barn
Wood
Gorse
Wood
Upper
Nashenden
Farm
1
Monk
Wood
B2097
ROCHESTER RD
64
ME5
M2
73
A
38
B
74
C

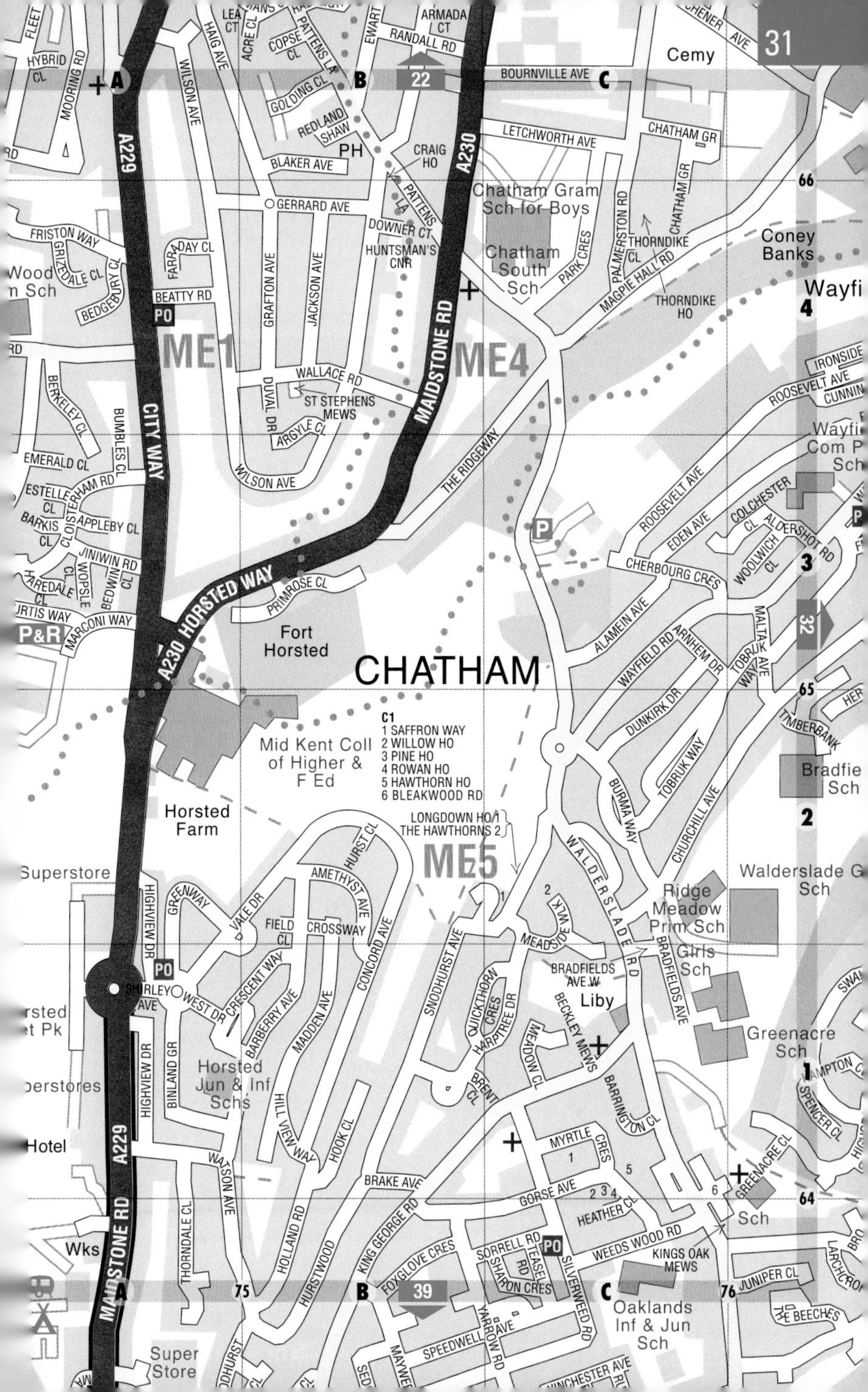
31
Cemy
BOURNVILLE AVE
RANDALL RD
ARMADA CT
EWART
LEA CT
ACRE CL
HAIG AVE
COPSE CL
PATTENS LA
GOLDING CL
REDLAND SHAW
HYBRID CL
MOORING RD
FLEET
WILSON AVE
22
A229
A230
PH
CRAIG HO
BLAKER AVE
LETCHWORTH AVE
CHATHAM GR
Chatham Gram Sch for Boys
Chatham South Sch
PALMERSTON RD
THORNDIKE CL
MAGPIE HALL RD
THORNDIKE HO
PARK CRES
Coney Banks
Wayfi
66
GERRARD AVE
PATTENS LA
DOWNER CT
HUNTSMAN'S CNR
FRISTON WAY
GRIZEDALE CL
BEDGEBURY CL
FARRADAY CL
BEATTY RD
PO
GRAFTON AVE
JACKSON AVE
ME1
ME4
MAIDSTONE RD
WALLACE RD
DUVAL DR
ST STEPHENS MEWS
ARGYLE CL
WILSON AVE
THE RIDGEWAY
BERKELEY CL
BUMBLES CL
CITY WAY
EMERALD CL
ESTELLE CL
CLOISTERHAM RD
BARKIS CL
APPLEBY CL
JINIWIN RD
WOPSLE CL
BEDWIN CL
HAREDALE CL
CURTIS WAY
MARCONI WAY
P&R
A230 HORSTED WAY
PRIMROSE CL
Fort Horsted
CHATHAM
P
IRONSIDE
ROOSEVELT AVE
CUNNIN
Wayfi Com P Sch
ROOSEVELT AVE
EDEN AVE
COLCHESTER CL
ALDERSHOT RD
WOOLWICH CL
CHERBOURG CRES
ALAMEIN AVE
WAYFIELD RD
ARNHEM DR
TOBRUK WAY
MALTA AVE
32
65
TIMBERBANK
DUNKIRK DR
TOBRUK WAY
BURMA WAY
CHURCHILL AVE
Bradfie Sch
Mid Kent Coll of Higher & F Ed
C1
1 SAFFRON WAY
2 WILLOW HO
3 PINE HO
4 ROWAN HO
5 HAWTHORN HO
6 BLEAKWOOD RD
LONGDOWN HO 1
THE HAWTHORNS 2
Horsted Farm
ME5
Superstore
HIGHVIEW DR
GREENWAY
VALE DR
HURST CL
AMETHYST AVE
FIELD CL
CROSSWAY
CONCORD AVE
SNODHURST AVE
WALDERSLADE RD
MEADSIDE WALK
Ridge Meadow Prim Sch
Walderslade G Sch
Girls Sch
BRADFIELDS AVE
BRADFIELDS AVE W
Liby
SHIRLEY AVE
WEST DR
CRESCENT WAY
BARBERRY AVE
MADDEN AVE
QUICKTHORN CRES
HARPTREE DR
MEADOW CL
BECKLEY MEWS
Greenacre Sch
Horsted Ret Pk
Superstores
Horsted Jun & Inf Schs
HIGHVIEW DR
BINLAND GR
HILL VIEW WAY
HOOK CL
BRENT CL
BARRINGTON CL
HAMPTON
SPENCER CL
Hotel
WATSON AVE
MYRTLE CRES
BRAKE AVE
GORSE AVE
HEATHER CL
GREENACRE CL
64
Sch
THORNDALE CL
HOLLAND RD
KING GEORGE RD
FOXGLOVE CRES
SORRELL RD
TEASEL RD
SHARON CRES
SILVERWEED RD
WEEDS WOOD RD
KINGS OAK MEWS
JUNIPER CL
LARCHCROFT
THE BEECHES
Wks
MAIDSTONE RD
A229
75
HURSTWOOD
39
76
Oaklands Inf & Jun Sch
SPEEDWELL AVE
YARROW RD
WINCHESTER AVE
Super Store

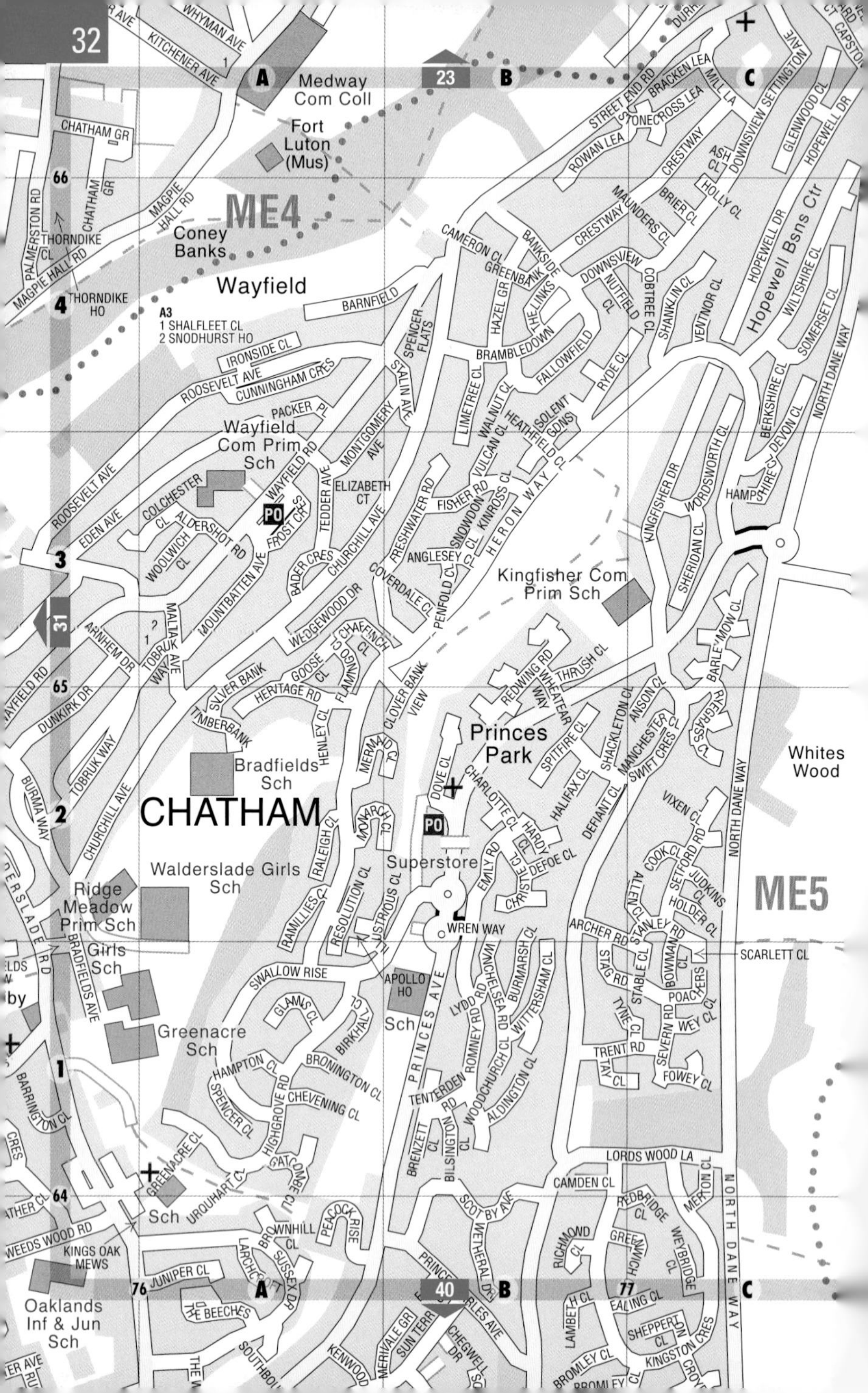
Medway
Com Coll
Fort
Luton
(Mus)
ME4
Coney
Banks
Wayfield
A3
1 SHALFLEET CL
2 SNODHURST HO
Wayfield
Com Prim
Sch
Kingfisher Com
Prim Sch
Princes
Park
Whites
Wood
Bradfields
Sch
CHATHAM
Walderslade Girls
Sch
Ridge
Meadow
Prim Sch
Girls
Sch
Greenacre
Sch
Superstore
APOLLO
HO
Sch
ME5
Hopewell Bsns Ctr
Oaklands
Inf & Jun
Sch
KINGS OAK
MEWS
THORNDIKE
HO
WHYMAN AVE
KITCHENER AVE
CHATHAM GR
PALMERSTON RD
THORNDIKE CL
MAGPIE HALL RD
IRONSIDE CL
ROOSEVELT AVE
CUNNINGHAM CRES
PACKER PL
BARNFIELD
SPENCER FLATS
STALIN AVE
MONTGOMERY AVE
EDEN AVE
COLCHESTER CL
ALDERSHOT RD
WOOLWICH CL
WAYFIELD RD
FROST CRES
TEDDER AVE
ELIZABETH CT
CHURCHILL AVE
BADER CRES
MOUNTBATTEN AVE
MALTA AVE
TOBRUK WAY
ARNHEM DR
DUNKIRK DR
BURMA WAY
WEDGEWOOD DR
CHAFFINCH CL
GOOSE CL
FLAMINGO CL
HERITAGE RD
SILVER BANK
TIMBERBANK
HENLEY CL
MERMAID CL
CLOVER BANK VIEW
COVERDALE CL
FRESHWATER RD
ANGLESEY CL
PENFOLD CL
FISHER RD
SNOWDON CL
KINROSS CL
HERON WAY
VULCAN CL
WALNUT CL
LIMETREE CL
HEATHFIELD CL
SOLENT GDNS
BRAMBLEDOWN
HAZEL GR
GREENBANK
THE LINKS
FALLOWFIELD
RYDE CL
CAMERON CL
BANKSIDE
DOWNSVIEW
NUTFIELD CL
COBTREE CL
SHANKLIN CL
VENTNOR CL
STREET END RD
BRACKEN LEA
STONECROSS LEA
ROWAN LEA
MILL LA
CRESTWAY
ASH CL
HOLLY CL
BRIER CL
MAUNDERS CL
DOWNSVIEW
SETTINGTON AVE
GLENWOOD CL
HOPEWELL DR
WILTSHIRE CL
SOMERSET CL
NORTH DANE WAY
BERKSHIRE CL
DEVON CL
HAMPSHIRE CL
WORDSWORTH CL
KINGFISHER DR
SHERIDAN CL
BARLEYMOW CL
RYEGRASS CL
REDWING RD
THRUSH CL
WHEATEAR WAY
SPITFIRE CL
SHACKLETON CL
ANSON CL
MANCHESTER CL
SWIFT CRES
HALIFAX CL
DEFIANT CL
VIXEN CL
DOVE CL
CHARLOTTE CL
HARDY CL
CHRISTIE CL
DEFOE CL
EMILY RD
RALEIGH CL
MONARCH CL
RESOLUTION CL
ILLUSTRIOUS CL
RAMILLIES CL
WREN WAY
COOK CL
SETFORD RD
JUDKINS CL
ALLEN CL
HOLDER CL
ARCHER RD
STANLEY RD
STAG RD
STABLE CL
BOWMAN CL
SCARLETT CL
POACHERS CL
TYNE CL
SEVERN RD
WEY CL
TRENT RD
TAY CL
FOWEY CL
SWALLOW RISE
GLAMIS CL
BIRKHALL CL
HAMPTON CL
BRONINGTON CL
SPENCER CL
HIGHGROVE RD
CHEVENING CL
GREENACRE CL
URQUHART CL
BALMORAL
GATCOMBE CL
PRINCES AVE
LYDD RD
WINCHELSEA RD
BURMARSH CL
WITTERSHAM CL
ROMNEY RD
WOODCHURCH CL
ALDINGTON CL
TENTERDEN RD
BRENZETT CL
BILSINGTON CL
LORDS WOOD LA
CAMDEN CL
MERTON CL
REDBRIDGE CL
RICHMOND CL
GREENWICH CL
WEYBRIDGE CL
SCOTBY AVE
WETHERAL DR
PEACOCK RISE
BROWNHILL CL
SUSSEX DR
LARCHCROFT
JUNIPER CL
THE BEECHES
SOUTHBOURNE
KENWOOD
MERIVALE GR
SUN TERR
CHEGWELL DR
CHARLES AVE
LAMBETH CL
EALING CL
SHEPPERTON CL
KINGSTON CRES
BROMLEY CL
WALDERSLADE RD
BRADFIELDS AVE
BARRINGTON CL
WEEDS WOOD RD
A
B
C
23
40
31
77
76
66
65
64
4
3
2
1

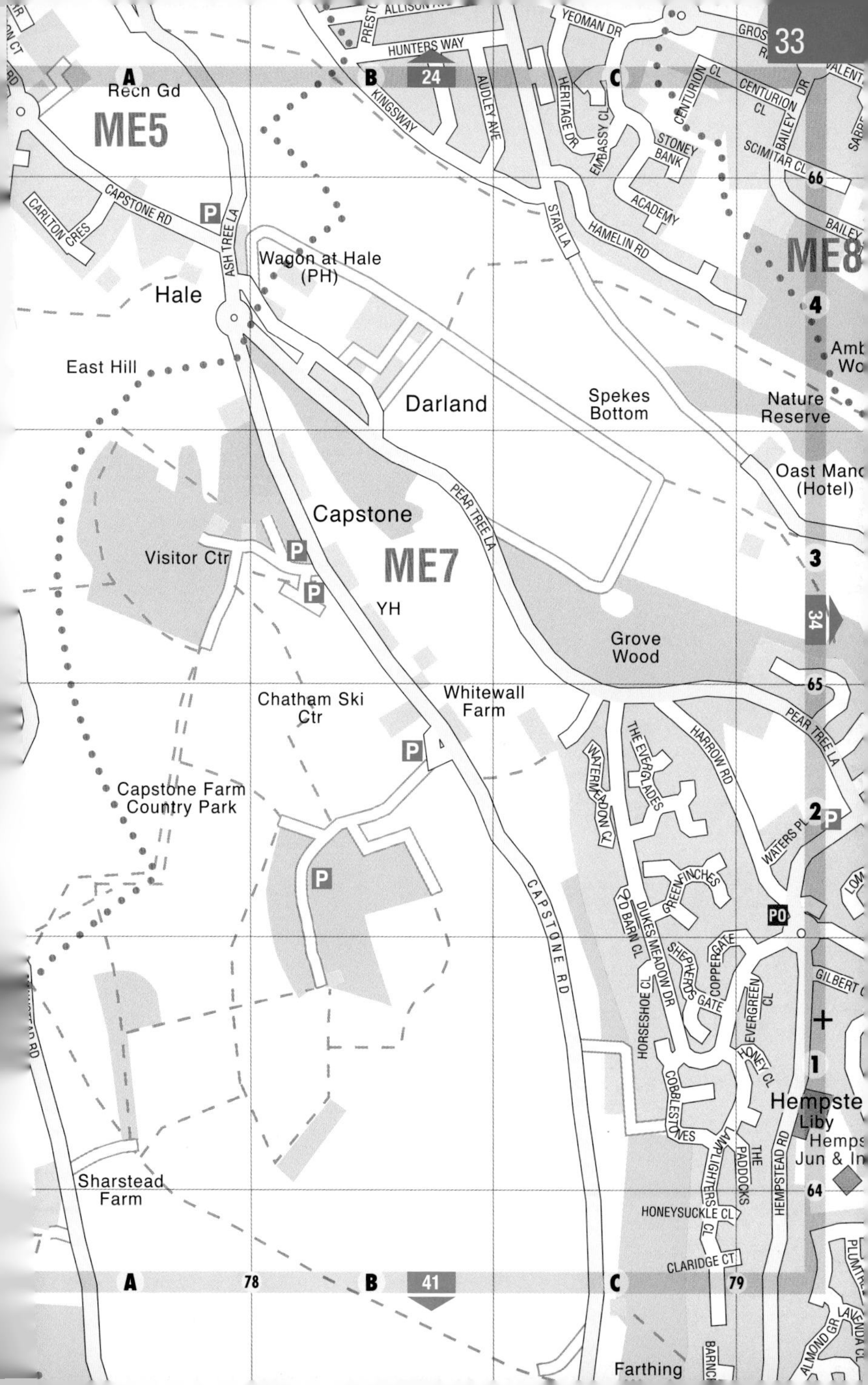
33
A
B
C
24
41
34
ME5
ME7
ME8
Recn Gd
Hale
East Hill
Darland
Spekes Bottom
Nature Reserve
Oast Manc
(Hotel)
Capstone
Visitor Ctr
YH
Grove Wood
Chatham Ski Ctr
Whitewall Farm
Capstone Farm Country Park
Sharstead Farm
Farthing
Hempste
Liby
Hemps
Jun & In
Wagon at Hale (PH)
CAPSTONE RD
CARLTON CRES
ASH TREE LA
KINGSWAY
HUNTERS WAY
ALLISON AVE
AUDLEY AVE
YEOMAN DR
HERITAGE DR
EMBASSY CL
STONEY BANK
ACADEMY
CENTURION CL
BAILEY DR
SCIMITAR CL
STAR LA
HAMELIN RD
PEAR TREE LA
HARROW RD
WATERMEADOW CL
THE EVERGLADES
GREENFINCHES
OLD BARN CL
DUKES MEADOW DR
SHEPHERDS GATE
COPPERGATE
EVERGREEN CL
HORSESHOE CL
HONEY CL
COBBLESTONES
LAMPLIGHTERS CL
THE PADDOCKS
HEMPSTEAD RD
HONEYSUCKLE CL
CLARIDGE CT
WATERS PL
GILBERT CL
ALMOND GR
LAVENDA CL
PO
P
78
79
64
65
66
1
2
3
4

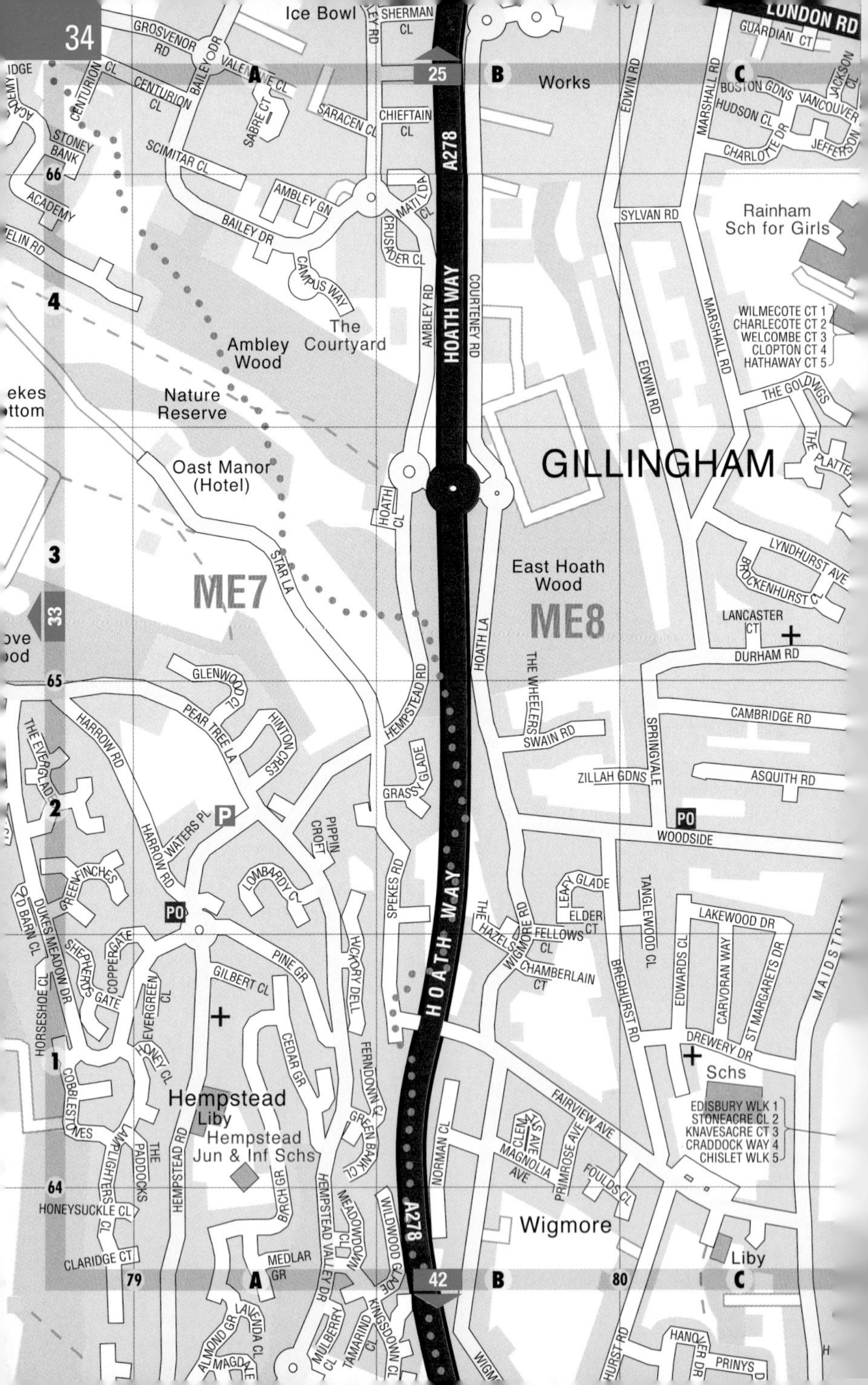

Ice Bowl
SHERMAN CL
LONDON RD
GUARDIAN CT
GROSVENOR RD
BAILEY DR
VALENTINE CL
CENTURION CL
CENTURION CL
SABRE CT
SARACEN CL
CHIEFTAIN CL
25
A
B
C
Works
EDWIN RD
MARSHALL RD
BOSTON GDNS
VANCOUVER
JACKSON CL
HUDSON CL
CHARLOTTE DR
JEFFERSON
STONEY BANK
ACADEMY
66
SCIMITAR CL
AMBLEY GN
MATILDA CL
A278
ACADEMY
BAILEY DR
CRUSADER CL
SYLVAN RD
Rainham Sch for Girls
CAMPUS WAY
AMBLEY RD
HOATH WAY
COURTENEY RD
4
The Courtyard
Ambley Wood
MARSHALL RD
EDWIN RD
WILMECOTE CT 1
CHARLECOTE CT 2
WELCOMBE CT 3
CLOPTON CT 4
HATHAWAY CT 5
THE GOLDINGS
Nature Reserve
THE PLATTERS
Oast Manor (Hotel)
GILLINGHAM
HOATH CL
3
STAR LA
East Hoath Wood
LYNDHURST AVE
BROCKENHURST CL
ME7
ME8
33
HOATH LA
THE WHEELERS
LANCASTER CT
DURHAM RD
65
GLENWOOD CL
PEAR TREE LA
HINTON CRES
HEMPSTEAD RD
HARROW RD
THE EVERGLADES
SWAIN RD
SPRINGVALE
CAMBRIDGE RD
GRASSY GLADE
ZILLAH GDNS
ASQUITH RD
2
P
WATERS PL
PIPPIN CROFT
PO
WOODSIDE
HARROW RD
GREENFINCHES
LOMBARDY CL
SPEKES RD
HOATH WAY
LEAFY GLADE
ELDER CT
TANGLEWOOD CL
OLD BARN CL
DUKES MEADOW DR
PO
HICKORY DELL
THE HAZELS
WIGMORE RD
FELLOWS CL
LAKEWOOD DR
SHEPHERDS GATE
COPPERGATE
PINE GR
CHAMBERLAIN CT
EDWARDS CL
CARVORAN WAY
ST MARGARETS DR
GILBERT CL
EVERGREEN CL
BREDHURST RD
MAIDSTONE
HORSESHOE CL
HONEY CL
CEDAR GR
FERNDOWN CL
DREWERY DR
1
Schs
COBBLESTONES
Hempstead Liby
FAIRVIEW AVE
Hempstead Jun & Inf Schs
EDISBURY WLK 1
STONEACRE CL 2
KNAVESACRE CT 3
CRADDOCK WAY 4
CHISLET WLK 5
LAMPLIGHTERS CL
THE PADDOCKS
HEMPSTEAD RD
GREEN BANK CL
NORMAN CL
CLEMENTS AVE
MAGNOLIA AVE
PRIMROSE AVE
FOULDS CL
64
BIRCH GR
HEMPSTEAD VALLEY DR
MEADOWDOWN CL
WILDWOOD GLADE
A278
HONEYSUCKLE CL
Wigmore
CLARIDGE CT
MEDLAR GR
Liby
79
A
42
B
80
C
LAVENDA CL
ALMOND GR
MAGDALEN
MULBERRY CL
TAMARIND CL
KINGSDOWN CL
BREDHURST RD
HANOVER DR
PRINYS DR

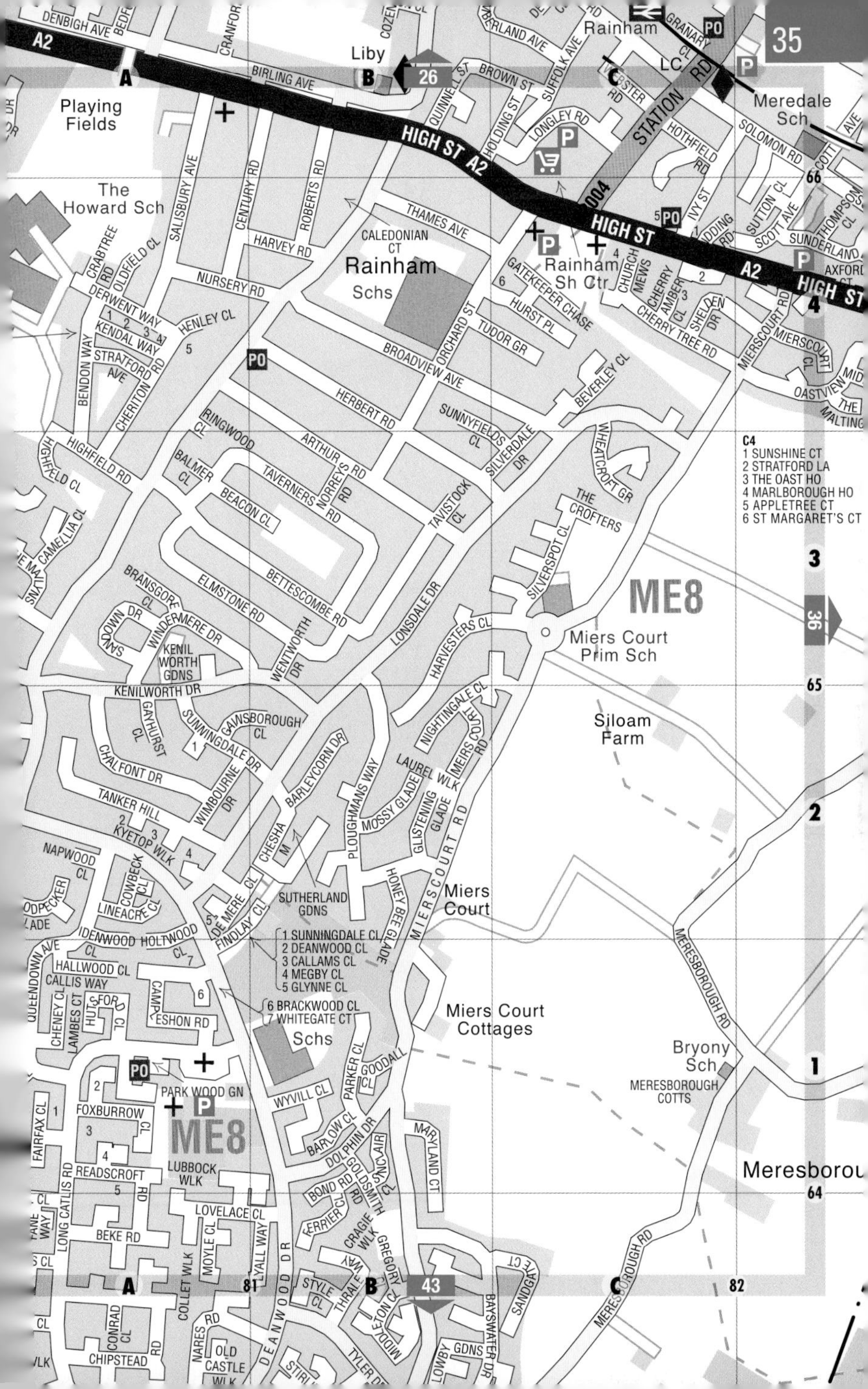

A2
DENBIGH AVE
BEDFORD
CRANFORD
Liby
26
Rainham
GRANARY CL
PO
LC
Playing Fields
BIRLING AVE
BROWN ST
SUFFOLK AVE
WEBSTER RD
STATION RD
Meredale Sch
HIGH ST A2
QUINNELL ST
HOLDING ST
LONGLEY RD
HOTHFIELD RD
SOLOMON RD
SCOTT AVE
66
The Howard Sch
SALISBURY AVE
CENTURY RD
ROBERTS RD
THAMES AVE
A2004
HIGH ST
IVY ST
SUTTON CL
THOMPSON CL
SUNDERLAND CL
AXFORD CT
CRABTREE RD
OLDFIELD CL
HARVEY RD
CALEDONIAN CT
Rainham Schs
Rainham Sh Ctr
CHURCH MEWS
CHERRY AMBER CL
SHELDEN DR
MIERSCOURT RD
NURSERY RD
DERWENT WAY
KENDAL WAY
HENLEY CL
STRATFORD AVE
BENDON WAY
CHERITON RD
GATEKEEPER CHASE
HURST PL
TUDOR GR
ORCHARD ST
CHERRY TREE RD
MIERSCOURT CL
OASTVIEW
THE MALTINGS
BROADVIEW AVE
BEVERLEY CL
HERBERT RD
SUNNYFIELDS CL
SILVERDALE DR
RINGWOOD CL
ARTHUR RD
NORREYS RD
HIGHFIELD RD
HIGHFIELD CL
BALMER CL
TAVERNERS RD
BEACON CL
TAVISTOCK CL
WHEATCROFT GR
THE CROFTERS
C4
1 SUNSHINE CT
2 STRATFORD LA
3 THE OAST HO
4 MARLBOROUGH HO
5 APPLETREE CT
6 ST MARGARET'S CT
CAMELLIA CL
SILVERSPOT CL
ME8
BRANSGORE CL
ELMSTONE RD
BETTESCOMBE RD
LONSDALE DR
36
SANDOWN DR
WINDERMERE DR
HARVESTERS CL
Miers Court Prim Sch
KENILWORTH GDNS
WENTWORTH DR
KENILWORTH DR
65
GAYHURST CL
GAINSBOROUGH CL
SUNNINGDALE DR
NIGHTINGALE CL
MIERS COURT RD
Siloam Farm
CHALFONT DR
BARLEYCORN DR
LAUREL WLK
PLOUGHMANS WAY
MOSSY GLADE
GLISTENING GLADE
TANKER HILL
WIMBOURNE DR
KYETOP WLK
CHESHAM
NAPWOOD CL
COWBECK CL
HONEY BEE GLADE
MIERSCOURT RD
Miers Court
LINEACRE CL
DEMERE CL
FINDLAY CL
SUTHERLAND GDNS
IDENWOOD CL
HOLTWOOD CL
QUEENDOWN AVE
HALLWOOD CL
CALLIS WAY
1 SUNNINGDALE CL
2 DEANWOOD CL
3 CALLAMS CL
4 MEGBY CL
5 GLYNNE CL
MERESBOROUGH RD
CHENEY CL
LAMBES CT
HUTSFORD CL
CAMPION CL
ESHON RD
6 BRACKWOOD CL
7 WHITEGATE CT
Schs
Miers Court Cottages
PARKER CL
GOODALL CL
Bryony Sch
MERESBOROUGH COTTS
PARK WOOD GN
FAIRFAX CL
FOXBURROW CL
WYVILL CL
BARLOW CL
DOLPHIN DR
SINCLAIR CL
MARYLAND CT
GOLDSMITH RD
BOND RD
READSCROFT RD
LUBBOCK WLK
Meresborough
64
LONG CATLIS RD
LOVELACE CL
FERRIER CL
CRAGIE WLK
GREGORY CL
BEKE RD
MOYLE CL
LYALL WAY
COLLET WLK
DEANWOOD DR
THRALE WAY
SANDGATE CT
A
81
STYLE CL
B
43
C
82
MIDDLETON CL
BAYSWATER DR
CONRAD CL
CHIPSTEAD RD
NARES RD
OLD CASTLE WLK
LOWBY GDNS
TYLER DR

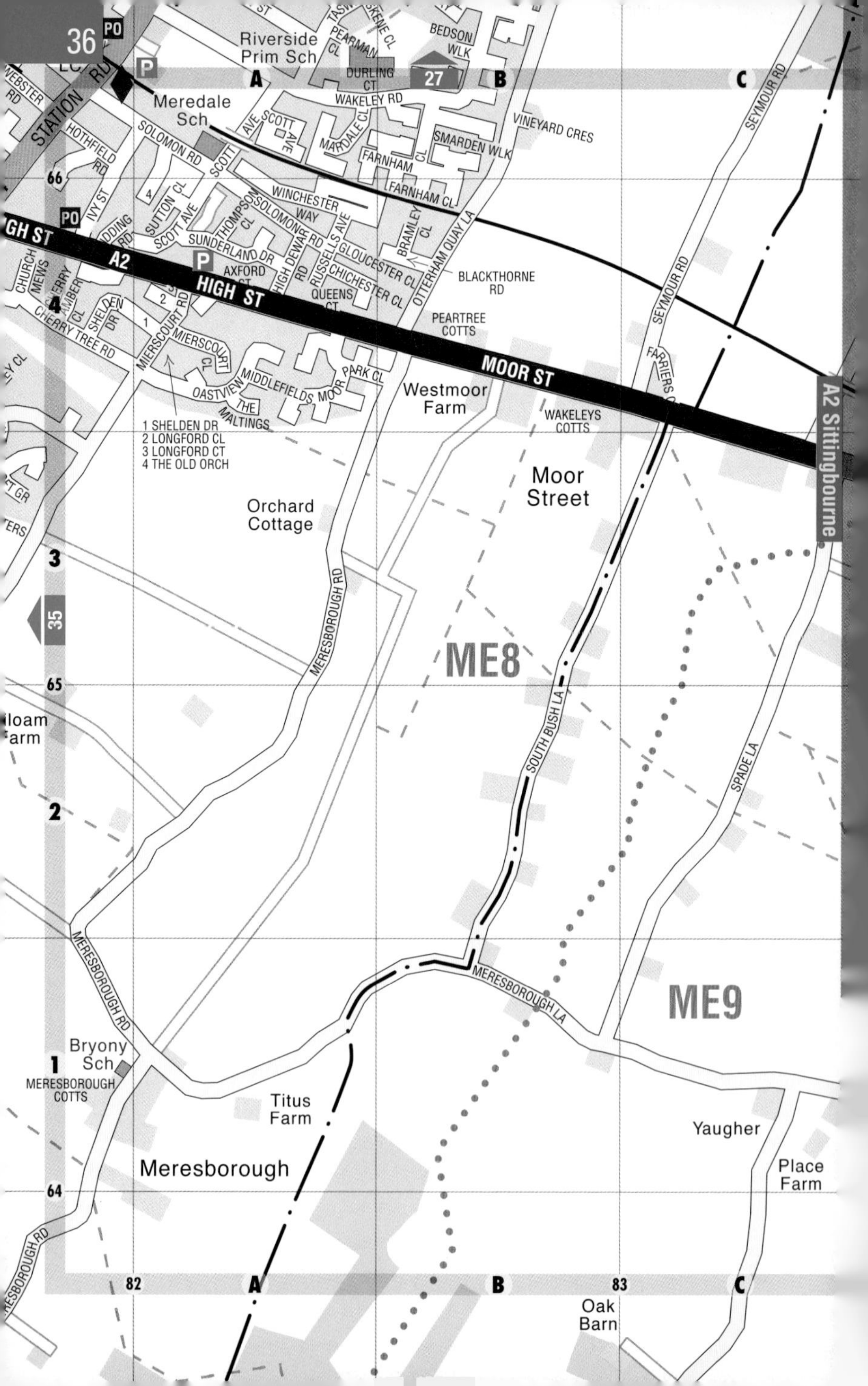
36
27
35
A2 Sittingbourne
Riverside Prim Sch
Meredale Sch
Westmoor Farm
Orchard Cottage
Moor Street
Bryony Sch
Titus Farm
Meresborough
Yaugher
Place Farm
Oak Barn
ME8
ME9
HIGH ST
A2
MOOR ST
STATION RD
SOLOMON RD
WINCHESTER WAY
GLOUCESTER CL
CHICHESTER CL
OTTERHAM QUAY LA
SEYMOUR RD
VINEYARD CRES
SMARDEN WLK
FARNHAM CL
WAKELEY RD
DURLING CT
BEDSON WLK
PEARMAN CL
BRAMLEY CL
BLACKTHORNE RD
PEARTREE COTTS
WAKELEYS COTTS
FARRIERS CL
MIERSCOURT RD
MIERSCOURT CL
CHERRY TREE RD
MIDDLEFIELDS
MOOR PARK CL
OASTVIEW
THE MALTINGS
MERESBOROUGH RD
MERESBOROUGH LA
SOUTH BUSH LA
SPADE LA
MERESBOROUGH COTTS
1 SHELDEN DR
2 LONGFORD CL
3 LONGFORD CT
4 THE OLD ORCH
82
83
64
65
66

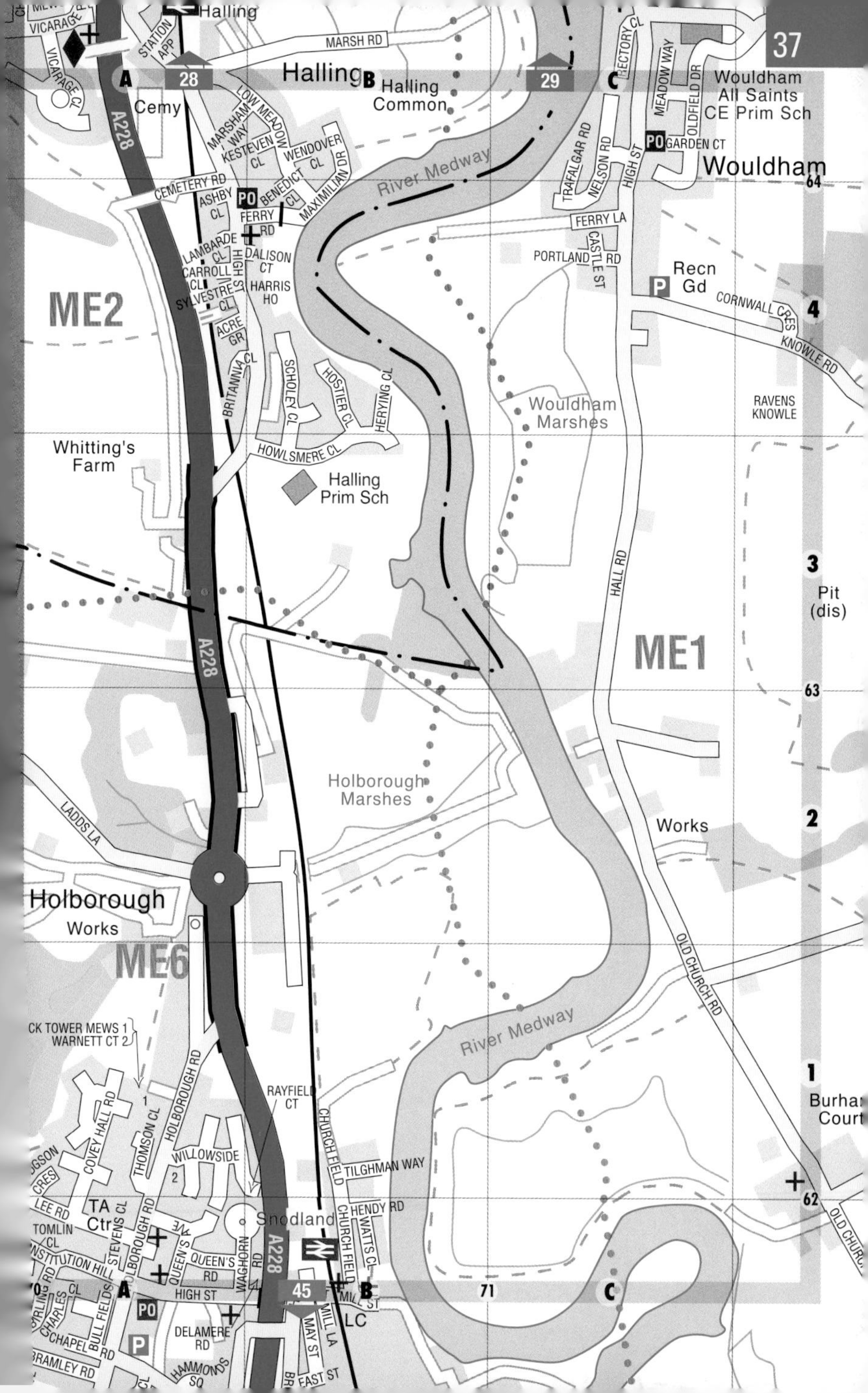
Halling
MARSH RD
VICARAGE
VICARAGE CL
STATION APP
28
29
A
B
C
Halling Common
Cemy
A228
LOW MEADOW
MARSHAM WAY
KESTEVEN CL
WENDOVER CL
BENEDICT CL
MAXIMILIAN DR
River Medway
RECTORY CL
MEADOW WAY
OLDFIELD DR
Wouldham All Saints CE Prim Sch
GARDEN CT
Wouldham
TRAFALGAR RD
NELSON RD
HIGH ST
64
CEMETERY RD
ASHBY CL
FERRY RD
LAMBARDE CL
CARROLL CL
SYLVESTRE CL
DALISON CT
HARRIS HO
HIGH ST
FERRY LA
PORTLAND RD
CASTLE ST
Recn Gd
CORNWALL CRES
KNOWLE RD
ME2
ACRE GR
BRITANNIA CL
SCHOLEY CL
HOSTIER CL
HERYING CL
HOWLSMERE CL
4
Wouldham Marshes
RAVENS KNOWLE
Whitting's Farm
Halling Prim Sch
HALL RD
3
Pit (dis)
ME1
63
Holborough Marshes
LADDS LA
Works
2
Holborough
Works
ME6
OLD CHURCH RD
River Medway
CK TOWER MEWS 1
WARNETT CT 2
RAYFIELD CT
HOLBOROUGH RD
THOMSON CL
COVEY HALL RD
WILLOWSIDE
CHURCH FIELD
TILGHMAN WAY
1
Burha
Court
HENDY RD
62
OLD CHUR
LEE RD
TA Ctr
STEVENS CL
HOLBOROUGH RD
QUEEN'S AVE
Snodland
TOMLIN CL
INSTITUTION HILL
QUEEN'S RD
WAGHORN RD
CHURCH FIELD
WATTS CL
HIGH ST
45
71
MILL ST
BULL FIELDS
CHARLES CL
CHAPEL RD
BRAMLEY RD
DELAMERE RD
HAMMONDS SQ
MAY ST
MILL LA
LC
EAST ST

Wood
Upper
Nashenden
Farm
A
30
B
C
Monk
Wood
ME1
M2
B2097
ROCHESTER RD
64
4
Syle
Wood
Middle
Hill
Middlehill
Wood
Bridge
Woods
3
Burham Hill
Farm
HILL RD
ME5
Buckmore
Park
63
Sports
Ctr
The Robin
Hood (PH)
2
Lord
Leas
Burham
Common
North Downs Way
COMMON RD
1
BRISLEY'S
ROW
ME1
NEW
RD
62
PO
Fleur de Lis
(PH)
73
A
46
B
74
C
47
BELL LA
BELL CRES
Burham

Ret Pk
Superstores
Hotel
Wks
Horsted Jun & Inf Schs
Greenacre Sch
Sch
Oaklands Inf & Jun Sch
ME5
Super Store
B4
1 LAVENDER CL
2 ASPEN WAY
3 HONEYSUCKLE CL
4 GENTIAN CL
Bridgewood Manor Hotel
SINDAL SHAW HO
MARSTON WLK
Taddington Wood
Kit Hill
Weeds Wood
C4
1 MALLOW WAY
2 JASMINE CL
3 HAREBELL CL
4 ROSEMARY CL
5 LINDEN HO
6 OAK HO
PRINCES AVE
Walderslade Prim Sch
WOODLANDS CT
GLENEAGLES CT
Walderslade
Tunbury Prim Sch
HEPPLEWHITE MEWS
FELDSPAR CL
PODKIN WOOD
Bluebell Hill
The Upper Bell Inn (PH)
Crem
Impton Wood
Frith Wood
The Alexan
MAIDSTONE RD
A229
M2
B2097
ROBIN HOOD LANE (UPPER)
ROBIN HOOD LANE (LOWER)
WALDERSLADE WOODS
KINGS OAK MEWS
31
40
47
48
75
76
62
63
64

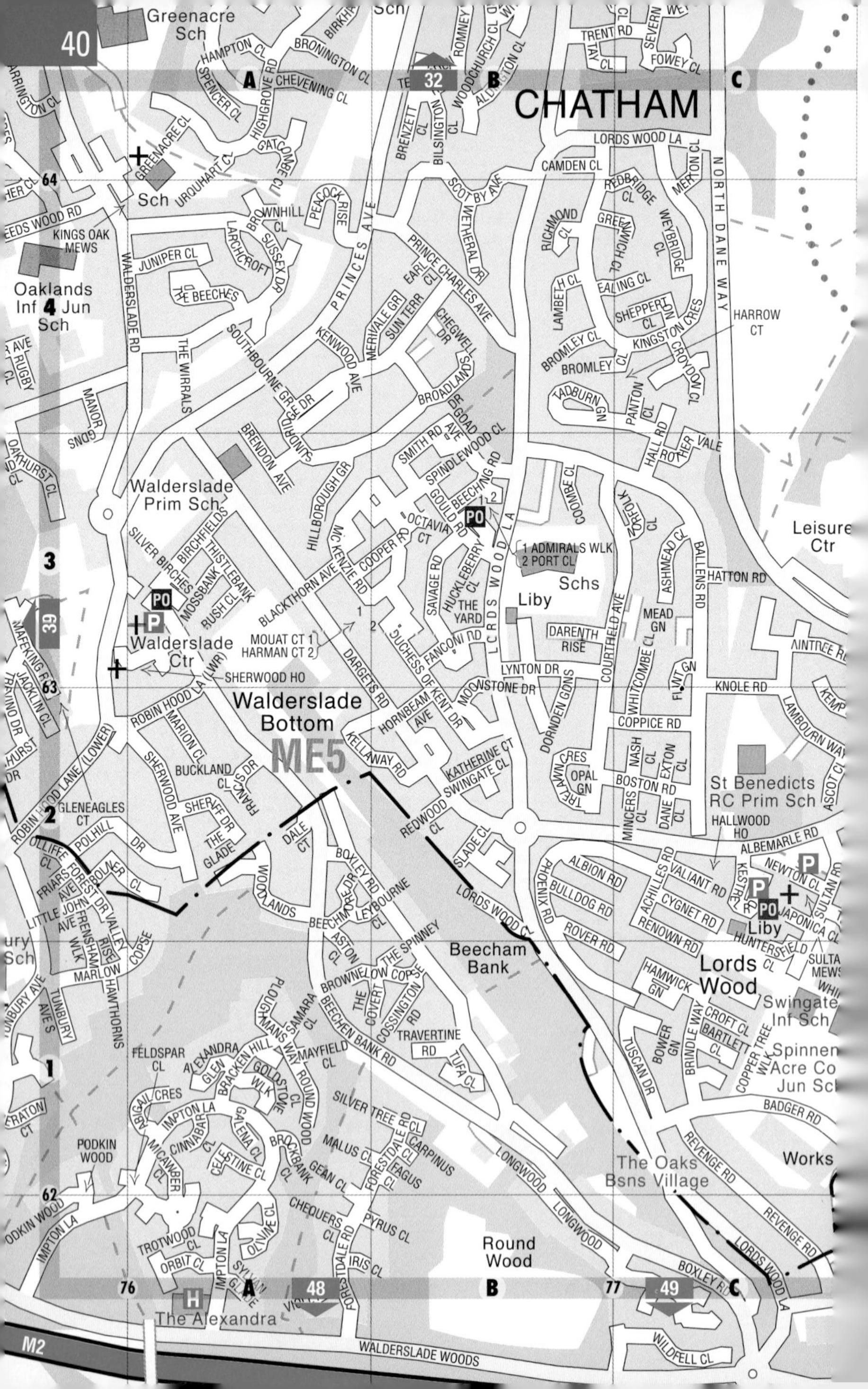
CHATHAM
Greenacre Sch
Oaklands Inf & Jun Sch
Walderslade Prim Sch
Walderslade Ctr
Walderslade Bottom
ME5
Leisure Ctr
Schs
Liby
St Benedicts RC Prim Sch
Lords Wood
Swingate Inf Sch
Spinnens Acre Com Jun Sch
Beecham Bank
The Oaks Bsns Village
Works
Round Wood
The Alexandra
PODKIN WOOD
M2
WALDERSLADE WOODS
PRINCES AVE
PRINCE CHARLES AVE
NORTH DANE WAY
LORDS WOOD LA
WALDERSLADE RD
ROBIN HOOD LANE (LOWER)
ROBIN HOOD LA (LWR)
BLACKTHORN AVE
LORDS WOOD CL
REVENGE RD
BOXLEY RD
LONGWOOD
BEECHEN BANK RD
KNOLE RD
ALBEMARLE RD
HATTON RD
BALLENS RD
COURTFIELD AVE
SOUTHBOURNE GR
DUCHESS OF KENT DR
DARGETS RD
SHERWOOD AVE
SHERWOOD HO
1 ADMIRALS WLK
2 PORT CL
MOUAT CT 1
HARMAN CT 2
KINGS OAK MEWS
HARROW CT
HALLWOOD HO
32
39
48
49
64
63
62
76
77
A
B
C
1
2
3
4

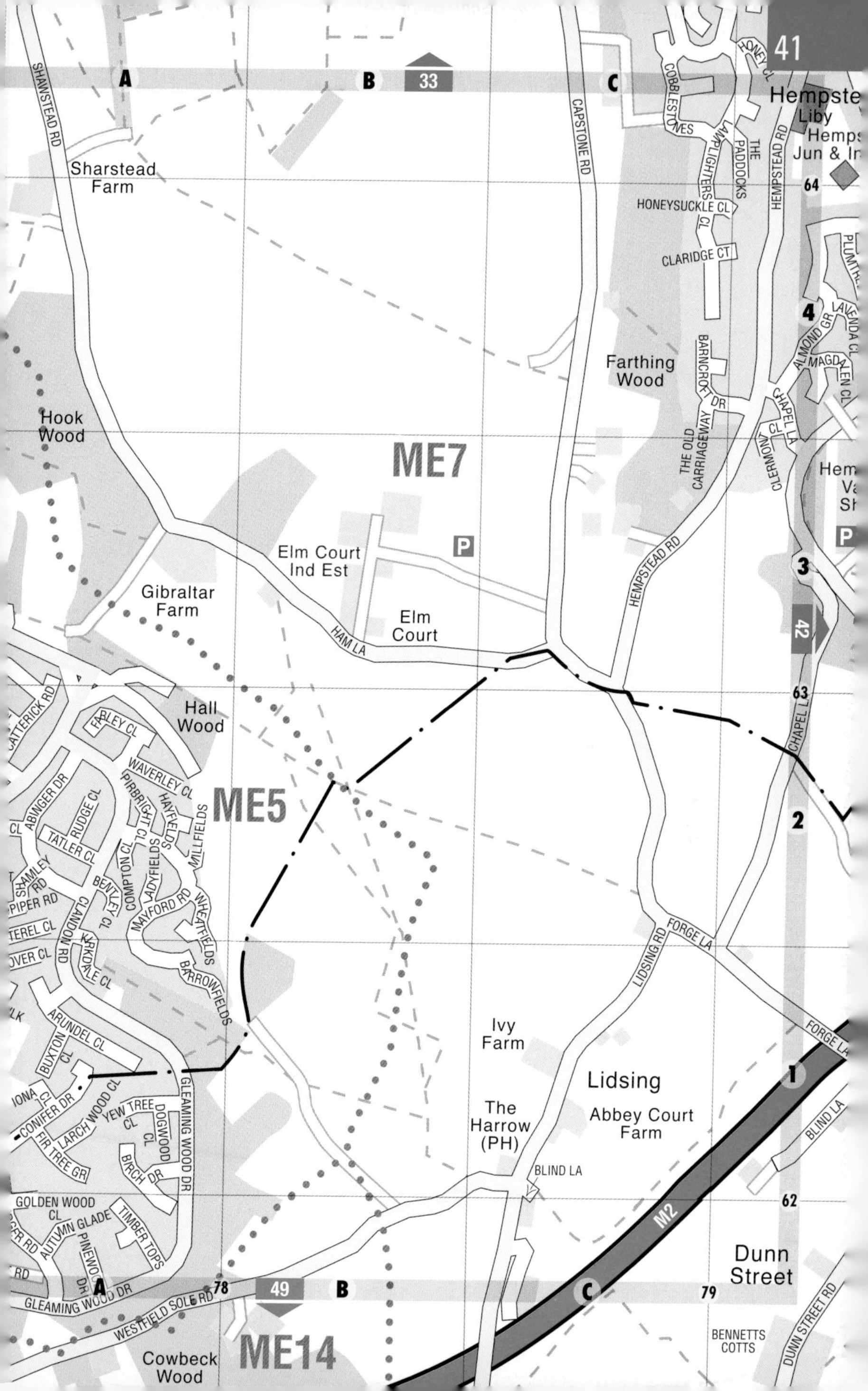

33
A
B
C
Sharstead Farm
SHAWSTEAD RD
CAPSTONE RD
COBBLESTONES
LAMPLIGHTERS CL
THE PADDOCKS
HONEY CL
HEMPSTEAD RD
Hempstead
Liby
Hempstead Jun & Inf
64
HONEYSUCKLE CL
CLARIDGE CT
4
LAVENDA CL
ALMOND GR
MAGDALEN CL
Farthing Wood
BARNCROFT DR
THE OLD CARRIAGEWAY
CHAPEL LA
CLERMONT CL
Hook Wood
ME7
Elm Court Ind Est
P
Gibraltar Farm
Elm Court
HAM LA
3
42
63
Hall Wood
CATTERICK RD
FARLEY CL
WAVERLEY CL
PIRBRIGHT CL
HAYFIELDS
ABINGER DR
RUDGE CL
ME5
MILLFIELDS
TATLER CL
COMPTON CL
LADYFIELDS
BENTLEY CL
MAYFORD RD
WHEATFIELDS
PIPER RD
CLANDON RD
KIRKDALE CL
BARROWFIELDS
2
FORGE LA
LIDSING RD
Ivy Farm
ARUNDEL CL
BUXTON CL
GLEAMING WOOD DR
Lidsing
CONIFER DR
LARCH WOOD CL
YEW TREE CL
DOGWOOD CL
The Harrow (PH)
Abbey Court Farm
1
BLIND LA
FIR TREE GR
BIRCH DR
GOLDEN WOOD CL
AUTUMN GLADE
TIMBER TOPS
M2
62
Dunn Street
A
78
49
B
C
79
GLEAMING WOOD DR
WESTFIELD SOLE RD
Cowbeck Wood
ME14
BENNETTS COTTS
DUNN STREET RD

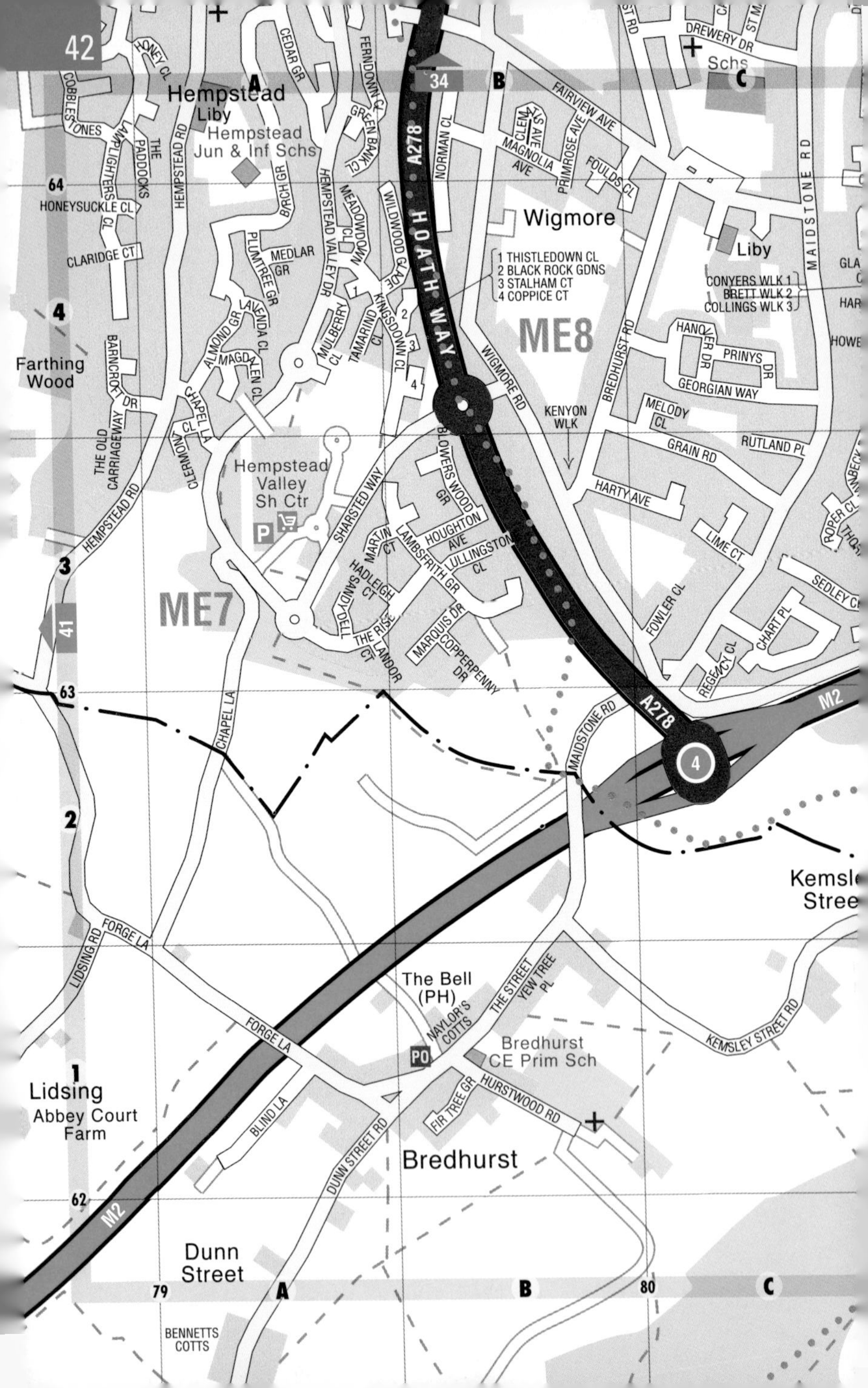

Hempstead
Liby
Hempstead Jun & Inf Schs
Wigmore
Liby
Schs
ME8
ME7
Farthing Wood
Hempstead Valley Sh Ctr
1 THISTLEDOWN CL
2 BLACK ROCK GDNS
3 STALHAM CT
4 COPPICE CT
CONYERS WLK 1
BRETT WLK 2
COLLINGS WLK 3
HOATH WAY
A278
M2
34
41
Kemsley Street
The Bell (PH)
Bredhurst CE Prim Sch
Bredhurst
Lidsing
Abbey Court Farm
Dunn Street
BENNETTS COTTS
HEMPSTEAD RD
CHAPEL LA
FORGE LA
LIDSING RD
MAIDSTONE RD
KEMSLEY STREET RD
THE STREET
HURSTWOOD RD
DUNN STREET RD
BLIND LA
FIR TREE GR
NAYLOR'S COTTS
YEW TREE PL
WIGMORE RD
BREDHURST RD
FAIRVIEW AVE
GEORGIAN WAY
GRAIN RD
HARTY AVE
SHARSTED WAY
FOWLER CL
DREWERY DR
64
63
62
79
80

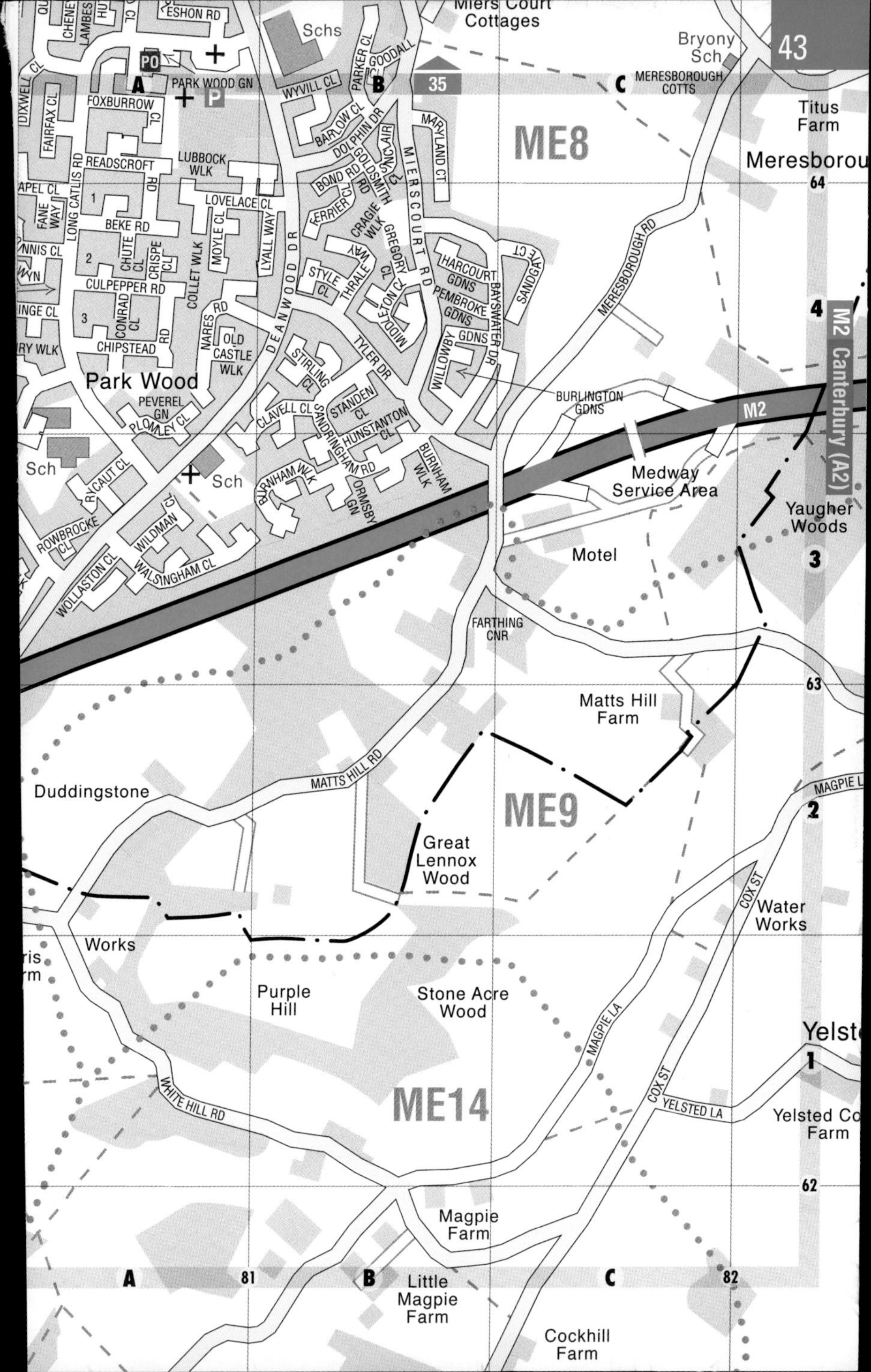
Miers Court
Cottages
Schs
Bryony
Sch
ESHON RD
CHENEY
LAMBES
PO
PARK WOOD GN
A
B
C
35
MERESBOROUGH
COTTS
WYVILL CL
PARKER CL
GOODALL
DIXWELL CL
FAIRFAX CL
FOXBURROW
CL
READSCROFT
RD
LONG CATLIS RD
LUBBOCK
WLK
BARLOW CL
DOLPHIN DR
BOND RD
GOLDSMITH
RD
SINCLAIR
CL
MIERSCOURT RD
MARYLAND CT
ME8
Titus
Farm
Meresborou
64
APEL CL
FANE
WAY
1
BEKE RD
LOVELACE CL
MOYLE CL
LYALL WAY
FERRIER CL
CRAGIE
WLK
GREGORY
CL
NNIS CL
WYN
2
CHUTE
CL
CRISPE
CL
COLLET WLK
DEANWOOD DR
STYLE
CL
THRALE
WAY
MIDDLETON CL
HARCOURT
GDNS
PEMBROKE
GDNS
BAYSWATER DR
SANDGATE CT
MERESBOROUGH RD
CULPEPPER RD
INGE CL
3
CONRAD
CL
RD
NARES
RD
OLD
CASTLE
WLK
TYLER DR
GDNS
WILLOWBY
4
M2 Canterbury (A2)
RY WLK
CHIPSTEAD
Park Wood
STIRLING
CL
STANDEN
CL
BURLINGTON
GDNS
M2
PEVEREL
GN
PLOMLEY CL
CLAVELL CL
SANDRINGHAM RD
HUNSTANTON
CL
Sch
RYCAUT CL
Sch
BURNHAM WLK
ORMSBY
GN
BURNHAM
WLK
Medway
Service Area
Yaugher
Woods
ROWBROCKE
CL
WILDMAN
CL
WALSINGHAM CL
WOLLASTON CL
Motel
3
FARTHING
CNR
63
Matts Hill
Farm
Duddingstone
MATTS HILL RD
ME9
MAGPIE LA
2
Great
Lennox
Wood
COX ST
Water
Works
Works
Purple
Hill
Stone Acre
Wood
MAGPIE LA
Yelst
1
WHITE HILL RD
ME14
COX ST
YELSTED LA
Yelsted Co
Farm
62
Magpie
Farm
A
81
B
Little
Magpie
Farm
C
82
Cockhill
Farm

Whitedyke Rd
Paddlesworth Farm
A
B
C
Mark Farm
PADDLESWORTH RD
TOWNSEND RD
62
ME6
Walnut Tree Farm
4
MIDSUMMER
GASSONS RD
ST BENEDICT RD
Stalks Wood
Dyke Place
STANGATE RD
RITCH RD
DOWLING
LUCAS RD
BUSBRIDGE RD
3
Langhold House
SNODLAND RD
MARY LAST CL
ME19
Austen's Farm
61
Parson's Corner
LEGGE LA
SANDY LA
Horn Street
2
Birling Lodge
Birling
Sandhole
Liby
PH
CH
BULL RD
BIRLING PK
THE CLOSE
RYARSH RD
1
MASTERS LA
Birling Ashes
RSPCA Animal Ctr
A228
60
BIRLING RD
Birling Ashes
Birling Wood
68
A
50
B
69
C
CASTLE WAY
Leybourne Lake
M20

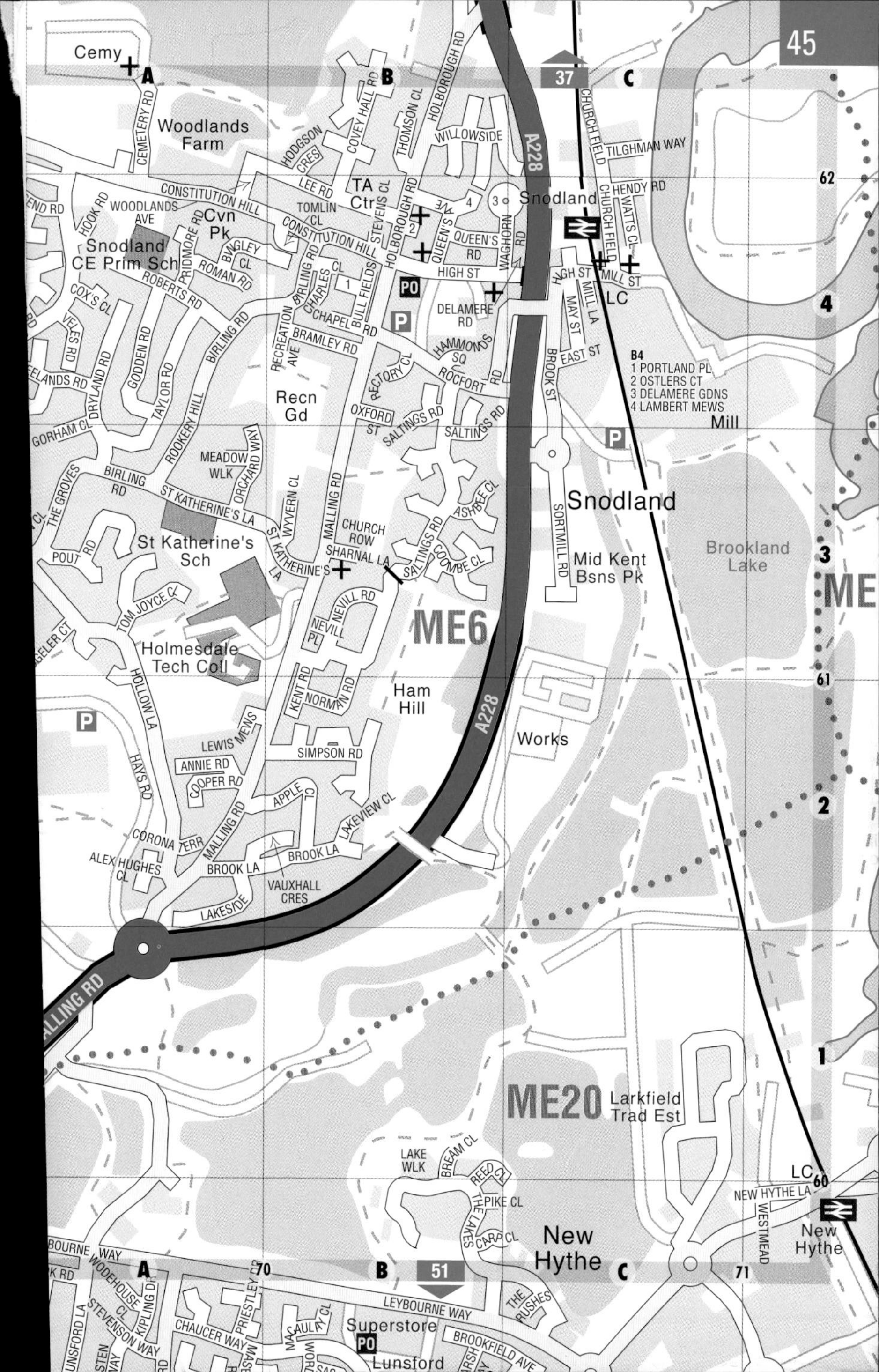

37
51
62
61
60
70
71

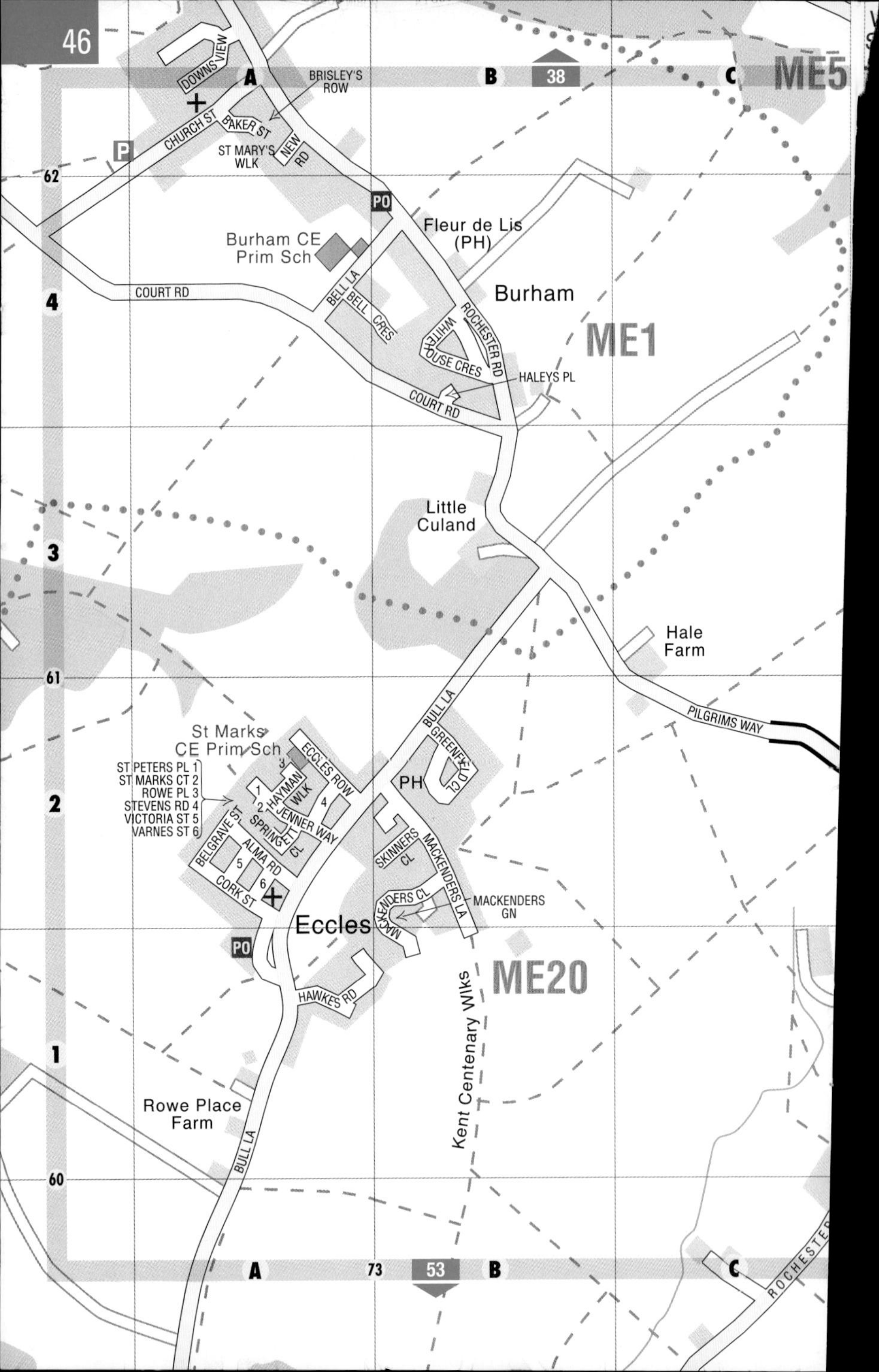
A
B
38
C
ME5
DOWNS VIEW
BRISLEY'S ROW
CHURCH ST
BAKER ST
ST MARY'S WLK
NEW RD
P
62
PO
Fleur de Lis (PH)
Burham CE Prim Sch
BELL LA
BELL CRES
COURT RD
Burham
4
WHITE HOUSE CRES
ROCHESTER RD
ME1
HALEYS PL
COURT RD
Little Culand
3
Hale Farm
61
BULL LA
PILGRIMS WAY
St Marks CE Prim Sch
ST PETERS PL 1
ST MARKS CT 2
ROWE PL 3
STEVENS RD 4
VICTORIA ST 5
VARNES ST 6
ECCLES ROW
GREENFIELD CL
HAYMAN WLK
JENNER WAY
SPRINGETT CL
BELGRAVE ST
ALMA RD
CORK ST
2
PH
SKINNERS CL
MACKENDERS LA
MACKENDERS CL
MACKENDERS GN
Eccles
PO
ME20
HAWKES RD
1
Kent Centenary Wlks
Rowe Place Farm
BULL LA
60
A
73
53
B
C
ROCHESTER

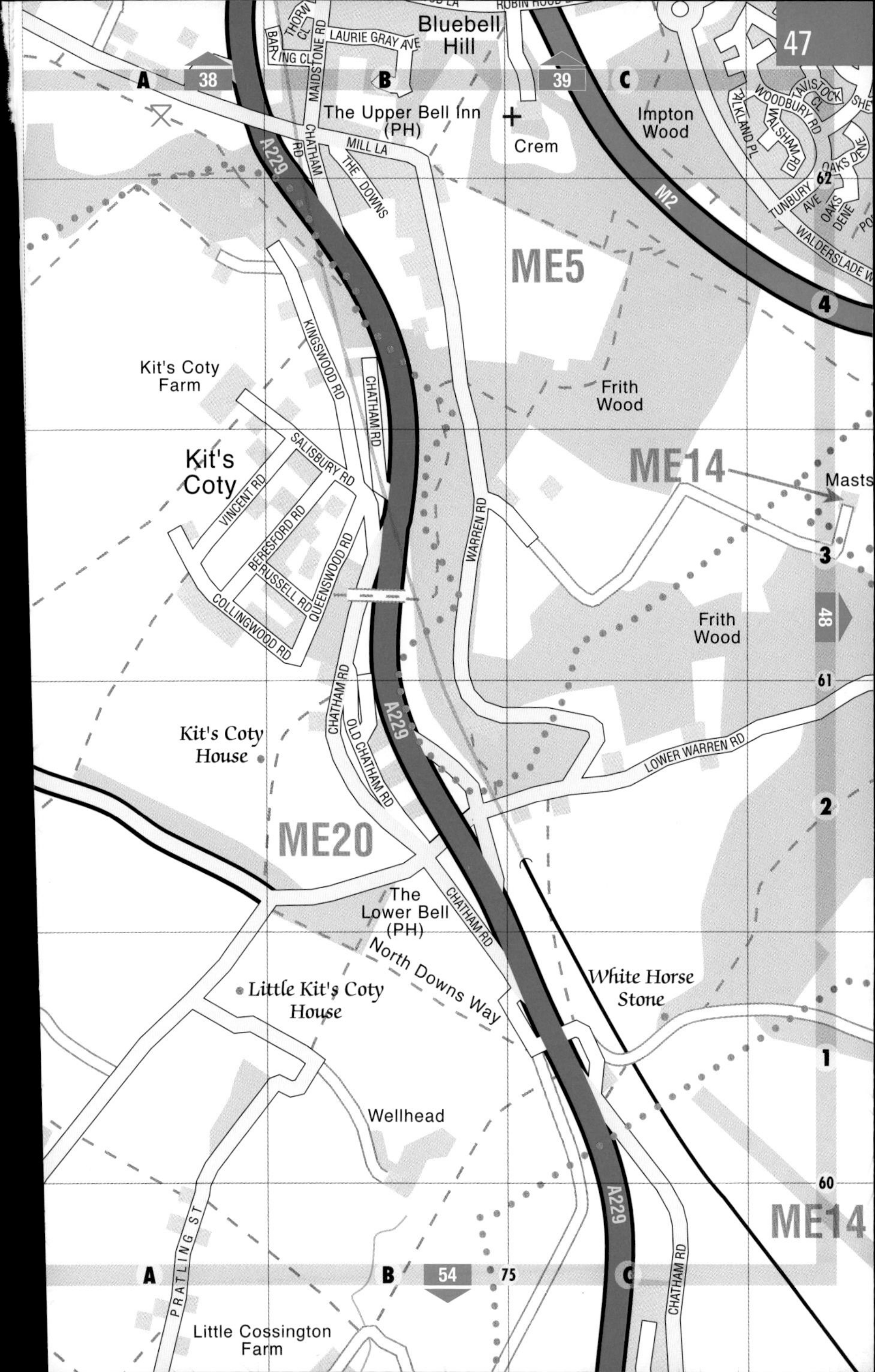
Bluebell Hill
LAURIE GRAY AVE
MAIDSTONE RD
The Upper Bell Inn (PH)
Crem
Impton Wood
CHATHAM RD
MILL LA
THE DOWNS
A229
M2
WOODBURY RD
TAVISTOCK CL
WALSHAM RD
TUNBURY AVE
OAKS DENE
WALDERSLADE
ME5
KINGSWOOD RD
Kit's Coty Farm
CHATHAM RD
Frith Wood
ME14
Masts
Kit's Coty
SALISBURY RD
VINCENT RD
BERESFORD RD
QUEENSWOOD RD
RUSSELL RD
COLLINGWOOD RD
WARREN RD
Frith Wood
Kit's Coty House
OLD CHATHAM RD
LOWER WARREN RD
ME20
The Lower Bell (PH)
North Downs Way
White Horse Stone
Little Kit's Coty House
Wellhead
ME14
PRATLING ST
Little Cossington Farm
A
B
C
38
39
48
54
4
3
2
1
62
61
60
75

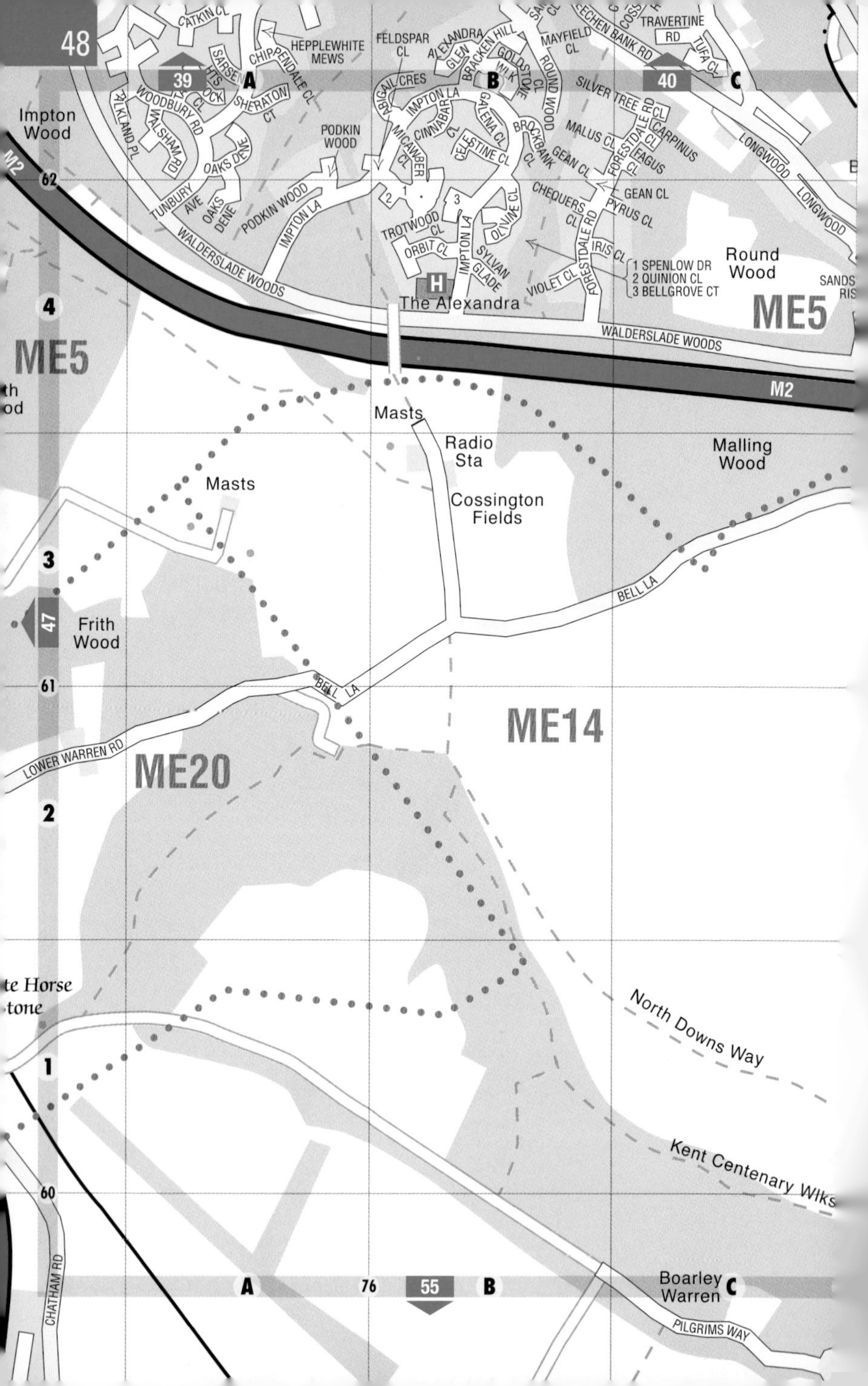

39
40
A
B
C
CATKIN CL
HEPPLEWHITE MEWS
FELDSPAR CL
ALEXANDRA GLEN
BRACKEN HILL
MAYFIELD CL
TRAVERTINE RD
TUFA CL
SARSEN
CHIPPENDALE CL
SHERATON CT
WOODBURY RD
WALSHAM RD
FALKLAND PL
ABIGAIL CRES
IMPTON LA
GOLDSTONE WLK
ROUND WOOD CL
SILVER TREE CL
FORESTDALE RD
CARPINUS CL
FAGUS CL
MALUS CL
GEAN CL
LONGWOOD
Impton Wood
PODKIN WOOD
CINNABAR CL
MICAWBER CL
CELESTINE CL
GALENA CL
BROCKBANK CL
OAKS DENE
TUNBURY AVE
PODKIN WOOD
M2
62
CHEQUERS CL
PYRUS CL
TROTWOOD CL
ORBIT CL
OLIVINE CL
SYLVAN GLADE
IRIS CL
VIOLET CL
1 SPENLOW DR
2 QUINION CL
3 BELLGROVE CT
Round Wood
WALDERSLADE WOODS
The Alexandra
ME5
4
ME5
Masts
Radio Sta
Malling Wood
Masts
Cossington Fields
3
BELL LA
47
Frith Wood
61
BELL LA
ME14
LOWER WARREN RD
ME20
2
te Horse
tone
North Downs Way
1
Kent Centenary Wlks
60
CHATHAM RD
A
76
55
B
Boarley Warren
C
PILGRIMS WAY

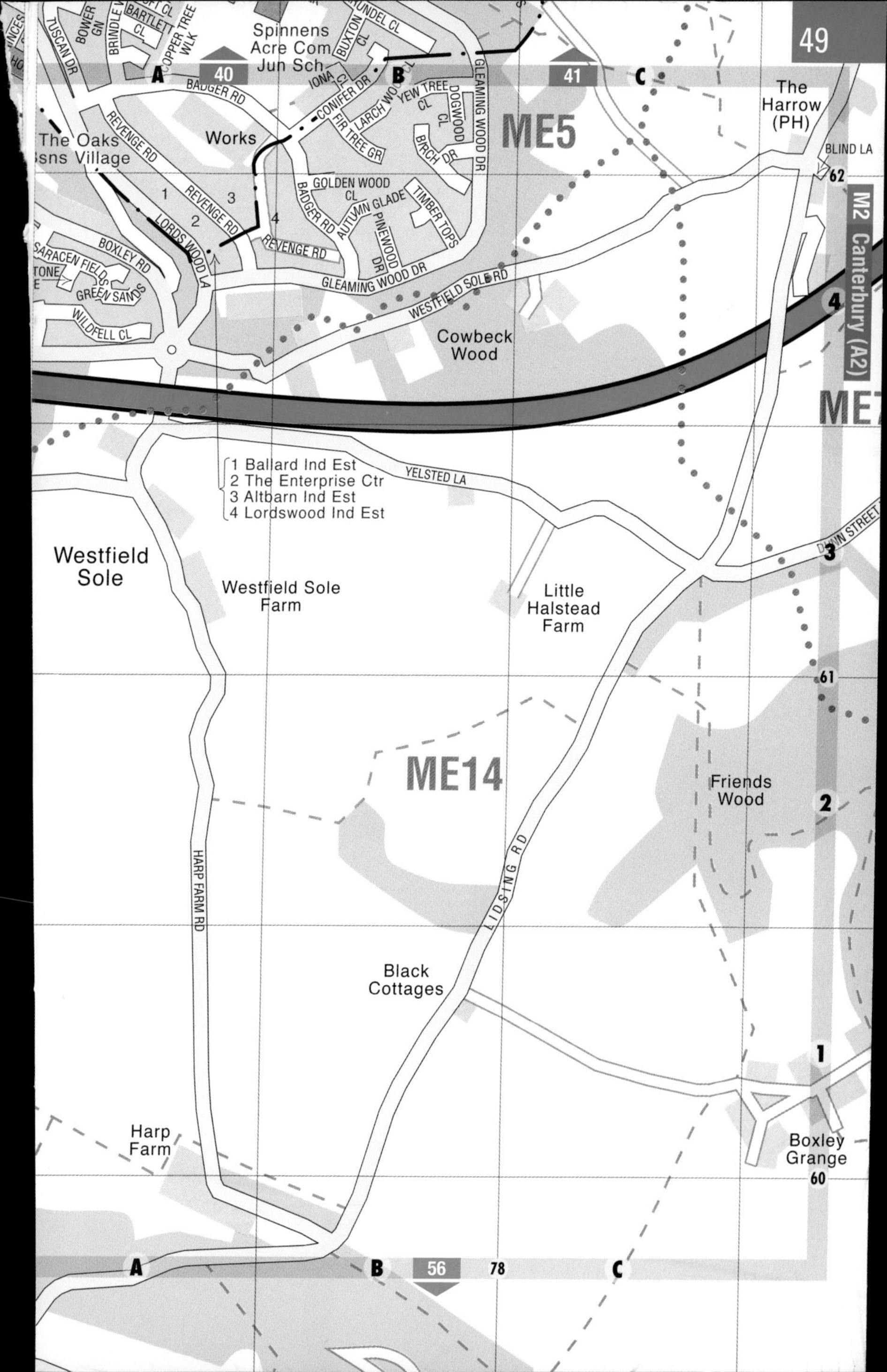
Spinnens
Acre Com
Jun Sch
A
40
B
41
C
The Harrow (PH)
BLIND LA
62
M2 Canterbury (A2)
ME5
The Oaks
Bsns Village
Works
BADGER RD
CONIFER DR
FIR TREE GR
LARCH WOOD CL
YEW TREE CL
DOGWOOD CL
BIRCH DR
GLEAMING WOOD DR
GOLDEN WOOD CL
AUTUMN GLADE
TIMBER TOPS
PINEWOOD DR
REVENGE RD
LORDS WOOD LA
BOXLEY RD
SARACEN FIELDS
GREEN SANDS
WILDFELL CL
TUSCAN DR
BOWER GN
BRINDLE WAY
BARTLETT CL
COPPER TREE WLK
BUXTON CL
IONA CL
WESTFIELD SOLE RD
Cowbeck Wood
ME7
4
YELSTED LA
1 Ballard Ind Est
2 The Enterprise Ctr
3 Altbarn Ind Est
4 Lordswood Ind Est
Westfield Sole
Westfield Sole Farm
Little Halstead Farm
DUNN STREET RD
3
61
ME14
Friends Wood
2
HARP FARM RD
LIDSING RD
Black Cottages
1
Harp Farm
Boxley Grange
60
A
B
56
78
C

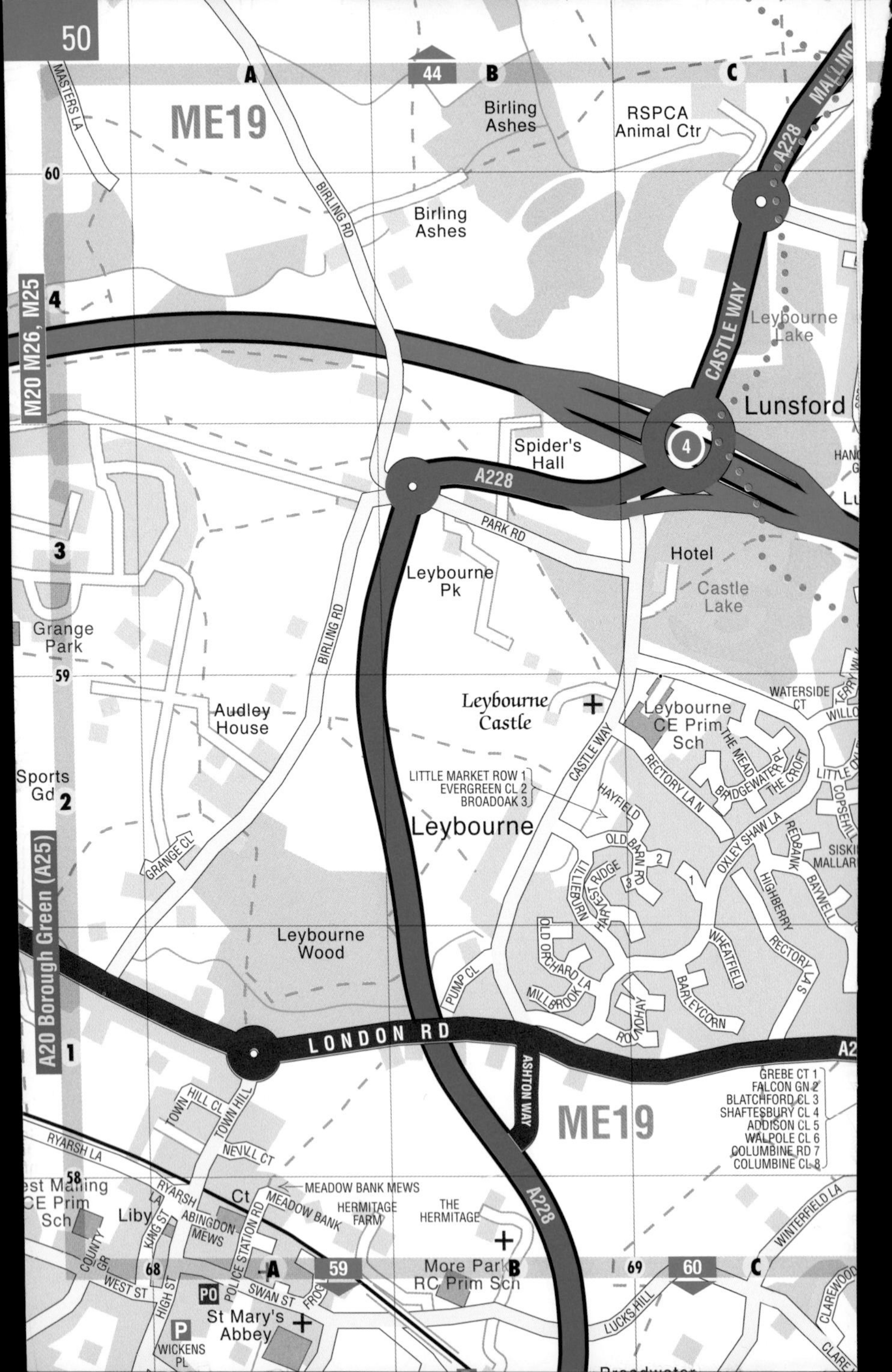
ME19
Birling Ashes
RSPCA Animal Ctr
Birling Ashes
Leybourne Lake
Lunsford
Spider's Hall
Hotel
Castle Lake
Leybourne Pk
Grange Park
Audley House
Leybourne Castle
Leybourne CE Prim Sch
LITTLE MARKET ROW 1
EVERGREEN CL 2
BROADOAK 3
Leybourne
Sports Gd
Leybourne Wood
LONDON RD
ME19
GREBE CT 1
FALCON GN 2
BLATCHFORD CL 3
SHAFTESBURY CL 4
ADDISON CL 5
WALPOLE CL 6
COLUMBINE RD 7
COLUMBINE CL 8
MEADOW BANK MEWS
HERMITAGE FARM
THE HERMITAGE
More Park RC Prim Sch
St Mary's Abbey
Liby
Ct
West Malling CE Prim Sch
A20 Borough Green (A25)
M20 M26, M25
CASTLE WAY
A228
PARK RD
BIRLING RD
MASTERS LA
RECTORY LA N
RECTORY LA S
OXLEY SHAW LA
HAYFIELD
OLD BARN RD
HARVEST RIDGE
LILLIEBURN
OLD ORCHARD LA
MILLBROOK
ROUNDHAY
BARLEYCORN
WHEATFIELD
HIGHBERRY
REDBANK
BAYWELL
THE MEAD
BRIDGEWATER PL
THE CROFT
WATERSIDE CT
PUMP CL
GRANGE CL
ASHTON WAY
TOWN HILL CL
TOWN HILL
NEVILL CT
RYARSH LA
RYARSH LA
ABINGDON MEWS
KING ST
MEADOW BANK
POLICE STATION RD
COUNTY GR
WEST ST
HIGH ST
SWAN ST
FROG
WICKENS PL
LUCKS HILL
WINTERFIELD LA
CLAREWOOD
PO
P
44
59
60
A
B
C
68
69
60
59
58
1
2
3
4

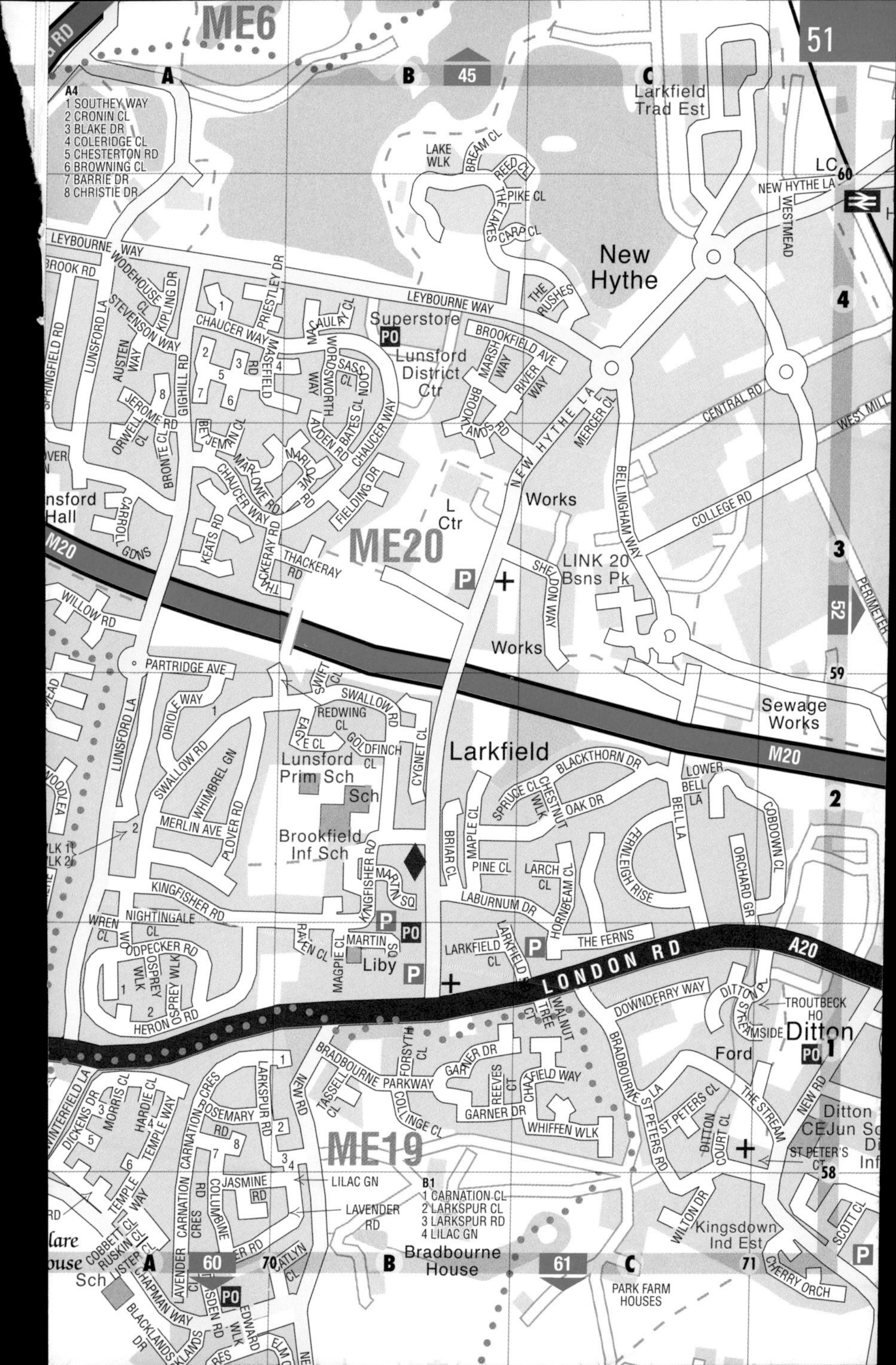
ME6
45
A4
1 SOUTHEY WAY
2 CRONIN CL
3 BLAKE DR
4 COLERIDGE CL
5 CHESTERTON RD
6 BROWNING CL
7 BARRIE DR
8 CHRISTIE DR
Larkfield Trad Est
LAKE WLK
BREAM CL
REED CL
PIKE CL
THE LAKES
CARP CL
NEW HYTHE LA
WESTMEAD
New Hythe
LEYBOURNE WAY
BROOK RD
WODEHOUSE CL
KIPLING DR
STEVENSON WAY
PRIESTLEY DR
THE RUSHES
CHAUCER WAY
MACAULAY CL
Superstore
MASEFIELD
WORDSWORTH WAY
SASSOON CL
Lunsford District Ctr
BROOKFIELD AVE
MARSH WAY
RIVER WAY
SPRINGFIELD RD
LUNSFORD LA
AUSTEN WAY
GIGHILL RD
JEROME RD
ORWELL CL
BRONTE CL
BETJEMAN CL
AUDEN RD
BATES CL
BROOKLANDS RD
MERCER CL
CENTRAL RD
WEST MILL
MARLOWE RD
FIELDING DR
BELLINGHAM WAY
Works
COLLEGE RD
Lunsford Hall
CARROLL GDNS
KEATS RD
THACKERAY RD
L Ctr
ME20
M20
LINK 20 Bsns Pk
SHELDON WAY
PERIMETER
52
WILLOW RD
PARTRIDGE AVE
ORIOLE WAY
SWIFT CL
SWALLOW RD
REDWING CL
EAGLE CL
GOLDFINCH CL
CYGNET CL
Larkfield
BLACKTHORN DR
Sewage Works
59
LOWER BELL LA
BELL LA
SWALLOW RD
WHIMBREL GN
Lunsford Prim Sch
Sch
SPRUCE CL
CHESTNUT WLK
OAK DR
COBDOWN CL
WOODLEA
MERLIN AVE
PLOVER RD
Brookfield Inf Sch
BRIAR CL
MAPLE CL
PINE CL
LARCH CL
HORNBEAM CL
FERNLEIGH RISE
ORCHARD GR
KINGFISHER RD
MARTIN SQ
LABURNUM DR
NIGHTINGALE CL
WREN CL
WOODPECKER RD
OSPREY WLK
RAVEN CL
MAGPIE CL
MARTIN SQ
Liby
LARKFIELD CL
THE FERNS
LONDON RD
A20
HERON RD
DOWNDERRY WAY
DITTON PL
TROUBECK HO
STREAMSIDE
Ditton
Ford
WINTERFIELD LA
DICKENS DR
MORRIS CL
HARDIE CL
TEMPLE WAY
LARKSPUR RD
NEW RD
BRADBOURNE PARKWAY
FORSYTH CL
GARNER DR
REEVES CT
CHATFIELD WAY
WALNUT TREE CT
BRADBOURNE LA
ST PETERS CL
THE STREAM
NEW RD
Ditton CE Jun Sch
ROSEMARY RD
CARNATION CRES
TASSELL CL
COLLINGE CL
GARNER DR
WHIFFEN WLK
ST PETERS RD
DITTON COURT CL
ST PETER'S CT
58
ME19
JASMINE RD
COLUMBINE RD
LILAC GN
LAVENDER RD
B1
1 CARNATION CL
2 LARKSPUR CL
3 LARKSPUR RD
4 LILAC GN
WILTON DR
Kingsdown Ind Est
SCOTT CL
COBBETT CL
RUSKIN CL
LISTER CL
Sch
60
70
CATLYN CL
Bradbourne House
61
71
CHERRY ORCH
PARK FARM HOUSES
CHAPMAN WAY
BLACKLANDS DR
EDWARD WLK
ELM CL

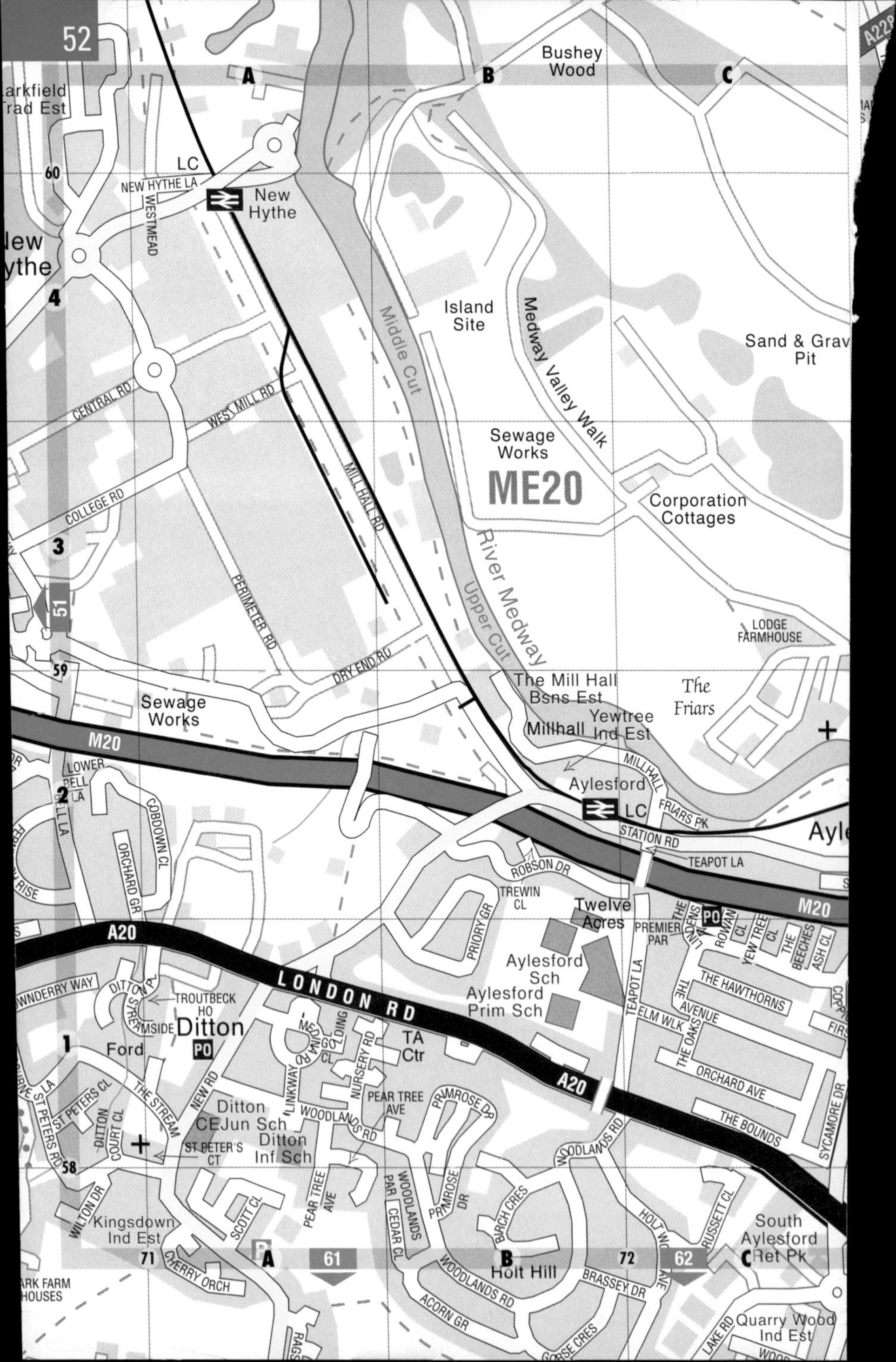

Bushey Wood
Larkfield Trad Est
LC
NEW HYTHE LA
WESTMEAD
New Hythe
Island Site
Medway Valley Walk
Sand & Grav Pit
Middle Cut
CENTRAL RD
WEST MILL RD
Sewage Works
ME20
COLLEGE RD
MILL HALL RD
Corporation Cottages
River Medway
Upper Cut
PERIMETER RD
LODGE FARMHOUSE
DRY END RD
The Mill Hall Bsns Est
The Friars
Sewage Works
Millhall
Yewtree Ind Est
M20
LOWER BELL LA
BELL LA
COBDOWN CL
MILL HALL
Aylesford
LC
FRIARS PK
STATION RD
Ayle
ORCHARD GR
RISE
ROBSON DR
TEAPOT LA
TREWIN CL
Twelve Acres
PRIORY GR
PREMIER PAR
THE LINDENS
PO
ROWAN CL
YEW TREE CL
THE BEECHES
ASH CL
M20
A20
Aylesford Sch
Aylesford Prim Sch
TEAPOT LA
THE HAWTHORNS
LONDON RD
DITTON PL
TROUTBECK HO
STREAMSIDE
Ditton
MEDINA RD
GOLDING CL
ELM WLK
THE AVENUE
THE OAKS
Ford
PO
NURSERY RD
TA Ctr
ORCHARD AVE
ST PETERS CL
THE STREAM
NEW RD
LINKWAY
PEAR TREE AVE
PRIMROSE DR
A20
SYCAMORE DR
ST PETERS RD
DITTON COURT CL
Ditton CE Jun Sch
Ditton Inf Sch
WOODLANDS RD
ST PETER'S CT
THE BOUNDS
WOODLANDS RD
WILTON DR
PEAR TREE AVE
WOODLANDS PAR
CEDAR CL
PRIMROSE DR
BIRCH CRES
HOLT WOOD AVE
RUSSETT CL
Kingsdown Ind Est
SCOTT CL
South Aylesford Ret Pk
CHERRY ORCH
Holt Hill
WOODLANDS RD
BRASSEY DR
ARK FARM HOUSES
ACORN GR
Quarry Wood Ind Est
LAKE RD
GORSE CRES

51
61
62

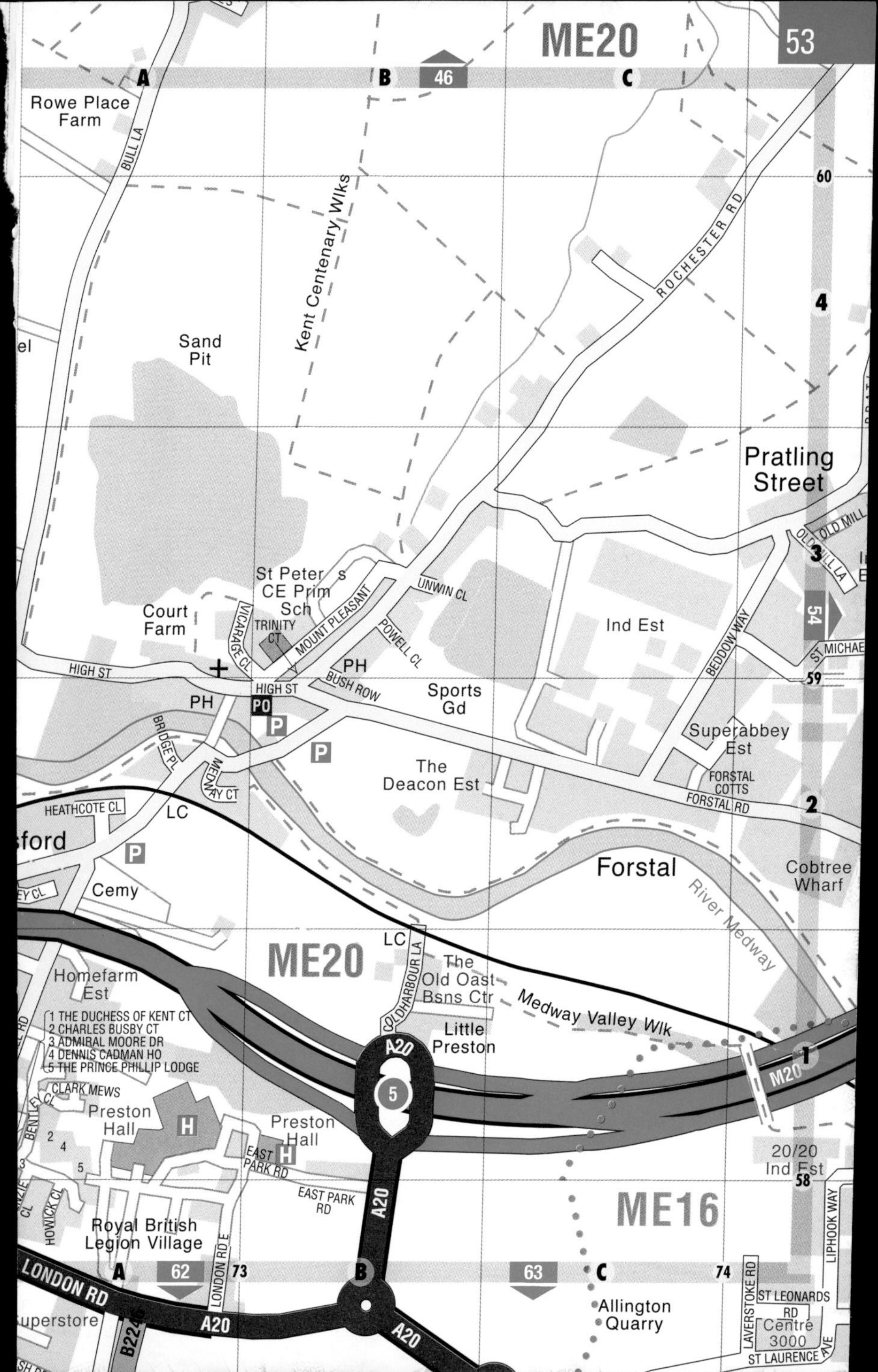
ME20
A
B
46
C
Rowe Place Farm
BULL LA
60
Kent Centenary Wlks
ROCHESTER RD
4
Sand Pit
Pratling Street
OLD MILL
OLD MILL LA
3
St Peter's CE Prim Sch
UNWIN CL
Court Farm
VICARAGE CL
TRINITY CT
MOUNT PLEASANT
POWELL CL
Ind Est
54
BEDDOW WAY
ST MICHAE
HIGH ST
PH
HIGH ST
BUSH ROW
Sports Gd
59
PH
PO
P
BRIDGE PL
P
Superabbey Est
MEDWAY CT
The Deacon Est
FORSTAL COTTS
FORSTAL RD
2
HEATHCOTE CL
LC
sford
P
Forstal
Cobtree Wharf
Cemy
River Medway
LC
ME20
COLDHARBOUR LA
The Old Oast Bsns Ctr
Homefarm Est
Medway Valley Wlk
1 THE DUCHESS OF KENT CT
2 CHARLES BUSBY CT
3 ADMIRAL MOORE DR
4 DENNIS CADMAN HO
5 THE PRINCE PHILLIP LODGE
Little Preston
A20
1
5
M20
CLARK MEWS
BENTLEY CL
Preston Hall
H
Preston Hall
EAST PARK RD
H
20/20 Ind Est
58
HOWICK CL
EAST PARK RD
A20
ME16
LIPHOOK WAY
Royal British Legion Village
LONDON RD E
A
62
73
B
63
C
74
LAVERSTOKE RD
LONDON RD
ST LEONARDS RD
Allington Quarry
uperstore
A20
Centre 3000
B2246
A20
ST LAURENCE AVE

White Horse Stone
47
A
B
C
Wellhead
A229
60
ROCHESTER RD
4
PRATLING ST
Little Cossington Farm
Great Cossington
CHATHAM RD
GREY WETHERS
TOLGATE WAY
HIGHAM VIEW
PILGRIMS VIEW
BAKERY COTTS
Tyland Cons
OLD MILL LA
Pratling Street
Ind Est
3
53
ME20
BEDDOW WAY
ST MICHAELS CL
CH
59
Superabbey Est
FORSTAL COTTS
ME14
Cobtree Manor
CRABTREE RDBT
2
FORSTAL RD
Forstal
Cobtree Wharf
River Medway
6
Museum of Kent Rural Life
LOCK LA
1
M20
P
Malta Inn (PH)
THE RUNNING HORSE RDBT
CHATHAM RD
CASTLE RD
20/20 Ind Est
58
LIPHOOK WAY
Allington
ME16
PINE COTTS
Allington Castle
74
LAVERSTOKE RD
63
75
64
Allington Quarry
ST LEONARDS RD
Centre 3000
ST LAURENCE AVE
BARNABAS CL

North Downs Way
Kent Centenary Wlks
48
A
B
C
60
Boarley
Warren
PILGRIMS WAY
4
Boarley
Farm
Barn Wildlife
ervation Ctr
ME14
3
56
TYLAND LA
BOARLEY LA
Curlews
Works
SHENLEY GR
59
King s Arms
(PH)
Abbey
Gate
Street
Farm
2
BOARLEY LA
Abbey
Farm
ABBEY
GATE
COTTS
Boxley Abbey
(rems of)
Donkey
Shaws
GRANGE LA
M20
Park
Wood
BOXLEY RD
GRANGE LA
1 FARTHINGS COTTS
2 YEW TREE COTTS
BOARLEY LA
Sandling
Cookes
Cottage
1
1 CUCKWOOD AVE
2 BOARLEY CT
BURLEIGH DR
SANDBOURNE DR
SANDLING LA
Harbourlands
Farm
58
BROOKBANK
M20
Harbourland
SANDLING LA
64
76
B
65
C
77
Invicta
Park
WOODCUT
BARNHURST RD
DOWNS CL
DOWNS VIEW RD
Sandling
Prim Sch
RAYMER RD
STOCKTON CL
CLEWSON RISE
NEVILLE CL
ERITH CL

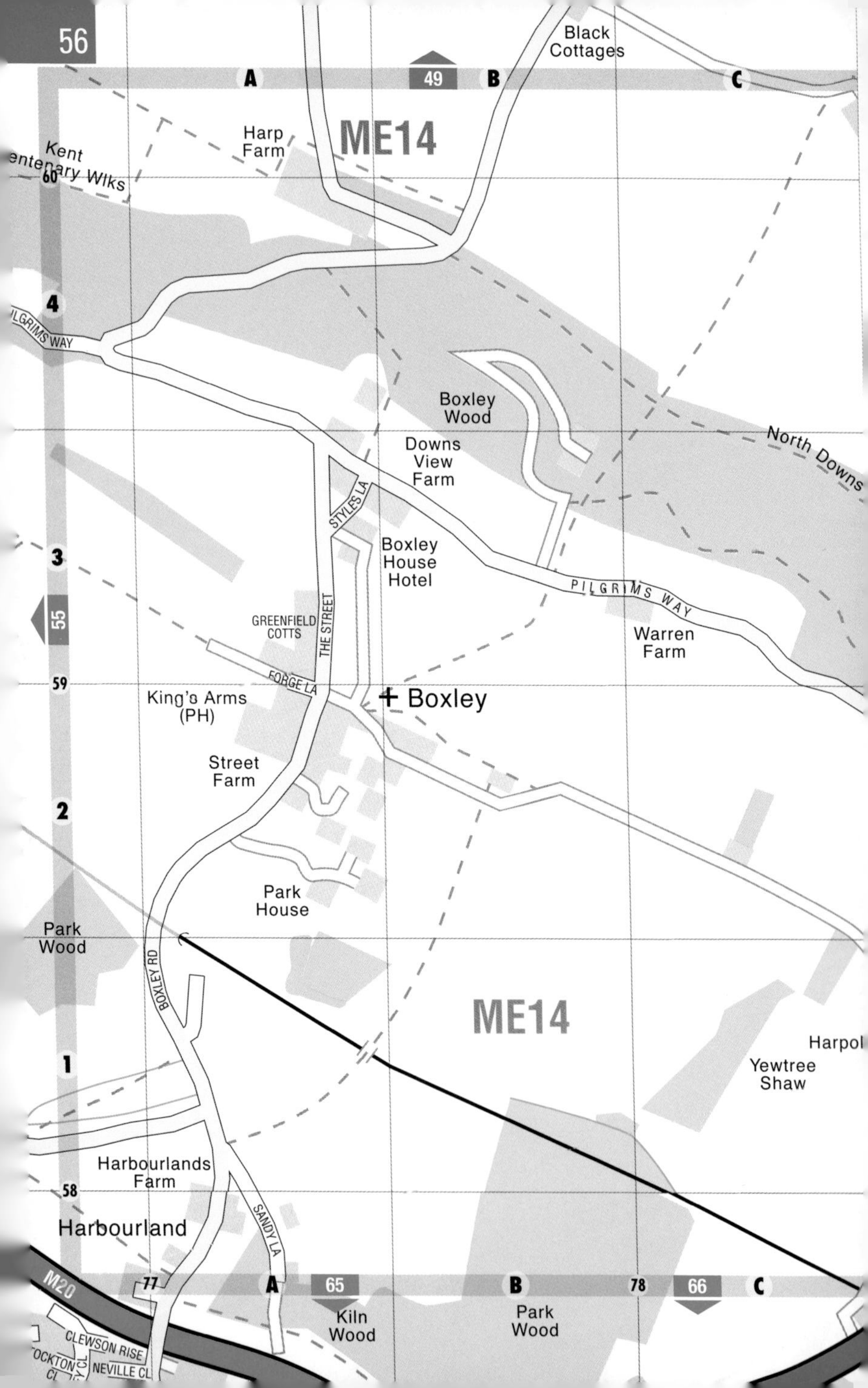
Black Cottages
A
49
B
C
Harp Farm
ME14
Kent Centenary Wlks
60
4
PILGRIMS WAY
Boxley Wood
North Downs
Downs View Farm
STYLES LA
Boxley House Hotel
3
55
GREENFIELD COTTS
THE STREET
PILGRIMS WAY
Warren Farm
59
FORGE LA
King's Arms (PH)
Boxley
Street Farm
2
Park House
Park Wood
BOXLEY RD
ME14
1
Harpol
Yewtree Shaw
Harbourlands Farm
58
Harbourland
SANDY LA
M20
77
A
65
B
78
66
C
Kiln Wood
Park Wood
CLEWSON RISE
NEVILLE CL

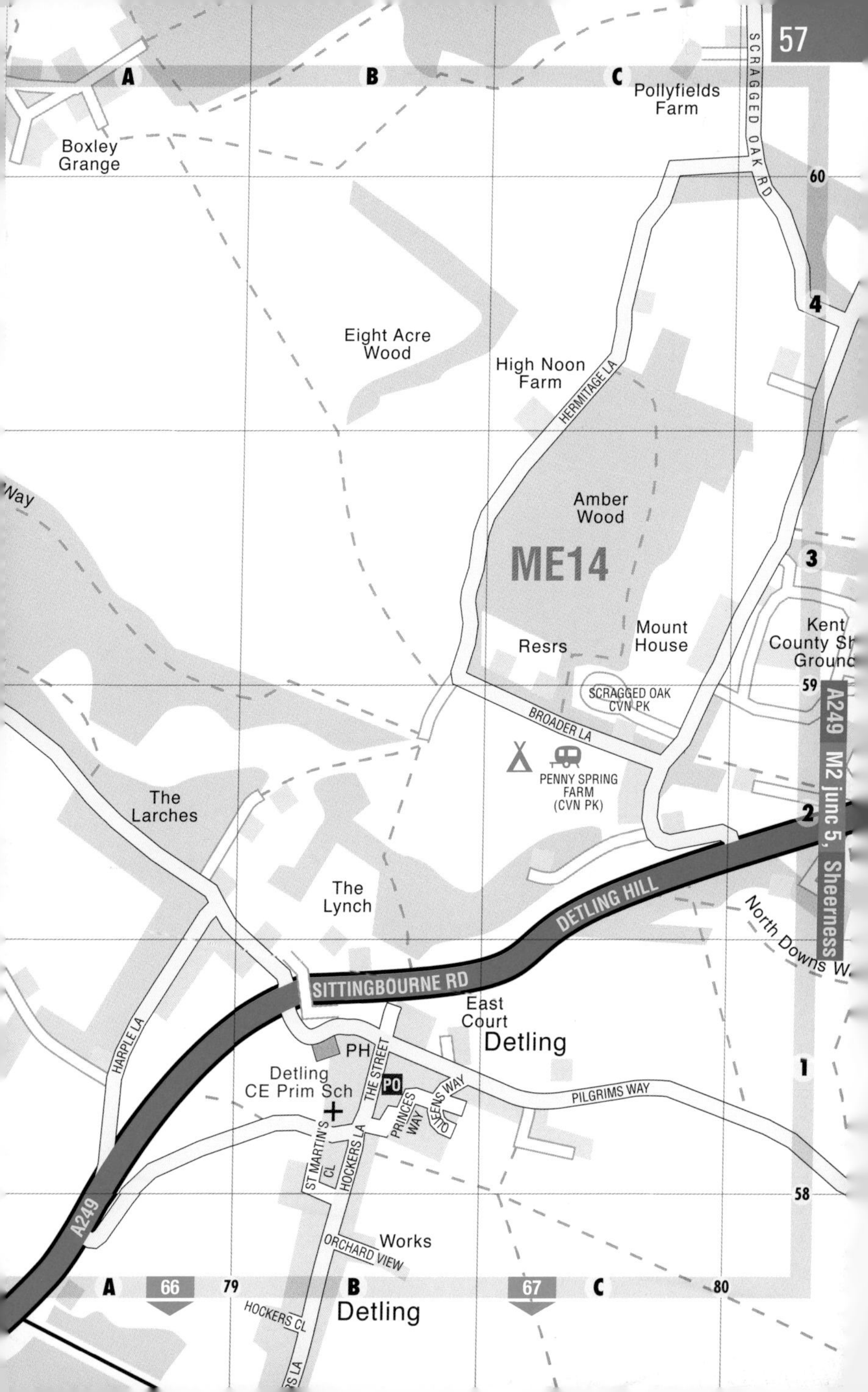
A
B
C
Pollyfields Farm
SCRAGGED OAK RD
Boxley Grange
60
4
Eight Acre Wood
High Noon Farm
HERMITAGE LA
Way
Amber Wood
ME14
3
Mount House
Resrs
Kent County Sh Ground
59
SCRAGGED OAK CVN PK
BROADER LA
A249 M2 junc 5, Sheerness
PENNY SPRING FARM (CVN PK)
2
The Larches
The Lynch
DETLING HILL
North Downs W
SITTINGBOURNE RD
East Court
Detling
PH
HARPLE LA
Detling CE Prim Sch
THE STREET
PO
QUEENS WAY
PILGRIMS WAY
1
ST MARTIN'S CL
HOCKERS LA
PRINCES WAY
58
A249
ORCHARD VIEW
Works
A
66
79
B
67
C
80
Detling
HOCKERS CL

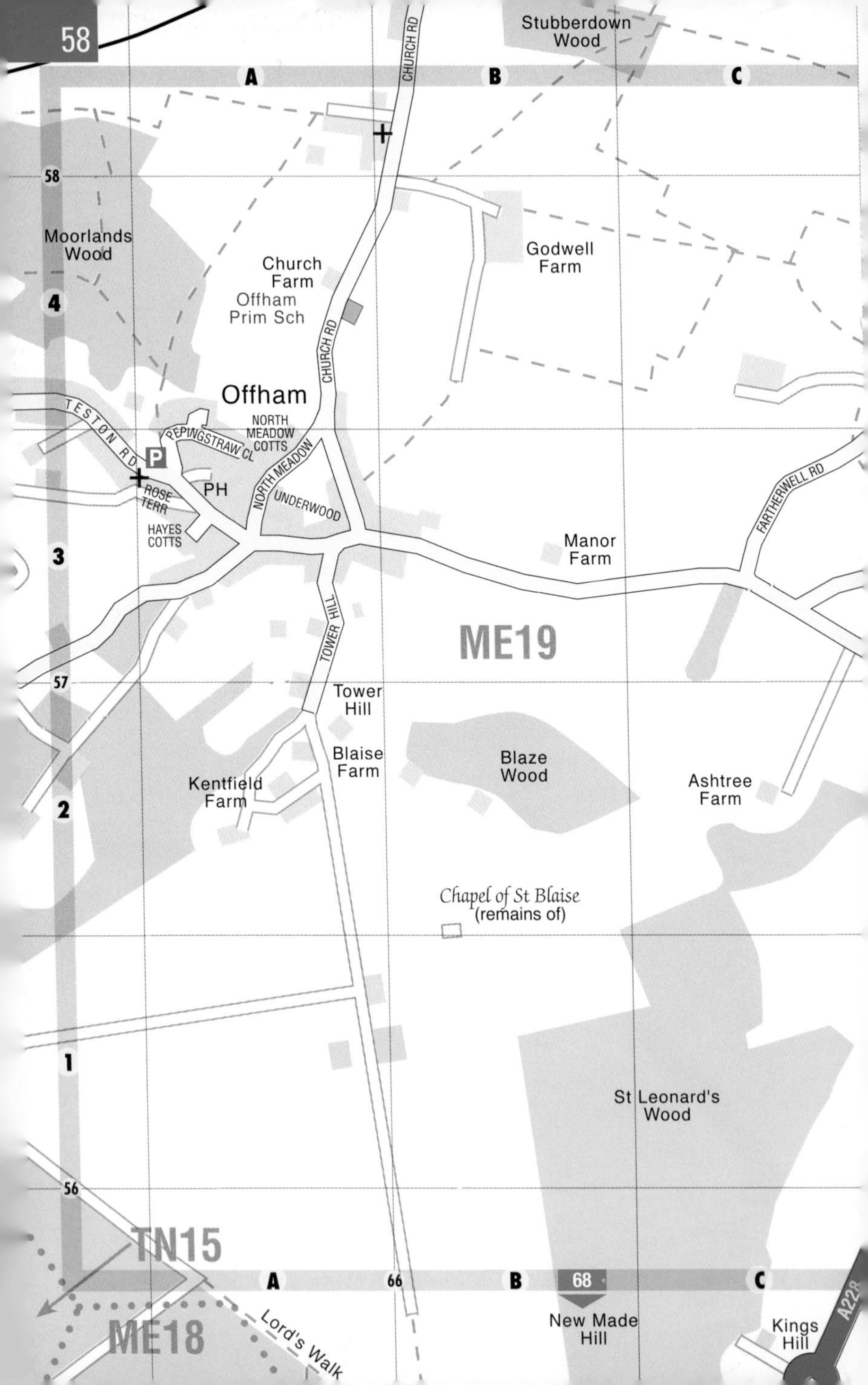

A
B
C
Stubberdown Wood
CHURCH RD
58
Moorlands Wood
Church Farm
Offham Prim Sch
Godwell Farm
4
Offham
TESTON RD
PEPINGSTRAW CL
NORTH MEADOW COTTS
NORTH MEADOW
P
PH
ROSE TERR
UNDERWOOD
HAYES COTTS
Manor Farm
FARTHERWELL RD
3
TOWER HILL
ME19
57
Tower Hill
Blaise Farm
Blaze Wood
Kentfield Farm
Ashtree Farm
2
Chapel of St Blaise
(remains of)
1
St Leonard's Wood
56
TN15
A
66
B
68
C
New Made Hill
Kings Hill
A228
ME18
Lord's Walk

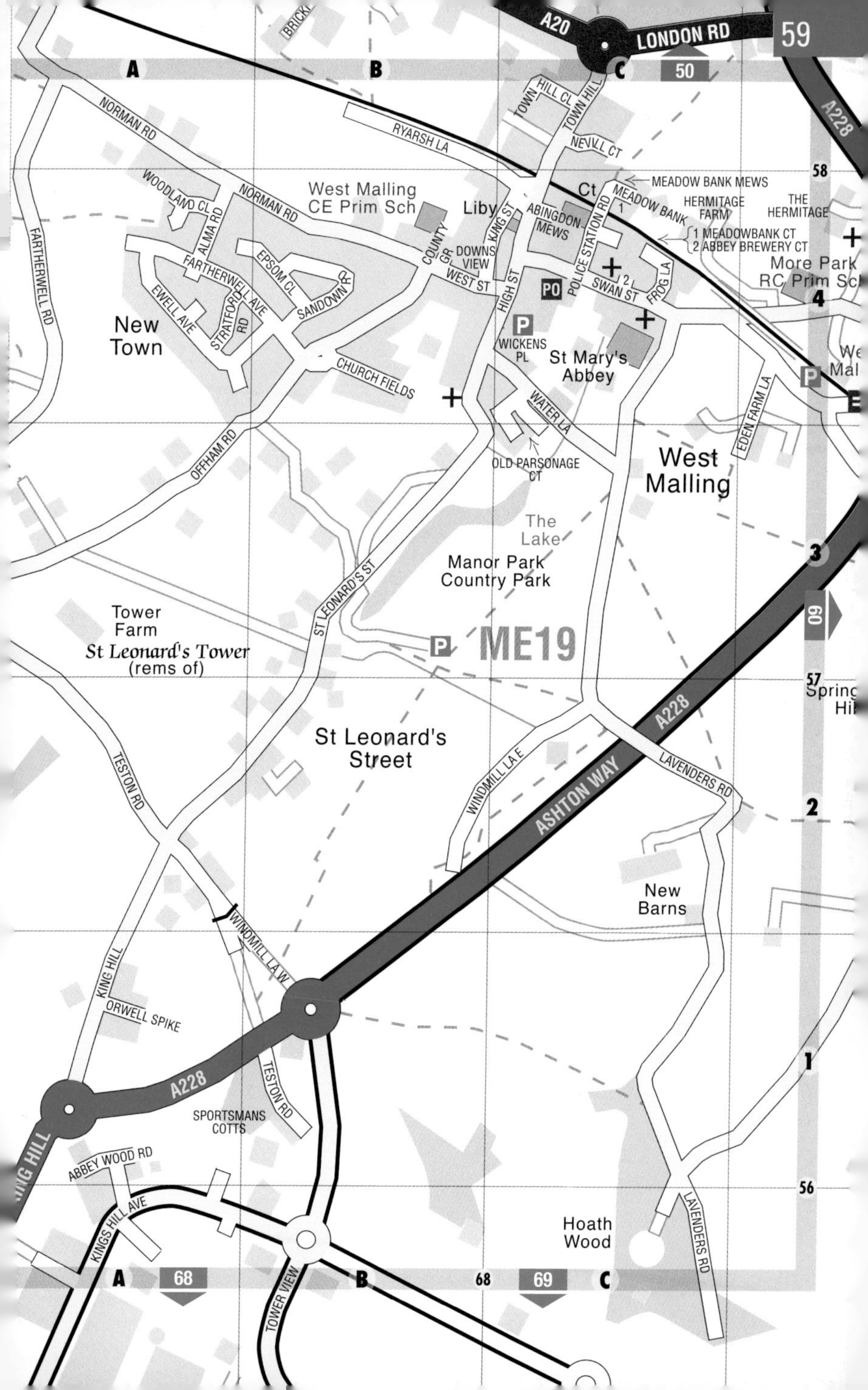
A20
LONDON RD
50
A228
A
B
C
NORMAN RD
RYARSH LA
TOWN HILL CL
TOWN HILL
NEVILL CT
MEADOW BANK MEWS
58
WOODLAND CL
NORMAN RD
West Malling
CE Prim Sch
Liby
KING ST
ABINGDON MEWS
Ct
MEADOW BANK
HERMITAGE FARM
THE HERMITAGE
1 MEADOWBANK CT
2 ABBEY BREWERY CT
FARTHERWELL RD
ALMA RD
FARTHERWELL AVE
EPSOM CL
SANDOWN RD
COUNTY GR
DOWNS VIEW
WEST ST
HIGH ST
PO
POLICE STATION RD
SWAN ST
FROG LA
More Park
RC Prim Sch
4
EWELL AVE
STRATFORD RD
New Town
WICKENS PL
St Mary's Abbey
CHURCH FIELDS
WATER LA
EDEN FARM LA
OFFHAM RD
OLD PARSONAGE CT
West Malling
The Lake
Manor Park
Country Park
3
ST LEONARD'S ST
60
Tower Farm
St Leonard's Tower
(rems of)
ME19
57
Spring Hi
St Leonard's Street
A228
WINDMILL LA E
LAVENDERS RD
TESTON RD
ASHTON WAY
2
New Barns
WINDMILL LA W
KING HILL
ORWELL SPIKE
1
A228
TESTON RD
SPORTSMANS COTTS
ABBEY WOOD RD
56
KINGS HILL AVE
Hoath Wood
LAVENDERS RD
TOWER VIEW
A
68
B
68
69
C

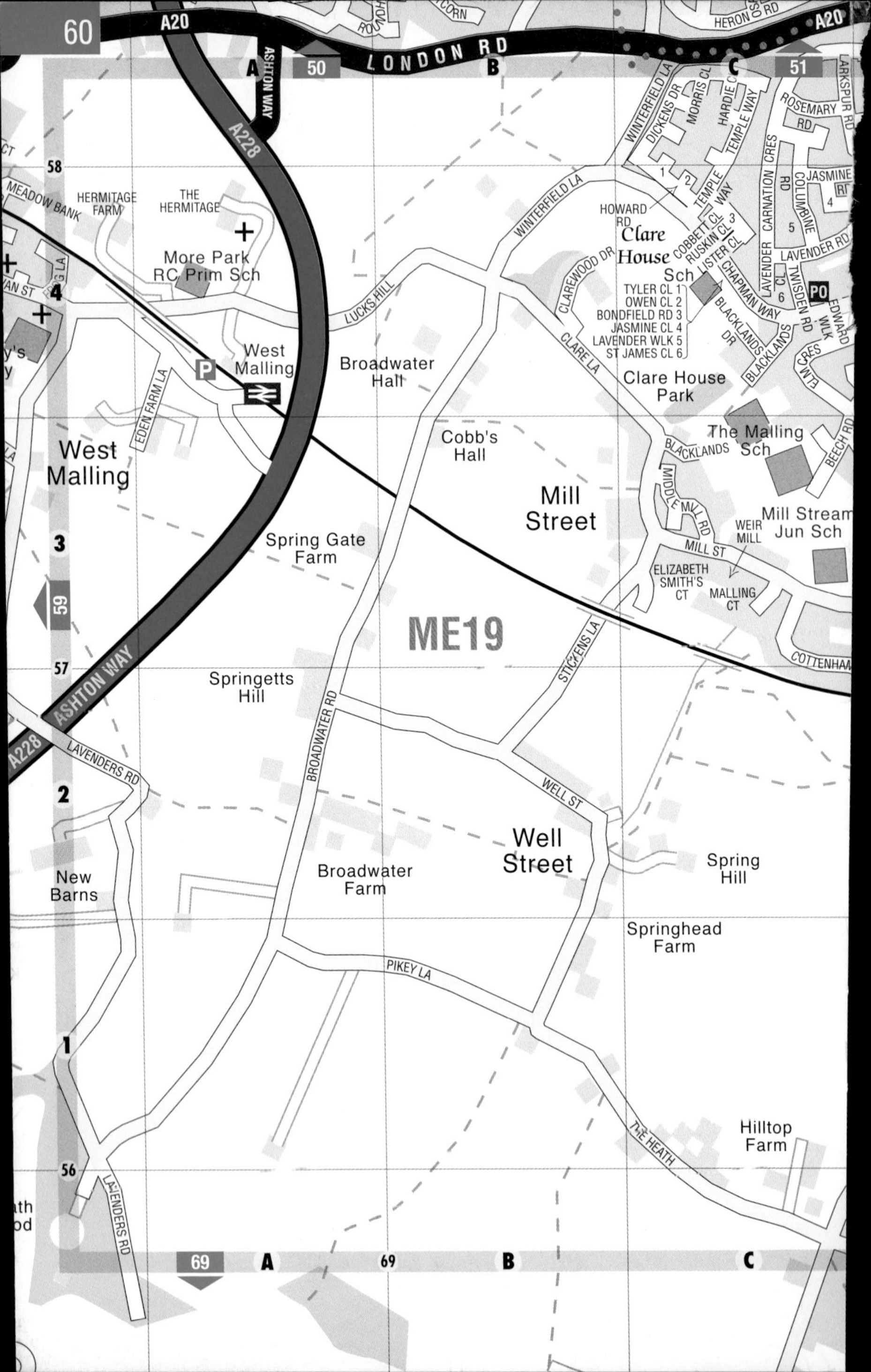
A20
LONDON RD
ASHTON WAY
A228
50
51
A
B
C
WINTERFIELD LA
DICKENS DR
MORRIS CL
HARDIE CL
TEMPLE WAY
ROSEMARY RD
LARKSPUR RD
JASMINE
CARNATION CRES
COLUMBINE RD
LAVENDER RD
HOWARD RD
Clare House
Sch
COBBETT CL
RUSKIN CL
LISTER CL
CLAREWOOD DR
TYLER CL 1
OWEN CL 2
BONDFIELD RD 3
JASMINE CL 4
LAVENDER WLK 5
ST JAMES CL 6
CHAPMAN WAY
BLACKLANDS DR
BLACKLANDS
TWISDEN RD
PO
EDWARD WLK
ELM CRES
CLARE LA
Clare House Park
The Malling Sch
BEECH RD
58
MEADOW BANK
HERMITAGE FARM
THE HERMITAGE
More Park RC Prim Sch
LUCKS HILL
West Malling
Broadwater Hall
P
EDEN FARM LA
Cobb's Hall
BLACKLANDS
MIDDLE MILL RD
Mill Street
West Malling
WEIR MILL
Mill Stream Jun Sch
MILL ST
3
Spring Gate Farm
ELIZABETH SMITH'S CT
MALLING CT
59
ME19
STICKENS LA
COTTENHAM
57
Springetts Hill
BROADWATER RD
LAVENDERS RD
2
WELL ST
Well Street
Spring Hill
New Barns
Broadwater Farm
Springhead Farm
PIKEY LA
1
THE HEATH
Hilltop Farm
56
LAVENDERS RD
69
A
69
B
C

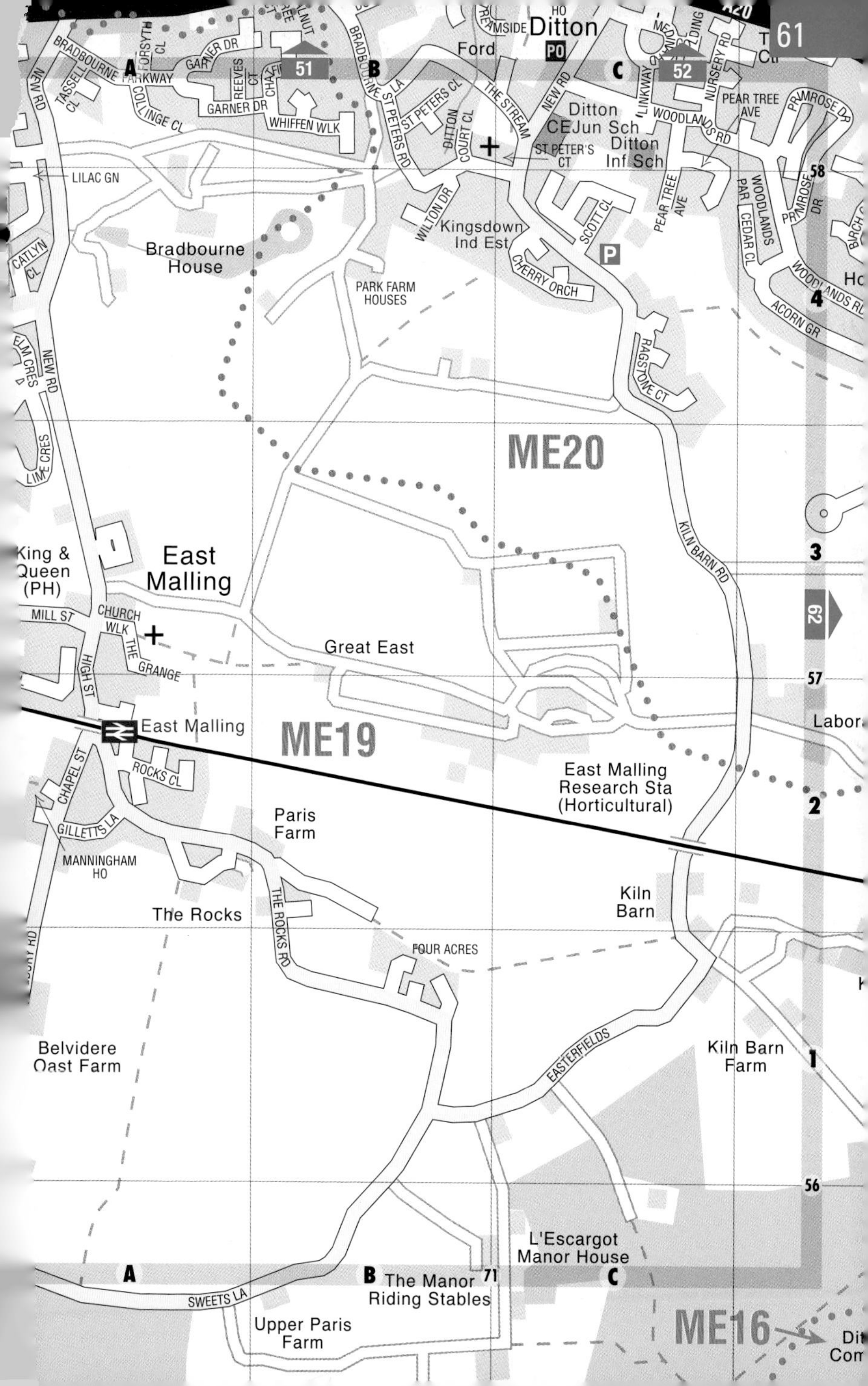

Ditton
Ford
PO
A
51
B
C
52
BRADBOURNE PARKWAY
NEW RD
TASSELL CL
FORSYTH CL
GARNER DR
REEVES CT
COLLINGE CL
WHIFFEN WLK
BRADBOURNE LA
ST PETERS RD
ST PETERS CL
DITTON COURT CL
THE STREAM
NEW RD
Ditton CE Jun Sch
Ditton Inf Sch
ST PETER'S CT
LINKWAY
NURSERY RD
PEAR TREE AVE
WOODLANDS RD
PRIMROSE DR
58
LILAC GN
Bradbourne House
WILTON DR
Kingsdown Ind Est
SCOTT CL
P
CHERRY ORCH
WOODLANDS PAR
CEDAR CL
ACORN GR
WOODLANDS RD
BIRCH
4
PARK FARM HOUSES
CATLYN CL
ELM CRES
NEW RD
RAGSTONE CT
ME20
LIME CRES
KILN BARN RD
3
King & Queen (PH)
East Malling
62
MILL ST
CHURCH WLK
THE GRANGE
HIGH ST
Great East
57
East Malling
ME19
CHAPEL ST
ROCKS CL
East Malling Research Sta (Horticultural)
2
Paris Farm
GILLETTS LA
MANNINGHAM HO
Kiln Barn
The Rocks
THE ROCKS RD
FOUR ACRES
Belvidere Oast Farm
EASTERFIELDS
Kiln Barn Farm
1
56
L'Escargot Manor House
A
B
71
C
The Manor Riding Stables
SWEETS LA
Upper Paris Farm
ME16

LONDON RD A20
Prim Sch
TA Ctr
NURSERY RD
LINKWAY
ELM WLK
AVENUE
THE OAKS
FIRS CL
HALL RD
A
52
B
C
53
ORCHARD AVE
THE BOUNDS
SYCAMORE DR
CLARK MEWS
BENTLEY CL
Preston Hall
H
PEAR TREE AVE
PRIMROSE DR
WOODLANDS RD
WOODLANDS PAR
CEDAR CL
BIRCH CRES
HOLT WOOD AVE
RUSSETT CL
South Aylesford Ret Pk
MCKENZIE CL
HOWICK CL
1 WILLIAM BAKER HO
2 CLIVE HO
Royal British Legion Village
LONDON RD E
LONDON RD
58
Holt Hill
BRASSEY DR
ACORN GR
GORSE CRES
FFINCH CL
LAKE RD
Quarry Wood Ind Est
BURNTASH RD
WOOD CL
Superstore
B2246
Euroway
4
RAGSTONE CT
WEALDEN WAY
Britannia Bsns Pk
MILLS RD
ME20
3
KILN BARN RD
61
HERMITAGE LA
57
Laboratories
East Malling Research Sta (Horticultural)
Barming
2
Kiln Barn
Broke Wood
Knoxes Shaw Farm
1
Kiln Barn Farm
ME19
HERMITAGE CT
ME16
Hermitage Farm
56
A
72
B
70
C
Fullingpits Wood
Ditton Common

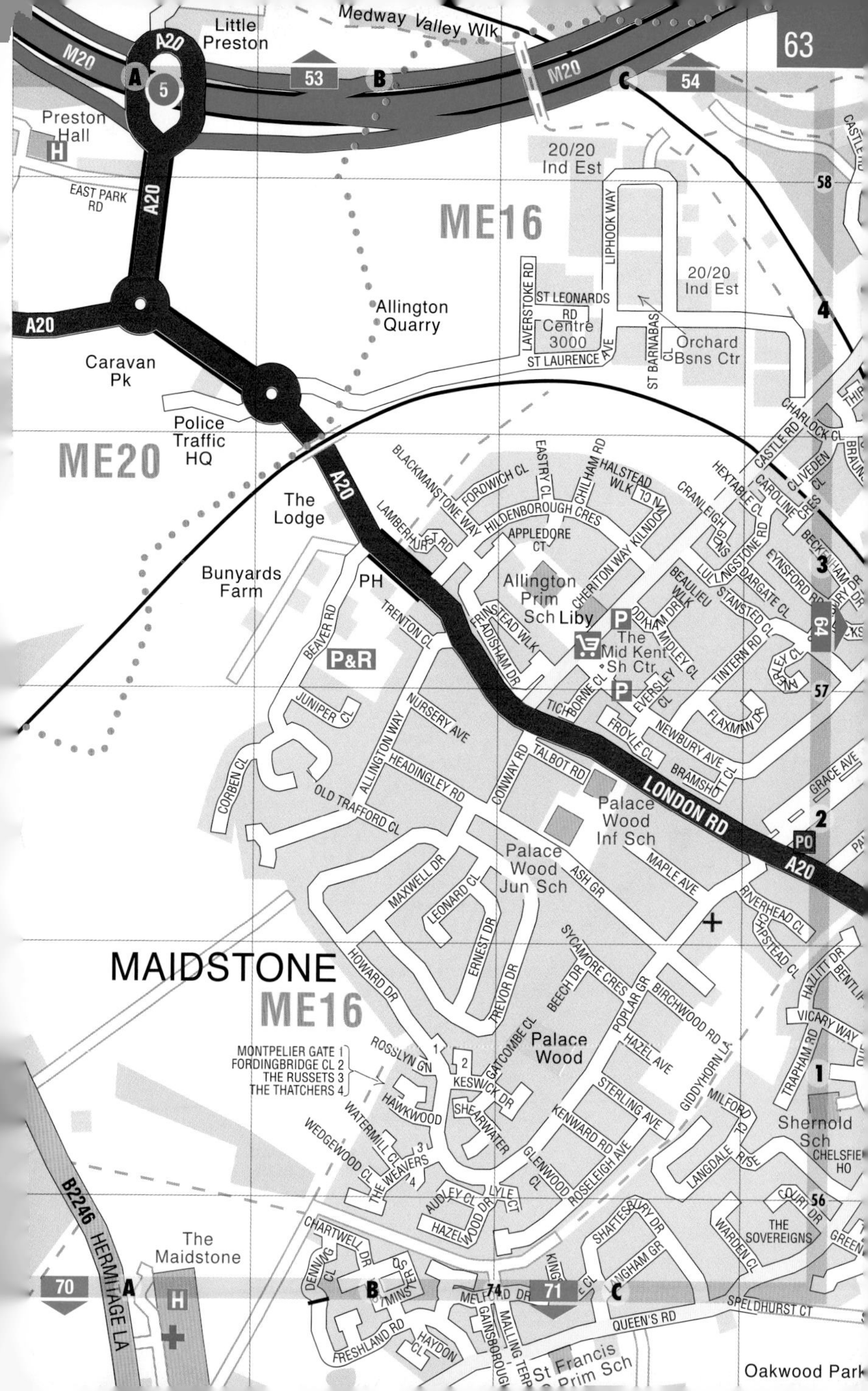
Medway Valley Wlk
Little Preston
M20
A20
53
54
Preston Hall
EAST PARK RD
ME16
20/20 Ind Est
LIPHOOK WAY
LAVERSTOKE RD
ST LEONARDS RD
Centre 3000
ST LAURENCE AVE
ST BARNABAS CL
Orchard Bsns Ctr
Allington Quarry
Caravan Pk
Police Traffic HQ
ME20
The Lodge
Bunyards Farm
PH
P&R
BEAVER RD
JUNIPER CL
CORBEN CL
TRENTON CL
NURSERY AVE
ALLINGTON WAY
HEADINGLEY RD
OLD TRAFFORD CL
BLACKMANSTONE WAY
FORDWICH CL
EASTRY CL
CHILHAM RD
HALSTEAD WLK
HILDENBOROUGH CRES
APPLEDORE CT
Allington Prim Sch
Liby
The Mid Kent Sh Ctr
CHERITON WAY
KILNDOWN CL
CRANLEIGH GDNS
HEXTABLE CL
CASTLE RD
CHARLOCK CL
CLIVEDEN CL
CAROLINE CRES
LULLINGSTONE RD
DARGATE CL
STANSTED CL
BEAULIEU WLK
MIDLEY CL
TINTERN RD
FLAXMAN DR
EVERSLEY CL
FROYLE CL
NEWBURY AVE
BRAMSHOTT CL
TICHBORNE CL
TALBOT RD
CONWAY RD
LONDON RD
A20
Palace Wood Inf Sch
Palace Wood Jun Sch
ASH GR
MAPLE AVE
GRACE AVE
PO
RIVERHEAD CL
CHIPSTEAD CL
MAXWELL DR
LEONARD CL
ERNEST DR
TREVOR DR
HOWARD DR
MAIDSTONE
ME16
SYCAMORE CRES
BEECH DR
POPLAR GR
BIRCHWOOD RD
HAZEL AVE
Palace Wood
GATCOMBE CL
ROSSLYN GN
MONTPELIER GATE 1
FORDINGBRIDGE CL 2
THE RUSSETS 3
THE THATCHERS 4
KESWICK DR
SHEARWATER
HAWKWOOD
WATERMILL CL
WEDGEWOOD CL
THE WEAVERS
AUDLEY CL
LYLE CT
HAZELWOOD DR
GLENWOOD CL
KENWARD RD
ROSELEIGH AVE
STERLING AVE
GIDDYHORN LA
MILFORD CL
LANGDALE RISE
VICARY WAY
TRAPHAM RD
HAZLITT DR
Shernold Sch
CHELSFIELD HO
THE SOVEREIGNS
WARDEN CL
SHAFTESBURY DR
LANGHAM GR
CHARTWELL DR
DENNING CL
MINSTER RD
B2246 HERMITAGE LA
The Maidstone
70
71
74
MELFORD DR
GAINSBOROUGH
MALLING TERR
QUEEN'S RD
SPELDHURST CT
FRESHLAND RD
HAYDON CL
St Francis Prim Sch
Oakwood Park
58
57
56
64

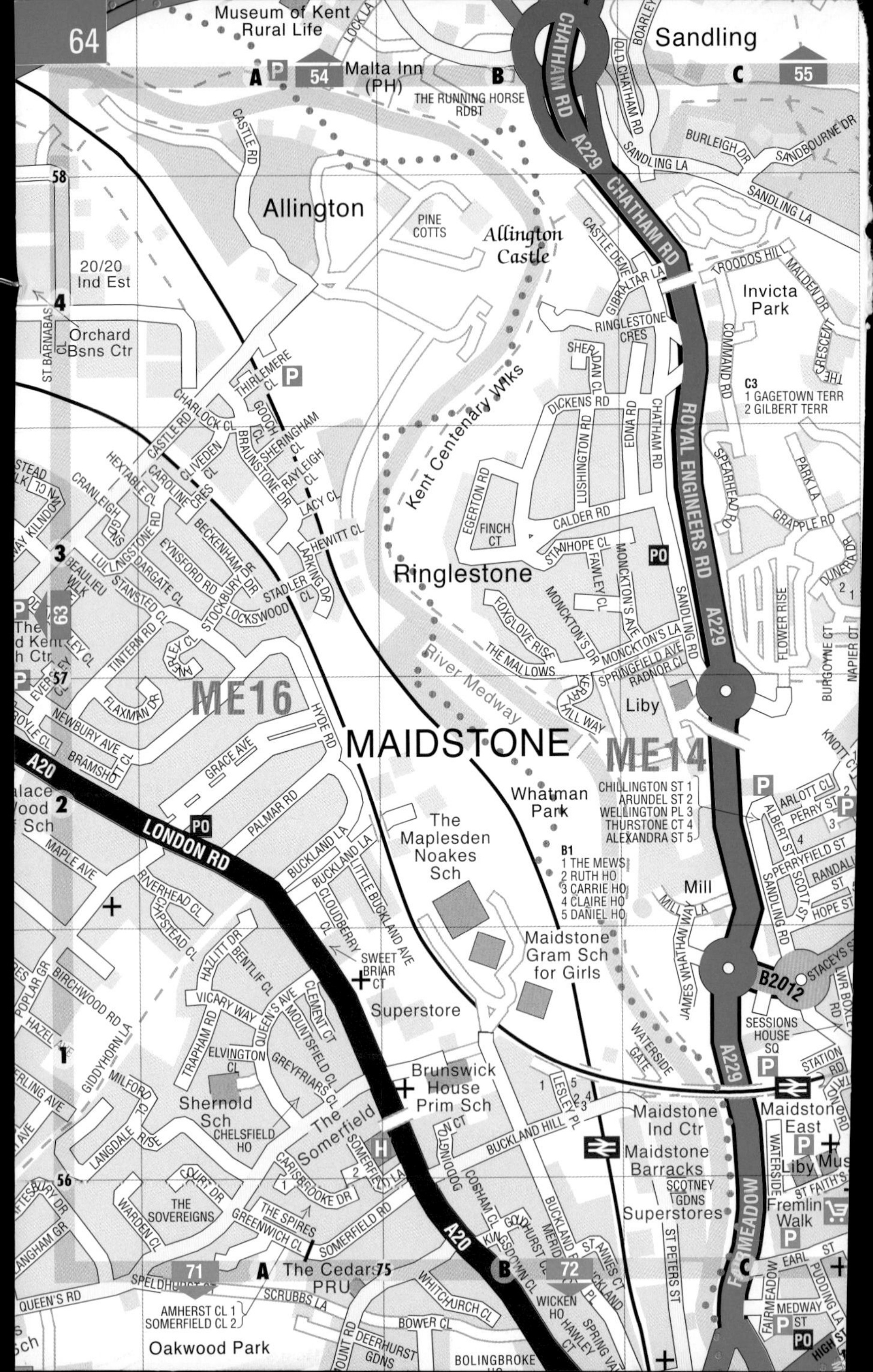

Museum of Kent
Rural Life
Malta Inn
(PH)
THE RUNNING HORSE
RDBT
Sandling
54
55
Allington
Allington
Castle
PINE
COTTS
20/20
Ind Est
Orchard
Bsns Ctr
Kent Centenary Wlks
Invicta
Park
C3
1 GAGETOWN TERR
2 GILBERT TERR
Ringlestone
River Medway
ME16
MAIDSTONE
ME14
Liby
CHILLINGTON ST 1
ARUNDEL ST 2
WELLINGTON PL 3
THURSTONE CT 4
ALEXANDRA ST 5
Whatman
Park
B1
1 THE MEWS
2 RUTH HO
3 CARRIE HO
4 CLAIRE HO
5 DANIEL HO
The
Maplesden
Noakes
Sch
Mill
Maidstone
Gram Sch
for Girls
Superstore
SWEET
BRIAR
CT
Brunswick
House
Prim Sch
Shernold
Sch
The
Somerfield
Maidstone
Ind Ctr
Maidstone
Barracks
Superstores
Maidstone
East
Liby Mus
Fremlin
Walk
SESSIONS
HOUSE
SQ
THE
SOVEREIGNS
The Cedars
PRU
AMHERST CL 1
SOMERFIELD CL 2
Oakwood Park
A20
LONDON RD
A229
CHATHAM RD
ROYAL ENGINEERS RD
B2012
63
71
72
75

Cookes Cottage
GRANGE LA
M20
A
55
B
C
56
BOXLEY RD
Harbourlands Farm
Harbourland
HARBOURLAND CL
SANDY LA
A1
1 MANDEVILLE CT
2 CRUNDALE
3 WALMER CT
4 PRIORY GATE
5 STARNES CT
6 KILBURN HO
7 LADBROOKE HO
8 LAMBARD HO
9 WINCHESTER PL
10 LOWER BOXLEY RD
58
Kiln Wood
4
A3
1 ADEN TERR
2 BARBADOS TERR
3 CANADA TERR
4 NORWAY TERR
5 MALTA TERR
6 LIBYA TERR
7 KENYA TERR
8 HONDURAS TERR
BROOKBANK
WOODCUT
BARNHURST RD
DOWNS CL
DOWNS VIEW RD
ASHBURNHAM RD
Sandling Prim Sch
RAYMER RD
CLEWSON RISE
STOCKTON CL
NEVILLE CL
BOXLEY CL
DOWNS RD
GOODWIN DR
STAPLERS CT
Viewpoint
ERITH CL
BECKSBOURNE CL
NEW BARNS RD
MALDEN DR
SANDLING LA
THE HEDGES
Sports Gd
GRAPPLE RD
ARCHIBALD HO
DHEKELIA CL
FIJI TERR
JAMAICA TERR
DUNERA DR
Jun Sch
WOODLANDS CL
WOODLAND WAY
ROBINS CT
SANDLING CT
PO
PENENDEN CT
WORDSWORTH RD
BYRON RD
NORTH WAY
BANNISTER RD
HILLARY RD
FARADAY RD
SANDY LA
Heath Wood
PENENDEN HEATH RD
HEATH FIELD AVE
SHAW CL
SITTINGBOURNE RD
3
Hotel
99
BEARSTED RD
57
HEATHFIELD CL
Penenden Heath
SILCHESTER CT
HEATHFIELD RD
NORTHDOWN CL
REDCLIFFE LA
BOXLEY RD
ST FRANCIS CL
CHATTENDEN CT
HOLLY GDNS
SAXONS DR
ROMAN HTS
WHATMAN CL
NORMAN CL
A249
LITTLEBOURNE RD
GARRINGTON CL
WEYHILL CL
EMSWORTH GR
NETLEY CL
Low Fullin Wo
2
1 ALDON CT
2 CHALLOCK
3 NEWINGTO
4 PLAISTOW
St Pauls Inf Sch
ROCK RD
TA Ctr
FINTONAGH DR
PINE GR
TUDOR AVE
BONNINGTON RD
FARNINGHAM CL
GLADSTONE RD
GRANVILLE RD
GRANVILLE CT
KNOWLE RD
A2
1 TELFORD HO
2 WALSHAW HO
3 WALSINGHAM HO
PARK HO
PARK AVE
ME14
STUART CL
CALEHILL CL
CRAYFORD CL
BLEAN SQ
COOLING CL
NEWENDEN CL
LUDDENHAM CL
TWYFORD CT
THE MEDLARS
BASMERE CL
ALDON CL
CUDHAM CL
HAMPTON RD
BEDGEBURY CL
KEWLANDS
LAKER HO
PEEL ST
JOHN ST
THORNHILL PL
CROSS ST
PENENDEN ST
HARDY ST
PO
SALISBURY RD
CURZON RD
HATHERALL RD
SITTINGBOURNE RD
RECREATION CL
WINDSOR CL
MATFIELD CRES
GUSTON RD
COWDEN RD
NORTHFLEET CL
BARGROVE RD
GRECIAN ST
WATERLOW RD
ST LUKES CT
QUARRY SQ
BLUETT ST
JAMES ST
CLIFTON CL
CHURCHLANDS
ST LUKE'S RD
SPORTSFIELD
BLENDON RD
ASHURST RD
SPINDLE GLADE
ELIZABETH HO
HM Prison
WELL RD
WHEELER ST
FOLEY ST
PO
HEATHORN ST
ALBANY ST
ST LUKE'S AVE
BARDEN CT
BREDGAR CL
MARSTON DR
EASTWELL CL
HADLOW RD
ARDENLEE DR
CEDAR CT
MULBERRY CT
Vinters Park
1
HEDLEY ST
ALLEN ST
PRINCES ST
CLAREMONT RD
COMMODORE RD
ALKHAM RD
HOLMOAKS
COUNTY RD
WOOLLETT ST
CAMDEN ST
LUCERNE ST
HOLLAND RD
B2012
BRACKLEY CL
MILSTEAD CL
LANGTON CL
LOMBARDY DR
JEFFREY ST
BREWER ST
KINGS WLK
Sch
CONSORT CL
SNOWDON PAR
SNOWDON AVE
BIRCHINGTON CL
OLD SCHOOL PL
CROMWELL RD
UNION ST
HANOVER CT
56
VINTERS RD
WYATT ST
TUFTON ST
ASTLEY ST
QUEEN ANNE RD
ALBION PL
GOLDTHORNE CL
MOSTYN RD
HUNTSMAN LA
LENFIELD AVE
Invicta
Playing Field
CHURCH ST
MARSHAM ST
WYKE
72
PO
73
ANDREW BROUGHTON WAY
KING ST
SQUARE HILL
SUNNINGDALE CT
Valley Park Com Sch
Chequers Ctr
GABRIEL'S HILL

Harpole
Yewtree Shaw
HARPLE LA
A 56 B C 57
A249
58
ME14
Park Wood
4 Kiln Wood
SITTINGBOURNE RD
A249
M20
7
Heath Wood
Horish Wood
HEATH FIELD AVE
3
SHAW CL
SITTINGBOURNE RD
P&R
65
Hotel
BEARSTED RD
A249
Newnham Court Farm
Works
PH
57
Lower Fullingpits Wood
Crem
Gidd's Pond Farm
GIDD'S POND COTTS
BEARSTED RD
Pope's Wood
POPES WOOD
GARRINGTON CL
WEYHILL CL
EMSWORTH GR
NETLEY CL
FARNINGHAM CL
NEWENDEN CL
2
LUDDENHAM CL
TWYFORD CT
THE MEDLARS
KEWLANDS
HAMPTON RD
BEDGEBURY CL
CUDHAM CL
HOCKERS LA
HEN COPPICE VIEW
LEY FIELDS
GATE DR
SHEPHERDS
HORSESHOE CL
EXTON GDNS
Television Studios
BRIARFIELDS
AVONDALE CT
HARROW WAY
SADDLERS CL
Weavering Street
WARE ST
ME14
NORTHFLEET CL
BARGROVE RD
THE MALTINGS
HAYRICK CL
THE HEDGEROW
GREENWAYS
WENTS WOOD
BARON CL
SHILLINGHELD CL
FULBERT
RAMPION CL
BILBERRY CL
SPINDLE GLADE
Vinters Park
LODGE RD
GRANARY CL
ORACHE DR
HENBANE CL
PO
GROVE GREEN RD
WYTHERLING CL
FITZWILLIAM RD
1
HOLMOAKS
ALKHAM RD
NEW CUT RD
THRESHERS DR
GENTIAN CL
Superstore
Grove Green
GROVEWOOD DR
HIGHRIDGE CL
MAXTON CL
BETONY GDNS
HAREBELL CL
FARRIER CL
SPEEDWELL CL
PENHURST CL
CAMOMILE
AVRANCHES RD
YARROW
LOMBARDY DR
MAIDSTONE
PROVENDER WAY
WINGROVE DR
GROVE GREEN LA
COLTSFOOT DR
56
COULTERS CL
CLARENCE CT
WEAVERING ST
TEASEL CL
St John's Sch
BARROW RD
HAYWAIN CL
HARVESTERS WAY
CROWNFIELDS
Playing Field
73 A 78 SHEARERS CL B 74 C
VINTNERS WAY
THISTLEDOWN
Valley Park Com Sch
WHEATFIELDS
BARLEY FIELDS
WAGONERS CL
SAMPHIRE CL
FALLOWFIELD
MEADOWDOWN
BARNCROFT CL
CORNFLOWER CL

Court
PH
Detling
CE Prim Sch
A
THE STREET
PO
QUEENS WAY
PRINCES WAY
57
B
PILGRIMS WAY
C
ST MARTIN'S CL
HOCKERS LA
Detling
Works
ORCHARD VIEW
ME14
HOCKERS CL
HOCKERS LA
58
CASTLE H
Black Horse (PH)
4
Thurnham Court
Thurnha
M20
Court Farm
3
THURNHAM LA
Gorewood Farm
Honeyhills Wood
57
Gore Wood
2
M25 Ashford, Folkestone, Channel Tunnel
Clayswood
Birling House
Chapel Lane Farm
ME14
1 PORT CL
2 AVERENCHES RD
3 CREVE COEUR CL
4 MAMIGNOT CL
CHAPEL LA
Ware Street
FANCY ROW
1
CH
LONGFIELDS DR
WARE ST
SHARSTED WAY
Bearsted
MOUNT PLEASANT DR
SANDY LA
SANDY MOUNT
Liby
Bearsted Green Bsns Ctr
BELL LA
HILL BROW
HOG HILL
PO
COLEGATE DR
56
PH
MYNN CRES
FULLERS CL
THE SPRIG
MONCRIF CL
WINDMILL HTS
FREMLINS RD
MALLINGS LA
MALLINGS DR
The Green
THE STREET
BIRLING AVE
74
A
THE ALMONDS
PIMPERNEL CL
B
BLAKENEY CL
80
75
C
Roseacre Jun Sch
ROSEACRE LA
Bearsted
THE ORCHARD
CHURCH LA
TRAPFIELD CL
THE LANDWAY
SPURWAY
Thurnham

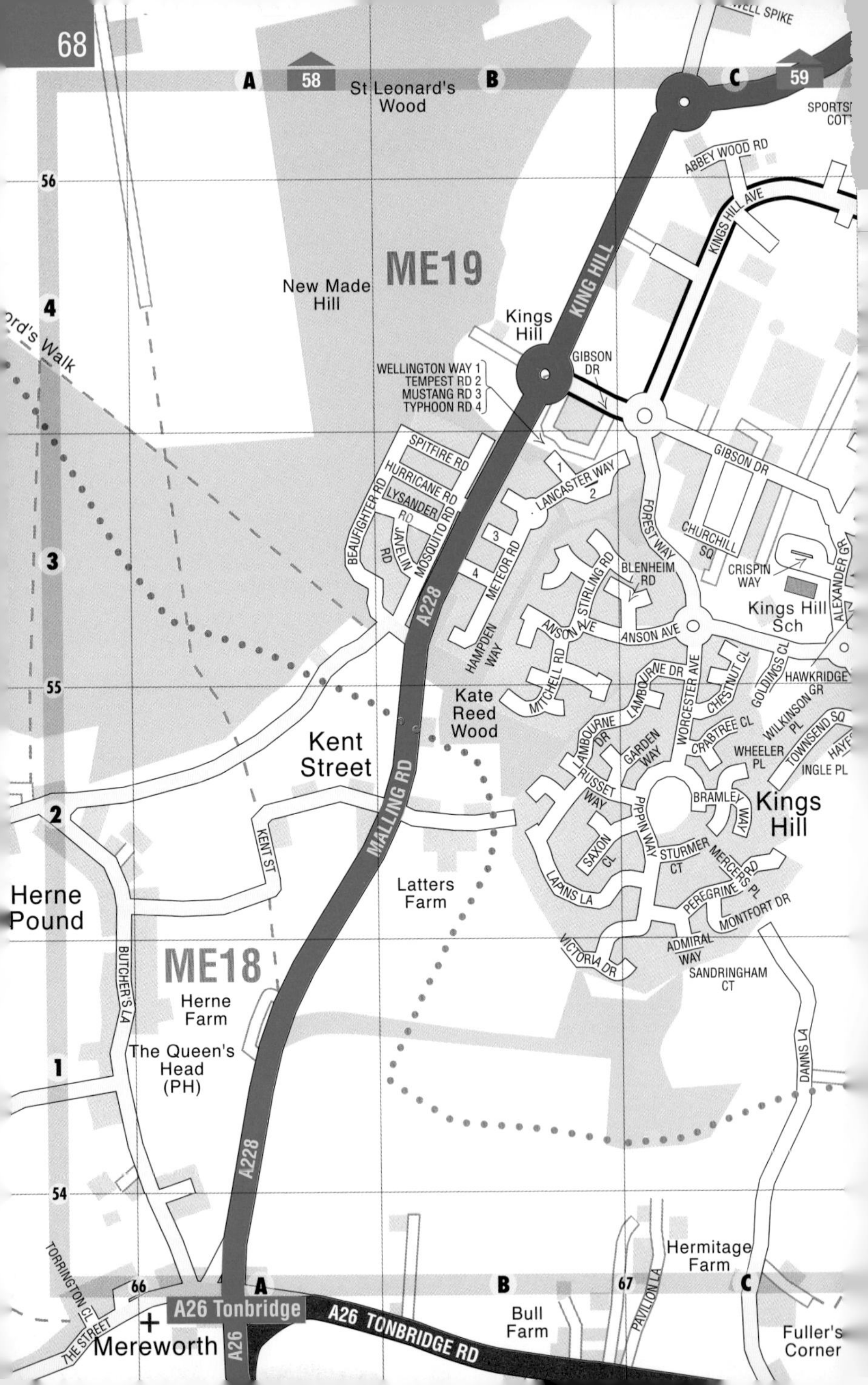
58
59
A
B
C
St Leonard's Wood
SPORTS COTT
ABBEY WOOD RD
KINGS HILL AVE
ME19
New Made Hill
KING HILL
Kings Hill
GIBSON DR
WELLINGTON WAY 1
TEMPEST RD 2
MUSTANG RD 3
TYPHOON RD 4
SPITFIRE RD
HURRICANE RD
LYSANDER RD
BEAUFIGHTER RD
JAVELIN RD
MOSQUITO RD
LANCASTER WAY
METEOR RD
HAMPDEN WAY
FOREST WAY
CHURCHILL SQ
CRISPIN WAY
ALEXANDER GR
Kings Hill Sch
STIRLING RD
BLENHEIM RD
ANSON AVE
MITCHELL RD
A228
Kate Reed Wood
Kent Street
LAMBOURNE DR
WORCESTER AVE
CHESTNUT CL
GOLDINGS CL
HAWKRIDGE GR
WILKINSON PL
TOWNSEND SQ
WHEELER PL
INGLE PL
CRABTREE CL
GARDEN WAY
RUSSET WAY
BRAMLEY WAY
PIPPIN WAY
SAXON CL
STURMER CT
MERCERS PL
PEREGRINE RD
MONTFORT DR
LAPINS LA
VICTORIA DR
ADMIRAL WAY
SANDRINGHAM CT
MALLING RD
KENT ST
Latters Farm
Herne Pound
ME18
BUTCHER'S LA
Herne Farm
The Queen's Head (PH)
DANNS LA
56
55
54
4
3
2
1
66
67
TORRINGTON CL
THE STREET
Mereworth
A26 Tonbridge
A26
A26 TONBRIDGE RD
Bull Farm
PAVILION LA
Hermitage Farm
Fuller's Corner

A
59
B
C
60
ME19
Hoath Wood
LAVENDERS RD
56
4
TOWER VIEW
Superstore
HAZEN RD
WOODFORD GR
CARDINAL WLK
GREENSLEEVES WAY
BAXTER WAY
KENDALL AVE
MAYPOLE DR
REGENT WAY
COBHAM DR
PEARL WAY
The Discovery Sch
3
QUEEN ST
LAXTON
MILTON CT
MILTON LA
FORTUNE WAY
WINSTON AVE
MELROSE AVE
MONARCH TERR
BOVARDE AVE
DAWN LA
ALFRISTON GR
BRAEBURN WAY
ALDERWICK GR
DISCOVERY DR
ELSTER PL
RUBIN PL
CLEEVE CT
CH
BANCROFT LA
OSLIN WLK
55
TESTON R
HAWTHORNDEN CL
ROUGEMONT
REDWELL GR
1 CARLTON CL
2 NIAGARA CL
3 LINDEL CT
4 AMES WAY
5 ANSIA CL
CLEMENS PL
BEACHAMWELL DR
HOLLANDBURY PK
KETRIDGE LA
2
Cattering Wood
Hoat Woo
Canon Court
Canon Court Farm
Flite Wood
CANON LA
1
BROOMSCROFT COTTS
Broomscroft
ME18
54
A
68
B
78
C
69

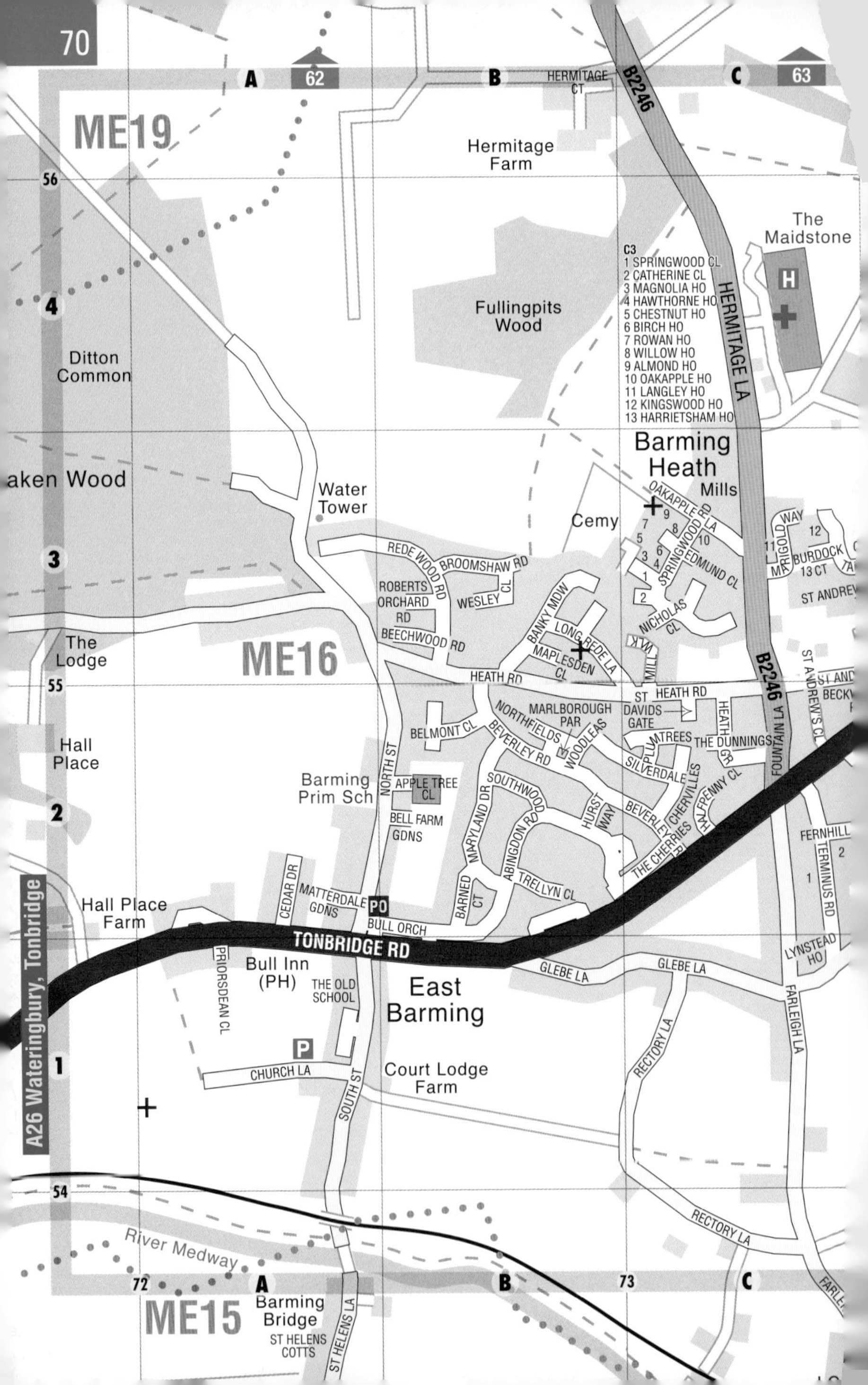
A
62
B
HERMITAGE CT
B2246
C
63
ME19
Hermitage Farm
56
The Maidstone
H
C3
1 SPRINGWOOD CL
2 CATHERINE CL
3 MAGNOLIA HO
4 HAWTHORNE HO
5 CHESTNUT HO
6 BIRCH HO
7 ROWAN HO
8 WILLOW HO
9 ALMOND HO
10 OAKAPPLE HO
11 LANGLEY HO
12 KINGSWOOD HO
13 HARRIETSHAM HO
HERMITAGE LA
4
Fullingpits Wood
Ditton Common
Barming Heath
aken Wood
Water Tower
Mills
OAKAPPLE LA
Cemy
SPRINGWOOD RD
EDMUND CL
MARIGOLD WAY
BURDOCK CT
ST ANDREW
3
REDE WOOD RD
BROOMSHAW RD
ROBERTS ORCHARD RD
WESLEY CL
BANKY MDW
LONG REDE LA
NICHOLAS CL
MILL WK
The Lodge
ME16
BEECHWOOD RD
MAPLESDEN CL
B2246
ST ANDREW'S CL
55
HEATH RD
ST DAVIDS GATE
HEATH RD
MARLBOROUGH PAR
HEATH GR
BECK
Hall Place
BELMONT CL
NORTHFIELDS
WOODLEAS
PLUMTREES
THE DUNNINGS
FOUNTAIN LA
BEVERLEY RD
SILVERDALE
Barming Prim Sch
NORTH ST
APPLE TREE CL
SOUTHWOOD
CHERVILLES
HALFPENNY CL
2
BELL FARM GDNS
MARYLAND DR
ABINGDON RD
HURST WAY
BEVERLEY RD
THE CHERRIES
FERNHILL
TERMINUS RD
A26 Wateringbury, Tonbridge
CEDAR DR
MATTERDALE GDNS
BARNED CT
TRELLYN CL
Hall Place Farm
PO
BULL ORCH
TONBRIDGE RD
LYNSTEAD HO
PRIORSDEAN CL
Bull Inn (PH)
THE OLD SCHOOL
East Barming
GLEBE LA
GLEBE LA
RECTORY LA
FARLEIGH LA
1
P
CHURCH LA
SOUTH ST
Court Lodge Farm
54
RECTORY LA
River Medway
72
A
B
73
C
ME15
Barming Bridge
ST HELENS COTTS
ST HELENS LA

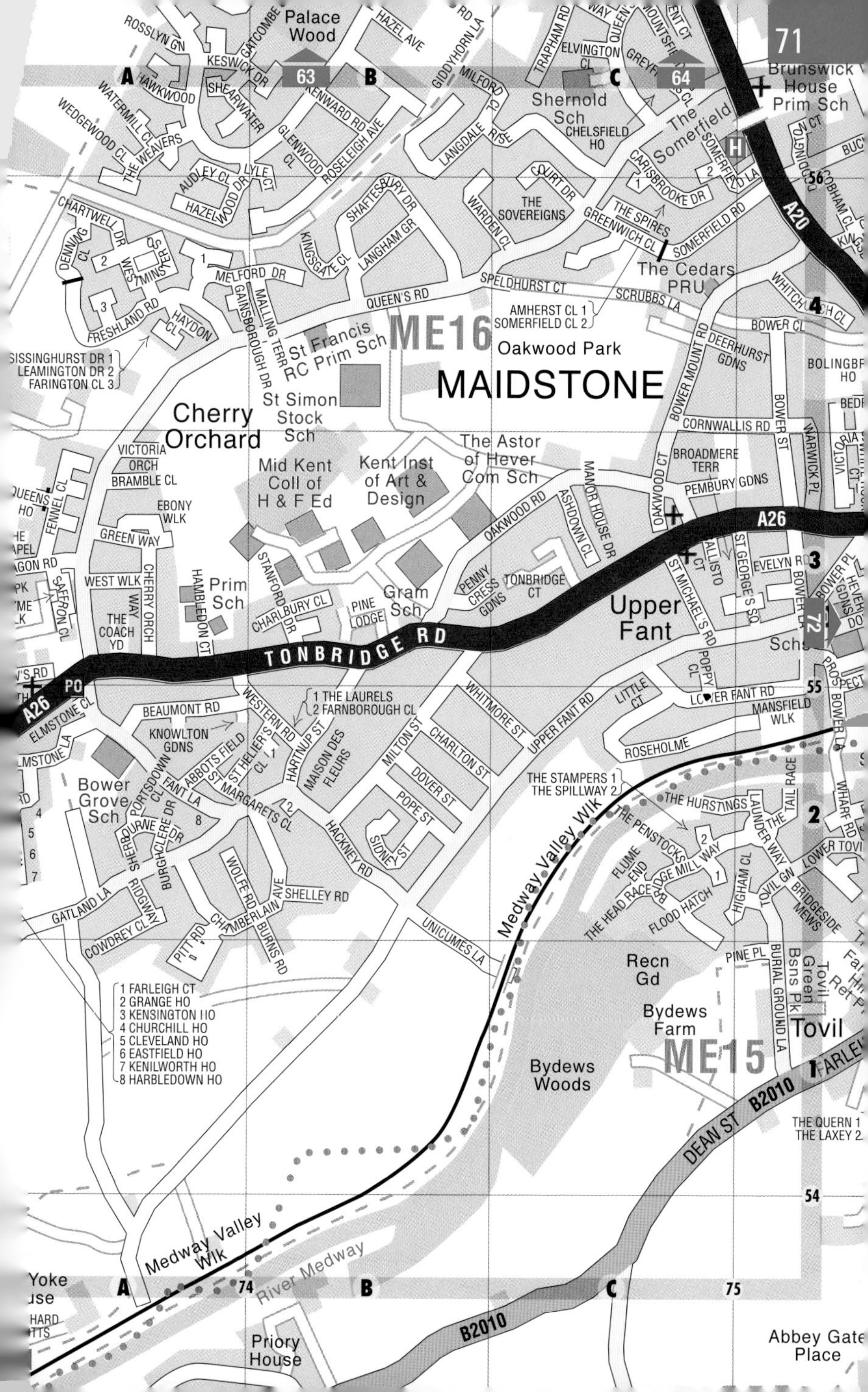

Palace Wood
63
64
A
B
C
Shernold Sch
Brunswick House Prim Sch
The Somerfield
The Sovereigns
The Cedars PRU
ME16
MAIDSTONE
Oakwood Park
St Francis RC Prim Sch
St Simon Stock Sch
Cherry Orchard
Mid Kent Coll of H & F Ed
Kent Inst of Art & Design
The Astor of Hever Com Sch
Prim Sch
Gram Sch
TONBRIDGE RD
A26
A20
Upper Fant
Bower Grove Sch
Medway Valley Wlk
Recn Gd
Bydews Farm
Bydews Woods
ME15
Tovil
Tovil Green Bsns Pk
B2010
DEAN ST
River Medway
Priory House
Abbey Gate Place
72
56
55
54
74
75
4
3
2
1
AMHERST CL 1
SOMERFIELD CL 2
SISSINGHURST DR 1
LEAMINGTON DR 2
FARINGTON CL 3
1 THE LAURELS
2 FARNBOROUGH CL
THE STAMPERS 1
THE SPILLWAY 2
1 FARLEIGH CT
2 GRANGE HO
3 KENSINGTON HO
4 CHURCHILL HO
5 CLEVELAND HO
6 EASTFIELD HO
7 KENILWORTH HO
8 HARBLEDOWN HO
THE QUERN 1
THE LAXEY 2

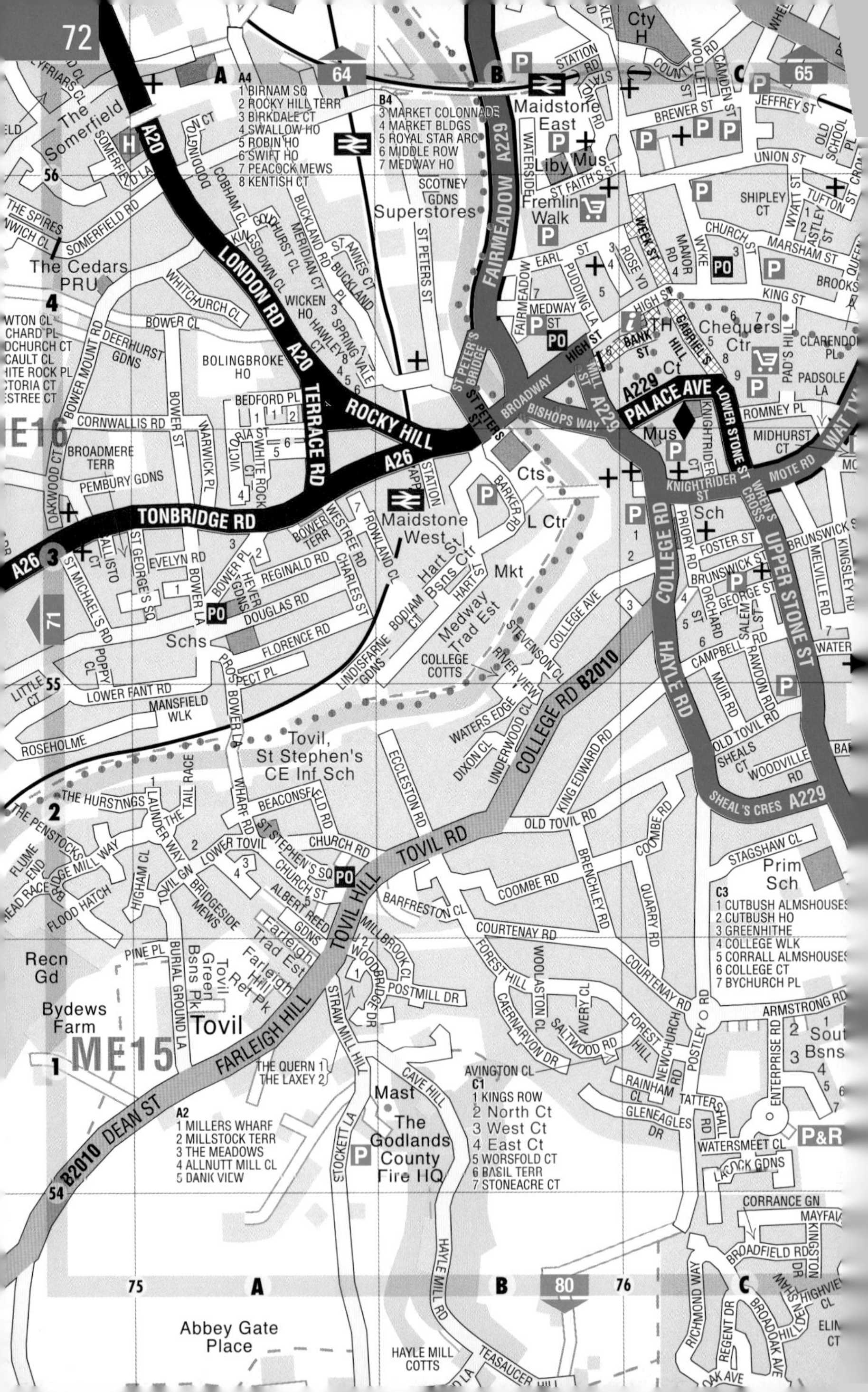

72
64
65
A
B
C
A4
1 BIRNAM SQ
2 ROCKY HILL TERR
3 BIRKDALE CT
4 SWALLOW HO
5 ROBIN HO
6 SWIFT HO
7 PEACOCK MEWS
8 KENTISH CT
B4
3 MARKET COLONNADE
4 MARKET BLDGS
5 ROYAL STAR ARC
6 MIDDLE ROW
7 MEDWAY HO
Cty H
Maidstone East
The Somerfield
A20
LONDON RD
ROCKY HILL
TERRACE RD
A26
TONBRIDGE RD
FAIRMEADOW
A229
Superstores
Fremlin Walk
Liby
Mus
The Cedars PRU
BOLINGBROKE HO
Maidstone West
Hart St Bsns Ctr
Medway Trad Est
Mkt
Cts
L Ctr
PALACE AVE
Chequers Ctr
HIGH ST
BROADWAY
BISHOPS WAY
COLLEGE RD
B2010
HAYLE RD
UPPER STONE ST
MOTE RD
ME16
71
Schs
Tovil, St Stephen's CE Inf Sch
TOVIL RD
TOVIL HILL
FARLEIGH HILL
DEAN ST
Recn Gd
Bydews Farm
Tovil
ME15
Tovil Green Bsns Pk
Farleigh Trad Est
Farleigh Hill Ret Pk
Prim Sch
C3
1 CUTBUSH ALMSHOUSES
2 CUTBUSH HO
3 GREENHITHE
4 COLLEGE WLK
5 CORRALL ALMSHOUSES
6 COLLEGE CT
7 BYCHURCH PL
A2
1 MILLERS WHARF
2 MILLSTOCK TERR
3 THE MEADOWS
4 ALLNUTT MILL CL
5 BANK VIEW
C1
1 KINGS ROW
2 North Ct
3 West Ct
4 East Ct
5 WORSFOLD CT
6 BASIL TERR
7 STONEACRE CT
Mast
The Godlands County Fire HQ
P&R
Sout Bsns
75
76
80
54
55
56
Abbey Gate Place
HAYLE MILL COTTS
HAYLE MILL RD
SHEAL'S CRES

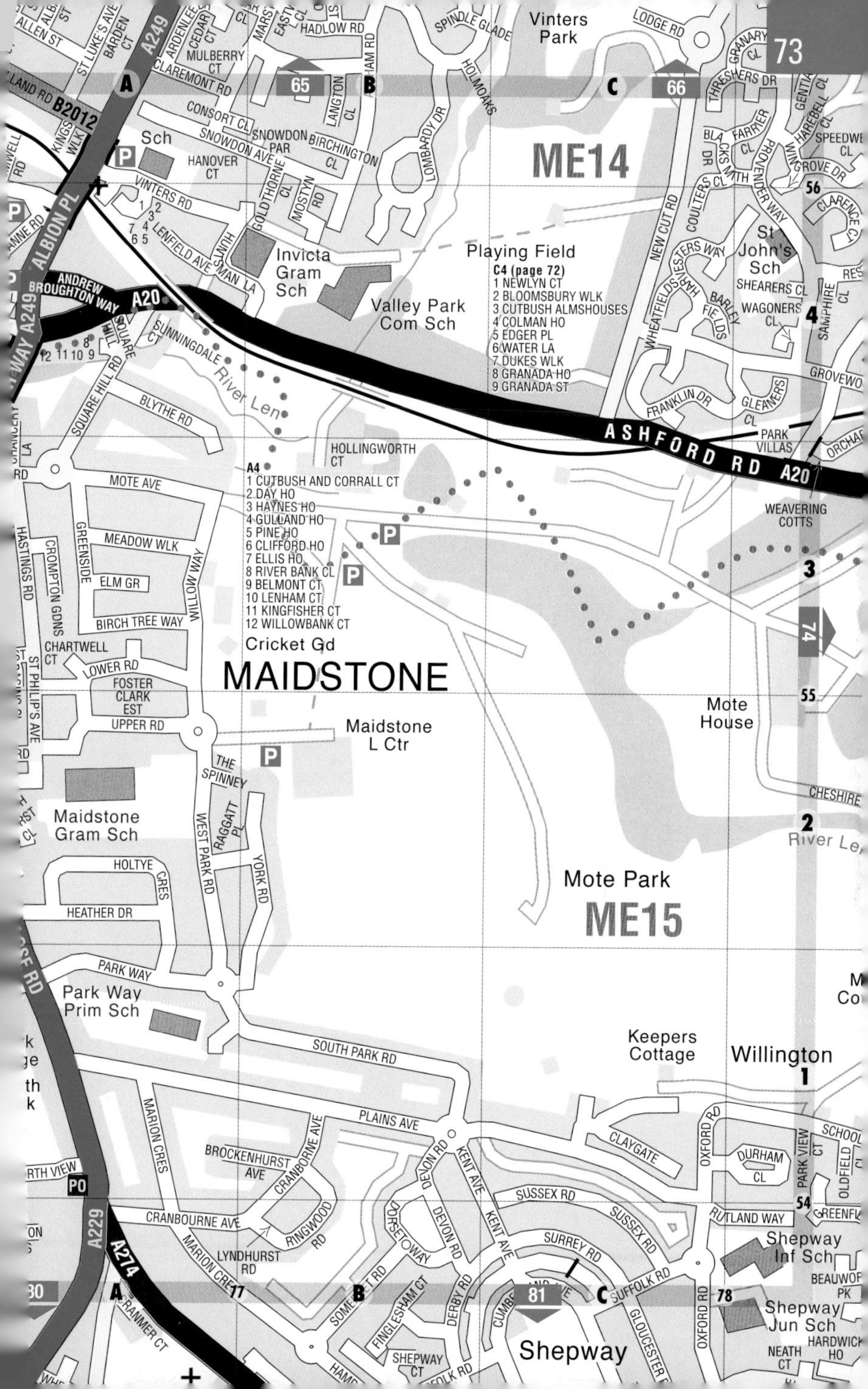

Vinters Park
ME14
Sch
Invicta Gram Sch
Valley Park Com Sch
Playing Field
C4 (page 72)
1 NEWLYN CT
2 BLOOMSBURY WLK
3 CUTBUSH ALMSHOUSES
4 COLMAN HO
5 EDGER PL
6 WATER LA
7 DUKES WLK
8 GRANADA HO
9 GRANADA ST
St John's Sch
A4
1 CUTBUSH AND CORRALL CT
2 DAY HO
3 HAYNES HO
4 GULLAND HO
5 PINE HO
6 CLIFFORD HO
7 ELLIS HO
8 RIVER BANK CL
9 BELMONT CT
10 LENHAM CT
11 KINGFISHER CT
12 WILLOWBANK CT
Cricket Gd
MAIDSTONE
Maidstone L Ctr
Maidstone Gram Sch
Mote House
Mote Park
ME15
Park Way Prim Sch
Keepers Cottage
Willington
Shepway Inf Sch
Shepway Jun Sch
Shepway
ASHFORD RD A20
A249
A20
B2012
A229
A274
ALBION PL
ANDREW BROUGHTON WAY
SQUARE HILL RD
BLYTHE RD
MOTE AVE
MEADOW WLK
ELM GR
BIRCH TREE WAY
WILLOW WAY
GREENSIDE
CROMPTON GDNS
HASTINGS RD
CHARTWELL CT
LOWER RD
FOSTER CLARK EST
UPPER RD
ST PHILIP'S AVE
THE SPINNEY
RAGGATT PL
WEST PARK RD
YORK RD
HOLTYE CRES
HEATHER DR
PARK WAY
SOUTH PARK RD
PLAINS AVE
MARION CRES
BROCKENHURST AVE
CRANBORNE AVE
CRANBOURNE AVE
RINGWOOD RD
LYNDHURST RD
DEVON RD
KENT AVE
DORSET WAY
SUSSEX RD
SURREY RD
SUFFOLK RD
GLOUCESTER RD
DERBY RD
FINGLESHAM CT
SHEPWAY CT
CLAYGATE
OXFORD RD
DURHAM CL
RUTLAND WAY
PARK VIEW CT
OLDFIELD CL
HOLLINGWORTH CT
SUNNINGDALE CT
River Len
HUNTSMAN LA
LENFIELD AVE
VINTERS RD
HANOVER CT
SNOWDON AVE
SNOWDON PAR
CONSORT CL
CLAREMONT RD
MULBERRY CT
CEDAR CT
ARDENLEE
ST LUKE'S AVE
BARDEN CT
ALLEN ST
HADLOW RD
BIRCHINGTON CL
GOLDTHORNE CL
MOSTYN RD
LANGTON CL
LOMBARDY DR
HOLMOAKS
SPINDLE GLADE
LODGE RD
NEW CUT RD
COULTERS CL
WHEATFIELDS
HARVESTERS WAY
BARLEY FIELDS
FRANKLIN DR
GLEANERS CL
PARK VILLAS
WEAVERING COTTS
BLACKSMITH DR
FARRIER CL
PROVENDER WAY
THRESHERS DR
GRANARY CL
SHEARERS CL
WAGONERS CL
SAMPHIRE CT
WINGROVE DR
CLARENCE CT
CHESHIRE
KINGS WLK
65
66
74
81

RAMPION CL
BILBERRY CL
HEDGEROW
GREENWAY
GRANARY CL
ORACHE DR
HENBANE
GENTIAN CL
THRESHERS DR
A
66
Grove Green
GROVEWOOD DR
HIGHRIDGE
GROVE GREEN RD
SHILLINGHELD CL
FULBERT DR
B
FITZWILLIAM RD
MAXTON CL
BETONY GDNS
PEVEREL DR
LONGFIELDS DR
C
67
WARE ST
MOUNT PLEASANT DR
BELL LA
HILL BROW
FARRIER CL
HAREBELL CL
SPEEDWELL CL
BLACKSMITH DR
PROVENDER WAY
GROVE DR
COULTERS CL
NEW CUT RD
56
GROVE GREEN LA
PENHURST CL
CAMOMILE DR
AVERENCHES RD
YARROW CT
PEVEREL DR
COLTSFOOT DR
MYNN CRES
FULLERS CL
THE SPRIG
HAMPSON WAY
BIRLING AVE
THE ALMONDS
CLARENCE CT
RESTHARROW RD
St John's Sch
WEAVERING ST
HAYWAIN CL
TEASEL CL
CROWNFIELDS
VINTNERS WAY
HARVESTERS WAY
SHEARERS CL
WAGONERS CL
BARLEY FIELDS
SAMPHIRE CL
MEADOWDOWN
BARNCROFT CL
THISTLEDOWN
ALDINGTON RD
Roseacre Jun Sch
FALLOWFIELD CL
NUTWOOD CL
CORNFLOWER CL
BIRLING AVE
BIRLING CL
AMES AVE
THE LANDWAY
SPURWAY
ROSEACRE
4
Thurnham CE Inf Sch
GROVEWOOD DR
FAUCHON'S LA
AVIEMORE GDNS
CLARENDON CL
FRANKLIN DR
GLEANERS CL
GROVEWOOD CT
ME14
Roseacre
PARK VILLAS
ORCHARD DR
FAUCHON'S CL
PLANTATION LA
ROSEACRE GDNS
ASHFORD RD A20
WEAVERING COTTS
LORD ROMNEY'S HILL
THE GROVE
OTTERIDGE
PO
3
BIDDENDEN CL
LAXTON CL
WINIFRED RD
ROSEMARY RD
ROMNEY CL
73
P&R
BRAMLEY CRES
ROYSTON RD
SHIRLEY WAY
BLENHEIM CL
COPSEWOOD
55
Mote House
MADGINFORD RD
MADGINFORD CL
MADGINFORD RD
GREYSTONES RD
LAMBOURNE RD
EGREMONT RD
EGREMONT RD
TYDEMAN RD
Liby
RAGSTONE RD
SPOT LA
CHESHIRE RD
YEOMAN WAY
2
Jun & Inf Schs
GREENSAND RD
River Len
Mote Park
MERTON RD
GAULT CL
LENSIDE DR
ME15
WILLINGTON ST
GRENADIER CL
WILLOW RISE 1
LEN VALLEY WLK 2
SPOT LA
COTSWOLD GDNS
MALLARDS WAY
BOURNEWOOD CL
SPOT LA
GRAMPIAN WAY
CHEVIOT GDNS
Mote Cottage
FOXDEN DR
DERINGWOOD DR
REINDEN GR
CHILTERN CL
PENNINE WAY
MAIDSTONE
PO
DERINGWOOD DR
Orchard Spo (PH)
Keepers Cottage
DERINGWOOD DR
GORHAM DR
1
LONGHAM COPSE
HORTON DOWNS
FRITHWOOD
MONKDOWN
MURRAIN DR
OTTERBOURNE PL
RHODEWOOD CL
SCHOOL LA
THE BEAMS
KINGS ACRE
CLAYGATE
OXFORD RD
DURHAM CL
PARK VIEW CT
OLDFIELD CL
CHURCH RD
1 ELLENSWOOD
2 REDSELLS CL
3 RAVENS DANE
54
RUTLAND WAY
GREENFIELDS
SUSSEX RD
Shepway Inf Sch
Willington
BEAUWORTH
SUFFOLK RD
78
81
A
B
82
79
C
Shepway Jun Sch
The Rectory
GLOUCESTER RD
OXFORD RD
NEATH CT
HARDWICK HO
CHAPMAN AVE
DENTON

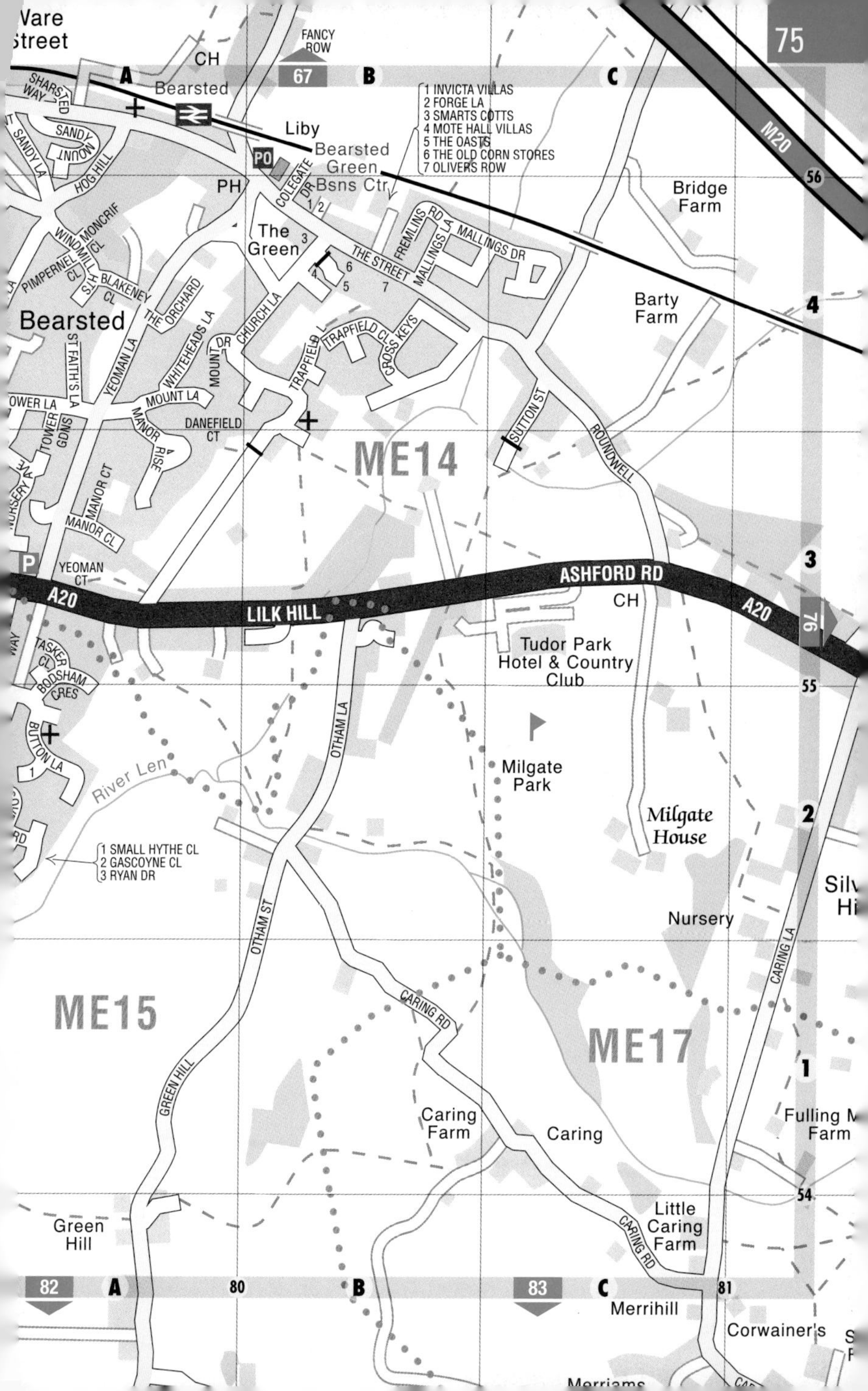
Ware Street
FANCY ROW
67
A
B
C
CH
Bearsted
SHARSTED WAY
SANDY MOUNT
SANDY LA
HOG HILL
Liby
Bearsted Green Bsns Ctr
PO
PH
COLEGATE DR
1 INVICTA VILLAS
2 FORGE LA
3 SMARTS COTTS
4 MOTE HALL VILLAS
5 THE OASTS
6 THE OLD CORN STORES
7 OLIVERS ROW
M20
56
Bridge Farm
The Green
MONCRIF CL
WINDMILL HTS
PIMPERNEL CL
BLAKENEY CL
THE ORCHARD
THE STREET
FREMLINS RD
MALLINGS LA
MALLINGS DR
Barty Farm
4
Bearsted
ST FAITH'S LA
YEOMAN LA
WHITEHEADS LA
MOUNT DR
CHURCH LA
TRAPFIELD L
TRAPFIELD CL
CROSS KEYS
TOWER LA
TOWER GDNS
MOUNT LA
MANOR RISE
DANEFIELD CT
SUTTON ST
ROUNDWELL
ME14
NURSERY AVE
MANOR CT
MANOR CL
P
YEOMAN CT
3
A20
LILK HILL
ASHFORD RD
CH
76
Tudor Park Hotel & Country Club
TASKER CL
BODSHAM CRES
55
BUTTON LA
OTHAM LA
Milgate Park
River Len
Milgate House
2
1 SMALL HYTHE CL
2 GASCOYNE CL
3 RYAN DR
OTHAM ST
Nursery
Silv Hi
CARING LA
ME15
CARING RD
ME17
1
GREEN HILL
Caring Farm
Caring
Fulling M Farm
54
Green Hill
Little Caring Farm
CARING RD
82
A
80
B
83
C
81
Merrihill
Corwainer's
Merriams

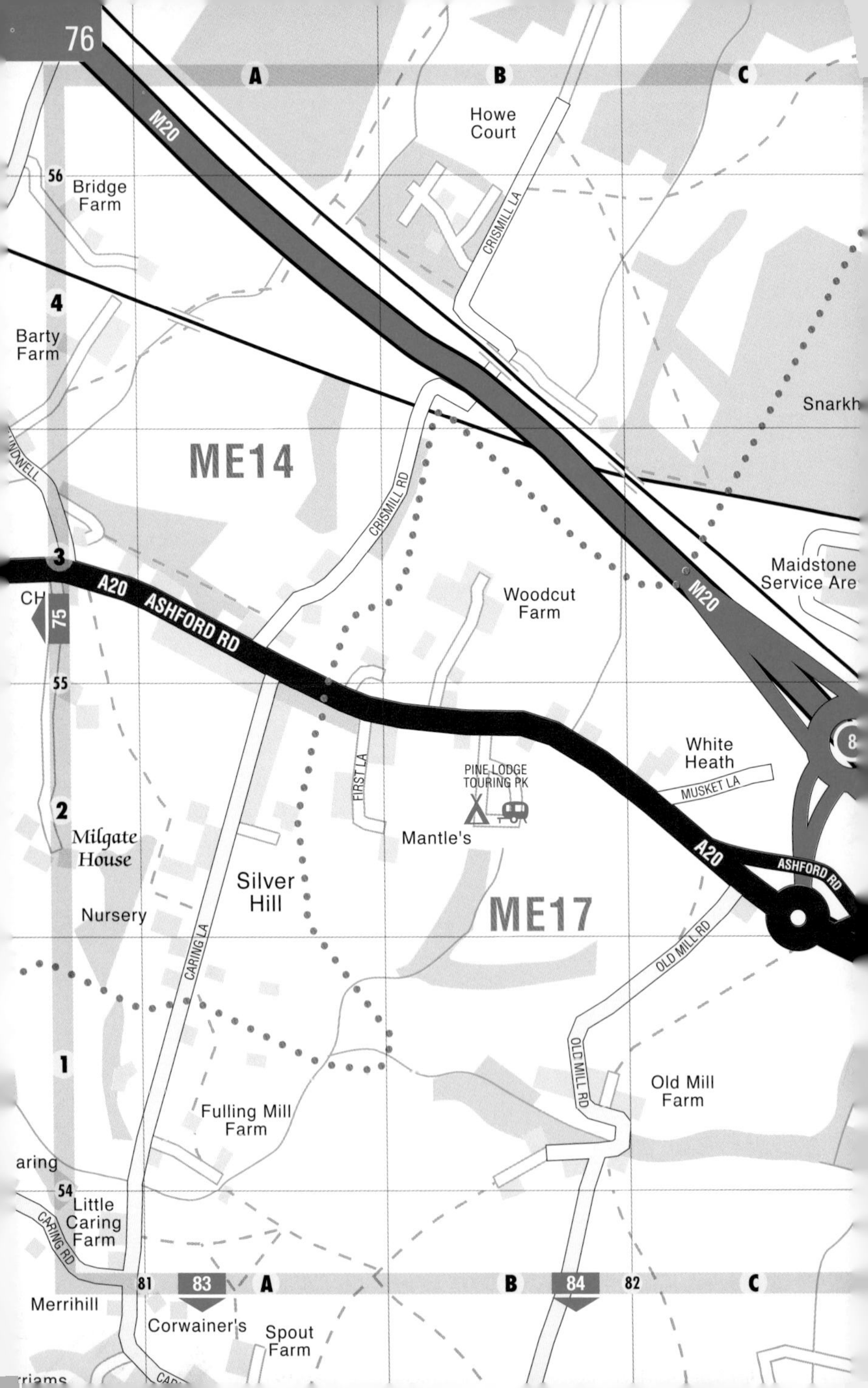
A
B
C
M20
Howe Court
56
Bridge Farm
CRISMILL LA
4
Barty Farm
Snarkh
ME14
CRISMILL RD
3
A20
ASHFORD RD
CH
75
Maidstone Service Are
Woodcut Farm
55
FIRST LA
PINE LODGE TOURING PK
White Heath
MUSKET LA
8
2
Milgate House
Mantle's
Silver Hill
ASHFORD RD
ME17
Nursery
CARING LA
OLD MILL RD
1
OLD MILL RD
Old Mill Farm
Fulling Mill Farm
aring
54
Little Caring Farm
CARING RD
81
83
84
82
Merrihill
Corwainer's
Spout Farm

A
B
C
ME17
Allington Farm
56
Little Allington
4
Newlands Wood
st Wood
Strickets Garden
3
Hollingbourne
Little Snagbrook
Hollingbourn
55
Hollingbourne Prim Sch
Eyhorne Farm
Eyhorne Street
ATHELSTAN GN
THE PAVINGS
MUSKET LA
BOURNESIDE TERR
EYHORNE ST
CLAYGATE
TILE FIELDS
HASTEDS
TROYS MEAD
CULPEPER CL
HADLEY GDNS
2
Godfrey House
PH
PO
Eyhorne Green
ASHFORD RD
ME17
1
Coom Woo
The Great Danes Hotel
PENFOLD HILL
B2163
Oakfield
er Len
A20
M20
54
P
84
A
83
B
85
C
84
HOSPITAL RD
Park Gate Inn (PH)

69
A
B
C
BROOMSCROFT COTTS
Broomscroft
ME18
54
CANON LA
4
A26 Tonbridge
TONBRIDGE RD
VINE CT
PO
RED HILL
PELICAN CT
BOORMAN MEWS
Cemy
Manor Farm
RED HOUSE GDNS
MILL LA
UPPER MILL
LODGE CL
LOVE LA
ALLINGTON GDNS
P
HANBURY CL
Hotel
FIELDS LA
OLD RD
HILLSIDE CT
COBBS CL
Wateringbury
GLEBE MDW
B2015
BOW TERR
THE BRUCKS
3
WARDEN MILL CL
LENEY RD
RIVERS CL
BOW RD
PHOENIX DR
53
SILVER BIRCH WLK
PHOENIX COTTS
Wateringbury CE Prim Sch
THE RETREAT CVN PK
ORCHARD CRES
WATERSIDE MEWS
PH
GLENLEIGH RD
HENRYS CL
Wateringbury
LC
2
Nettlestead
Rock Farm
KING'S COTTS
Bow Bridge
BRYANT CL
BISHOPS CL
ROCK FARM OASTHOUSE
SCHOOL VILLAS
GIBBS HILL
ME18
MAIDSTONE RD
BOW HILL
1
Nettlestead Court Farm
NETTLESTEAD CT
Nettlestead Place
52
B2015
68
69

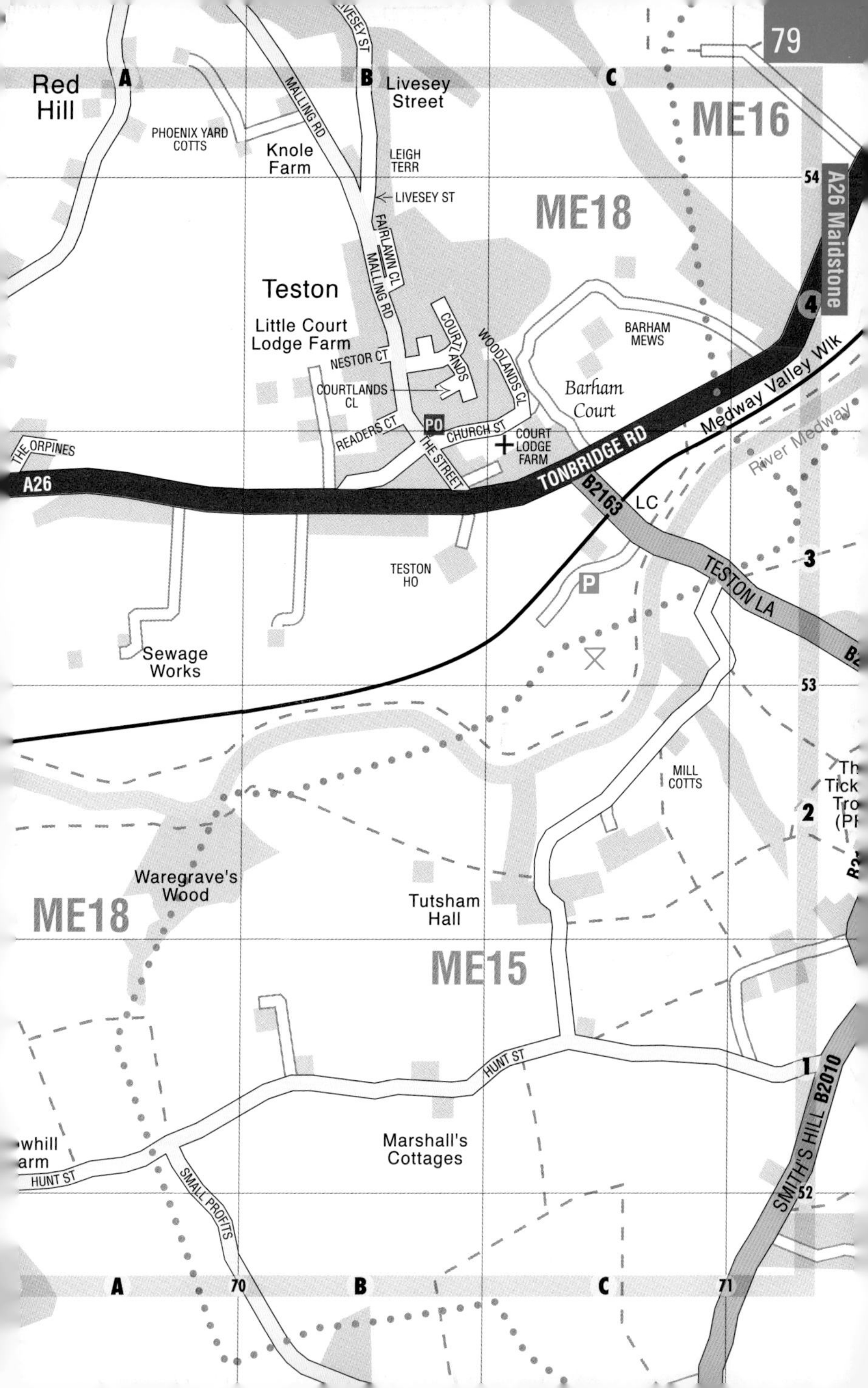
Red Hill
Livesey Street
PHOENIX YARD COTTS
Knole Farm
LEIGH TERR
LIVESEY ST
MALLING RD
FAIRLAWN CL
ME16
ME18
A26 Maidstone
Teston
Little Court Lodge Farm
NESTOR CT
COURTLANDS
COURTLANDS CL
WOODLANDS CL
BARHAM MEWS
Barham Court
READERS CT
PO
CHURCH ST
THE STREET
COURT LODGE FARM
THE ORPINES
A26
TONBRIDGE RD
Medway Valley Wlk
River Medway
B2163
LC
TESTON HO
TESTON LA
P
Sewage Works
MILL COTTS
Waregrave's Wood
ME18
Tutsham Hall
ME15
HUNT ST
Marshall's Cottages
SMALL PROFITS
SMITH'S HILL B2010
54
53
52
70
71
A
B
C
1
2
3
4

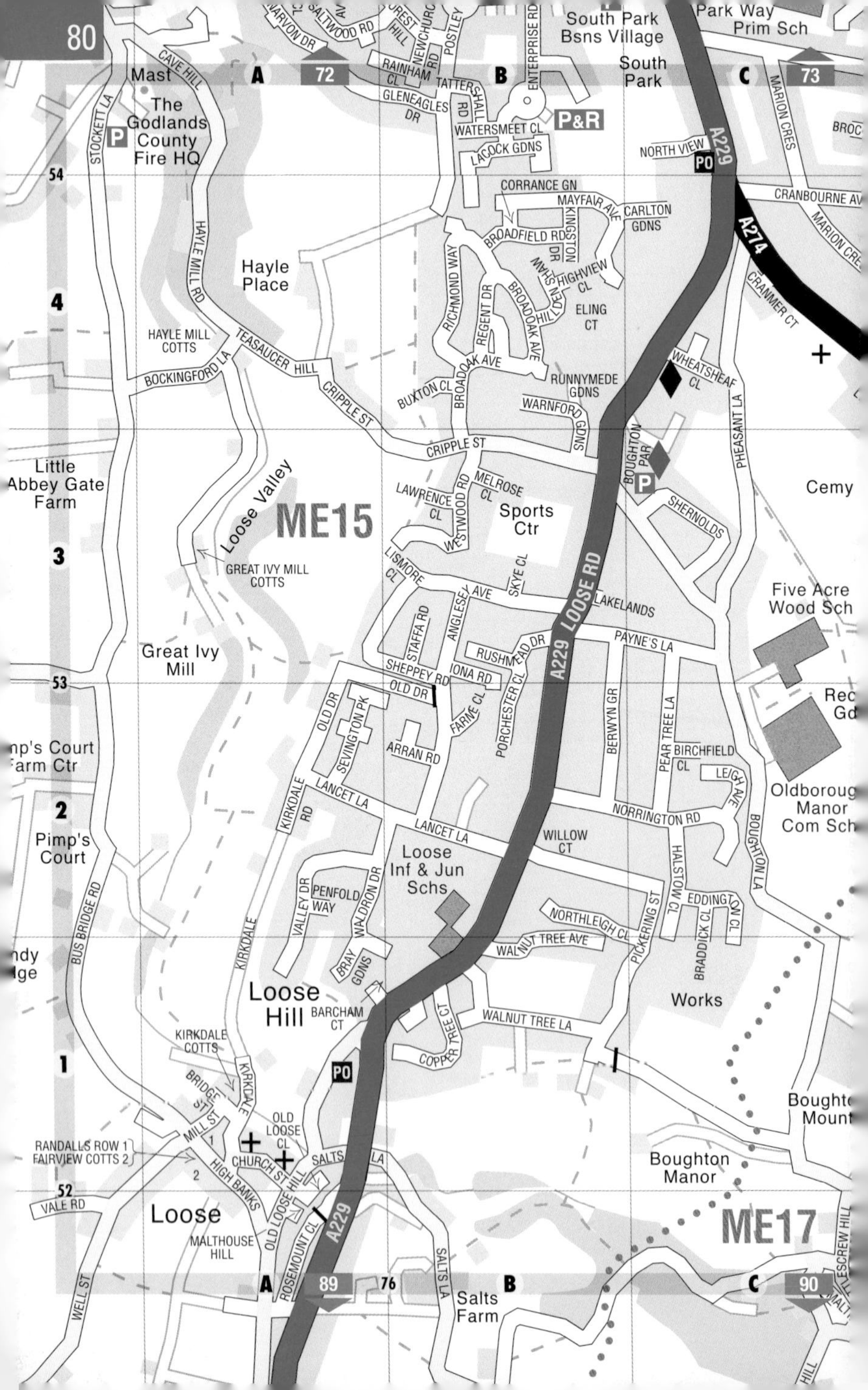
72
73
89
90
76
South Park Bsns Village
Park Way Prim Sch
South Park
Mast
The Godlands County Fire HQ
Hayle Place
HAYLE MILL COTTS
Little Abbey Gate Farm
Loose Valley
ME15
GREAT IVY MILL COTTS
Great Ivy Mill
Sports Ctr
Five Acre Wood Sch
Cemy
Oldborough Manor Com Sch
Loose Inf & Jun Schs
Pimp's Court
Loose Hill
KIRKDALE COTTS
RANDALLS ROW 1
FAIRVIEW COTTS 2
Loose
Works
Boughton Manor
ME17
Salts Farm
A229
A274
LOOSE RD
P&R
PO
CAVE HILL
STOCKETT LA
HAYLE MILL RD
TEASAUCER HILL
BOCKINGFORD LA
CRIPPLE ST
GLENEAGLES DR
WATERSMEET CL
LACOCK GDNS
ENTERPRISE RD
NORTH VIEW
CRANBOURNE AV
MARION CRES
CRANMER CT
CORRANCE GN
MAYFAIR AVE
CARLTON GDNS
BROADFIELD RD
KINGSTON DR
HIGHVIEW CL
ELING CT
RICHMOND WAY
REGENT DR
BROADOAK AVE
RUNNYMEDE GDNS
WHEATSHEAF CL
BUXTON CL
WARNFORD GDNS
BOUGHTON PAR
PHEASANT LA
SHERNOLDS
MELROSE CL
LAWRENCE CL
WESTWOOD RD
LISMORE CL
ANGLESEY AVE
SKYE CL
LAKELANDS
PAYNE'S LA
STAFFA RD
RUSHMEAD DR
SHEPPEY RD
IONA RD
OLD DR
FARNE CL
PORCHESTER CL
BERWYN GR
PEAR TREE LA
BIRCHFIELD CL
SEVINGTON PK
ARRAN RD
LEIGH AVE
LANCET LA
KIRKDALE RD
NORRINGTON RD
WILLOW CT
BOUGHTON LA
VALLEY DR
PENFOLD WAY
WALDRON DR
HALSTOW CL
EDDINGTON CL
NORTHLEIGH CL
PICKERING ST
BRADDICK CL
WALNUT TREE AVE
BRAY GDNS
BARCHAM CT
WALNUT TREE LA
COPPER TREE CT
BUS BRIDGE RD
KIRKDALE
BRIDGE ST
MILL ST
OLD LOOSE CL
CHURCH ST
SALTS LA
HIGH BANKS
OLD LOOSE HILL
VALE RD
MALTHOUSE HILL
ROSEMOUNT CL
WELL ST
LINTON HILL

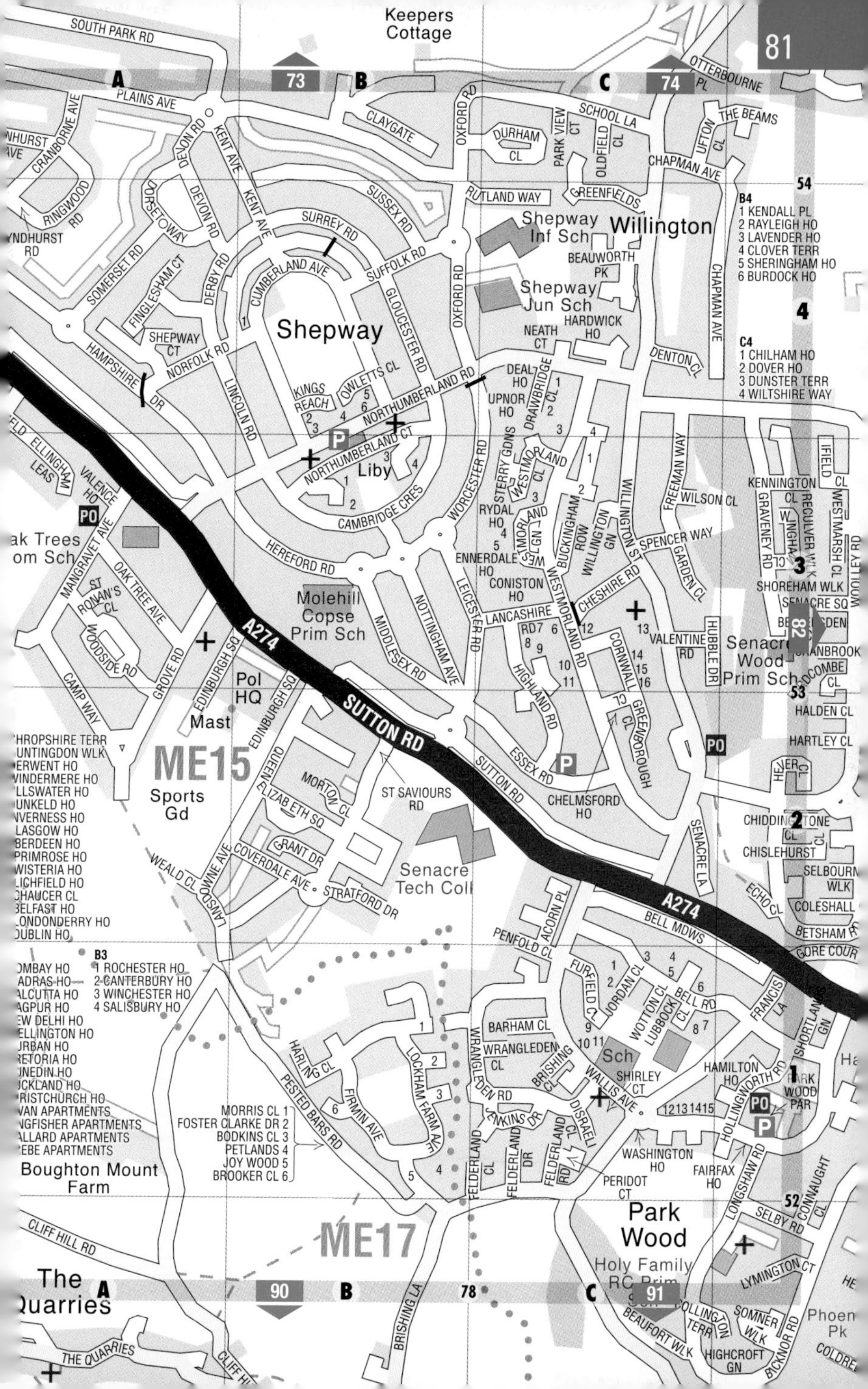

Keepers Cottage
SOUTH PARK RD
PLAINS AVE
A
73
B
C
74
OTTERBOURNE PL
CLAYGATE
OXFORD RD
SCHOOL LA
THE BEAMS
DURHAM CL
PARK VIEW CT
OLDFIELD CL
UFTON CL
CHAPMAN AVE
CRANBORNE AVE
RINGWOOD RD
DEVON RD
KENT AVE
DORSET WAY
SUSSEX RD
RUTLAND WAY
GREENFIELDS
54
B4
1 KENDALL PL
2 RAYLEIGH HO
3 LAVENDER HO
4 CLOVER TERR
5 SHERINGHAM HO
6 BURDOCK HO
LYNDHURST RD
SURREY RD
Shepway Inf Sch
Willington
BEAUWORTH PK
SOMERSET RD
DERBY RD
CUMBERLAND AVE
SUFFOLK RD
Shepway Jun Sch
FINGLESHAM CT
GLOUCESTER RD
HARDWICK HO
4
Shepway
SHEPWAY CT
NEATH CT
DENTON CL
C4
1 CHILHAM HO
2 DOVER HO
3 DUNSTER TERR
4 WILTSHIRE WAY
HAMPSHIRE DR
NORFOLK RD
LINCOLN RD
OWLETTS CL
KINGS REACH
NORTHUMBERLAND RD
DEAL HO
DRAWBRIDGE CL
UPNOR HO
NORTHUMBERLAND CT
ELLINGHAM LEAS
VALENCE HO
Liby
WORCESTER RD
STERRY GDNS
WESTMORLAND CL
FREEMAN WAY
WILSON CL
KENNINGTON CL
IFIELD CL
GRAVENEY RD
RECULVER WLK
WESTMARSH CL
PO
CAMBRIDGE CRES
RYDAL HO
WESTMORLAND GN
BUCKINGHAM ROW
WILLINGTON GN
WILLINGTON ST
SPENCER WAY
GARDEN CL
Oak Trees Com Sch
MANGRAVET AVE
HEREFORD RD
ENNERDALE HO
CONISTON HO
3
WOOLLEY RD
ST RONAN'S CL
OAK TREE AVE
Molehill Copse Prim Sch
MIDDLESEX RD
NOTTINGHAM AVE
LEICESTER RD
LANCASHIRE RD
CHESHIRE RD
WESTMORLAND RD
SHOREHAM WLK
SENACRE SQ
A274
WOODSIDE RD
GROVE RD
EDINBURGH SQ
Pol HQ
HIGHLAND RD
CORNWALL CL
VALENTINE RD
HUBBLE DR
Senacre Wood Prim Sch
82
CRANBROOK
CAMP WAY
Mast
SUTTON RD
GREENBOROUGH CL
53
HALDEN CL
HARTLEY CL
SHROPSHIRE TERR
HUNTINGDON WLK
DERWENT HO
WINDERMERE HO
ULLSWATER HO
DUNKELD HO
INVERNESS HO
GLASGOW HO
ABERDEEN HO
PRIMROSE HO
WISTERIA HO
LICHFIELD HO
CHAUCER CL
BELFAST HO
LONDONDERRY HO
DUBLIN HO
ME15
Sports Gd
QUEEN ELIZABETH SQ
MORTON CL
ST SAVIOURS RD
ESSEX RD
CHELMSFORD HO
SENACRE LA
CHIDDINGSTONE CL
CHISLEHURST CL
2
SELBOURNE WLK
ECHO CL
COLESHALL
GRANT DR
WEALD CL
LANSDOWNE AVE
COVERDALE AVE
STRATFORD DR
Senacre Tech Coll
ACORN PL
BELL MDWS
BETSHAM
GORE COURT
PENFOLD CL
B3
1 ROCHESTER HO
2 CANTERBURY HO
3 WINCHESTER HO
4 SALISBURY HO
BOMBAY HO
MADRAS HO
CALCUTTA HO
NAGPUR HO
NEW DELHI HO
WELLINGTON HO
DURBAN HO
PRETORIA HO
DUNEDIN HO
AUCKLAND HO
CHRISTCHURCH HO
SWAN APARTMENTS
KINGFISHER APARTMENTS
MALLARD APARTMENTS
GREBE APARTMENTS
FURFIELD CL
JORDAN CL
BELL RD
FRANCIS LA
SHORTLANDS GN
BARHAM CL
WOTTON CL
LUBBOCK CL
HARLING CL
LOCKHAM FARM AVE
WRANGLEDEN CL
Sch
BRISHING CL
SHIRLEY CT
HAMILTON HO
HOLLINGWORTH RD
PARK WOOD PAR
1
MORRIS CL 1
FOSTER CLARKE DR 2
BODKINS CL 3
PETLANDS 4
JOY WOOD 5
BROOKER CL 6
PESTED BARS RD
FIRMIN AVE
WRANGLEDEN RD
JENKINS DR
WALLIS AVE
DISRAELI CL
WASHINGTON HO
FAIRFAX HO
Boughton Mount Farm
FELDERLAND CL
FELDERLAND DR
FELDERLAND RD
PERIDOT CT
LONGSHAW RD
CONNAUGHT CL
52
Park Wood
SELBY RD
CLIFF HILL RD
ME17
Holy Family RC Prim Sch
LYMINGTON CT
The Quarries
90
78
91
BRISHING LA
COLLINGTON TERR
SOMNER WLK
BEAUFORT WLK
HIGHCROFT GN
BICKNOR RD
Phoenix Pk
THE QUARRIES
CLIFF HILL

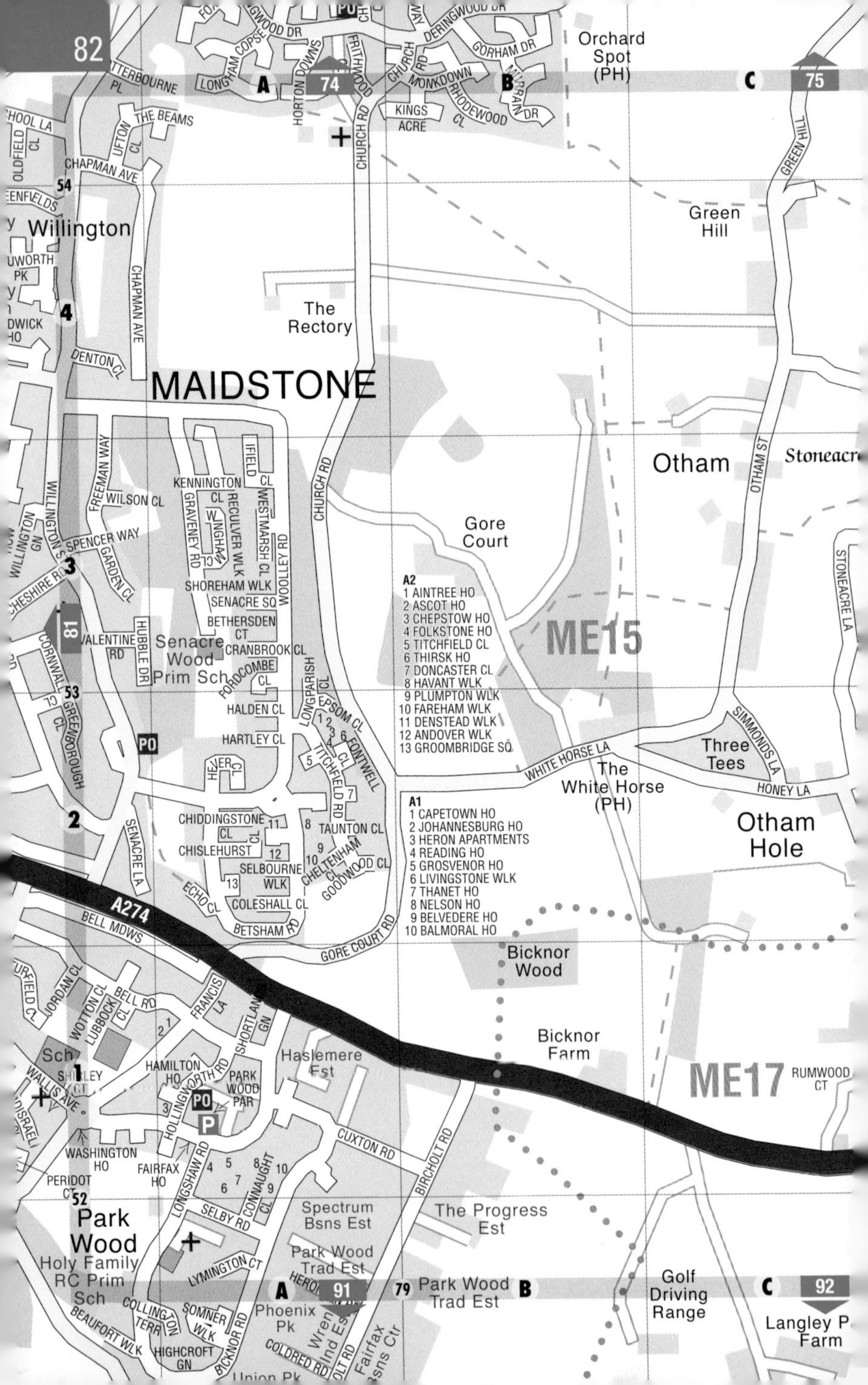
MAIDSTONE
Willington
Orchard Spot (PH)
Green Hill
The Rectory
Otham
Stoneacre
Gore Court
ME15
ME17
Senacre Wood Prim Sch
The White Horse (PH)
Three Tees
Otham Hole
Bicknor Wood
Bicknor Farm
Haslemere Est
Spectrum Bsns Est
The Progress Est
Park Wood Trad Est
Park Wood
Holy Family RC Prim Sch
Phoenix Pk
Golf Driving Range
Langley P Farm
RUMWOOD CT
A274
A2
1 AINTREE HO
2 ASCOT HO
3 CHEPSTOW HO
4 FOLKSTONE HO
5 TITCHFIELD CL
6 THIRSK HO
7 DONCASTER CL
8 HAVANT WLK
9 PLUMPTON WLK
10 FAREHAM WLK
11 DENSTEAD WLK
12 ANDOVER WLK
13 GROOMBRIDGE SQ
A1
1 CAPETOWN HO
2 JOHANNESBURG HO
3 HERON APARTMENTS
4 READING HO
5 GROSVENOR HO
6 LIVINGSTONE WLK
7 THANET HO
8 NELSON HO
9 BELVEDERE HO
10 BALMORAL HO
CHURCH RD
WHITE HORSE LA
HONEY LA
OTHAM ST
GREEN HILL
SIMMONDS LA
STONEACRE LA
GORE COURT RD
CHAPMAN AVE
WILLINGTON ST
SPENCER WAY
FREEMAN WAY
WOOLLEY RD
SENACRE LA
BELL MDWS
CUXTON RD
BIRCHOLT RD
LONGSHAW RD
HOLLINGWORTH RD
SELBY RD
LYMINGTON CT
BICKNOR RD
DERINGWOOD DR
GORHAM DR
MONKDOWN
RHODEWOOD CL
KINGS ACRE
HORTON DOWNS
LONGHAM COPSE
OTTERBOURNE PL
THE BEAMS
74
75
81
91
92
79

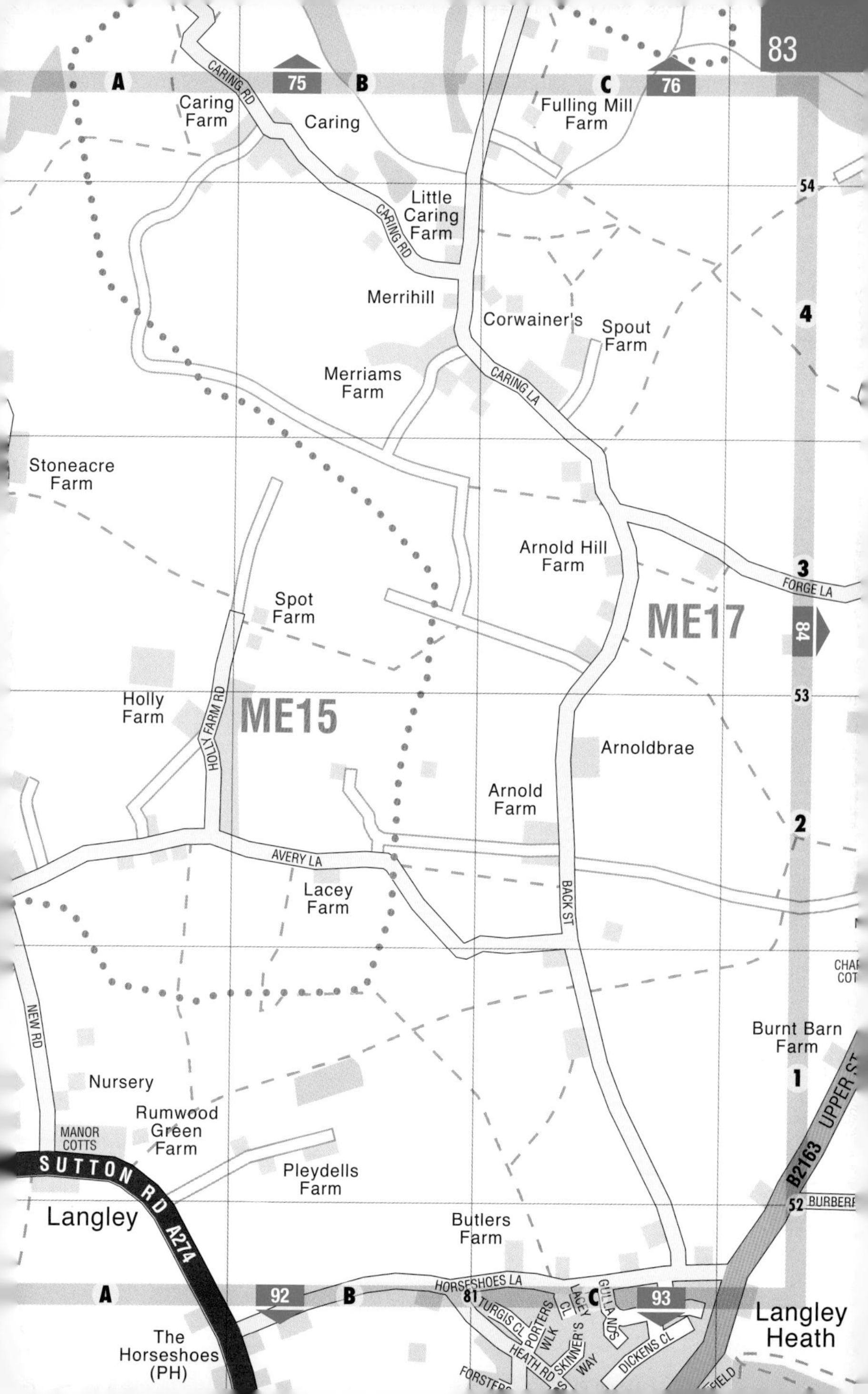

A
75
B
C
76
CARING RD
Caring Farm
Caring
Fulling Mill Farm
54
Little Caring Farm
CARING RD
Merrihill
Corwainer's
Spout Farm
4
Merriams Farm
CARING LA
Stoneacre Farm
Arnold Hill Farm
3
FORGE LA
Spot Farm
ME17
84
53
Holly Farm
HOLLY FARM RD
ME15
Arnoldbrae
Arnold Farm
2
AVERY LA
Lacey Farm
BACK ST
CHAR COT
NEW RD
Burnt Barn Farm
Nursery
1
UPPER ST
Rumwood Green Farm
MANOR COTTS
B2163
SUTTON RD A274
Pleydells Farm
52
BURBERR
Langley
Butlers Farm
A
92
B
HORSESHOES LA
81
C
93
TURGIS CL
PORTERS WLK
LACEY CL
GUILLANDS
SKINNER'S WAY
HEATH RD
DICKENS CL
Langley Heath
The Horseshoes (PH)

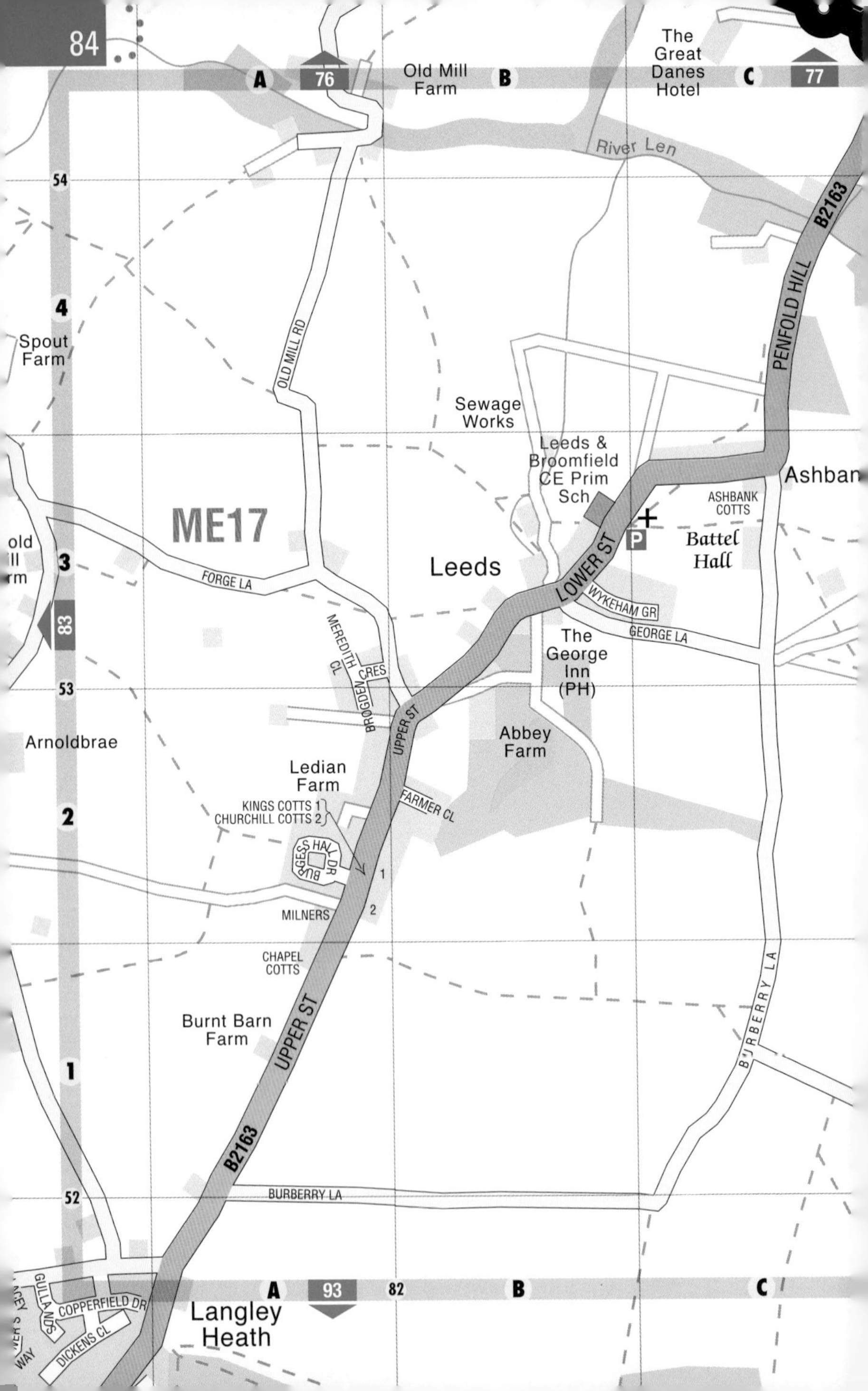

A
76
Old Mill Farm
B
The Great Danes Hotel
C
77
River Len
54
B2163
PENFOLD HILL
4
Spout Farm
OLD MILL RD
Sewage Works
Leeds & Broomfield CE Prim Sch
Ashban
ASHBANK COTTS
ME17
P
Battel Hall
old
ll
rm
3
Leeds
LOWER ST
FORGE LA
WYKEHAM GR
83
MEREDITH CL
The George Inn (PH)
GEORGE LA
BROGDEN CRES
53
UPPER ST
Arnoldbrae
Abbey Farm
Ledian Farm
FARMER CL
KINGS COTTS 1
CHURCHILL COTTS 2
2
BURGESS HALL DR
1
2
MILNERS
CHAPEL COTTS
BURBERRY LA
Burnt Barn Farm
UPPER ST
1
B2163
52
BURBERRY LA
A
93
82
B
C
GULLANDS
COPPERFIELD DR
DICKENS CL
WAY
Langley Heath

A20
M20
A
77
B
C
Oakfield
Coombe
Wood
HARPSWOOD
54
P
ME17
HOSPITAL RD
4
Park Gate
Inn
(PH)
Warren
Wood
CH
ASHFORD RD
Leeds
Castle
A20
M20
3
Forge
House
98
53
The
Great
Water
2
River Len
Church
Farm
Broomfield
Roses
Farm
1
Park Barn
Farm
PARK BARN RD
ME17
52
BROOMFIELD RD
Scrub
Wood
A
B
84
C
CHEGWORTH

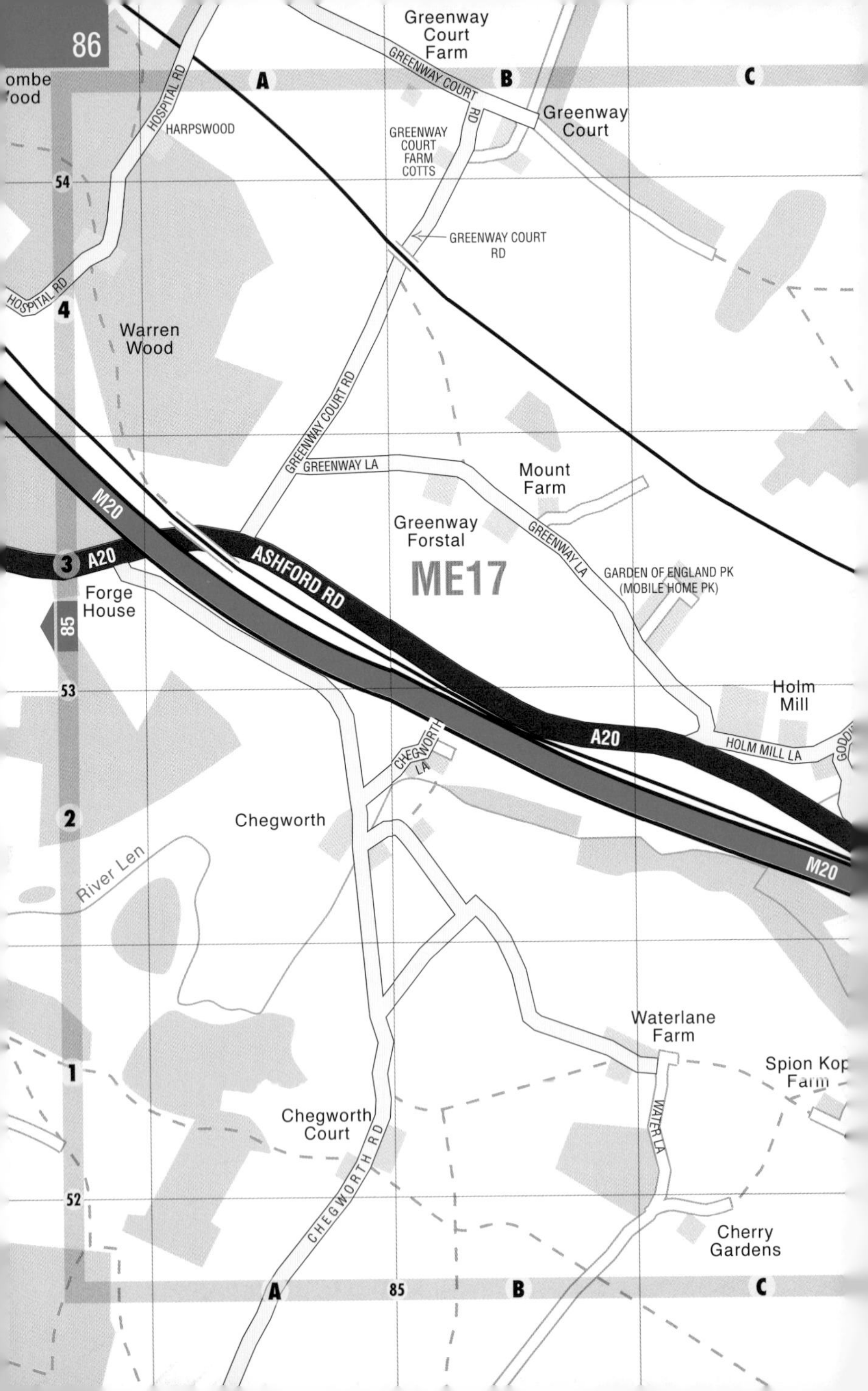
Greenway Court Farm
GREENWAY COURT RD
Greenway Court
HOSPITAL RD
HARPSWOOD
GREENWAY COURT FARM COTTS
GREENWAY COURT RD
Warren Wood
GREENWAY COURT RD
GREENWAY LA
Mount Farm
Greenway Forstal
GREENWAY LA
GARDEN OF ENGLAND PK (MOBILE HOME PK)
ME17
M20
A20
ASHFORD RD
Forge House
Holm Mill
A20
HOLM MILL LA
CHEGWORTH LA
Chegworth
River Len
M20
Waterlane Farm
Spion Kop Farm
WATER LA
Chegworth Court
CHEGWORTH RD
Cherry Gardens
A
B
C
54
4
3
85
53
2
1
52

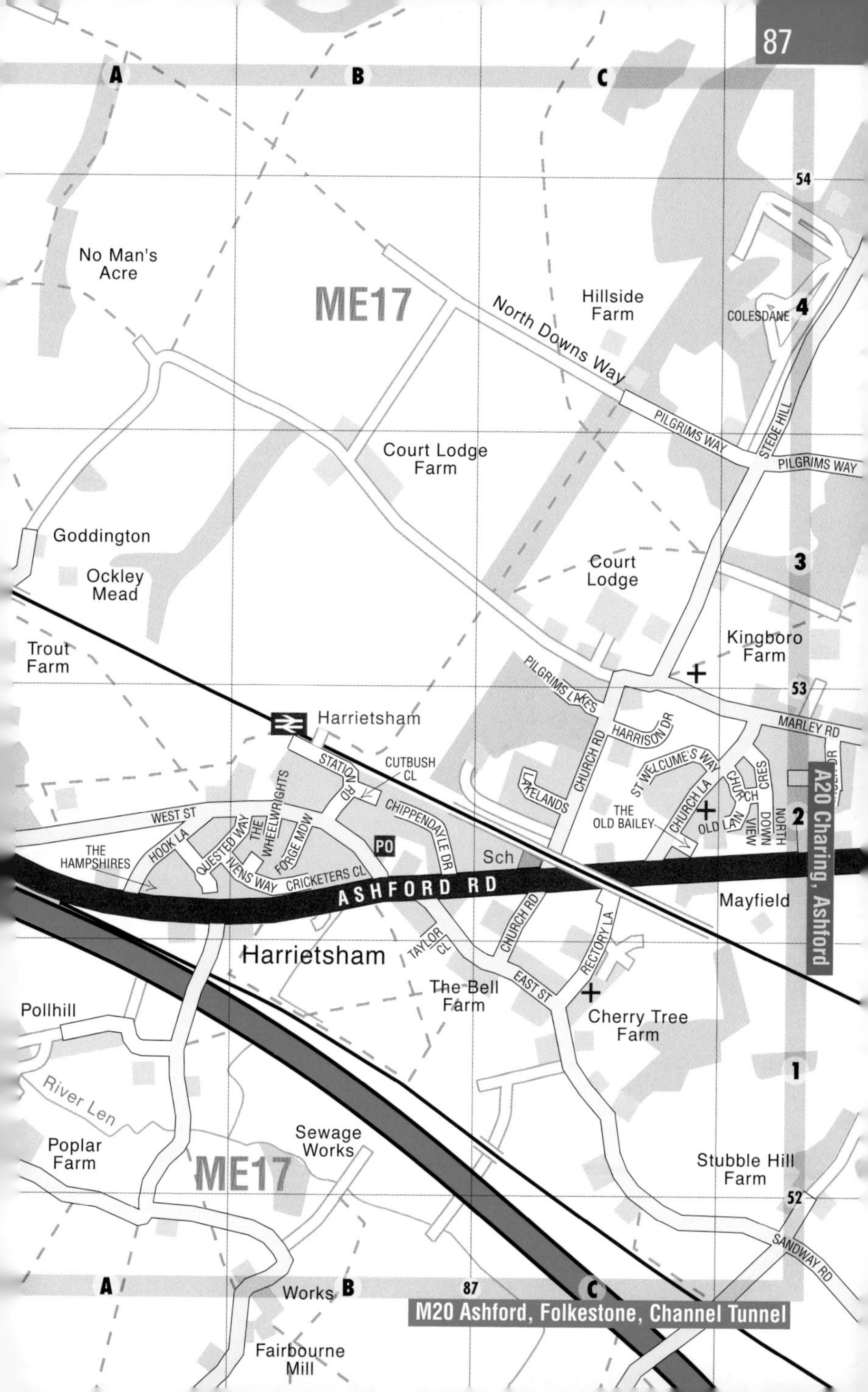

A
B
C
54
No Man's Acre
ME17
North Downs Way
Hillside Farm
COLESDANE
4
Court Lodge Farm
PILGRIMS WAY
STEDE HILL
PILGRIMS WAY
Goddington
Ockley Mead
Court Lodge
3
Trout Farm
Kingboro Farm
PILGRIMS LAKES
53
Harrietsham
HARRISON DR
MARLEY RD
CHURCH RD
STATION RD
CUTBUSH CL
LAKELANDS
ST WELCUME'S WAY
CHURCH LA
CHURCH LAN
CRES
A20 Charing, Ashford
WEST ST
QUESTED WAY
THE WHEELWRIGHTS
FORGE MDW
CHIPPENDAYLE DR
THE OLD BAILEY
OLD LAN
VIEW
DOWN
NORTH
2
THE HAMPSHIRES
HOOK LA
NEVENS WAY
CRICKETERS CL
PO
Sch
ASHFORD RD
Mayfield
CHURCH RD
RECTORY LA
TAYLOR CL
Harrietsham
The Bell Farm
EAST ST
Pollhill
Cherry Tree Farm
1
River Len
Sewage Works
Poplar Farm
ME17
Stubble Hill Farm
52
SANDWAY RD
A
Works
B
87
C
M20 Ashford, Folkestone, Channel Tunnel
Fairbourne Mill

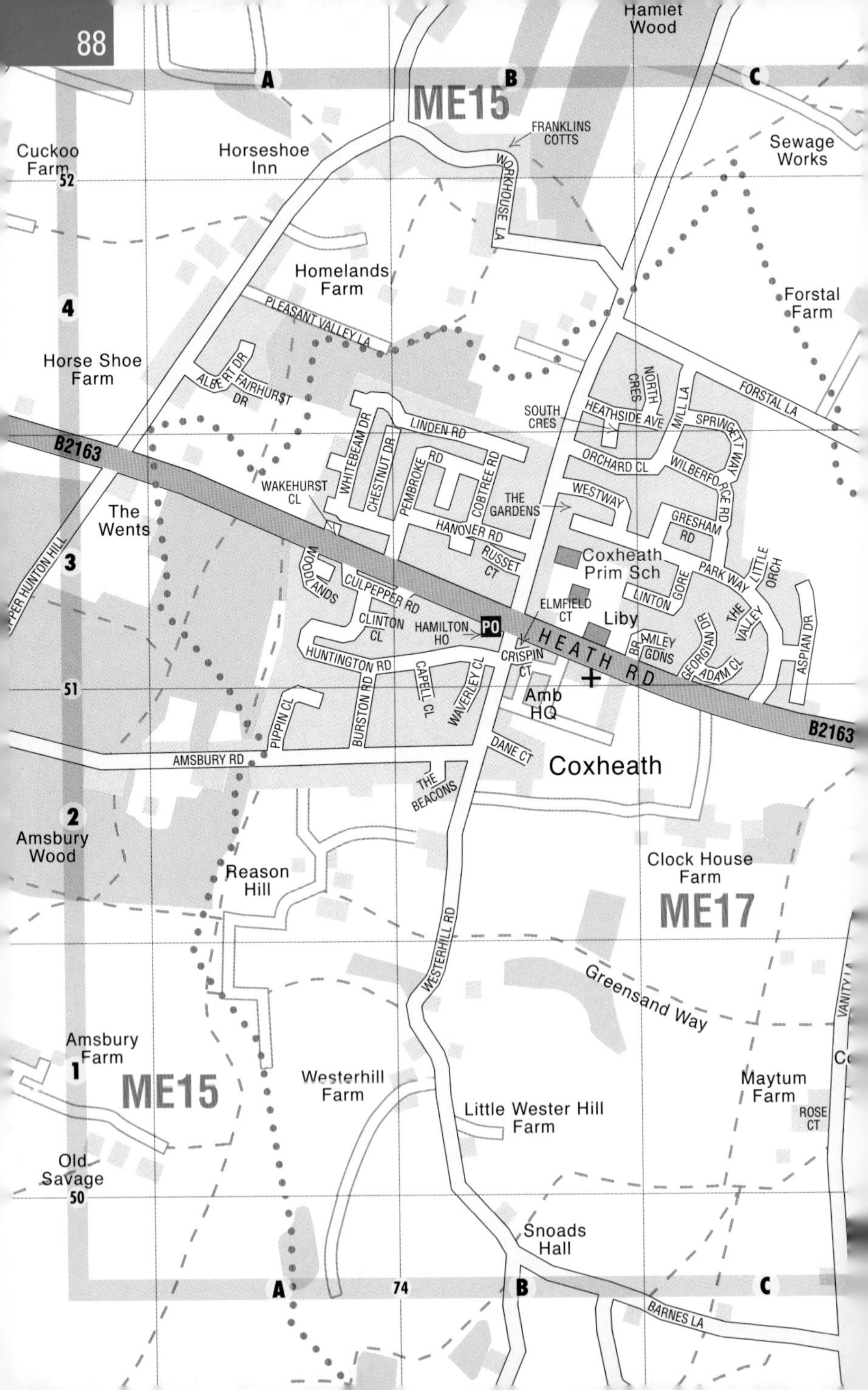

Hamlet Wood
A
B
C
ME15
FRANKLINS COTTS
Sewage Works
Cuckoo Farm
52
Horseshoe Inn
WORKHOUSE LA
Homelands Farm
Forstal Farm
4
PLEASANT VALLEY LA
Horse Shoe Farm
ALBERT DR
FAIRHURST DR
NORTH CRES
MILL LA
FORSTAL LA
SOUTH CRES
HEATHSIDE AVE
SPRINGETT WAY
B2163
LINDEN RD
WHITEBEAM DR
CHESTNUT DR
PEMBROKE RD
COBTREE RD
ORCHARD CL
WILBERFORCE RD
WAKEHURST CL
THE GARDENS
WESTWAY
The Wents
HANOVER RD
GRESHAM RD
3
UPPER HUNTON HILL
WOODLANDS
RUSSET CT
Coxheath Prim Sch
LITTLE ORCH
PARK WAY
CULPEPPER RD
LINTON
GORE
ELMFIELD CT
Liby
THE VALLEY
CLINTON CL
HAMILTON HO
PO
HEATH RD
BRAMLEY GDNS
GEORGIAN DR
ASPIAN DR
HUNTINGTON RD
CRISPIN CT
ADAM CL
CAPELL CL
WAVERLEY CL
51
PIPPIN CL
BURSTON RD
Amb HQ
B2163
DANE CT
AMSBURY RD
Coxheath
THE BEACONS
2
Amsbury Wood
Reason Hill
Clock House Farm
ME17
WESTERHILL RD
Greensand Way
VANITY LA
Amsbury Farm
1
ME15
Westerhill Farm
Little Wester Hill Farm
Maytum Farm
ROSE CT
Old Savage
50
Snoads Hall
A
74
B
C
BARNES LA

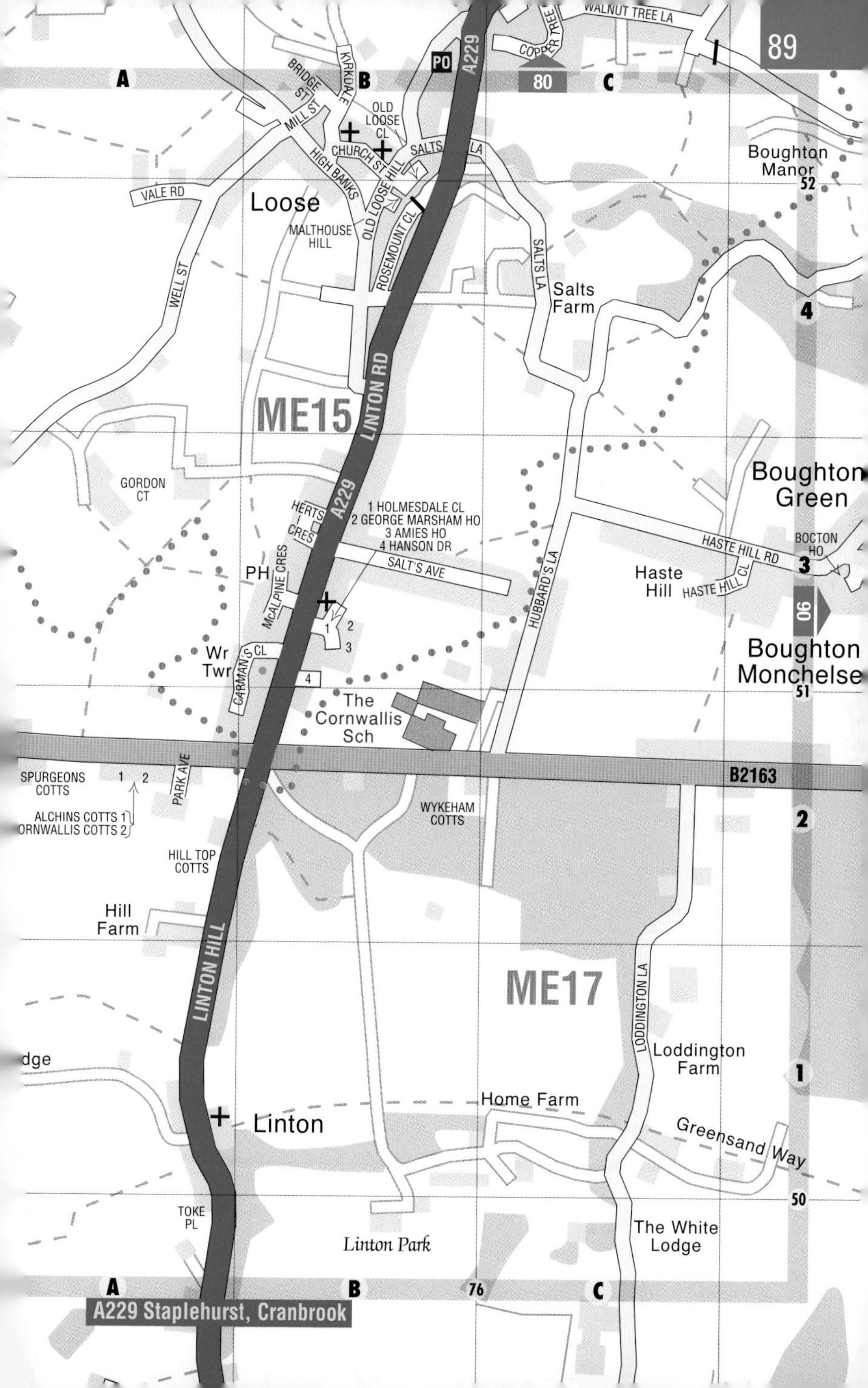

WALNUT TREE LA
COPPER TREE
80
A
B
C
KIRKDALE
BRIDGE ST
MILL ST
OLD LOOSE CL
CHURCH ST
SALTS LA
HIGH BANKS
OLD LOOSE HILL
ROSEMOUNT CL
VALE RD
Loose
MALTHOUSE HILL
WELL ST
SALTS LA
Salts Farm
Boughton Manor
52
4
ME15
LINTON RD
A229
GORDON CT
HERTS CRES
1 HOLMESDALE CL
2 GEORGE MARSHAM HO
3 AMIES HO
4 HANSON DR
SALT'S AVE
Boughton Green
BOCTON HO
HASTE HILL RD
3
Haste Hill
HASTE HILL CL
HUBBARD'S LA
McALPINE CRES
PH
06
Boughton Monchelsea
51
Wr Twr
CARMAN'S CL
The Cornwallis Sch
B2163
SPURGEONS COTTS
PARK AVE
ALCHINS COTTS 1
ORNWALLIS COTTS 2
WYKEHAM COTTS
2
HILL TOP COTTS
Hill Farm
LINTON HILL
ME17
LODDINGTON LA
Loddington Farm
1
dge
Home Farm
Linton
Greensand Way
50
TOKE PL
Linton Park
The White Lodge
76
A229 Staplehurst, Cranbrook

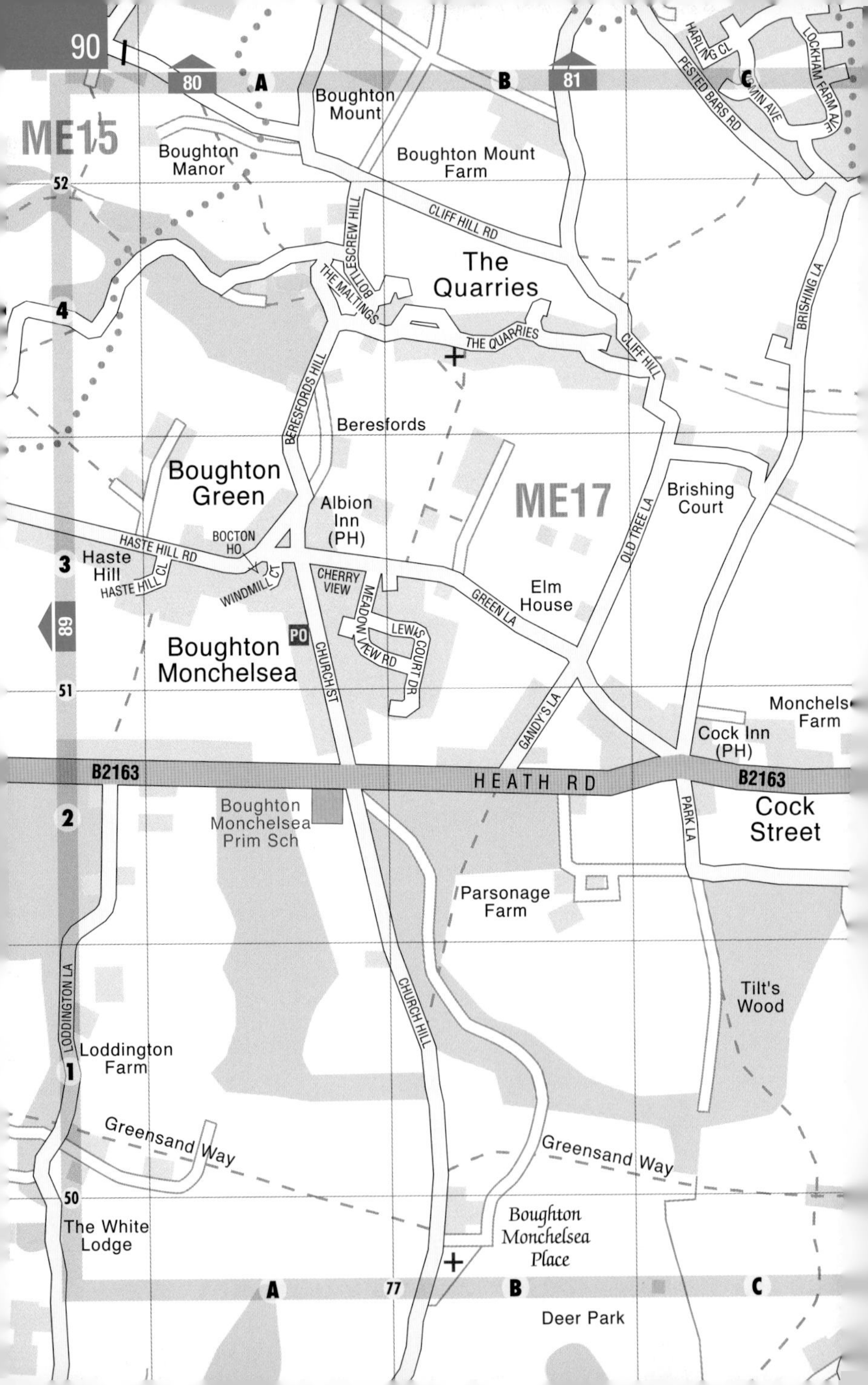

80
A
B
81
C
ME15
Boughton Mount
Boughton Manor
Boughton Mount Farm
HARLING CL
PESTED BARS RD
LOCKHAM FARM AVE
CLIFF HILL RD
BOTTLESCREW HILL
THE MALTINGS
The Quarries
THE QUARRIES
CLIFF HILL
BRISHING LA
BERESFORDS HILL
Beresfords
Boughton Green
Albion Inn (PH)
ME17
Brishing Court
OLD TREE LA
HASTE HILL RD
BOCTON HO
Haste Hill
HASTE HILL CL
WINDMILL CT
CHERRY VIEW
MEADOW VIEW RD
LEWIS COURT DR
GREEN LA
Elm House
89
PO
Boughton Monchelsea
CHURCH ST
GANDY'S LA
Cock Inn (PH)
B2163
HEATH RD
PARK LA
Cock Street
Boughton Monchelsea Prim Sch
Parsonage Farm
CHURCH HILL
Tilt's Wood
LODDINGTON LA
Loddington Farm
Greensand Way
Greensand Way
The White Lodge
Boughton Monchelsea Place
Deer Park
77
52
51
50
4
3
2
1

BARHAM CL
WRANGLEDEN CL
BRISHING
Sch
SHIRLEY CT
WALLIS AVE
DISRAELI
JENKINS DR
FELDERLAND CL
FELDERLAND DR
FELDERLAND RD
81
A
HAMILTON HO
HOLLINGWORTH RD
PARK WOOD PAR
PO
P
B
82
Haslemere Est
A274
C
Bicknor Farm
WASHINGTON HO
PERIDOT CT
FAIRFAX HO
LONGSHAW RD
CONNAUGHT CL
CUXTON RD
BIRCHOLT RD
Park Wood
SELBY RD
Spectrum Bsns Est
The Progress Est
Holy Family RC Prim Sch
LYMINGTON CT
Park Wood Trad Est
HERONDEN RD
Park Wood Trad Est
COLLINGTON TERR
SOMNER WLK
Phoenix Pk
Wren Ind Est
Fairfax Bsns Ctr
BEAUFORT WLK
HIGHCROFT GN
BICKNOR RD
COLDRED RD
Union Pk
BIRCHOLT RD
ME15
Palace Ind Est
Target Bsns Ctr
BIRCHOLT RD
CHRISTEN WAY
Boxmend Ind Est 1
Orchard Ind Est 2
BRISHING RD
Golf Driving Range
52
4
ME17
Langley Loch
3
92
51
Mount Pleasant Farm
Iden Farm
Marlpit
2
MARLPIT COTTS
Marlpit Farm
FOUR WENTS
PLOUGH WENTS RD
Pleasant Farm
ME17
BACK LA
WIERTON LA
B2163
LESTED LA
Chart Sutton
COBFIELD
LAXTON DR
AMBER WAY
PO
CHART CNR
AMBER LA
PH
Amberfield
Wierton Grange
CHART HILL RD
MARSHAM CRES
MERCER WAY
50
ALMERY COTTS
Wierton Place
Wierton Hall Farm
A
B
79
C
Wierton
Greensand Way
Ambercourt
Ladds Court Farm

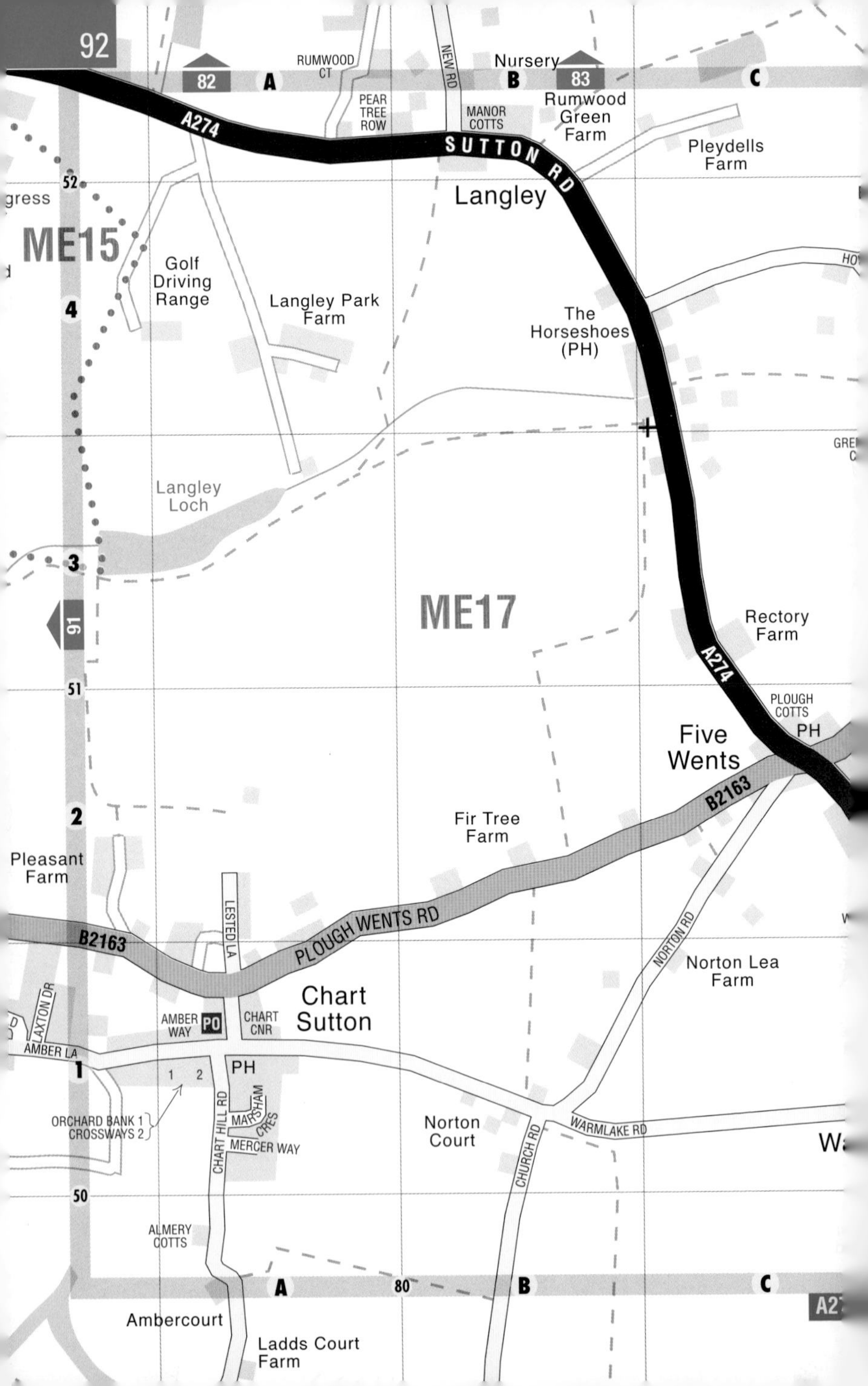
82
A
RUMWOOD CT
NEW RD
Nursery
83
B
C
A274
PEAR TREE ROW
MANOR COTTS
Rumwood Green Farm
SUTTON RD
Pleydells Farm
52
gress
Langley
ME15
Golf Driving Range
Langley Park Farm
4
The Horseshoes (PH)
Langley Loch
3
ME17
91
Rectory Farm
A274
51
PLOUGH COTTS
PH
Five Wents
B2163
2
Fir Tree Farm
Pleasant Farm
PLOUGH WENTS RD
LESTED LA
B2163
NORTON RD
Norton Lea Farm
LAXTON DR
Chart Sutton
AMBER WAY
PO
CHART CNR
AMBER LA
1
PH
ORCHARD BANK 1
CROSSWAYS 2
CHART HILL RD
MARSHAM CRES
MERCER WAY
Norton Court
CHURCH RD
WARMLAKE RD
50
ALMERY COTTS
A
80
B
C
Ambercourt
Ladds Court Farm

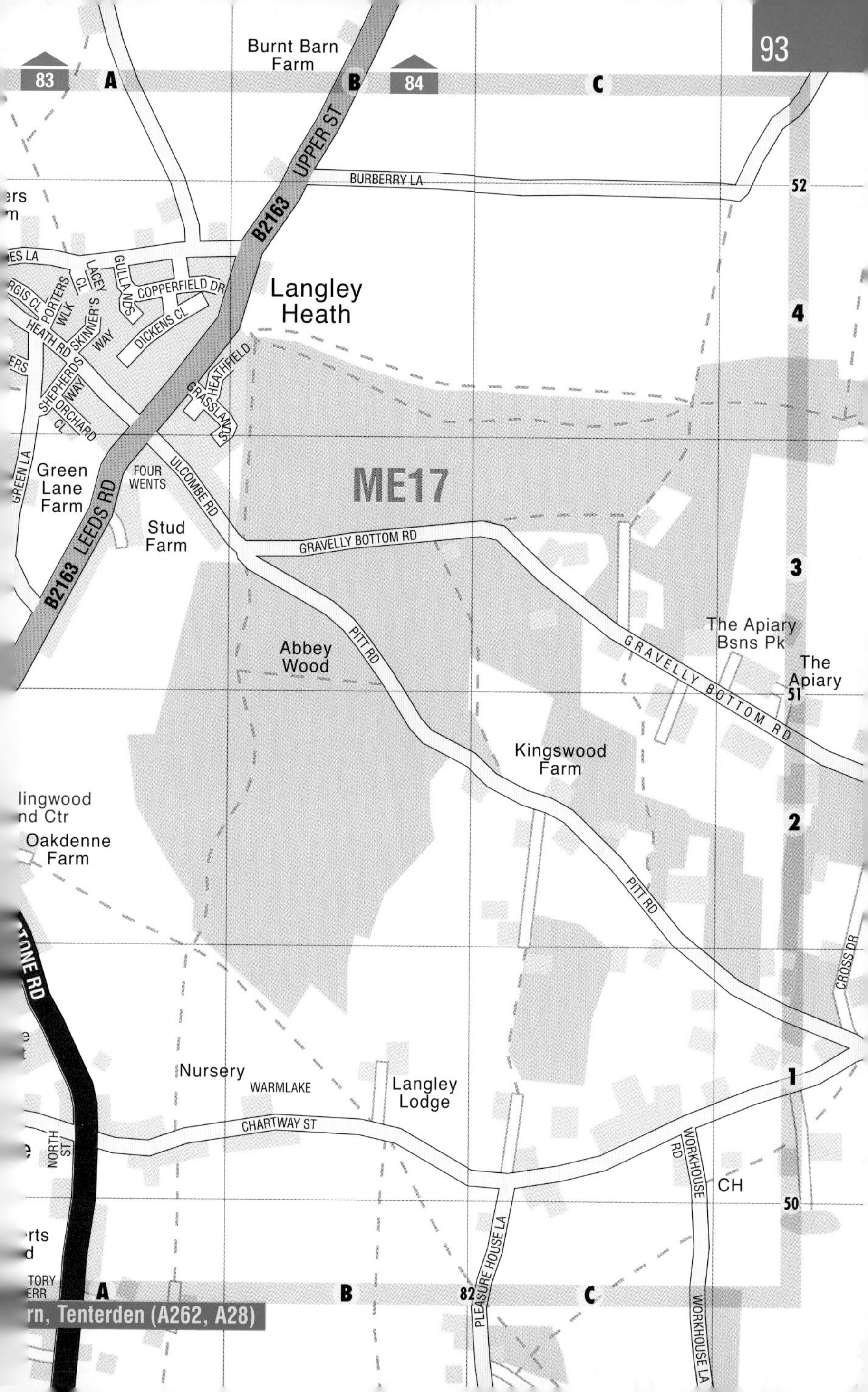
Burnt Barn
Farm
83
A
B
84
C
UPPER ST
BURBERRY LA
52
B2163
Langley
Heath
4
LACEY
CL
GULLANDS
COPPERFIELD DR
PORTERS
WLK
SKINNER'S
WAY
DICKENS CL
HEATH RD
SHEPHERDS
WAY
ORCHARD
CL
HEATHFIELD
GRASSLANDS
GREEN LA
Green
Lane
Farm
FOUR
WENTS
ULCOMBE RD
ME17
LEEDS RD
B2163
Stud
Farm
GRAVELLY BOTTOM RD
3
Abbey
Wood
PITT RD
The Apiary
Bsns Pk
The
Apiary
51
GRAVELLY BOTTOM RD
Kingswood
Farm
Oakdenne
Farm
2
PITT RD
CROSS DR
Nursery
WARMLAKE
Langley
Lodge
1
CHARTWAY ST
NORTH
ST
WORKHOUSE
RD
CH
50
PLEASURE HOUSE LA
A
B
82
C
WORKHOUSE LA
rn, Tenterden (A262, A28)

A
B
C
Garrison Point
LB Sta
SLIPWAY RD
BOATHOUSE RD
JETTY RD
GARRISON RD
Docks
ANCHOR LA
STOREHOUSE WHARF
ANCHOR LA
MAIN RD
Sheerness Harbour Est
ARCHWAY RD
ARCHWAY RD
1 NAVAL TERR
2 REGENCY CL
3 BENTHAM SQ
4 The Duke of Clarence
5 EDWARD ST
The Moat
Superstore
Coll
BEACH TERR
BRIDGE RD
A250
VICTORY ST
Jetty
Sheerness Harbour Est
GREAT BASIN RD
KING'S HEAD ALLEY
HIGH ST
CHARLES ST
CHAPEL ST
EAST LA
UNION ST
WEST ST
KING ST
WEST PAS
SHEPPEY ST
A249
Sheerness-on-Sea
Works
Blue Town
1 ROYAL FOUNTAIN MEWS
2 WEST LA
3 FOUNTAIN LA
LC
RAILWAY RD
PEPYS AVE
SHORT ST
RUSSELL ST
HOPE ST
ROSE ST
BROAD ST
HERO HO 1
LAUREL HO 2
LABURNUM HO 3
CEDAR HO 4
WILLOW HO 5
BIRCH HO 6
Rose Street Prim Sch
Piers
ME12
BRIELLE WAY
St Edward's RC Prim Sch
NEW ST
KENT RD
THAMES AVE
SWALE AVE
FLEET AVE
ESTUARY RD
Mile Town
New Road Ind Est
GRACE RD
Regis Bsns Pk
NEW RD
MEDWAY RD
CECIL AVE
CARLTON AVE
WHEATSHEAF GDNS
Works
Allot Gdns
MONTAGUE CT
MIRANDA CT
BRITON CT
DIAMOND CT
The Lappel
ST GEORGE'S CT
DORSET RD
West Minster Prim Sch
BRIDGEWATER RD
TRIBUNE CT
SHEARWATER CT
ST GEORGE'S AVE
RULE CT
NEW RD
NELSON CL
The Fleet
DAVIE CT
BONETTA CT
DAVIE CL
QUEEN'S WAY
CHERRY TREE CL
HAWTHORN AVE
LARCH TERR
ALDER CL
ALMOND TREE CL
COATS AVE
PO
CHILHAM CL
APPLEDORE AVE
EDENBRIDGE DR
BREDHURST CL
MILSTEAD CL
West Minster
LINDEN DR
LINDEN DR
NEWLAND RD
CROMWELL RD
BOXLEY CL
DETLING CL
HARTLIP CL
Diggs Marshes
91
96
75
74
4
3
2
1

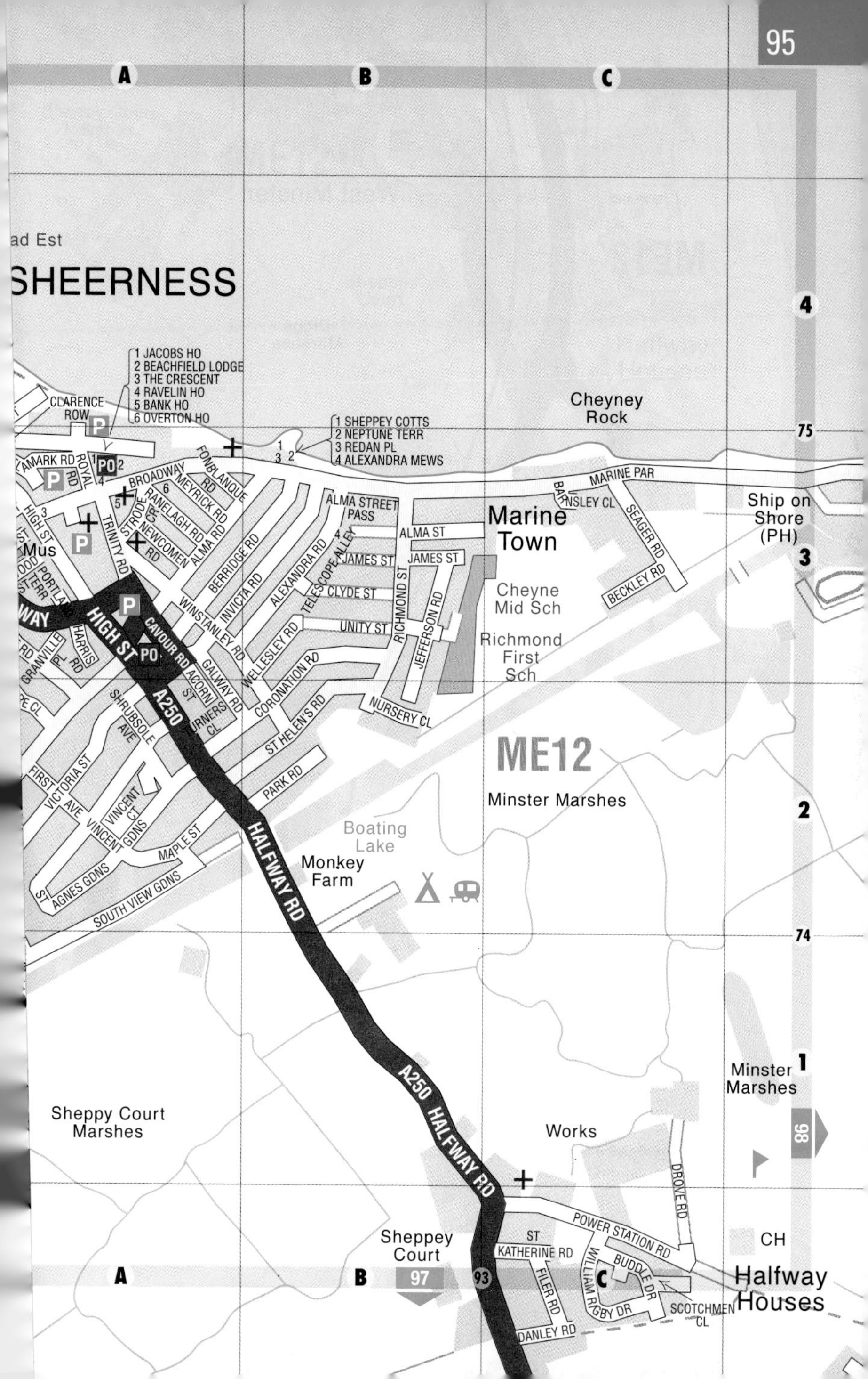
A
B
C
SHEERNESS
ad Est
1 JACOBS HO
2 BEACHFIELD LODGE
3 THE CRESCENT
4 RAVELIN HO
5 BANK HO
6 OVERTON HO
CLARENCE ROW
1 SHEPPEY COTTS
2 NEPTUNE TERR
3 REDAN PL
4 ALEXANDRA MEWS
Cheyney Rock
75
MARINE PAR
BARNSLEY CL
SEAGER RD
BECKLEY RD
Ship on Shore (PH)
Marine Town
Cheyne Mid Sch
Richmond First Sch
ALMA STREET PASS
ALMA ST
JAMES ST
CLYDE ST
UNITY ST
TELESCOPE ALLEY
RICHMOND ST
JEFFERSON RD
NURSERY CL
ALEXANDRA RD
INVICTA RD
BERRIDGE RD
WELLESLEY RD
CORONATION RD
ST HELEN'S RD
PARK RD
FOMBLANQUE RD
BROADWAY
MEYRICK RD
RANELAGH RD
ALMA RD
NEWCOMEN RD
STRODE CR
TRINITY RD
WINSTANLEY RD
GALWAY RD
ACORN ST
TURNERS CL
CAVOUR RD
HIGH ST
A250
HALFWAY RD
ROYAL RD
HIGH ST
Mus
PORTLAND TERR
HARRIS RD
GRANVILLE RD
SHRUBSOLE AVE
VICTORIA ST
FIRST AVE
VINCENT CT
VINCENT GDNS
MAPLE ST
AGNES GDNS
SOUTH VIEW GDNS
ME12
Minster Marshes
Boating Lake
Monkey Farm
74
Sheppy Court Marshes
A250 HALFWAY RD
Works
Minster Marshes
96
DROVE RD
POWER STATION RD
CH
Sheppey Court
KATHERINE RD
FILER RD
WILLIAM RD
BUDDLE DR
DANLEY RD
SCOTCHMEN CL
Halfway Houses
97
93
4
3
2
1

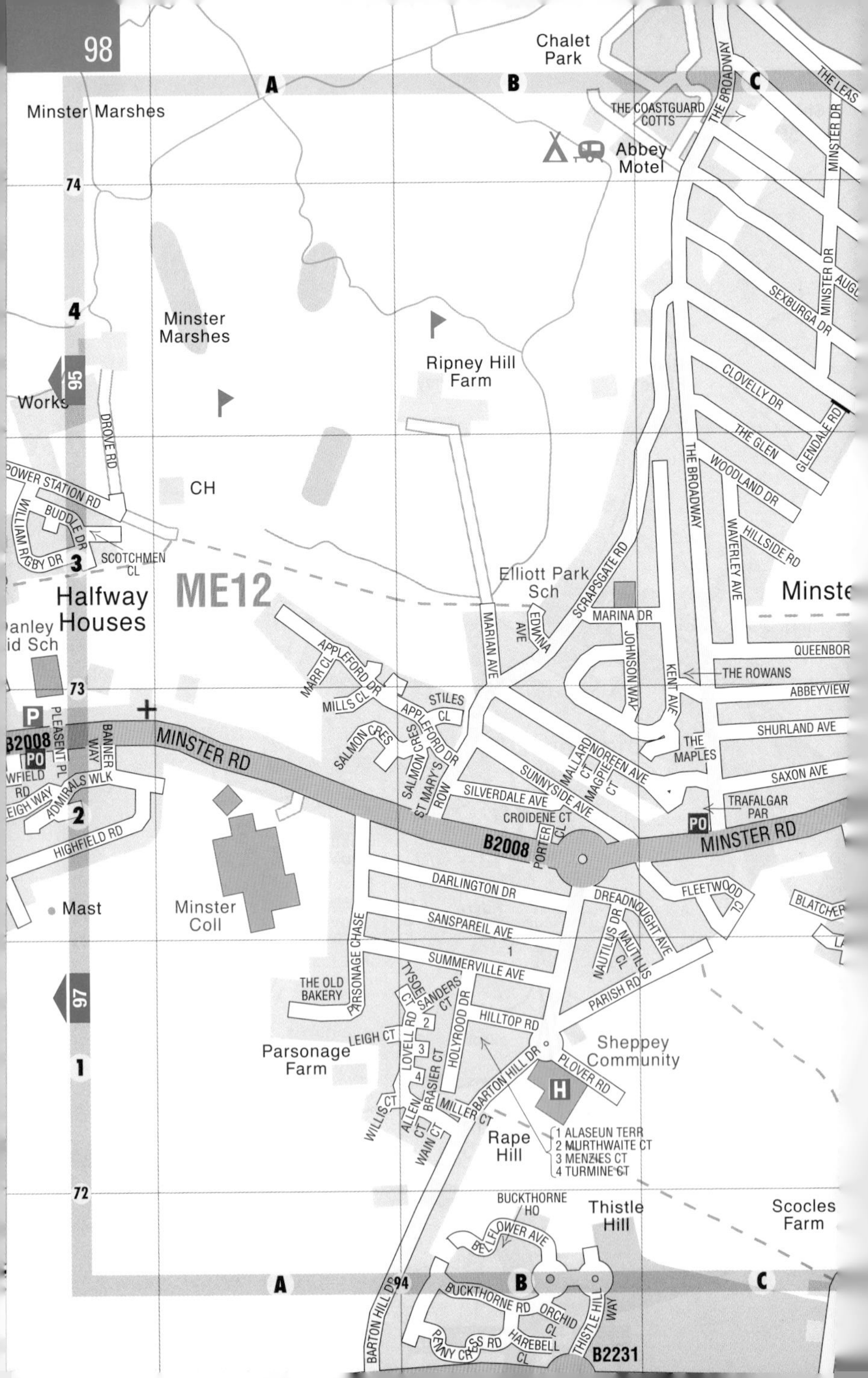
Chalet Park
Minster Marshes
THE COASTGUARD COTTS
THE BROADWAY
THE LEAS
Abbey Motel
MINSTER DR
74
4
Minster Marshes
SEXBURGA DR
AUGU
Ripney Hill Farm
95
Works
CLOVELLY DR
GLENDALE RD
THE GLEN
DROVE RD
WOODLAND DR
CH
POWER STATION RD
BUDDLE DR
WILLIAM RIGBY DR
SCOTCHMEN CL
3
HILLSIDE RD
WAVERLEY AVE
SCRAPSGATE RD
Elliott Park Sch
ME12
Halfway Houses
Minste
MARINA DR
MARIAN AVE
EDWINA AVE
JOHNSON WAY
KENT AVE
QUEENBOR
THE ROWANS
ABBEYVIEW
73
APPLEFORD DR
MARR CL
MILLS CL
STILES CL
B2008
PLEASENT PL
BANNER WAY
MINSTER RD
SALMON CRES
SHURLAND AVE
THE MAPLES
MALLARD CT
NOREEN AVE
MAGPIE CT
SAXON AVE
SUNNYSIDE AVE
SILVERDALE AVE
ST MARY'S ROW
ADMIRALS WLK
HIGHFIELD RD
2
CROIDENE CT
PORTER CL
TRAFALGAR PAR
PO
P
MINSTER RD
DARLINGTON DR
FLEETWOOD CL
Mast
Minster Coll
DREADNOUGHT AVE
BLATCHER
SANSPAREIL AVE
NAUTILUS DR
NAUTILUS CL
SUMMERVILLE AVE
PARISH RD
PARSONAGE CHASE
THE OLD BAKERY
TYSOE CT
SANDERS CT
HOLYROOD DR
97
HILLTOP RD
Sheppey Community
Parsonage Farm
LEIGH CT
LOVELL RD
BRASIER CT
BARTON HILL DR
PLOVER RD
1
WILLIS CT
ALLEN CT
WAIN CT
MILLER CT
H
Rape Hill
1 ALASEUN TERR
2 MURTHWAITE CT
3 MENZIES CT
4 TURMINE CT
72
BUCKTHORNE HO
Thistle Hill
Scocles Farm
BELLFLOWER AVE
A
94
B
C
BUCKTHORNE RD
ORCHID CL
THISTLE HILL WAY
PENNY CRESS RD
HAREBELL CL
B2231

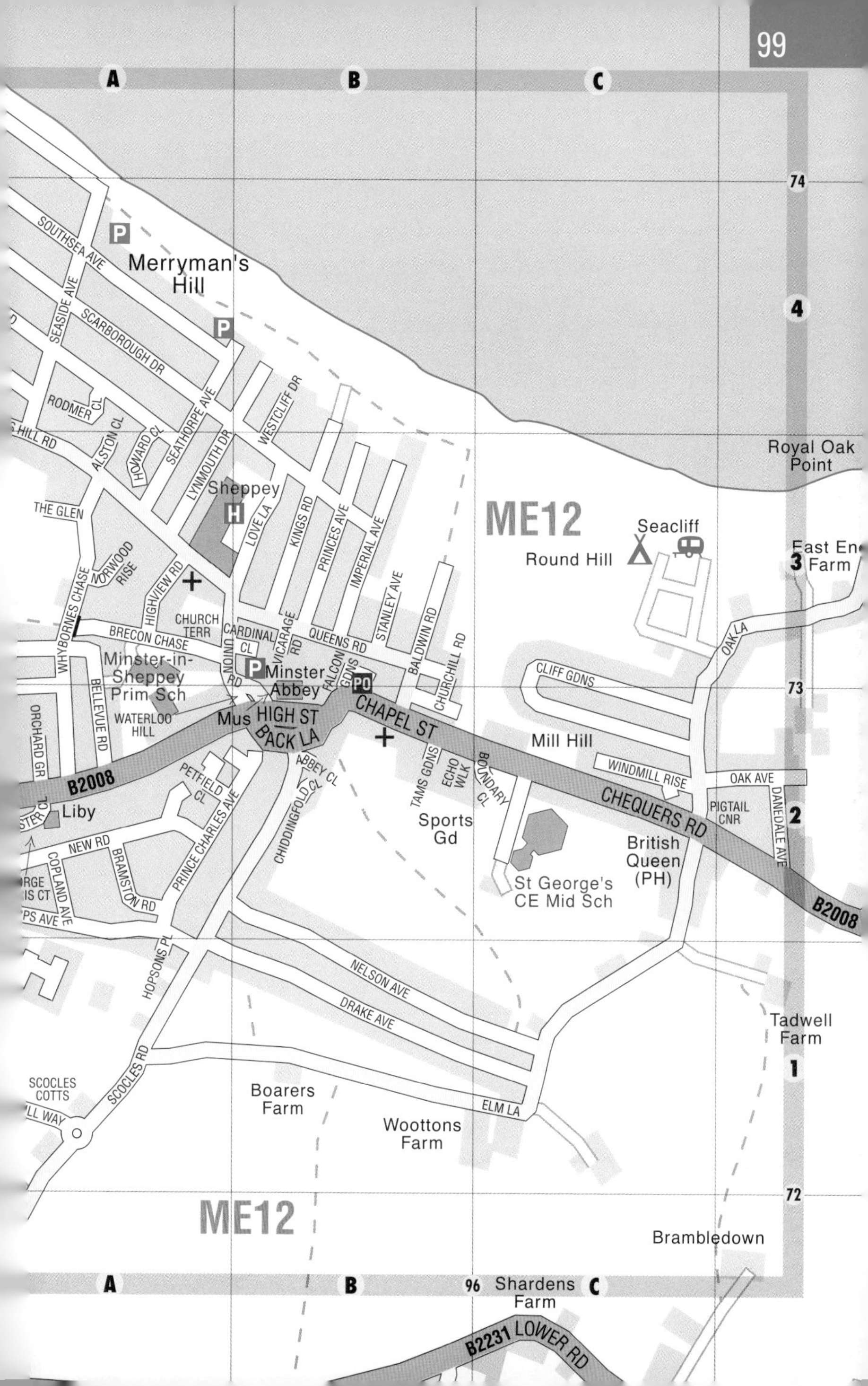

A
B
C
74
4
73
3
2
1
72
96
Merryman's Hill
SOUTHSEA AVE
SEASIDE AVE
SCARBOROUGH DR
RODMER CL
ALSTON CL
HOWARD CL
SEATHORPE AVE
LYNMOUTH DR
WESTCLIFF DR
Sheppey
THE GLEN
NORWOOD RISE
HIGHVIEW RD
WHYBORNES CHASE
BRECON CHASE
CHURCH TERR
CARDINAL CL
UNION RD
VICARAGE RD
LOVE LA
KINGS RD
PRINCES AVE
IMPERIAL AVE
QUEENS RD
STANLEY AVE
BALDWIN RD
CHURCHILL RD
FALCON GDNS
Minster-in-Sheppey Prim Sch
Minster Abbey
PO
Mus
HIGH ST
BACK LA
CHAPEL ST
WATERLOO HILL
BELLEVUE RD
ORCHARD GR
B2008
Liby
PETFIELD CL
PRINCE CHARLES AVE
ABBEY CL
CHIDDINGFOLD CL
TAMS GDNS
ECHO WLK
BOUNDARY CL
Sports Gd
NEW RD
BRAMSTON RD
COPLAND AVE
HOPSONS PL
ME12
Royal Oak Point
Seacliff
Round Hill
East End Farm
OAK LA
CLIFF GDNS
Mill Hill
WINDMILL RISE
OAK AVE
PIGTAIL CNR
DANEDALE AVE
CHEQUERS RD
British Queen (PH)
St George's CE Mid Sch
B2008
NELSON AVE
DRAKE AVE
ELM LA
Tadwell Farm
SCOCLES COTTS
SCOCLES RD
Boarers Farm
Woottons Farm
ME12
Brambledown
Shardens Farm
B2231 LOWER RD

Culnell's Cottages
Coleshall Farm
PINTAIL DR
A
B
C
Coleshall
67
FEATHERBED LA
B2005
Culnells
4
GROVEHURST RD
SHEPPEY WAY
Corbiere
ME10
Kemsley
Pheasants Farm
3
ME9
BRAMBLEFIELD LA
WOODSHOLE COTTS
LAYFIELD COTTS
A249
Kemsley
66
Howt Green
Stickfast Farm
PH
STICKFAST LA
Upper Toes
Nether Toes
2
PASTIME CL
ECLIPSE DR
ATTLEE WAY
BURNHAM CL
ESTHER CT
PHILLIPPA CT
SITTINGBOURNE
BRITANNIA CL
ALEXANDRA CL
JESSICA MEWS
VOLANTE DR
RICHMOND DR
GENESTA CL
FOXGROVE
CHALLENGER CL
CARDINE CL
SHEPPEY WAY
Quinton Farm House
Church Farm
1
1 SUNSTONE DR
2 SAPPHIRE CL
3 JADE CL
4 OLIVINE CL
QUINTON RD
LORIMAR CT
DENBIGH CL
MILBOURNE GR
Regis Mano Com Prim Sch
Bobbing Village Sch
AMBER RISE
SONORA WAY
ME10
GLENBROOK GR
THE MEADS AVE
THE MEADS AVE
KNIGHTSFIELD RD
ROBERTS CL
MIDDLETUNE AVE
NEWBRIDGE AVE
FROBISHER CL
BALAS DR
ANATASE CL
DYNGLEY CL
65
CINNABAR DR
ARGENT WAY
FELDSPAR CL
PIPPIN CL
VICARAGE RD
SPROTSH
DOBBIE CL
TOURMALINE DR
GALENA CL
TOPAZ DR
FORGE RD
A249 Maidstone, M2
89
A
103
B
90
C
104
LAXTON WAY
WORCESTER DR
Recn Gd
Milton Regis
CHERRY CL
Mus
HIGH ST
MOONSTONE SQ
DERBY CL
BEECHWOOD
LAMMAS DR
DEAN RD
PO

A249 Sheerness
ME9
ME9
ME10
ME10
LC
1 OSTEND CT
2 BRUGES CT
3 MELLOR ROW
The Kemsley Arms (PH)
THE CRESCENT
Chy
Chy
Mill
Kemsley Mill Railway Mus
Kemsley Marshes
Kemsley Down
Kemsley Down
Conveyor
MENIN RD
MONS CT
THE SQUARE
RIDHAM AVE
FLANDERS CL
COLDHARBOUR LA
WEST GN
EAST GN
LIEGE CL
YPRES DR
GODWIN CL
CASTLE ROUGH LA
GROVEHURST AVE
GLOVER CL
MARSH RISE
RECREATION WAY
MOONFLEET CL
EADRED WAY
COLEMAN DR
THE WILLOWS
PAVILION DR
SAXON SHORE
CRICKETERS CL
Sittingbourne & Kemsley Light Rly
Castle Rough
Blue Houses
BEAUVOIR DR
GROVEHURST RD
MERLEBURGH DR
AYLEWYN GN
CHEYNE CL
DONEMOWE DR
PUTTNEY DR
EDYNGHAM CL
COLFE WAY
NEWMAN DR
INGLEDEN CL
AUSTIN CL
CLERKE DR
TODD CRES
WALSBY DR
YEATES DR
MILLER CL
VAUGHAN DR
BURKESTON CL
GREGORY CL
ADISHAM GN
TAILLOUR CL
WHIMBREL CL
RETTENDON DR
TURNER CL
GREEN PORCH CL
SAFFRON WAY
Kemsley Marshes
Church Marshes Country Park
HINDE CL
TRINITY RD
Trinity Trad Est
Superstore
Trinity Trad Est
LANGLEY RD
TRIBUNE DR
Court Sch
Milton Regis
Milton Creek
Saxon Shore Way
Works
MILL WAY
B2005
Sewage Works
D2 Trad Est
GAS RD
STADIUM WAY
104
105
91
92
65
66
67
A
B
C
1
2
3
4

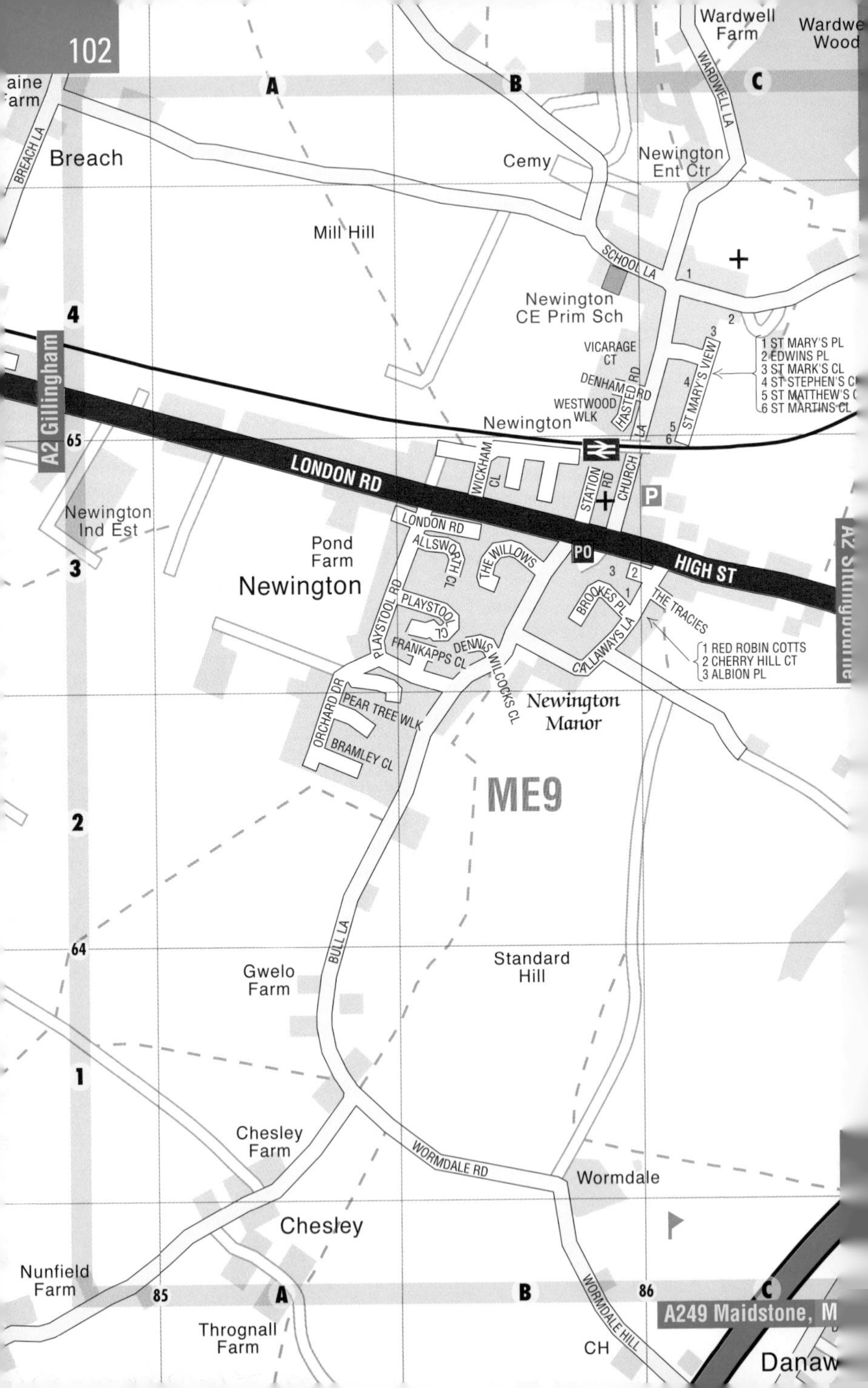
A
B
C
aine
Farm
Wardwell
Farm
Wardwe
Wood
WARDWELL LA
BREACH LA
Breach
Cemy
Newington
Ent Ctr
Mill Hill
SCHOOL LA
Newington
CE Prim Sch
4
A2 Gillingham
VICARAGE
CT
DENHAM RD
HASTED RD
WESTWOOD
WLK
ST MARY'S VIEW
1 ST MARY'S PL
2 EDWINS PL
3 ST MARK'S CL
4 ST STEPHEN'S CL
5 ST MATTHEW'S CL
6 ST MARTINS CL
Newington
65
LONDON RD
WICKHAM CL
STATION RD
CHURCH LA
P
Newington
Ind Est
LONDON RD
Pond
Farm
ALLSWORTH CL
THE WILLOWS
PO
HIGH ST
A2 Sittingbourne
3
Newington
PLAYSTOOL RD
PLAYSTOOL CL
BROOKES PL
THE TRACIES
CALLAWAYS LA
FRANKAPPS CL
DENNIS
WILCOCKS CL
1 RED ROBIN COTTS
2 CHERRY HILL CT
3 ALBION PL
ORCHARD DR
PEAR TREE WLK
BRAMLEY CL
Newington
Manor
ME9
2
BULL LA
64
Gwelo
Farm
Standard
Hill
1
Chesley
Farm
WORMDALE RD
Wormdale
Chesley
Nunfield
Farm
85
A
B
86
C
WORMDALE HILL
A249 Maidstone, M
Thrognall
Farm
CH
Danaw

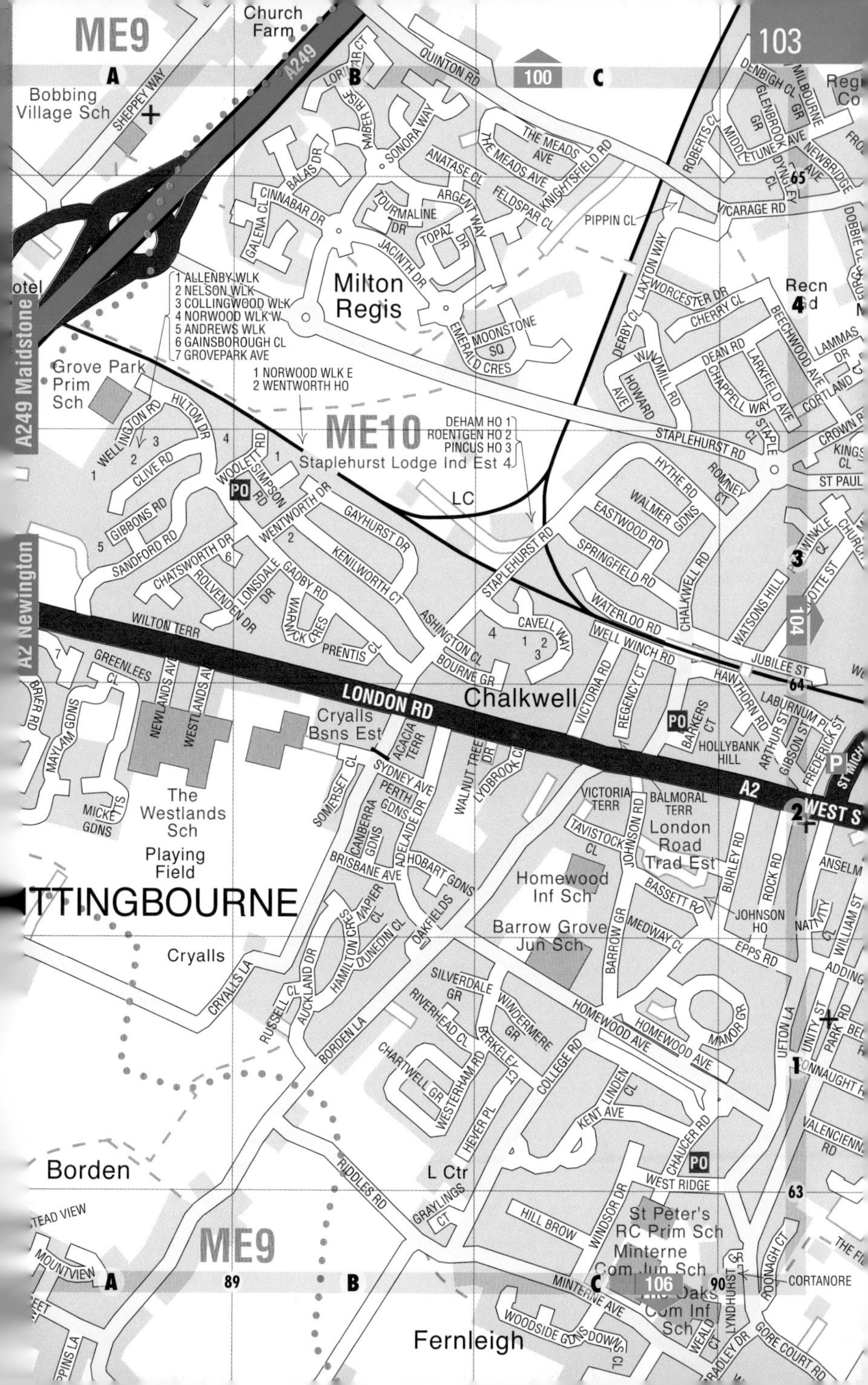
ME9
Church Farm
A
B
C
100
A249
Bobbing Village Sch
SHEPPEY WAY
QUINTON RD
LORIMAR CT
AMBER RISE
SONORA WAY
BALAS DR
CINNABAR DR
GALENA CL
TOURMALINE DR
TOPAZ DR
ARGENT WAY
JACINTH DR
ANATASE CL
THE MEADS AVE
FELDSPAR CL
KNIGHTSFIELD RD
PIPPIN CL
Milton Regis
EMERALD CRES
MOONSTONE SQ
1 ALLENBY WLK
2 NELSON WLK
3 COLLINGWOOD WLK
4 NORWOOD WLK W
5 ANDREWS WLK
6 GAINSBOROUGH CL
7 GROVEPARK AVE
1 NORWOOD WLK E
2 WENTWORTH HO
DENBIGH CL
MILBOURNE GR
GLENBROOK GR
ROBERTS CL
MIDDLETUNE AVE
NEWBRIDGE AVE
DYNGLEY CL
65
VICARAGE RD
LAXTON WAY
WORCESTER DR
CHERRY CL
BEECHWOOD AVE
Recn Gd
4
DERBY CL
WINDMILL RD
HOWARD AVE
DEAN RD
CHAPPELL WAY
LARKFIELD AVE
LAMMAS DR
CORTLAND CL
CROWN RD
STAPLE CL
STAPLEHURST RD
KINGS CL
ST PAUL
otel
A249 Maidstone
Grove Park Prim Sch
WELLINGTON RD
HILTON DR
CLIVE RD
WOOLETT RD
SIMPSON RD
ME10
DEHAM HO 1
ROENTGEN HO 2
PINCUS HO 3
Staplehurst Lodge Ind Est 4
LC
HYTHE RD
ROMNEY CT
WALMER GDNS
EASTWOOD RD
SPRINGFIELD RD
CHALKWELL RD
WATERLOO RD
WATSONS HILL
PERIWINKLE CL
CHURCH
3
COTTE ST
104
PO
GIBBONS RD
SANDFORD RD
WENTWORTH DR
GAYHURST DR
KENILWORTH CT
CHATSWORTH DR
ROLVENDEN DR
LONSDALE DR
GADBY RD
WARWICK CRES
PRENTIS CL
ASHINGTON CL
STAPLEHURST RD
CAVELL WAY
BOURNE GR
WELL WINCH RD
JUBILEE ST
64
A2 Newington
WILTON TERR
GREENLEES CL
BRIER RD
MAYLAM GDNS
NEWLANDS AVE
WESTLANDS AVE
LONDON RD
Chalkwell
VICTORIA RD
REGENCY CT
BARKERS CT
HAWTHORN RD
LABURNUM PL
ARTHUR ST
GIBSON ST
FREDERICK ST
HOLLYBANK HILL
P
ST MICHAEL
Cryalls Bsns Est
ACACIA TERR
SYDNEY AVE
SOMERSET CL
PERTH GDNS
WALNUT TREE DR
LYDBROOK CL
VICTORIA TERR
BALMORAL TERR
A2
WEST ST
2
MICKLETS GDNS
The Westlands Sch
Playing Field
CANBERRA GDNS
ADELAIDE DR
HOBART GDNS
BRISBANE AVE
TAVISTOCK CL
JOHNSON RD
London Road Trad Est
BURLEY RD
ROCK RD
ANSELM
Homewood Inf Sch
BASSETT RD
JOHNSON HO
NATIVITY CL
WILLIAM ST
ITTINGBOURNE
NAPIER CL
HAMILTON CRES
DUNEDIN CL
OAKFIELDS
Barrow Grove Jun Sch
BARROW GR
MEDWAY CL
EPPS RD
ADDING
Cryalls
CRYALLS LA
AUCKLAND DR
RUSSELL CL
BORDEN LA
SILVERDALE GR
RIVERHEAD CL
WINDERMERE GR
HOMEWOOD AVE
MANOR GR
UFTON LA
UNITY ST
PARK RD
CHARTWELL GR
WESTERHAM RD
BERKELEY CT
COLLEGE RD
KENT AVE
LINDEN CL
1
CONNAUGHT R
HEVER PL
CHAUCER RD
PO
VALENCIENNES RD
Borden
L Ctr
RIDDLES RD
GRAYLINGS CT
WEST RIDGE
63
HILL BROW
WINDSOR DR
St Peter's RC Prim Sch
Minterne Com Jun Sch
TEAD VIEW
ME9
MOUNTVIEW
A
89
B
C
106
90
CORTANORE
ROONAGH CT
LYNDHURST GR
MINTERNE AVE
The Oaks Com Inf Sch
WEALD CT
WOODSIDE GDNS
DOWNS CL
Fernleigh
BRADLEY DR
GORE COURT RD
THE FI
PIPPINS LA
STREET

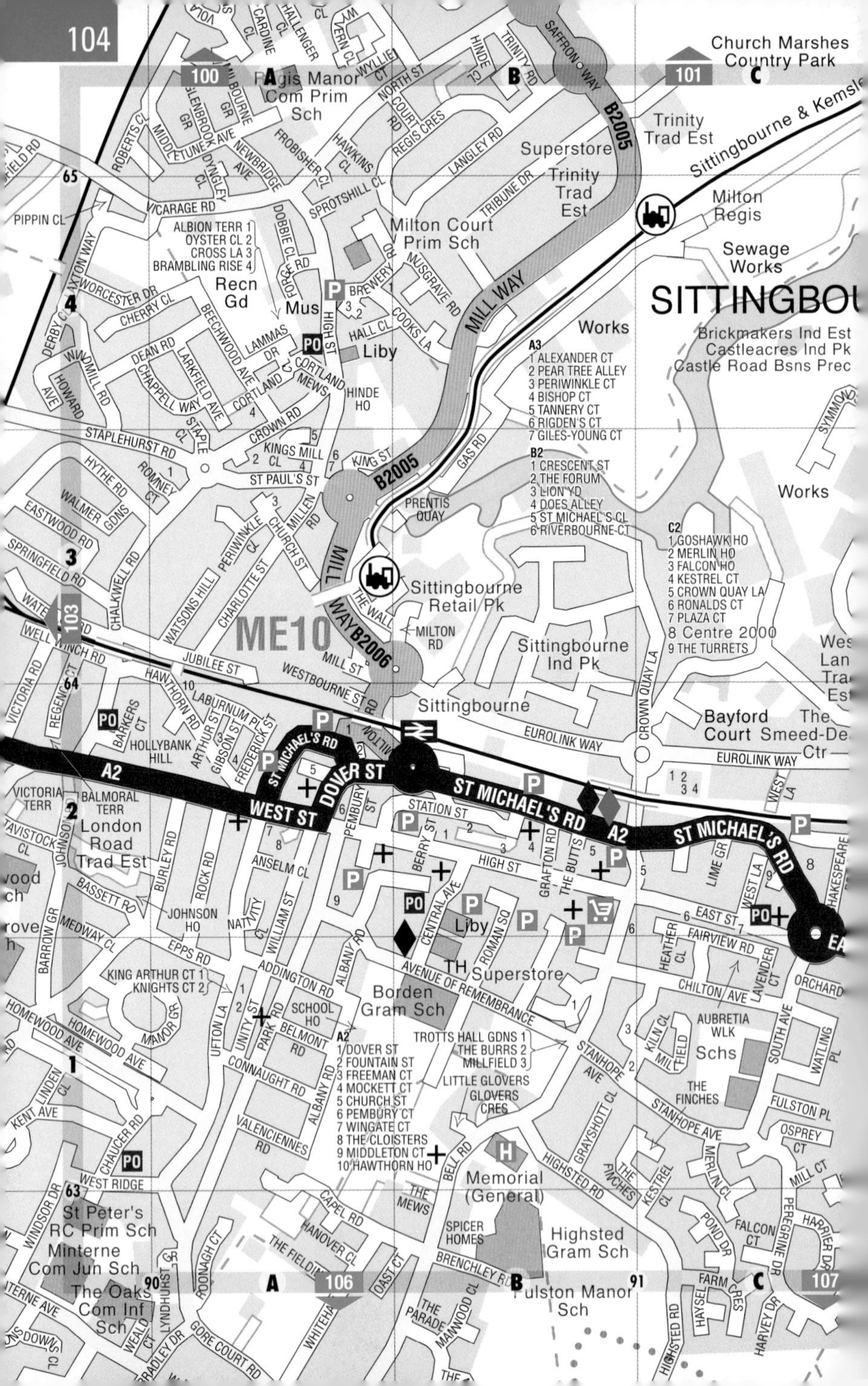
100
101
103
106
107
A
B
C
1
2
3
4
63
64
65
90
91
Church Marshes Country Park
Regis Manor Com Prim Sch
Trinity Trad Est
Superstore
Milton Regis
Sewage Works
SITTINGBOU
Brickmakers Ind Est
Castleacres Ind Pk
Castle Road Bsns Prec
Works
Milton Court Prim Sch
Recn Gd
Mus
Liby
HINDE HO
ME10
Sittingbourne Retail Pk
Sittingbourne Ind Pk
Sittingbourne
Bayford Court
The Smeed-Dean Ctr
London Road Trad Est
Borden Gram Sch
Superstore
TH
Aubretia Wlk
Schs
Memorial (General)
Highsted Gram Sch
Fulston Manor Sch
St Peter's RC Prim Sch
Minterne Com Jun Sch
The Oaks Com Inf Sch
SCHOOL HO
JOHNSON HO
SPICER HOMES
PO
P
B2005
B2006
A2
MILL WAY
SAFFRON WAY
Sittingbourne & Kemsley
ST MICHAEL'S RD
WEST ST
DOVER ST
EUROLINK WAY
CROWN QUAY LA
HIGH ST
EAST ST
VICARAGE RD
STAPLEHURST RD
CHURCH ST
JUBILEE ST
WESTBOURNE ST
AVENUE OF REMEMBRANCE
STANHOPE AVE
HIGHSTED RD
BELL RD
A3
1 ALEXANDER CT
2 PEAR TREE ALLEY
3 PERIWINKLE CT
4 BISHOP CT
5 TANNERY CT
6 RIGDEN'S CT
7 GILES-YOUNG CT
B2
1 CRESCENT ST
2 THE FORUM
3 LION YD
4 DOES ALLEY
5 ST MICHAEL'S CL
6 RIVERBOURNE CT
C2
1 GOSHAWK HO
2 MERLIN HO
3 FALCON HO
4 KESTREL CT
5 CROWN QUAY LA
6 RONALDS CT
7 PLAZA CT
8 Centre 2000
9 THE TURRETS
ALBION TERR 1
OYSTER CL 2
CROSS LA 3
BRAMBLING RISE 4
KING ARTHUR CT 1
KNIGHTS CT 2
TROTTS HALL GDNS 1
THE BURRS 2
MILLFIELD 3
A2
1 DOVER ST
2 FOUNTAIN ST
3 FREEMAN CT
4 MOCKETT CT
5 CHURCH ST
6 PEMBURY CT
7 WINGATE CT
8 THE CLOISTERS
9 MIDDLETON CT
10 HAWTHORN HO

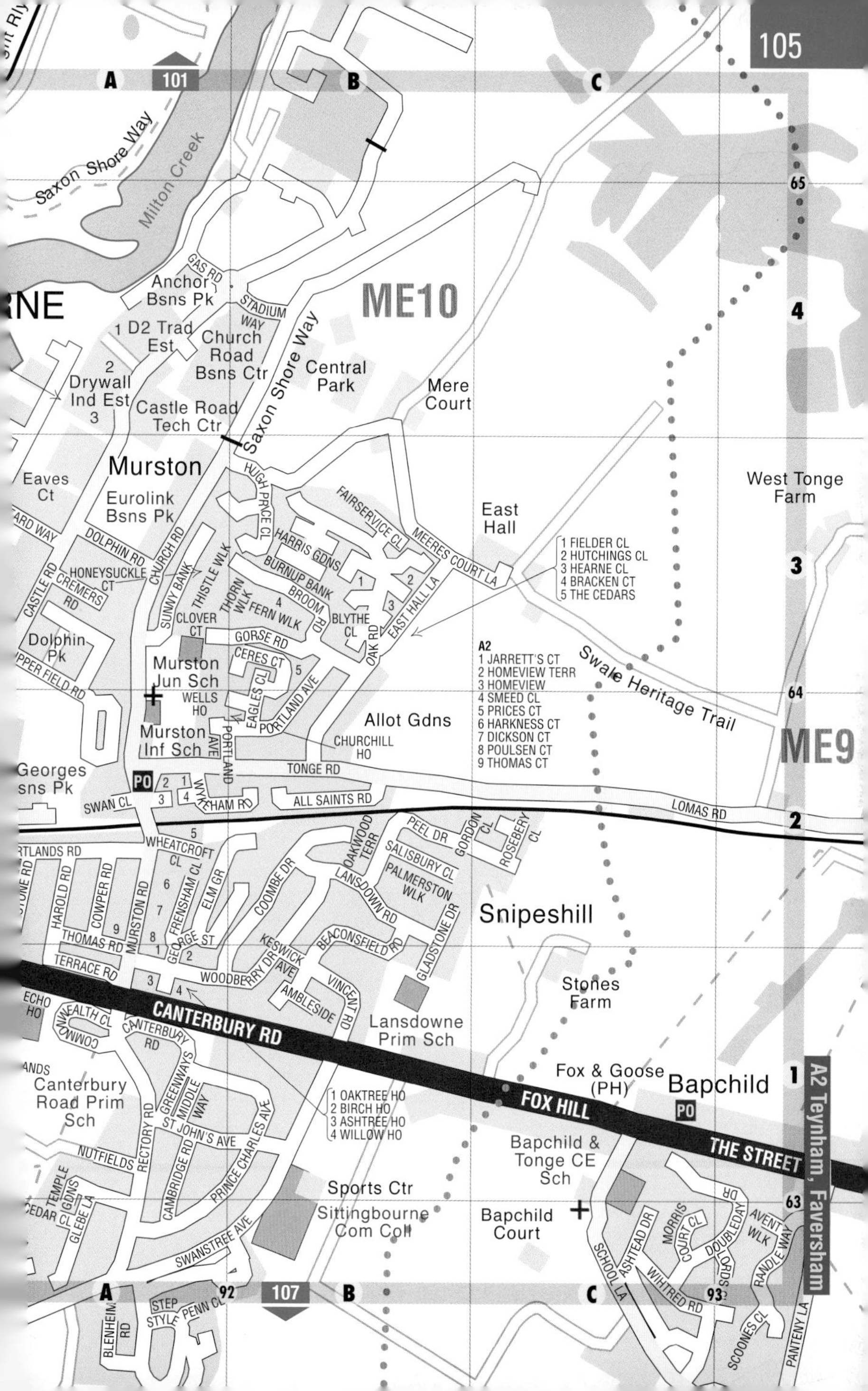
A
101
B
C
Saxon Shore Way
Milton Creek
GAS RD
Anchor
Bsns Pk
STADIUM
WAY
ME10
RNE
1 D2 Trad
Est
Church
Road
Bsns Ctr
Saxon Shore Way
Central
Park
2
Drywall
Ind Est
3
Castle Road
Tech Ctr
Mere
Court
Murston
Eaves
Ct
Eurolink
Bsns Pk
HUGH PRICE CL
FAIRSERVICE CL
East
Hall
West Tonge
Farm
HARRIS GDNS
MEERES COURT LA
DOLPHIN RD
CHURCH RD
THISTLE WLK
BURNUP BANK
1 FIELDER CL
2 HUTCHINGS CL
3 HEARNE CL
4 BRACKEN CT
5 THE CEDARS
HONEYSUCKLE
CT
SUNNY BANK
THORN
WLK
BROOM
RD
EAST HALL LA
CREMERS
RD
CASTLE RD
FERN WLK
BLYTHE
CL
CLOVER
CT
OAK RD
Dolphin
Pk
GORSE RD
A2
1 JARRETT'S CT
2 HOMEVIEW TERR
3 HOMEVIEW
4 SMEED CL
5 PRICES CT
6 HARKNESS CT
7 DICKSON CT
8 POULSEN CT
9 THOMAS CT
Swale Heritage Trail
Murston
Jun Sch
CERES CT
EAGLES CL
PORTLAND AVE
WELLS
HO
Allot Gdns
64
ME9
Murston
Inf Sch
PORTLAND
AVE
CHURCHILL
HO
Georges
Bsns Pk
TONGE RD
PO
WYKEHAM RD
SWAN CL
ALL SAINTS RD
LOMAS RD
WHEATCROFT
CL
OAKWOOD
TERR
PEEL DR
GORDON
CL
ROSEBERY
CL
SALISBURY CL
HAROLD RD
COWPER RD
MURSTON RD
FRENSHAM CL
ELM GR
COOMBE DR
LANSDOWN RD
PALMERSTON
WLK
Snipeshill
THOMAS RD
GEORGE ST
KESWICK
AVE
BEACONSFIELD RD
GLADSTONE DR
TERRACE RD
WOODBERRY DR
Stones
Farm
AMBLESIDE
VINCENT RD
ECHO
HO
COMMONWEALTH CL
CANTERBURY RD
CANTERBURY
RD
Lansdowne
Prim Sch
Fox & Goose
(PH)
Bapchild
Canterbury
Road Prim
Sch
GREENWAYS
MIDDLE
WAY
1 OAKTREE HO
2 BIRCH HO
3 ASHTREE HO
4 WILLOW HO
FOX HILL
PO
RECTORY RD
ST JOHN'S AVE
Bapchild &
Tonge CE
Sch
THE STREET
A2 Teynham, Faversham
NUTFIELDS
CAMBRIDGE RD
PRINCE CHARLES AVE
Sports Ctr
TEMPLE
GDNS
GLEBE LA
CEDAR CL
Sittingbourne
Com Coll
Bapchild
Court
ASHTEAD DR
MORRIS
COURT CL
DOUBLEDAY
DR
AVENT
WLK
RANDLE WAY
SWANSTREE AVE
SCHOOL LA
WHITRED RD
LORDS
63
A
92
107
B
C
93
STEP
STYLE
PENN CL
BLENHEIM
RD
SCOONES CL
PANTENY LA
65
4
3
2
1

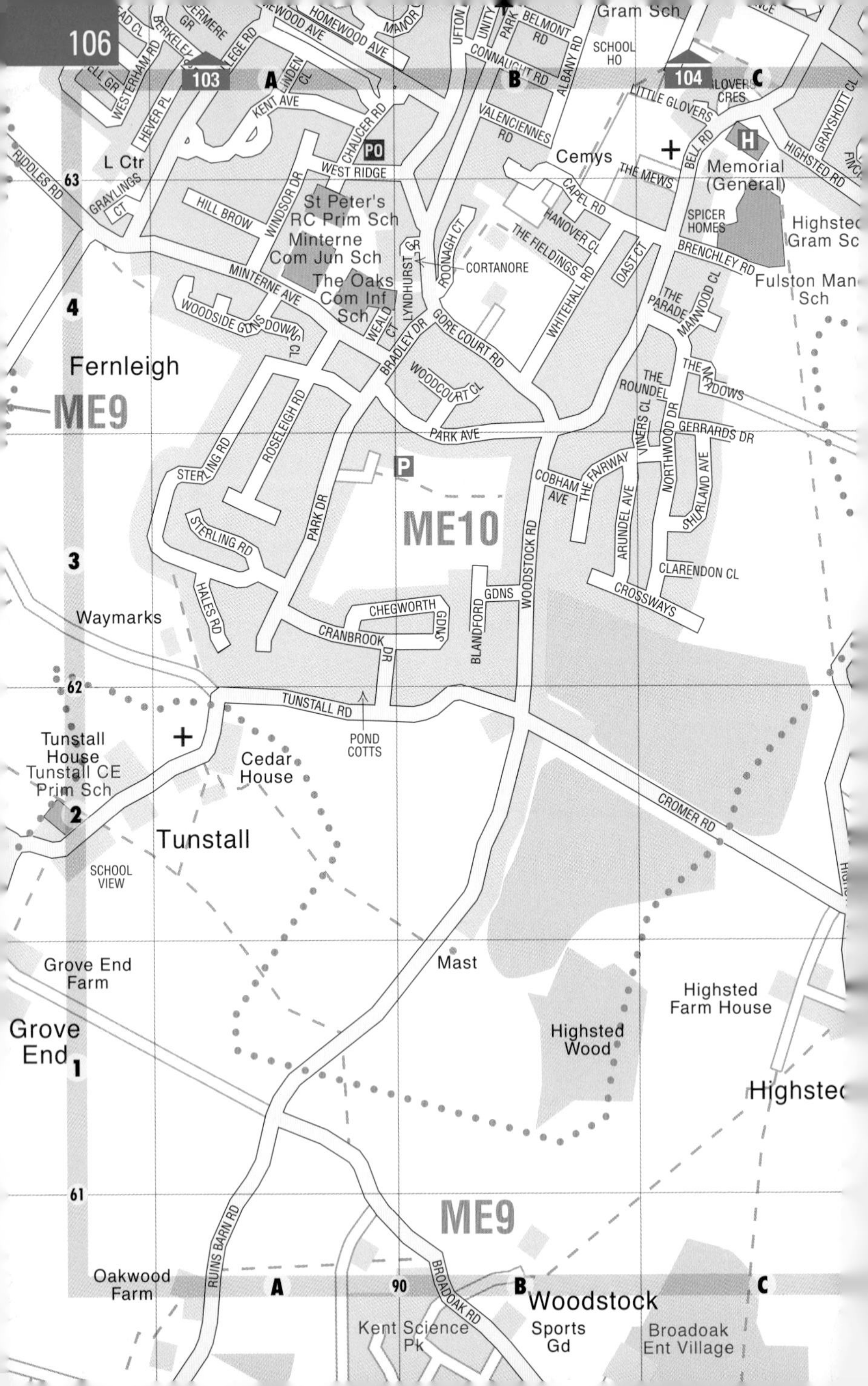
103
104
A
B
C
63
62
61
4
3
2
1
90
Fernleigh
ME9
ME10
ME9
L Ctr
Waymarks
Tunstall House
Tunstall CE Prim Sch
Cedar House
Tunstall
SCHOOL VIEW
Grove End Farm
Grove End
Mast
Highsted Wood
Highsted Farm House
Highsted
Oakwood Farm
Woodstock
Sports Gd
Kent Science Pk
Broadoak Ent Village
Cemys
Memorial (General)
SPICER HOMES
Fulston Manor Sch
SCHOOL HO
Gram Sch
St Peter's RC Prim Sch
Minterne Com Jun Sch
The Oaks Com Inf Sch
CORTANORE
POND COTTS
WEST RIDGE
CHAUCER RD
KENT AVE
LINDEN CL
HOMEWOOD AVE
MANOR
UFTON
UNITY
PARK
BELMONT RD
CONNAUGHT RD
ALBANY RD
VALENCIENNES RD
LITTLE GLOVERS
GLOVERS CRES
BELL RD
GRAYSHOTT CL
HIGHSTED RD
THE MEWS
CAPEL RD
HANOVER CL
THE FIELDINGS
WHITEHALL RD
OAST CT
BRENCHLEY RD
THE PARADE
MANWOOD CL
THE MEADOWS
THE ROUNDEL
VINERS CL
NORTHWOOD DR
GERRARDS DR
SHURLAND AVE
THE FAIRWAY
COBHAM AVE
ARUNDEL AVE
CLARENDON CL
CROSSWAYS
WOODSTOCK RD
BLANDFORD GDNS
CHEGWORTH GDNS
CRANBROOK DR
TUNSTALL RD
CROMER RD
PARK AVE
PARK DR
WOODCOURT CL
GORE COURT RD
BRADLEY DR
WEALD CT
LYNDHURST GR
ROONAGH CT
MINTERNE AVE
WOODSIDE GDNS
DOWNS CL
ROSELEIGH RD
STERLING RD
HALES RD
HILL BROW
WINDSOR DR
GRAYLINGS CT
RIDDLES RD
HEVER PL
WESTERHAM RD
BERKELEY CT
COLLEGE RD
RUINS BARN RD
BROADOAK RD

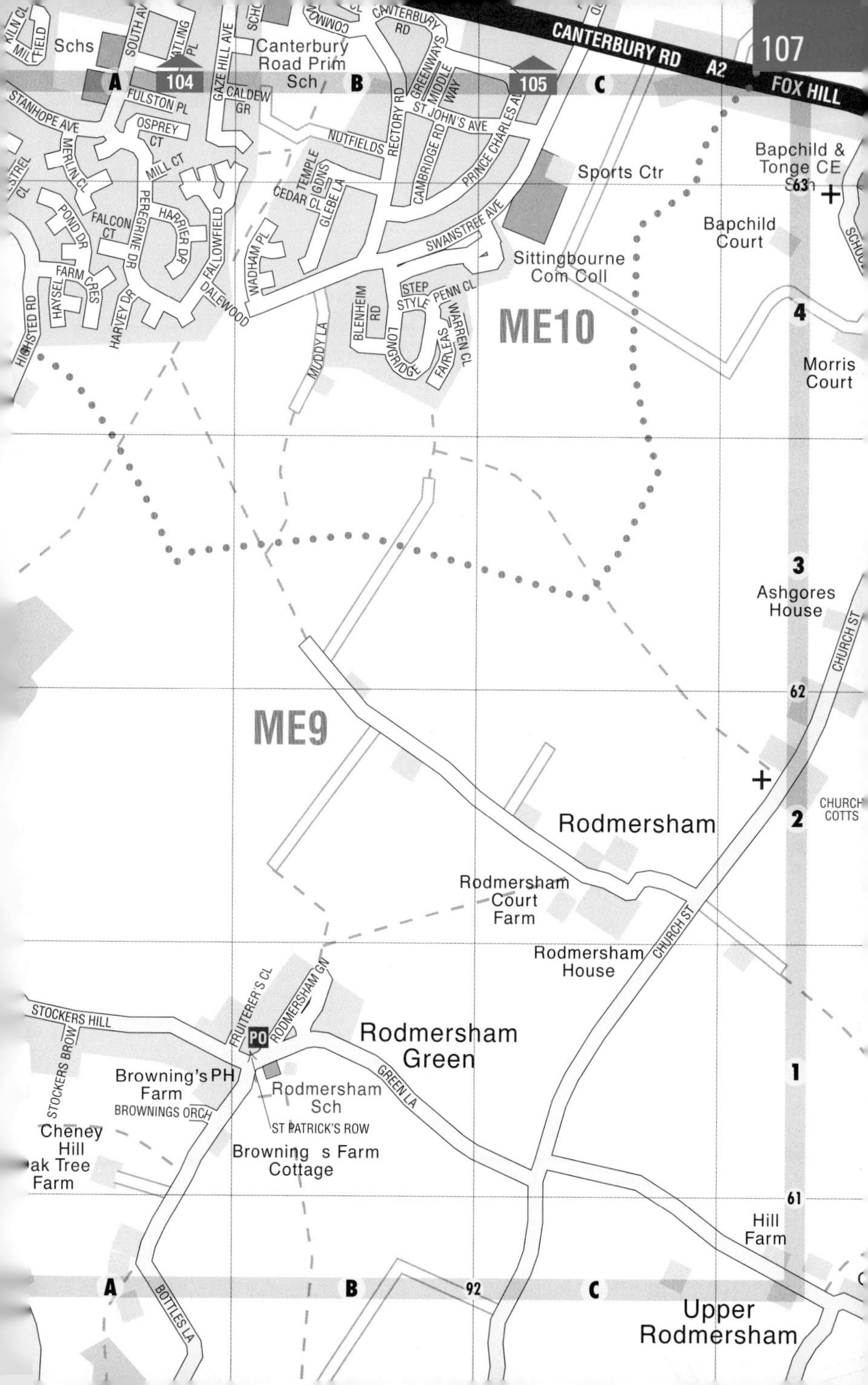
CANTERBURY RD A2
FOX HILL
Schs
Canterbury Road Prim Sch
104
105
A
B
C
FULSTON PL
STANHOPE AVE
OSPREY CT
MILL CT
CALDEW GR
GAZE HILL AVE
SOUTH AV
NUTFIELDS
RECTORY RD
GREENWAYS
MIDDLE WAY
ST JOHN'S AVE
CAMBRIDGE RD
PRINCE CHARLES AV
TEMPLE GDNS
CEDAR CL
GLEBE LA
MERLIN CL
POND DR
FALCON CT
PEREGRINE DR
HARRIER DR
FALLOWFIELD
DALEWOOD
WADHAM PL
SWANSTREE AVE
FARM CRES
HAYSEL
HARVEY DR
HIGHSTED RD
Sports Ctr
Sittingbourne Com Coll
Bapchild & Tonge CE Sch
Bapchild Court
Morris Court
63
4
BLENHEIM RD
STEP STYLE
PENN CL
WARREN CL
FAIRLEAS
LONGRIDGE
MUDDY LA
ME10
ME9
3
Ashgores House
CHURCH ST
62
2
CHURCH COTTS
Rodmersham
Rodmersham Court Farm
Rodmersham House
STOCKERS HILL
STOCKERS BROW
FRUITERER'S CL
RODMERSHAM GN
PO
Rodmersham Green
GREEN LA
Browning's PH Farm
BROWNINGS ORCH
Rodmersham Sch
ST PATRICK'S ROW
Cheney Hill
Oak Tree Farm
Browning s Farm Cottage
1
61
Hill Farm
BOTTLES LA
92
Upper Rodmersham

Index

Street names are listed alphabetically and show the locality, the Postcode district, the page number and a reference to the square in which the name falls on the map page

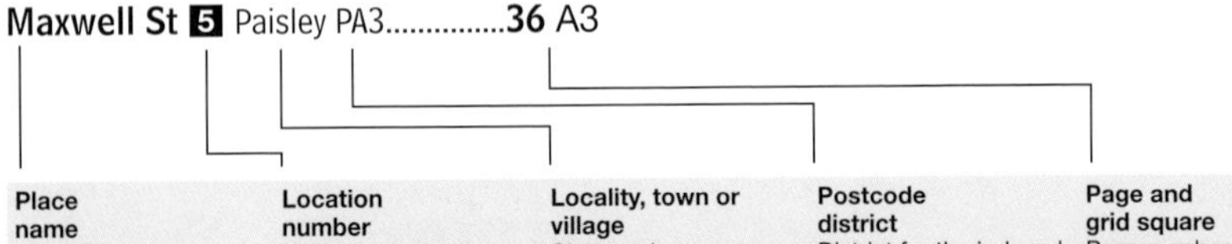

Place name
May be abbreviated on the map

Location number
Present when a number indicates the place's position in a crowded area of mapping

Locality, town or village
Shown when more than one place has the same name

Postcode district
District for the indexed place

Page and grid square
Page number and grid reference for the standard mapping

Towns and villages are listed in CAPITAL LETTERS

Public and commercial buildings are highlighted in **magenta. Places of interest** are highlighted in blue with a star*

Abbreviations used in the index

Acad	**Academy**	Ct	**Court**	Hts	**Heights**	Pl	**Place**
App	**Approach**	Ctr	**Centre**	Ind	**Industrial**	Prec	**Precinct**
Arc	**Arcade**	Ctry	**Country**	Inst	**Institute**	Prom	**Promenade**
Ave	**Avenue**	Cty	**County**	Int	**International**	Rd	**Road**
Bglw	**Bungalow**	Dr	**Drive**	Intc	**Interchange**	Recn	**Recreation**
Bldg	**Building**	Dro	**Drove**	Junc	**Junction**	Ret	**Retail**
Bsns, Bus	**Business**	Ed	**Education**	L	**Leisure**	Sh	**Shopping**
Bvd	**Boulevard**	Emb	**Embankment**	La	**Lane**	Sq	**Square**
Cath	**Cathedral**	Est	**Estate**	Liby	**Library**	St	**Street**
Cir	**Circus**	Ex	**Exhibition**	Mdw	**Meadow**	Sta	**Station**
Cl	**Close**	Gd	**Ground**	Meml	**Memorial**	Terr	**Terrace**
Cnr	**Corner**	Gdn	**Garden**	Mkt	**Market**	TH	**Town Hall**
Coll	**College**	Gn	**Green**	Mus	**Museum**	Univ	**University**
Com	**Community**	Gr	**Grove**	Orch	**Orchard**	Wk, Wlk	**Walk**
Comm	**Common**	H	**Hall**	Pal	**Palace**	Wr	**Water**
Cott	**Cottage**	Ho	**House**	Par	**Parade**	Yd	**Yard**
Cres	**Crescent**	Hospl	**Hospital**	Pas	**Passage**		
Cswy	**Causeway**	HQ	**Headquarters**	Pk	**Park**		

Index of towns, villages, streets, hospitals, industrial estates, railway stations, schools, shopping centres, universities and places of interest

20/–All

20/20 Ind Est ME16 . . 63 C4

A

Abbeville Ho ME1. . . . . 21 C4
Abbey Brewery Ct
ME19. . . . . 59 C4
Abbey Cl ME12. . . . . 99 B2
Abbey Court Specl Sch
ME2. . . . . 13 B4
Abbey Gate Cotts
ME14. . . . . 55 A2
Abbey Rd
Gillingham ME8. . . . . 25 A2
Rochester ME2. . . . . 13 C4
Abbeyview Dr ME12. . . 98 C2
Abbey Wood Rd
ME19. . . . . 59 A1
Abbots Court Rd ME3 . 11 C4
Abbots Field ME16. . . . 71 A2
Abbotts Cl ME1 . . . . 21 B3
Aberdeen Ho 9
ME15. . . . . 81 C3
Abigail Cres ME5 . . . . . 40 A1
Abingdon Mews
ME19. . . . . 59 C4
Abingdon Rd ME16 . . . 70 B2
Abinger Dr ME5 . . . . . . 41 A2
Absalom Ct ME8 . . . . . . 25 C2
Acacia Terr ME10 . . . . 103 B2
Academy Dr ME7 . . . . . 24 C1
Achilles Rd ME5 . . . . . . 40 C2
Acorn Gr ME20 . . . . 62 A4
Acorn Pl ME15. . . . . 81 C2
Acorn Rd ME7 . . . . 24 C4
Acorn St ME12. . . . . 95 A2
Acorn Wharf Rd ME1. . 14 C2
Acre Cl ME1 . . . . 22 B1
Acre Gr ME2. . . . . 37 A4
Adam Cl ME17 . . . . 88 C3
Adbert Dr ME15 . . . . . . 88 A4
Addington Rd ME10. . 104 A1
Addison Cl ME19. . . . . . 51 A1
Adelaide Dr ME10. . . . 103 B2
Adelaide Gdns ME12 . . 97 C3
Adelaide Rd ME7 . . . . . 23 C4
Aden Terr 1 ME14 . . . . 65 A3
Adisham Dr ME16. . . . . 63 B3
Adisham Gn ME10 . . . 101 A2
Admiral Ct ME7. . . . . . . 17 A2
Admiral Moore Dr
ME20. . . . . 53 A1
Admirals Wlk
Chatham ME5. . . . . 40 B3
Halfway Houses ME12 . . 97 C3
Admiral's Wlk ME4 . . . 15 C3
Admiralty Rd ME2 . . . . . 9 C1
Admiralty Terr
Chatham ME7. . . . . 16 A3
Rochester ME2. . . . . 9 C1
Admiral Way ME19. . . . 68 C1
Afghan Rd ME4 . . . . 22 B4
Ailsa Mews ME1 . . . . . . 20 C2
Aintree Ho 1 ME15 . . . 82 A2
Aintree Rd ME5. . . . . . . 40 C3
Ajax Rd ME1. . . . . 30 C4
Alamein Ave ME5 . . . . . 31 C3
Alaseun Terr ME12 . . . . 98 B1
Albany Rd
Chatham ME4 . . . . 23 B2
Gillingham ME7. . . . . 24 A4
Rochester ME1. . . . . 21 C4
Sittingbourne ME10 . . . 104 A1
Albany St ME14. . . . . . . 65 B1
Albany Terr
Chatham ME4 . . . . 22 B4
Gillingham ME7. . . . . 24 A4
Albatross Ave ME2. . . . 12 C2
Albemarle Rd ME5. . . . 40 C2
Albert Manor ME7 . . . . 16 B1
Albert Pl ME2 . . . . 14 B3
Albert Rd
Chatham ME4 . . . . 23 A3
Gillingham ME7. . . . . 23 C4
Rochester ME1. . . . . 21 C3
Albert Reed Gdns
ME15. . . . . 72 A2
Albert St ME14 . . . . 64 C2
Albion Pl
Chattenden ME2. . . . . . . 10 A3
Maidstone ME14. . . . . . . 73 A4
Newington ME9 . . . . . . 102 B3
Albion Rd ME5. . . . . 40 B2
Albion Terr ME10 . . . . 104 A4
Albury Cl ME5 . . . . 41 A2
Alchins Cotts ME17 . . . 89 A2
Alder Cl ME12 . . . . 94 B1
Aldershot Rd ME5 . . . . 32 A3
Alderwick Gr ME18 . . . 69 B3
Aldington Cl ME5 . . . . . 32 B1
Aldington Rd ME14 . . . 74 B4
Aldon Cl ME14. . . . . 65 C2
Aldon Ct ME14. . . . . 65 C2
Alexander Ct
1 Rochester ME2 . . . . . 14 B4
1 Sittingbourne
ME10. . . . . 104 A3
Alexander Gr ME18 . . . 68 C3
Alexandra Ave ME7 . . . 24 B4
Alexandra Cl ME10. . . 100 C1
Alexandra Glen ME5 . . 40 A1
Alexandra Hospl The
ME5. . . . . 48 B4
Alexandra Mews
ME12. . . . . 95 B3
Alexandra Rd
Chatham ME4 . . . . 23 B2
Sheerness ME12 . . . . . . 95 B3
Alexandra St ME14. . . . 64 C2
Alex Hughes Cl ME6 . . 45 A2
Alfred Cl ME4. . . . . 23 B2
Alfriston Gr ME19. . . . . 69 B3
Alkham Rd ME14 . . . . . 65 C1
Allenby Wlk ME10 . . . 103 A3
Allen Cl ME5 . . . . 32 C2
Allen Ct ME12 . . . . 98 B1
Allen St ME14 . . . . 65 B1
ALLINGTON. 64 A4
Allington Dr ME2 . . . . . 13 B4
Allington Gdns ME18. . 78 C3
Allington Prim Sch
ME16. . . . . 63 C3
Allington Rd ME8 . . . . . 25 A3
Allington Way ME16 . . 63 B2
Allison Ave ME7 . . . . . . 24 B1

Allnutt Mill Cl 4 ME15 . . . 72 A2
All Saints CE Prim Sch ME15 . . . 72 C3
All Saints' CE Prim Sch ME4 . . . 23 A3
All Saints Rd ME10 . . . 105 B2
Allsworth Cl ME9 . . . 102 B3
Alma Pl ME2 . . . 14 A3
Alma Rd
Eccles ME20 . . . 46 A2
Sheerness ME12 . . . 95 A3
West Malling ME19 . . . 59 A4
Alma St ME12 . . . 95 B3
Alma Street Pas ME12 . . . 95 B3
Almond Gr ME7 . . . 42 A4
Almond Ho 9 ME16 . . . 70 C3
Almonds The ME14 . . . 74 C4
Almond Tree Cl ME12 . 94 B1
Almon Pl ME1 . . . 15 A1
Alston Cl ME12 . . . 99 A3
Altbarn Ind Est ME5 . . 49 A4
Alton Ave ME19 . . . 68 C3
Amanda Cl ME5 . . . 39 C3
Amber Ct ME7 . . . 17 A1
Amber La ME17 . . . 91 C1
Amber Rise ME10 . . . 100 A1
Amber Way ME17 . . . 92 A1
Ambleside ME10 . . . 105 B1
Ambley Gn ME8 . . . 34 A4
Ambley Rd ME8 . . . 34 B4
Ambley Wood Nature Reserve* ME7, ME8 . . 34 A4
Ambrose Hill ME5 . . . 23 C2
Ames Ave ME14 . . . 74 C4
Ames Way ME18 . . . 69 A3
Amethyst Ave ME5 . . . 31 B2
Amherst Cl ME16 . . . 71 C4
Amherst Hill ME7 . . . 16 A2
Amherst Rd ME1 . . . 22 A3
Amherst Redoubt ME4 . . . 16 A1
Amies Ho ME15 . . . 89 B3
Amsbury Rd ME15, ME17 . . . 88 A2
Anatase Cl ME10 . . . 100 A1
Anchor Bsns Pk ME10 . . . 105 A4
Anchor Ho ME1 . . . 21 B4
Anchor La ME12 . . . 94 B4
Anchor Rd ME1 . . . 21 C1
Andover Wlk 12 ME15 . . . 82 A2
Andrew Broughton Way ME14 . . . 73 A4
Andrew Manor ME7 . . . 16 C2
Andrews Wlk ME10 . . 103 A3
Anerley Cl ME16 . . . 64 A3
Angel Cotts ME8 . . . 27 A2
Anglesey Ave ME15 . . . 80 B3
Anglesey Cl ME5 . . . 32 B3
Annie Rd ME6 . . . 45 A2
Annvera Ho 2 ME7 . . . 16 C3
Ansell Ave ME4 . . . 23 A1
Anselm Cl ME10 . . . 104 A2
Ansia Cl ME18 . . . 69 A3
Anson Ave M18, ME19 . 68 B3
Anson Cl ME5 . . . 32 C2
Anthonys Way ME2 . . . 15 B4
Apollo Ho ME5 . . . 32 A2
Apollo Way ME4 . . . 10 C2
Appleby Cl ME1 . . . 31 A3
Apple Cl ME6 . . . 45 B2
Applecross Cl ME1 . . . 21 B4
Appledore Ave ME12 . . 94 C1
Appledore Ct ME16 . . . 63 C3
Appledore Rd ME8 . . . 25 A3
Appleford Dr ME12 . . . 98 A3
Apple Tree Cl ME16 . . . 70 B2
Appletree Ct 5 ME8 . . 35 C4
Archer Ho ME3 . . . 3 C2
Archer Rd ME5 . . . 32 B2
Archery Cl ME3 . . . 2 B3
Archibald Ho ME14 . . . 65 A3
Archway Ct 4 ME2 . . . 14 B4
Archway Rd ME12 . . . 94 B4
Arden Bsns Pk ME2 . . . 15 B3
Arden Jun Sch ME7 . . 17 A2
Ardenlee Dr ME14 . . . 65 B1
Arden St ME7 . . . 16 C2
Arethusa Rd ME1 . . . 30 C4
Argent Way ME10 . . . 103 B4
Argyle Cl ME1 . . . 31 B4
Arlott Cl ME14 . . . 64 C2
Armada Ct ME4 . . . 22 B1
Armada Way ME4 . . . 22 C3
Armstrong Rd ME15 . . 72 C1
Armytage Cl ME3 . . . 11 B4
Arnhem Dr ME5 . . . 31 C3
Arnolde Cl ME2 . . . 15 B3
Arran Gn ME2 . . . 12 C2
Arran Rd ME15 . . . 80 B2
Arthur Rd
Gillingham ME8 . . . 35 B3
Rochester ME1 . . . 22 A3
Arthur St ME10 . . . 104 A2
Arundel Ave ME10 . . . 106 B3
Arundel Cl ME5 . . . 41 A1
Arundel St ME14 . . . 64 C2
Ascot Cl ME5 . . . 40 C2
Ascot Ho 2 ME15 . . . 82 A2
ASHBANK . . . 84 C3
Ashbank Cotts ME17 . . 84 C3
Ashbee Cl ME6 . . . 45 B3
Ashburnham Rd ME14 . . . 65 B4
Ashburn Mews ME7 . . . 24 B3
Ashby Cl ME2 . . . 37 A4
Ash Cl
Aylesford ME20 . . . 52 C1
Chatham ME5 . . . 23 C1
Gillingham ME8 . . . 25 B3
Ash Cres ME3 . . . 6 C3
Ashcroft Rd ME2 . . . 8 B2
Ashdown Cl ME16 . . . 71 C3
Ashenden Cl ME2 . . . 8 C2
Ashford Rd
Harrietsham ME17 . . . 87 A2
Maidstone, Grove Green ME14 . . . 73 C4
Maidstone ME14 . . . 75 C3
Ash Gr ME16 . . . 63 C2
Ashington Cl ME10 . . . 103 B3
Ashley Cl ME12 . . . 97 A2
Ashley Rd ME8 . . . 25 C2
Ashmead Cl ME5 . . . 40 C3
Ash Rd ME2 . . . 13 C2
Ashton Way ME19 . . . 59 C2
Ashtree Ho ME10 . . . 105 A1
Ash Tree La ME5 . . . 24 A1
Ashurst Rd ME14 . . . 65 C1
Ashwood Cl ME3 . . . 2 C3
Aspen Way 2 ME5 . . . 39 B4
Aspian Dr ME17 . . . 88 C3
Asquith Rd ME8 . . . 34 C2
Association Wlk ME1 . 30 C3
Aster Rd ME3 . . . 11 B3
Astley St ME14 . . . 72 C4
Aston Cl ME5 . . . 40 A2
Astor of Hever Com Sch The ME16 . . . 71 B3
Athelstan Gn ME17 . . . 77 B2
Athelstan Rd ME4 . . . 22 C2
Atlanta Ct ME4 . . . 22 A3
Attlee Way ME10 . . . 100 C2
Aubretia Wlk ME10 . . 104 C1
Auckland Dr ME10 . . . 103 B1
Auckland Ho 10 ME15 . . . 81 C1
Auden Rd ME20 . . . 51 B3
Audley Ave ME7 . . . 24 B1
Audley Cl ME16 . . . 63 B1
Augusta Cl 1 ME7 . . . 16 C3
Augustine Rd ME12 . . . 98 C4
Austell Manor 5 ME7 . . . 16 C2
Austen Way ME20 . . . 51 A4
Austin Cl
Gillingham ME5 . . . 24 B2
Sittingbourne ME10 . . . 101 B2
Autumn Glade ME5 . . . 49 B4
Aveling Cl ME3 . . . 5 A2
Aveling Ct 2 ME2 . . . 14 B3
Avenue of Remembrance ME10 . . . 104 B1
Avenue The
Aylesford ME20 . . . 52 C1
St Mary's Island ME4 . . . 10 C2
Averenches Rd ME14 . . 66 C1
Avery Cl ME15 . . . 72 B1
Avery La ME15, ME17 . . 83 B2
Aviemore Gdns ME14 . 74 B4
Avington Cl ME15 . . . 72 B1
Avocet Wlk ME5 . . . 41 A2
Avondale Ct ME14 . . . 66 B1
Avondale Rd ME7 . . . 17 A1
Axford Ct ME8 . . . 36 A4
AYLESFORD . . . 52 C2
Aylesford Cres ME8 . . . 25 B4
Aylesford Prim Sch ME20 . . . 52 B1
Aylesford Sch ME20 . . 52 B1
Aylesford Sta ME20 . . . 52 B2
Aylewyn Gn ME10 . . . 101 A2

B

Backfields ME1 . . . 21 B4
Back La
Maidstone ME17 . . . 91 A1
Minster (Sheppey) ME12 . . . 99 B2
Back St ME17 . . . 83 C2
Baden Rd ME7 . . . 17 A3
Bader Cres ME5 . . . 32 A3
Badger Rd ME5 . . . 40 C1
Baffin Cl ME4 . . . 22 C2
Bailey Dr ME7 . . . 25 A1
Bakenham Ho 1 ME1 . . . 21 C1
Baker St ME1 . . . 21 C3
Baker's Wlk ME1 . . . 14 C2
Bakery Cotts ME14 . . . 54 C3
Balas Dr ME10 . . . 100 A1
Baldwin Rd ME12 . . . 99 B3
Balfour Inf Sch ME1 . . 22 B1
Balfour Jun Sch ME4 . 22 B2
Balfour Rd ME4 . . . 22 B2
Ballard Bsns Pk ME2 . . 13 C1
Ballard Ind Est ME5 . . . 49 A4
Ballens Rd ME5 . . . 40 C3
Balls Cotts ME3 . . . 9 C4
Balmer Cl ME8 . . . 35 A3
Balmoral Ho 10 ME15 . 82 A1
Balmoral Rd ME7 . . . 17 A1
Balmoral Terr ME10 . . 103 C2
Bancroft La ME18 . . . 69 B2
Bangor Rd ME2 . . . 13 A2
Bank Ho ME12 . . . 95 A3
Bankside ME5 . . . 32 B4
Banks Rd ME2 . . . 14 C4
Bank St
Chatham ME4 . . . 23 B3
Maidstone ME14 . . . 72 C4
Bank View 5 ME15 . . . 72 A2
Banky Fields Cl ME8 . . 27 B1
Banky Mdw ME16 . . . 70 B3
Banner Way ME12 . . . 97 C3
Banning St ME2 . . . 14 B4
Bannister Rd ME14 . . . 65 A3
Bapchild & Tonge CE Prim Sch ME9 . . . 105 C1
Barbados Terr 2 ME14 . . . 65 A3
Barberry Ave ME5 . . . 31 B1
Barcham Ct ME15 . . . 80 A1
Bardell Terr ME1 . . . 15 A1
Barden Ct ME14 . . . 65 B1
Barfleur Manor 3 ME7 . . . 16 A2
Barfreston Cl ME15 . . . 72 B2
Bargrove Rd ME14 . . . 65 C1
Barham Cl ME15 . . . 81 C1
Barham Mews ME18 . . 79 C4
Barker Rd ME16 . . . 72 B3
Barkers Ct ME10 . . . 103 C2
Barkis Cl ME1 . . . 31 A3
Barler Pl ME11 . . . 96 B2
Barleycorn ME19 . . . 50 C1
Barleycorn Dr ME8 . . . 35 B2
Barley Fields ME14 . . . 73 C4
Barleymow Cl ME5 . . . 32 C3
Barling Cl ME5 . . . 39 A1
Barlow Cl ME8 . . . 35 B1
BARMING HEATH . . . 70 C3
Barming Prim Sch ME16 . . . 70 B2
Barming Sta ME16 . . . 62 C2
Barnaby Terr ME1 . . . 22 A2
Barnard Ct ME4 . . . 23 A2
Barncroft Cl ME14 . . . 74 B4
Barncroft Dr ME7 . . . 41 C4
Barned Ct ME16 . . . 70 B2
Barnfield ME5 . . . 32 A4
Barnhurst Rd ME14 . . . 65 A4
Barnsley Cl ME12 . . . 95 C3
Barnsole Inf Sch ME7 24 B4
Barnsole Jun Sch ME7 . . . 24 B4
Barnsole Rd ME7 . . . 24 B3
Barnwell Pl ME7 . . . 16 C1
Barnwood Cl ME1 . . . 30 B4
Baron Cl
Gillingham ME7 . . . 17 B3
Maidstone ME14 . . . 66 C1
Barrack Rd ME4 . . . 16 B4
Barrie Dr 7 ME20 . . . 51 A4
Barrier Rd ME4 . . . 15 C1
Barrington Cl ME5 . . . 31 C1
Barrowfields ME5 . . . 41 A1
Barrow Gr ME10 . . . 103 C1
Barrow Grove Jun Sch ME10 . . . 103 C1
Bartlett Cl ME5 . . . 40 C1
Bartletts Cl ME12 . . . 97 A2
Barton Hill Dr ME12 . . . 98 B1
Barton Rd
Maidstone ME15 . . . 72 C2
Rochester ME2 . . . 14 A3
Basi Cl ME2 . . . 8 C1
Basil Terr 6 ME15 . . . 72 C1
Basing Cl ME15 . . . 73 A3
Basmere Cl ME14 . . . 65 C2
Bassett Rd ME10 . . . 103 C2
Batchelor St ME4 . . . 23 A4
Bates Cl ME20 . . . 51 B3
Bath Hard ME1 . . . 15 A1
Battlesmere Rd ME3 . . . 2 B4
Baxter Way ME18 . . . 69 B3
Bay Cl ME3 . . . 11 B3
Bayford Rd ME10 . . . 104 C2
Bayswater Dr ME8 . . . 43 B4
Baywell ME19 . . . 50 C2
Beachamwell Dr ME18 . . . 69 B2
Beachfield Lodge ME12 . . . 95 A3
Beach St ME12 . . . 94 C2
Beach Terr ME12 . . . 94 C2
Beacon Cl ME8 . . . 35 A3
Beacon Hill ME5 . . . 24 A2
Beacon Hill La ME3 . . . 9 C4
Beacon Rd ME5 . . . 23 C2
Beaconsfield Ave ME7 . . . 17 B1
Beaconsfield Rd
Chatham ME4 . . . 22 C3
Maidstone ME15 . . . 72 A2
Sittingbourne ME10 . . . 105 B2
Beacons The ME17 . . . 88 B2
Beams The ME15 . . . 74 B1
BEARSTED . . . 75 A4
Bearsted Cl ME8 . . . 25 B3
Bearsted Green Bsns Ctr ME14 . . . 75 B4
Bearsted Rd ME14 . . . 66 B2
Bearsted Sta ME14 . . . 67 B1
Beatty Ave ME7 . . . 24 C4
Beatty Rd ME1 . . . 31 A4
Beaufighter Rd ME19 . 68 A3
Beaufort Ct ME2 . . . 15 B2
Beaufort Rd ME2 . . . 13 B4
Beaufort Wlk ME15 . . . 91 A4
Beaulieu Rise ME1 . . . 22 A1
Beaulieu Wlk ME16 . . . 63 C3
Beaumont Rd ME16 . . . 71 A2
Beauvoir Dr ME10 . . . 101 B2
Beauworth Pk ME15 . . 81 C4
Beaver Rd ME16 . . . 63 B3
Beckenham Dr ME16 . . 64 A3
Beckley Mews ME5 . . . 31 C1
Beckley Rd ME12 . . . 95 C3
Becksbourne Cl ME14 . . . 65 A4
Beckworth Pl ME16 . . . 71 A2
Beddow Way ME20 . . . 53 C3
Bedford Ave ME8 . . . 26 A1
Bedford Pl ME16 . . . 72 A4
Bedgebury Cl
Maidstone ME14 . . . 65 C2
Rochester ME1 . . . 31 A4
Bedson Wlk ME8 . . . 27 B1
Bedwin Cl ME1 . . . 31 A3
Beech Dr ME16 . . . 63 C1
Beechen Bank Rd ME5 . . . 40 A1
Beeches The
Aylesford ME20 . . . 52 C1
Chatham ME5 . . . 40 A4
Beech Gr ME3 . . . 6 C4
Beech Hurst Cl ME15 . . 73 A2
Beeching Rd ME5 . . . 40 B3
Beechings Gn ME8 . . . 25 C3
Beechings Way ME8 . . 25 C3
Beechings Way Ind Ctr ME8 . . . 25 B4
Beechmore Dr ME5 . . . 40 A2
Beech Rd
East Malling ME19 . . . 60 C3
Hoo St Werburgh ME3 . . 11 B3
Rochester ME2 . . . 13 C2
Beechwood Ave
Gillingham ME5 . . . 24 A2
Sittingbourne ME10 . . . 104 A4
Beechwood Rd ME16 . 70 B3
Begonia Ave ME8 . . . 25 C2
Beke Rd ME8 . . . 43 A4
Belfast Ho 14 ME15 . . . 81 C3
Belgrave Rd ME12 . . . 97 A2
Belgrave St ME20 . . . 46 A2
Bell Cres
Burham ME1 . . . 46 A4
Burham ME1 . . . 46 B4
Bellevue Rd ME12 . . . 99 A2
Bell Farm Gdns ME16 . 70 B2
Bellflower Ave ME12 . . 98 B1
Bellgrove Ct ME5 . . . 48 B4
Bellingham Way ME20 . . . 51 C3
Bell La
Burham ME1 . . . 46 A4
Burham ME1 . . . 46 B4
Chatham ME14 . . . 48 C3
Larkfield ME20 . . . 51 C2
Maidstone ME14 . . . 67 A1
Bell Mdw ME15 . . . 81 C2
Bell Rd
Maidstone ME15 . . . 81 C1
Sittingbourne ME10 . . . 104 B1
Bell Sh Ctr ME10 . . . 104 B2
Bell's La ME3 . . . 5 B2
Bell Wood Prim Sch ME15 . . . 81 C1
Belmont Cl ME16 . . . 70 B2
Belmont Ct 9 ME15 . . . 73 A4
Belmont Rd
Gillingham ME7 . . . 23 C4
Halfway Houses ME12 . . 97 C3
Sittingbourne ME10 . . . 104 A1
Belvedere Ho 9 ME15 . . . 82 A1
Bendon Way ME8 . . . 35 A4
Benedict Cl ME2 . . . 37 B4
Benenden Manor ME8 . . . 25 B3
Benenden Rd ME2 . . . 8 C1
Bentham Sq ME12 . . . 94 B4
Bentley Cl
Aylesford ME20 . . . 53 A1
Chatham ME5 . . . 41 A2
Bentlif Cl ME16 . . . 64 A1
Berber Rd ME2 . . . 14 B4
Berengrave La ME8 . . . 26 C2
Berengrave Nature Reserve* ME8 . . . 27 A3
Beresford Ave ME1 . . . 22 B2
Beresford Rd
Gillingham ME7 . . . 24 A4
Kit's Coty ME20 . . . 47 B3
Beresfords Hill ME17 . . 90 A4
Bergland Pk ME2 . . . 15 A4
Berkeley Cl ME1 . . . 31 A4
Berkeley Ct ME10 . . . 103 C1
Berkeley Mount 8 ME4 . . . 22 C4
Berkshire Cl ME5 . . . 32 C4
Berridge Rd ME12 . . . 95 A3
Berry Rd ME3 . . . 11 B3
Berry St ME10 . . . 104 B2
Berwyn Gr ME15 . . . 80 B2
Best St ME4 . . . 22 C4
Bethersden Ct ME15 . . 82 A3
Betjeman Cl ME20 . . . 51 A3
Betony Gdns ME14 . . . 66 C1
Betsham Rd ME15 . . . 82 A2

Bettescombe Rd ME8 . 35 B3
Beverley Cl ME8 . . . . . . 35 C4
Beverley Rd
Maidstone ME16. . . . . . . 70 B2
Maidstone ME16. . . . . . . 70 C2
Bicknor Rd ME15 . . . . . 91 B4
Biddenden Cl ME15 . . . 74 B3
Bilberry Cl ME14. . . . . . 66 B1
Bill Street Rd
Rochester ME2. . . . . 8 C1
1 Rochester ME2 . . . . . 14 C4
Bilsington Cl ME5. . . . . 32 B1
Bingham Rd ME2 . . . . . . 8 C1
Bingley Cl ME6 . . . . 45 A4
Bingley Rd 1 ME1 . . . . 22 B4
Binland Gr ME5. . . . . . . 31 A1
Binnacle Rd ME1 . . . . . 30 C4
Birch Cres ME20 . . . . . . 62 A4
Birch Dr ME5 . . . . 41 A1
Birchfield Cl ME15 . . . . 80 C2
Birchfields ME5 . . . . . . 40 A3
Birch Gr ME7 . . . . 42 A4
Birch Ho
6 Maidstone ME16. . . . 70 C3
Sheerness ME12 . . . . . . 94 C2
Sittingbourne ME10 . . . 105 A1
Birchington Cl ME14 . . 65 C1
Bircholt Rd ME15 . . . . . 91 B4
Birch Rd ME3. . . . . 11 B3
Birch Tree Way ME15 . . 73 A3
Birchwood Rd ME16 . . 63 C1
Birkdale Ct 3 ME16 . . 72 A4
Birkhall Cl ME5. . . . . . . 32 A1
BIRLING. 44 A2
Birling Ave
Gillingham ME8. . . . . 26 B1
Maidstone ME14. . . . . . . 74 C4
Birling Cl ME14 . . . . 74 C4
Birling Pk ME19 . . . . . . 44 A1
Birling Rd
Leybourne ME19. . . . . . . 50 A3
Snodland ME6. . . . . 45 A3
Birnam Sq 1 ME16 . . . 72 A4
Bishopbourne Gn
ME8. . . . . 25 B4
Bishop Ct 4 ME10 . . . 104 A3
Bishops Cl ME18. . . . . . 78 B2
Bishops Way ME15. . . . 72 B4
Bishops Wlk ME1 . . . . . 14 C1
Blacklands
East Malling ME19 . . . . . 60 C3
East Malling ME19 . . . . . 61 C4
Blacklands Dr ME19 . . 61 C4
Blackman Cl ME3. . . . . . 5 A3
Blackmanstone Way
ME16. . . . . 63 B3
Black Rock Gdns
ME7. . . . . 42 B4
Blacksmith Dr ME14 . . 66 A1
Blackthorn Ave ME5 . . 40 A3
Blackthorn Dr ME20 . . 51 C2
Blackthorne Rd ME8 . . 36 B4
Blainey Ho ME3. . . . . 3 C2
Blake Dr 3 ME20 . . . . . 51 A4
Blakeney Cl ME14. . . . . 75 A4
Blaker Ave ME1. . . . . . . 22 B1
Blandford Gdns
ME10. . . . . 106 B3
Blatcher Cl ME12 . . . . . 98 C2
Blatchford Cl ME19 . . . 51 A1
Bleakwood Rd 6
ME5. . . . . 31 C1
Blean Rd ME8 . . . . 25 C2
Blean Sq ME14 . . . . 65 C2
Blendon Rd ME14. . . . . 65 C1
Blenheim Ave ME4. . . . 22 B2
Blenheim Cl ME15 . . . . 74 B3
Blenheim Ct ME4 . . . . . 22 B3
Blenheim Rd ME10. . . 107 B4
Bligh Inf Sch ME2 . . . . 12 C3
Bligh Jun Sch ME2 . . . 12 C3
Bligh Way ME2 . . . . 13 A2
Blind La
Bredhurst ME7. . . . . 42 A1
Gillingham ME7. . . . . 41 C1
Blockmakers Ct ME4 . . 23 B1
Bloomsbury Wlk 2
ME15. . . . . 72 C4
Bloors La ME8. . . . . 26 A1
Bloors Wharf Rd ME7 . 26 C4
Blowers Wood Gr
ME7. . . . . 42 B3
Bluebell Cl ME7 . . . . . . 17 C2
BLUEBELL HILL 39 A1
Blue Boar La ME1. . . . . 15 A1
BLUE TOWN 94 C2
Bluett St ME14. . . . . 65 A1
Blythe Cl ME10 . . . . . . 105 B3
Blythe Rd ME15. . . . . . . 73 A4
Boarley Ct ME14 . . . . . . 55 A1
Boarley La ME14 . . . . . . 55 A2
Boathouse Rd ME12 . . 94 A4
Bockingford La ME15 . 80 A4
Bocton Ho ME17. . . . . . 90 A3
Bodiam Cl ME8 . . . . 25 C3
Bodiam Ct ME16. . . . . . 72 B3
Bodkins Cl ME17. . . . . . 81 B1
Bodsham Cres ME15 . . 75 A3
Bogarde Dr ME2. . . . . . . 8 B2
Boley Hill ME1. . . . . 14 C2
Bolingbroke Ho
ME16. . . . . 72 A3
Bolner Cl ME5 . . . . 39 C2
Bombay Ho 1 ME15 . . 81 C1
Bondfield Rd ME19 . . . 61 C4
Bond Rd ME8. . . . . 35 B1
Bonetta Ct ME12. . . . . . 94 C1
Bonham Dr ME10 . . . . 105 A3
Bonnington Gn ME8 . . 25 C3
Bonnington Rd ME14 . 65 C2
Boorman's Mews
ME18. . . . . 78 C3
Bootham Cl ME2. . . . . . 13 A1
Booth Rd ME4 . . . . 22 C2
BORDEN 103 A1
Borden Gram Sch
ME10. . . . . 104 B1
Borden La ME10,
ME9. . . . . 103 B1
Borough Rd
Gillingham ME7. . . . . 24 A4
Queenborough ME11 . . . 96 C1
BORSTAL. 21 B2
Borstal HM Prison &
Youth Custody Ctr
ME1. . . . . 21 B1
Borstal Manor Com Sch
ME1. . . . . 20 C2
Borstal Mews ME1. . . . 21 A2
Borstal Rd ME1. . . . . . . 21 B3
Borstal St ME1 . . . . 21 A2
Boston Gdns ME8. . . . . 25 C1
Boston Rd ME5 . . . . 40 C2
Bottlescrew Hill
ME17. . . . . 90 A4
Boughton Cl ME8 . . . . . 25 B3
BOUGHTON GREEN . . 90 A3
Boughton La ME15. . . . 80 C2
BOUGHTON
MONCHELSEA 90 A3
Boughton Monchelsea
Prim Sch ME17 . . . . . . 90 A2
Boughton Par ME15. . . 80 B3
Boundary Cl ME12 . . . . 99 C2
Boundary Rd ME4 . . . . 22 B3
Bounds The ME20. . . . . 52 C1
Bourne Ct ME1 . . . . 15 A1
Bourne Gr ME10 . . . . . 103 B3
Bourneside Terr
ME17. . . . . 77 C2
Bournewood Cl ME15 . 74 B1
Bournville Ave ME4 . . . 22 C1
Bovarde Ave ME19 . . . . 69 B3
Bower Cl ME16 . . . . 72 A4
Bower Gn ME5. . . . . 40 C1
Bower Grove Sch
ME16. . . . . 71 A2
Bower La ME16 . . . . 72 A3
Bower Mount Rd
ME16. . . . . 71 C4
Bower Pl ME16 . . . . 72 A3
Bowers Ho ME7 . . . . . . 17 B3
Bower St ME16 . . . . 72 A4
Bower Terr ME16 . . . . . 72 A3
Bowes Rd ME2 . . . . 14 B4
Bow Hill ME18. . . . . 78 B1
Bowman Cl ME5 . . . . . . 32 C1
Bow Rd ME18. . . . . 78 C3
Bow Terr ME18. . . . . 78 C3
BOXLEY 56 B2
Boxley Cl
Maidstone ME14. . . . . . . 65 B4
West Minster ME12 . . . . 96 C4
Boxley Rd
Chatham ME5 . . . . 40 B2
Maidstone ME14. . . . . . . 65 B3
Boxmend Ind Est
ME15. . . . . 91 B3
Brabourne Ave ME8. . . 25 C3
Bracken Ct ME10 . . . . 105 B3
Bracken Hill ME5 . . . . . 40 A1
Bracken Lea ME5 . . . . . 23 C1
Brackley Cl ME14 . . . . . 65 C1
Brackwood Cl ME8 . . . 35 A1
Bradbourne La ME20. . 51 C1
Bradbourne Parkway
ME19. . . . . 51 B1
Braddick Cl ME15. . . . . 80 C2
Bradfields Ave ME5 . . . 31 C1
Bradfields Ave W
ME5. . . . . 31 C1
Bradfields Sch ME5. . . 32 A2
Bradfords Cl ME4 . . . . . 10 B2
Bradley Dr ME10. . . . . 106 B4
Bradley Rd ME2 . . . . . . 28 A1
Braeburn Way ME19 . . 69 B3
Braes The ME3. . . . . 6 C3
Braithwaite Ct ME7 . . . 18 A1
Brake Ave ME5 . . . . 31 B1
Bramble Cl ME16 . . . . . 71 A3
Brambledown ME5 . . . 32 B4
Bramblefield La ME10,
ME9. . . . . 100 C3
Brambletree Cotts
ME1. . . . . 20 B2
Brambletree Cres
ME1. . . . . 20 C2
Brambling Rise
ME10. . . . . 104 A4
Bramley Cl
Gillingham ME8. . . . . 36 B4
Newington ME9 . . . . . . 102 A2
Bramley Cres ME15 . . . 74 B3
Bramley Gdns ME17. . . 88 B3
Bramley Rd ME6. . . . . . 45 B4
Bramley Rise ME2 . . . . 13 B4
Bramley Way ME19 . . . 68 C2
Bramshott Cl ME16 . . . 63 C2
Bramston Rd ME12 . . . 99 A2
Bransgore Cl ME8 . . . . 35 A3
Brasenose Rd ME7. . . . 24 B4
Brasier Ct ME12 . . . . . . 98 B1
Brassey Dr ME20. . . . . . 62 A4
Brasted Ct ME2. . . . . 8 A1
Braunstone Dr ME16 . . 64 A3
Bray Gdns ME15 . . . . . . 80 A1
Bream Cl ME20 . . . . 45 B1
Brecon Chase ME12. . . 99 A3
Bredgar Cl ME14. . . . . . 65 C1
Bredgar Rd ME8 . . . . . . 25 B4
BREDHURST. 42 B1
Bredhurst CE Prim Sch
ME7. . . . . 42 B1
Bredhurst Cl ME12. . . . 96 C4
Bredhurst Rd ME8 . . . . 42 B4
Brenchley Cl ME1. . . . . 22 A2
Brenchley Rd
Gillingham ME8. . . . . 25 B2
Maidstone ME15. . . . . . . 72 B2
Sittingbourne ME10 . . . 106 C4
Brendon Ave ME5. . . . . 40 A3
Brennan Ct ME7 . . . . . . 17 A2
Brent Cl ME5 . . . . 31 B1
Brenzett Cl ME5 . . . . . . 32 B1
Breton Rd ME1 . . . . 21 C2
Brett Wlk ME8. . . . . 43 A4
Brewer Rd ME3. . . . . 2 B3
Brewer St ME14 . . . . . . 65 A1
Brewery Rd ME10. . . . 104 A4
Briar Cl ME20. . . . . 51 B2
Briar Dale ME3 . . . . 6 B4
Briar Fields ME14. . . . . 66 B1
Brice Rd ME3. . . . . 6 B3
Brick Field View ME2. . . 8 C1
Brickmakers Ind Est
ME10. . . . . 105 A4
Bridge Ho ME1 . . . . 21 B4
Bridge Mill Way
ME15. . . . . 71 C2
Bridge Pl ME20 . . . . 53 A2
Bridge Rd
Gillingham ME7. . . . . 16 C3
Bridge Rd *continued*
Rochester ME1. . . . . 21 C2
Sheerness ME12 . . . . . . 94 C2
Bridgeside Mews
ME15. . . . . 72 A2
Bridge St ME15 . . . . 80 A1
Bridgewater Pl ME19 . 50 C2
Bridgewater Rd
ME12. . . . . 94 C1
Brielle Way
Queenborough ME11,
ME12. . . . . 96 B3
Sheerness ME12 . . . . . . 94 B3
Brier Cl ME5. . . . . 32 C4
Brier Rd ME10 . . . . 103 A2
Bright Rd 3 ME4 . . . . . 23 B2
Brindle Way ME5 . . . . . 40 C1
Brisbane Ave ME10 . . 103 B2
Brisbane Rd ME4 . . . . . 23 A3
Brishing Cl ME15 . . . . . 81 C1
Brishing La ME17 . . . . . 90 C4
Brishing Rd ME15 &
ME17. . . . . 91 B3
Brissenden Cl ME2. . . . 10 A3
Bristol Cl ME2 . . . . 13 A1
Britannia Bsns Pk
ME20. . . . . 62 B3
Britannia Cl
Halling ME2 . . . . 37 A4
Sittingbourne ME10 . . . 100 C1
Briton Ct ME12 . . . . 94 C1
Britton St ME7. . . . . 16 B1
Broader La ME14 . . . . . 57 C2
Broadfield Rd ME15. . . 80 B4
Broadlands Dr ME5 . . . 40 B4
Broadmere Terr
ME16. . . . . 71 C3
Broadoak ME19. . . . . . . 50 C2
Broadoak Ave ME15. . . 80 B4
Broad St ME12. . . . . 94 C2
BROAD STREET. 4 B1
Broadview Ave ME8. . . 35 B4
Broadwater Rd ME19 . 60 A2
Broadway
Gillingham ME8. . . . . 25 A3
Maidstone ME14. . . . . . . 72 B4
Sheerness ME12 . . . . . . 95 A3
Broadway The ME12 . . 98 C3
Broadwood Rd ME3. . . 10 A4
Brockbank Cl ME5 . . . . 40 A1
Brockenhurst Ave
ME15. . . . . 73 B1
Brockenhurst Cl ME8 . 34 C3
Brogden Cres ME17. . . 84 A3
Bromley Cl ME5 . . . . . . 40 B4
BROMPTON 16 A1
Brompton Farm Rd
ME2. . . . . 8 A2
Brompton Hill ME4 . . . 15 C2
Brompton La ME2 . . . . 14 A4
Brompton Rd ME7 . . . . 16 B2
Brompton-Westbrook
Prim Sch ME7 . . . . 16 A1
Bronington Cl ME5 . . . 32 A1
Bronte Cl ME20. . . . . . . 51 A3
Brookbank ME14 . . . . . 65 A4
Brooker Cl ME17. . . . . . 81 B1
Brookes Pl ME9. . . . . . 102 B3
Brookfield Ave ME20 . . 51 B4
Brookfield Inf Sch
ME20. . . . . 51 B2
Brookfield Jun Sch
ME20. . . . . 51 B2
Brook La ME6 . . . . 45 B2
Brooklands Rd ME20 . . 51 B4
Brooklyn Paddock
ME7. . . . . 17 A2
Brookmead Rd ME3. . . . 2 B3
Brook Rd ME20 . . . . 51 A4
Brookside ME3 . . . . 5 B1
Brooks Pl ME14. . . . . . . 72 C4
Brook St ME6. . . . . 45 C4
Brook The ME4 . . . . 23 A4
Broomcroft Rd ME8. . . 26 C2
BROOMFIELD. 85 B1
Broom Hill Rd ME2 . . . 13 C4
Broom Rd ME10 . . . . . 105 B3
Broomscroft Cotts
ME18. . . . . 69 B1
Broomshaw Rd ME16 . 70 B3
Brownelow Copse
ME5. . . . . 40 B1
Brownhill Cl ME5 . . . . . 40 A4
Browning Cl 6 ME20 . 51 A4
Brownings Orch
ME9. . . . . 107 A1
Brown St ME8 . . . . 26 C1
Brucks The ME18 . . . . . 78 C3
Bruges Ct ME10 . . . . . 101 A3
Brunel Way ME4. . . . . . 16 A3
Brunswick House Prim
Sch ME16 . . . . 64 B1
Brunswick St E ME15 . 72 C3
Brunswick St ME15 . . . 72 C3
Bryant Cl ME18 . . . . 78 B2
Bryant Rd ME2 . . . . 14 A3
Bryant St ME4 . . . . 23 A3
Bryony Sch ME8. . . . . . 35 C1
Buckingham Rd ME7. . 17 A1
Buckingham Row
ME15. . . . . 81 C3
Buckland Cl ME5 . . . . . 40 A2
Buckland Hill ME16 . . . 64 B1
Buckland La ME16 . . . . 64 A2
Buckland Pl ME16 . . . . 72 A4
Buckland Rd
Cliffe Woods ME3. . . . . . . 2 A4
Maidstone ME16. . . . . . . 72 A4
Buckthorne Ho ME12 . 98 B1
Buckthorne Rd ME12 . 98 B1
Buddle Dr ME12 . . . . . . 97 C4
Bulldog Rd ME5 . . . . . . 40 B2
Buller Rd ME4 . . . . 22 C2
Bull Fields ME6. . . . . . . 45 B4
Bull La
Eccles ME20 . . . . 46 A1
Eccles ME20. . . . . 46 B2
Bull Orch ME16 . . . . 70 B2
Bull Rd ME19 . . . . 44 A1
Bulrush Cl ME5 . . . . 39 C3
Bumbles Cl ME1 . . . . . . 31 A3
Bunters Hill Rd ME3 . . . 8 B4
Burberry La ME17. . . . . 84 C1
Burdock Ct ME16 . . . . . 70 C3
Burdock Ho 6 ME15. . 81 B4
Burgess Hall Dr
ME17. . . . . 84 A2
Burgess Rd ME2 . . . . . . 14 B3
Burghclere Dr ME16 . . 71 A2
Burgoyne Ct ME14 . . . . 64 C3
BURHAM. 46 B4
Burham CE Prim Sch
ME1. . . . . 46 A4
Burial Ground La
ME15. . . . . 72 A1
Burkeston Cl ME10. . . 101 B2
Burleigh Cl ME2 . . . . . . 13 B4
Burleigh Dr ME14. . . . . 55 A1
Burley Rd ME10. . . . . . 104 A2
Burlington Gdns ME8 . 43 B4
Burmarsh Cl ME5 . . . . . 32 B1
Burma Way ME5 . . . . . . 31 C2
Burnham Cl ME10. . . . 100 C2
Burnham Wlk ME8. . . . 43 B3
Burns Rd ME16 . . . . 71 B2
Burn's Rd ME7. . . . . 16 C3
Burntash Rd ME20 . . . . 62 C4
Burnt House Cl ME2 . . . 8 C2
Burnt Oak Terr ME7 . . . 17 A2
Burnup Bank ME10 . . 105 B3
Burritt Mews ME1 . . . . 21 C3
Burrs The ME10. . . . . . 104 B1
Burrstock Way ME8. . . 27 B2
Burston Rd ME17 . . . . . 88 A2
Burton Cl ME3. . . . . 8 C3
Busbridge Rd ME6. . . . 44 C3
Bushmeadow Rd
ME8. . . . . 26 C2
Bush Rd ME2 . . . . 19 B2
Bush Row ME20 . . . . . . 53 B3
Buttermere Cl ME7 . . . 18 A1
Butt Haw Cl ME3. . . . . . . 5 B1
Button Ho ME3 . . . . 3 C2
Button La ME15. . . . . . . 75 A2
Butts The ME10 . . . . . 104 B2
Buxton Cl
Chatham ME5 . . . . 41 A1
Loose ME15 . . . . 80 B4
Bychurch Pl 7 ME15. . 72 C3
Byron Prim Sch ME7. . 23 C3
Byron Rd
Gillingham ME7. . . . . 23 C3
Maidstone ME14. . . . . . . 65 B3
Bythorne Ct ME8 . . . . . 27 B1

C

Cadnam Cl ME2 . . . . . . 13 B4
Caernarvon Dr ME15 . . 72 B1
Cagney Cl ME3 . . . . 8 C3
Calcutta Ho [3] ME15 . . 81 C1
Caldecote Cl ME8 . . . . . 27 B1
Calder Rd ME14 . . . . . . 64 B3
Caldew Ave ME8 . . . . . . 25 C1
Caldew Gr ME10 . . . . . 104 C1
Caledonian Ct ME8 . . . 35 B4
Calehill Cl ME14 . . . . . . 65 C2
Callams Cl ME8 . . . . 35 A2
Callaways La ME9 . . . 102 B3
Callisto Ct ME16 . . . . . . 71 C3
Callis Way ME8 . . . . 35 A1
Camborne Manor [2] ME7 . . . . 16 C2
Cambria Ave ME1 . . . . . 20 C2
Cambridge Cres ME15 . . . . 81 B3
Cambridge Rd
Gillingham ME8 . . . . 34 C2
Rochester ME2 . . . . 14 A4
Sittingbourne ME10 . . . 105 A1
Cambridge Terr [1] ME4 . . . . 22 C4
Camden Cl ME5 . . . . . . 32 B1
Camden Rd ME7 . . . . . . 17 A3
Camden St ME14 . . . . . 65 A1
Camellia Cl ME8 . . . . . . 35 A3
Cameron Cl ME5 . . . . . . 32 B4
Camomile Dr ME14 . . . 66 C1
Campbell Ho ME3 . . . . . 3 C2
Campbell Rd ME15 . . . . 72 C3
Camperdown Manor [5] ME7 . . . . 16 A2
Campion Cl ME5 . . . . . . 39 B3
Campleshon Rd ME8 . . 35 A1
Campus Way ME8 . . . . . 34 A4
Camp Way ME15 . . . . . . 81 A2
Canada Terr [3] ME14 . . 65 A3
Canadian Ave ME7 . . . . 24 C4
Canal Rd ME2 . . . . 14 C3
Canberra Gdns ME10 . . . . 103 B2
Canning St ME14 . . . . . 65 A2
Canon Cl ME1 . . . . 21 B2
Canon La ME18 . . . . 69 B1
Canterbury Ho [2] ME15 . . . . 81 B3
Canterbury La ME8, ME9 . . . . 27 C1
Canterbury Rd ME10 . . . . 105 A1
Canterbury Road Prim Sch ME10 . . . . 105 A1
Canterbury St ME7 . . . . 23 C4
Capel Cl ME8 . . . . 43 A4
Capell Cl ME17 . . . . 88 B3
Capel Rd ME10 . . . . . . 106 B4
Capetown Ho [1] ME15 . . . . 82 A1
CAPSTONE 33 B3
Capstone Farm Country Pk* ME7 . . . . 33 A1
Capstone Rd
Chatham ME5 . . . . 24 A1
Gillingham ME7 . . . . 33 C2
Cardens Rd ME3 . . . . 2 B4
Cardinal Cl ME12 . . . . . 99 B3
Cardinal Wlk ME18 . . . 69 B3
Cardine Cl ME10 . . . . . 100 C1
Caring La ME14, ME17 . 76 A1
Caring Rd ME15, ME17 . 75 B1
Carisbrooke Dr ME16 . 71 C4
Carisbrooke Rd ME2 . . . 7 B1
Carlisle Cl ME2 . . . . 12 C2
Carlton Ave ME7 . . . . . . 24 B4
Carlton Cl ME18 . . . . . . 69 A3
Carlton Cres ME5 . . . . . 33 A4
Carlton Gdns ME15 . . . 80 C4
Carman's Cl ME15, ME17 . . . . 89 B3
Carnation Cl [1] ME19 . 51 B1
Carnation Cres ME19 . 51 A1
Carnation Rd ME2 . . . . 13 A3
Caroline Cres ME16 . . . 64 A3
Carp Cl ME20 . . . . 51 B4
Carpeaux Cl ME4 . . . . . 23 A4
Carpenters Cl ME1 . . . . 22 B2
Carpinus Cl ME5 . . . . . . 40 B1
Carrie Ho [3] ME16 . . . . 64 B1
Carrington Cl ME7 . . . . 17 C2
Carroll Cl ME2 . . . . 37 A4
Carroll Gdns ME20 . . . . 51 A3
Carton Cl ME1 . . . . 22 A2
Carton Rd ME3 . . . . 6 B3
Carvoran Way ME8 . . . 34 C1
Castleacres Ind Pk ME10 . . . . 105 A4
Castle Ave ME1 . . . . 21 C4
Castle Dene ME14 . . . . 64 C4
Castle Hill ME1 . . . . 14 C2
Castle Hill Ct ME1 . . . . 14 C2
Castlemaine Ave ME7 17 C2
Castlemere Ave ME11 . . . . 96 C2
Castle Rd
Chatham ME4 . . . . 23 B2
Maidstone ME16 . . . . 64 A3
Sittingbourne ME10 . . . 105 A3
Castle Road Bsns Prec ME10 . . . . 105 A4
Castle Road Tech Ctr ME10 . . . . 105 A4
Castle Rough La ME10 . . . . 101 A3
Castle St
Queenborough ME11 . . . . 96 B2
Rochester ME2 . . . . 9 B1
Wouldham ME1 . . . . 37 C4
Castle View Bsns Ctr ME1 . . . . 14 C2
Castle View Mews ME1 . . . . 14 C2
Castle View Rd ME2 . . . 14 A3
Castle Way ME19 . . . . . 50 B2
Catherine Cl [2] ME16 . 70 C3
Catherine St ME1 . . . . . 22 A3
Catkin Cl ME5 . . . . 39 C1
Catlyn Cl ME19 . . . . 61 A4
Catterick Rd ME5 . . . . . 41 A2
Caulkers Ho [7] ME4 . . . 23 B2
Cave Hill ME15 . . . . 72 B1
Cavell Way ME10 . . . . 103 C3
Cavendish Ave ME7 . . . 17 B2
Cavendish Rd ME1 . . . . 22 A3
Cavendish Way ME15 . 75 A3
Caversham Cl ME8 . . . . 26 C1
Cavour Rd ME12 . . . . . . 95 A3
Cazeneuve St ME1 . . . . 14 C1
Cecil Ave
Gillingham ME8 . . . . 25 A2
Rochester ME2 . . . . 14 B4
Cecil Rd ME1 . . . . 21 C3
Cedar Cl
Ditton ME20 . . . . 62 A4
Sittingbourne ME10 . . . 107 B4
Cedar Ct ME14 . . . . 65 B1
Cedar Dr ME16 . . . . 70 A2
Cedar Gr ME7 . . . . 34 A1
Cedar Ho ME12 . . . . 94 C2
Cedar Rd
Hoo St Werburgh ME3 . . . . 11 B3
Rochester ME2 . . . . 13 C2
Cedars PRU The ME16 . . . . 71 C4
Cedars Sch The ME1 . . 21 C4
Cedars The ME10 . . . . 105 B3
Celestine Cl ME5 . . . . . 40 A1
Celt Cl ME10 . . . . 101 A2
Cemetery Rd ME2 . . . . 37 A4
Central Ave
Chatham ME4 . . . . 16 B4
Sittingbourne ME10 . . . 104 B2
Central Bsns Pk ME2 . 15 B3
Central Par ME1 . . . . . . 22 A2
Central Park Gdns ME4 . . . . 22 B2
Central Rd
New Hythe ME20 . . . . . . 51 C4
Rochester ME2 . . . . 14 A3
Central Terr ME3 . . . . 3 C2
Centre 2000
Maidstone ME16 . . . . 63 C4
[8] Sittingbourne ME10 . . . . 104 C2
Centre Ct ME2 . . . . 15 B3
Centurion Cl ME8 . . . . . 24 C1
Century Ct ME1 . . . . 14 C1
Century Rd ME8 . . . . . . 35 A4
Ceres Ct ME10 . . . . 105 B3
Chada Ave ME7 . . . . 24 B3
Chaffinch Cl ME5 . . . . . 32 A3
Chalfont Dr ME8 . . . . . . 35 A2
Chalgrove Mews ME2 28 C1
Chalkenden Ave ME8 . 25 A2
Chalkers Way ME8 . . . . 25 B4
Chalk Pit Hill ME4 . . . . 23 A3
Chalk Rd ME11 . . . . 96 B2
CHALKWELL 103 C2
Chalkwell Rd ME10 . . 103 C3
Chalky Bank Rd ME8 . . 26 C2
Challenger Cl ME10 . . 100 C1
Challock Wlk ME14 . . . 65 C2
Chalmers Way ME8 . . . 25 A4
Chamberlain Ave ME16 . . . . 71 B2
Chamberlain Ct ME8 . . 34 B1
Chamberlain Rd ME4 . 23 B2
Chancery La ME15 . . . . 73 A3
Chandlers Wharf ME1 . . . . 14 B1
Chapel Cotts ME17 . . . . 84 A1
Chapel La
Bredhurst ME7 . . . . 42 A2
Gillingham ME7 . . . . 42 A4
Maidstone ME14 . . . . 67 A1
Chapel Rd ME6 . . . . 45 B4
Chapel St
East Malling ME19 . . . . . 61 A2
Minster (Sheppey) ME12 . . . . 99 B2
Sheerness ME12 . . . . . . 94 B3
Chapel The ME16 . . . . . 71 A3
Chaplin Cl ME3 . . . . 8 C3
Chapman Ave ME15 . . . 81 C4
Chapman Way ME19 . . 61 C4
Chappell Way ME10 . . 104 A4
Chapter Rd ME2 . . . . . . 13 C4
Chapter Sch ME2 . . . . . 13 A3
Charing Rd ME8 . . . . . . 25 B3
Chariot Way ME2 . . . . . 20 C4
Charlbury Cl ME16 . . . . 71 B3
Charlecote Ct ME8 . . . . 35 A4
Charles Busby Ct ME20 . . . . 53 A1
Charles Cl ME6 . . . . 45 B4
Charles Dickens Ave ME3 . . . . 6 C2
Charles Dr ME2 . . . . 19 B2
Charles St
Chatham ME4 . . . . 22 B3
Maidstone ME16 . . . . 72 A3
Rochester ME2 . . . . 14 A3
Sheerness ME12 . . . . . . 94 B4
Charlock Cl ME16 . . . . . 64 A4
Charlotte Cl ME5 . . . . . 32 B2
Charlotte Dr ME8 . . . . . 25 C1
Charlotte St ME10 . . . 104 A3
Charlton Manor ME7 . . 16 B1
Charlton St ME16 . . . . . 71 B2
Chart Cnr ME17 . . . . 92 A1
Charter St
Chatham ME4 . . . . 22 C2
Gillingham ME7 . . . . 16 C3
Chart Hill Rd ME17 . . . . 92 A1
Chart Pl ME8 . . . . 42 C3
CHART SUTTON 92 A1
Chartwell Cl ME2 . . . . . . 8 B1
Chartwell Ct
Chatham ME4 . . . . 22 B4
Maidstone ME15 . . . . 73 A3
Chartwell Dr ME16 . . . . 71 A4
Chartwell Gr ME10 . . . 103 B1
Chase The
Chatham ME4 . . . . 22 A2
Gillingham ME8 . . . . 25 A2
Chatfield Way ME19 . . . 51 C1
CHATHAM 15 B1
Chatham Gr ME4 . . . . . 22 C1
Chatham Gram Sch for Boys ME4 . . . . 31 C4
Chatham Gram Sch for Girls ME5 . . . . 23 C2
Chatham Hill ME4 . . . . 23 B3
Chatham Rd
Kit's Coty ME20 . . . . 47 B2
Maidstone ME14 . . . . 54 C1
Sandling ME14 . . . . 54 C4
Chatham Ski Ctr ME7 33 B2
Chatham South Sch ME4 . . . . 31 C4
Chatham Sta ME4 . . . . 22 B4
Chatsworth Dr
Rochester ME2 . . . . 8 B1
Sittingbourne ME10 . . . 103 A3
Chatsworth Rd [10] ME7 . . . . 16 C2
CHATTENDEN 9 C4
Chattenden Barracks Royal Sch of Military Engineering ME3 . . . . . 3 C1
Chattenden Ct ME14 . . 65 B2
Chattenden La ME3 . . . . 3 C1
Chattenden Prim Sch ME3 . . . . 9 C4
Chattenden Terr ME3 . . 9 C4
Chatwell Ct ME7 . . . . . . 16 C1
Chaucer Cl
[13] Maidstone ME15 . . . . 81 C3
Rochester ME2 . . . . 15 B4
Chaucer Rd
Gillingham ME7 . . . . 24 A3
Sittingbourne ME10 . . . 103 C1
Chaucer Way ME20 . . . 51 B3
Cheffins Ho ME7 . . . . . . 17 B3
Chegwell Dr ME5 . . . . . 40 B4
Chegworth Gdns ME10 . . . . 106 B3
Chegworth La ME17 . . 86 B2
Chegworth Rd ME17 . . 86 A1
Cheldoc Rise ME4 . . . . 10 C2
Chelmar Rd ME7 . . . . . . 23 B4
Chelmsford Ho ME15 . 81 C2
Chelmsford Rd ME2 . . . 13 A2
Chelsfield Ho ME16 . . . 64 A1
Cheltenham Cl ME15 . . 82 A2
Cheney Cl ME8 . . . . 35 A1
Chepstow Ho [3] ME15 . . . . 82 A2
Chequers Cl ME5 . . . . . 48 B4
Chequers Ct ME2 . . . . . . 8 A1
Chequers Ctr ME15 . . . 72 C4
Chequers Rd ME12 . . . . 99 C2
Cherbourg Cres ME5 . . 31 C3
Cheriton Rd ME8 . . . . . 35 A4
Cheriton Way ME16 . . . 63 C3
Cherries The ME16 . . . . 70 C2
Cherry Amber Cl ME8 35 C4
Cherry Cl ME10 . . . . . . 103 C4
Cherry Hill Ct ME9 . . . 102 B3
Cherry Orch ME20 . . . . 61 C4
CHERRY ORCHARD . . 71 A4
Cherry Orchard Way ME16 . . . . 71 A3
Cherry Rd ME3 . . . . 11 B3
Cherry Tree Cl ME12 . . 94 B1
Cherry Tree Rd ME8 . . . 35 C4
Cherry View ME17 . . . . . 90 A3
Chervilles ME16 . . . . . . 70 C2
Chesham Dr ME8 . . . . . 35 B2
Cheshire Rd
Maidstone ME15 . . . . 81 C3
Maidstone, Willington ME15 . . . . 74 A2
Chester Cl ME2 . . . . 13 A2
Chester Rd ME7 . . . . . . 24 A2
Chesterton Rd [5] ME20 . . . . 51 A4
Chestfield Cl ME8 . . . . . 26 B2
Chestnut Ave ME5 . . . . 39 C3
Chestnut Cl ME19 . . . . . 68 C2
Chestnut Dr ME17 . . . . 88 A3
Chestnut Ho [5] ME16 . 70 C3
Chestnut Rd ME2 . . . . . 13 B2
Chestnut Wlk ME20 . . . 51 C2
Chetney Cl ME2 . . . . 12 C3
Chevening Cl ME5 . . . . 32 A1
Cheviot Gdns ME15 . . . 74 C1
Cheyne Cl ME10 . . . . . 101 A2
Cheyne Mid Sch The ME12 . . . . 95 B3
Chicago Ave ME7 . . . . . 17 C1
Chichester Cl ME8 . . . . 36 A4
Chickfield Gdns [4] ME5 . . . . 23 C2
Chiddingfold Cl ME12 . 99 B2
Chiddingstone Cl ME15 . . . . 82 A2
Chieftain Cl ME7 . . . . . . 25 B1
Childscroft Rd ME8 . . . 26 C2
Chilham Cl
Chatham ME4 . . . . 22 B3
West Minster ME12 . . . . 94 C1
Chilham Ho
[1] Maidstone ME15 . . . . 81 C4
Rochester ME2 . . . . 8 C1
Chilham Rd
Gillingham ME8 . . . . 25 A3
Maidstone ME16 . . . . 63 C3
Chillington St ME14 . . . 64 C2
Chilliwack Rd ME3 . . . . . 3 C1
Chiltern Cl ME15 . . . . . . 74 B1
Chilton Ave ME10 . . . . 104 C1
Chilton Ct ME8 . . . . 26 B1
Chilton Dr ME3 . . . . 6 B3
Chimes The ME1 . . . . . . 14 C1
Chippendale Cl ME5 . . 39 C1
Chippendayle Dr ME17 . . . . 87 B2
Chipstead Cl ME16 . . . . 64 A2
Chipstead Rd ME8 . . . . 43 A4
Chislehurst Cl ME15 . . 82 A2
Chislet Wlk ME8 . . . . . . 35 A1
Christchurch Ct [3] ME5 . . . . 23 C2
Christchurch Ho [11] ME15 . . . . 81 C1
Christen Way ME15 & ME17 . . . . 91 B3
Christian Ct [3] ME2 . . . 14 C4
Christie Cl ME5 . . . . 32 B2
Christie Dr [8] ME20 . . . 51 A4
Christmas St ME7 . . . . . 17 B3
Church Farm Cl ME3 . . 11 B4
Church Field ME6 . . . . . 37 B1
Church Fields ME19 . . . 59 B4
Churchfields Terr ME1 . . . . 21 B4
Church Gn ME2 . . . . 14 C4
Church Hill
Chatham ME5 . . . . 23 C2
Loose ME17 . . . . 90 B1
Churchill Ave ME5 . . . . 32 A3
Churchill Cotts ME17 . 84 A2
Churchill Ho
Maidstone ME16 . . . . 71 A2
Sittingbourne ME10 . . . 105 B2
Churchill Rd ME12 . . . . 99 B2
Churchill Sq ME19 . . . . 68 C3
Church La
Chatham ME4 . . . . 15 C2
Harrietsham ME17 . . . . . 87 C2
Maidstone, Bearsted ME14 . . . . 75 B4
Maidstone ME16 . . . . 70 A1
Newington ME9 . . . . . . 102 B3
Churchlands ME14 . . . . 65 B1
Church Marshes Ctry Pk* ME10 . . . . 101 B1
Church Mews ME8 . . . . 35 C4
Church Path ME7 . . . . . 17 B2
Church Rd
Chart Sutton ME17 . . . . . 92 B1
Harrietsham ME17 . . . . . 87 C2
Maidstone ME15 . . . . 82 A3
Maidstone, Tovil ME15 . . 72 A2
Offham ME18 . . . . 58 A4
Sittingbourne, Murston ME10 . . . . 105 A3
Church Road Bsns Ctr ME10 . . . . 105 A4
Church Row ME6 . . . . . 45 B3
Church St
Chatham ME4 . . . . 23 A4
Gillingham ME7 . . . . 17 B2
Hoo St Werburgh ME3 . . . 5 B1
Maidstone, Boughton Monchelsea ME17 . . . . 90 A2
Maidstone, Loose ME15 . . . . 80 A1
Maidstone ME14 . . . . 72 C4
Maidstone, Tovil ME15 . . 72 A2
Rochester ME1 . . . . 22 A4
Rodmersham ME9 . . . . 107 C2
[5] Sittingbourne ME10 . . . . 104 A2
Sittingbourne ME10 . . . 104 A3
Teston ME18 . . . . 79 B4
Church Terr
Chatham ME5 . . . . 23 C2
Minster (Sheppey) ME12 . . . . 99 A3

Church Wlk ME19 ..... 61 A3
Chute Cl ME8 ..... 43 A4
Cinnabar Cl ME5 ..... 40 A1
Cinnabar Dr ME10 ... 103 B4
City Way ME1 ..... 22 A2
Claire Ho [4] ME16 .... 64 B1
Clandon Rd ME5 ..... 41 A2
Clare La ME19 ..... 60 B4
Claremont Rd ME14 ... 65 B1
Claremont Way [2]
ME4 ..... 22 C3
Clarence Ave ME1 .... 21 C4
Clarence Ct ME14 ..... 74 A4
Clarence Rd ME4 ..... 23 B2
Clarence Row ME12 ... 94 C2
Clarendon Cl
Maidstone ME14 ..... 74 C4
Sittingbourne ME10 ... 106 C3
Clarendon Dr ME2 ..... 8 A1
Clarendon Pl ME14 ... 72 C4
Clarewood Dr ME19 ... 60 B4
Claridge Ct ME7 ..... 41 C4
Clark Mews ME20 ..... 53 A1
Clavell Cl ME8 ..... 43 B4
Claygate
Eyhorne Street
ME17 ..... 77 C2
Maidstone ME15 ..... 73 C1
Cleave Rd ME7 ..... 24 B3
Cleeve Ct ME19 ..... 69 A3
Clematis Ave ME8 .... 34 B1
Clemens Pl ME18 ..... 69 B2
Clement Cl ME10 .... 100 C2
Clement Ct ME16 ..... 64 A1
Clerke Dr ME10 ..... 101 B2
Clermont Cl ME7 ..... 42 A4
Cleveland Ho ME16 ... 71 A2
Cleveland Rd ME7 .... 17 A2
Clewson Rise ME14 ... 65 B4
Cliffe Rd
Rochester ME2 ..... 8 A1
Rochester ME2 ..... 14 B4
CLIFFE WOODS 2 B3
Cliffe Woods Prim Sch
ME3 ..... 2 C4
Cliff Gdns ME12 ..... 99 C3
Cliff Hill ME17 ..... 90 C4
Cliff Hill Rd ME17 ..... 90 B4
Clifford Ho [6] ME14 ... 73 A4
Clifton Cl
Maidstone ME14 ..... 65 B1
Rochester ME2 ..... 13 C3
Clifton Rd ME7 ..... 16 C3
Clinton Ave ME2 ..... 13 B4
Clinton Cl ME17 ..... 88 A3
Clipper Cl ME2 ..... 15 B3
Clipper Ct ME2 ..... 15 B3
Cliveden Cl ME16 ..... 64 A3
Clive Ho ME20 ..... 62 C4
Clive Rd
Rochester ME1 ..... 21 C3
Sittingbourne ME10 ... 103 A3
Clock Tower Mews
ME6 ..... 37 A1
Cloisterham Rd ME1 .. 31 A3
Cloisters The [8]
ME10 ..... 104 A2
Clopton Ct ME8 ..... 35 A4
Close The ME1 ..... 21 C4
Cloudberry Cl ME16 ... 64 A2
Cloudesley Cl ME1 .... 21 B1
Clovelly Dr ME12 ..... 98 C4
Clover Bank View
ME5 ..... 32 B2
Clover Ct ME10 ..... 105 A3
Clover Lay ME8 ..... 27 B2
Cloverlay Ind Pk ME8 27 C1
Clover Rd ME3 ..... 11 B3
Clover St [3] ME4 ..... 22 C4
Clover Terr [4] ME15 ... 81 B4
Clyde St ME12 ..... 95 B3
Coach Yd The ME16 ... 71 A3
Coats Ave ME12 ..... 94 B1
Cobb Cl ME2 ..... 13 A4
Cobbett Cl ME19 ..... 61 C4
Cobblestones ME7 .... 33 C1
Cobbs Cl ME18 ..... 78 C3
Cobden Rd [4] ME4 .... 23 B2
Cobdown Cl ME20 .... 52 A2
Cobdown Gr ME8 ..... 27 A2
Cobfield ME17 ..... 91 C1
Cobham Ave ME10 ... 106 B3
Cobham Cl
Maidstone ME16 ..... 72 A4
Rochester ME2 ..... 13 B3
Cobham Dr ME18 ..... 69 B3
Cobham Rise ME7 .... 17 C1
Cobtree Cl ME5 ..... 32 C4
Cobtree Rd ME17 ..... 88 B3
Cobtree Wharf ME20 . 54 A2
COCK STREET 90 C2
Colchester Cl ME5 .... 32 A3
Coldharbour La
Forstal ME20 ..... 53 B1
Sittingbourne ME10 ... 101 A3
Coldred Rd ME15 ..... 91 B4
Colegate Dr ME14 .... 75 B4
Coleman Dr ME10 .... 101 A3
Coleridge Cl [4] ME20 . 51 A4
Colesdane ME17 ..... 87 C4
Coleshall Cl ME15 .... 82 A2
Colewood Dr ME2 .... 12 B4
Colfe Way ME10 ..... 101 B2
College Ave
Gillingham ME7 ..... 23 B4
Maidstone ME15 ..... 72 B3
College Cotts ME16 ... 72 B3
College Ct [6] ME15 ... 72 C3
College Rd
Chatham ME4 ..... 16 A3
Maidstone ME15 ..... 72 B2
New Hythe ME20 ..... 51 C3
Sittingbourne ME10 ... 103 C1
College Wlk [4] ME15 .. 72 C3
College Yd ME1 ..... 14 C2
Collet Wlk ME8 ..... 43 A4
Collinge Cl ME19 ..... 51 B1
Collings Wlk ME8 ..... 43 A4
Collington Terr ME15 .. 91 A4
Collingwood Ind Ctr
ME17 ..... 93 A2
Collingwood Rd
ME20 ..... 47 A3
Collingwood Wlk
ME10 ..... 103 A3
Collis St ME2 ..... 14 A4
Colman Ho [4] ME14 ... 72 C4
Coltsfoot Dr ME14 .... 74 B4
Columbine Cl
Rochester ME2 ..... 13 B3
West Malling ME19 .... 51 A1
Columbine Rd
East Malling ME19 ..... 61 C4
Rochester ME2 ..... 13 B3
Command Rd ME14 ... 64 C4
Commercial Rd ME2 .. 14 B3
Commissioners Ct
ME4 ..... 15 C2
Commissioner's Rd
ME2 ..... 14 C4
Commodore Rd
ME14 ..... 65 C1
Common Rd
Burham ME5 ..... 38 B1
Cliffe Woods ME3 ..... 2 B1
Common The ME1 .... 14 C2
Commonwealth Cl
ME10 ..... 105 A1
Compass Cl ME1 ..... 21 C1
Compass Ctr ME4 .... 16 A4
Compton Cl ME5 ..... 41 A2
Concord Ave ME5 ..... 31 B1
Coney Mews ME4 ..... 23 A1
Conifer Dr ME5 ..... 41 A1
Coniston Cl ME7 ..... 18 A2
Coniston Ho ME15 .... 81 C3
Connaught Cl ME15 ... 91 B4
Connaught Mews [2]
ME4 ..... 23 C2
Connaught Rd
Chatham ME4 ..... 23 C2
Gillingham ME7 ..... 17 A1
Sittingbourne ME10 ... 104 A1
Conquest Ind Est
ME2 ..... 14 A1
Conrad Cl ME8 ..... 43 A4
Consort Cl ME14 ..... 65 B1
Constitution Hill
[8] Chatham ME5 ..... 23 B3
Snodland ME6 ..... 45 B4
Constitution Rd ME5 .. 23 B2
Conway Cl ME2 ..... 7 B1
Conway Hall [16] ME7 .. 16 A2
Conway Mews ME7 ... 16 A2
Conway Rd ME16 ..... 63 C2
Conyers Wlk ME8 ..... 43 A4
Cooden Cl ME8 ..... 27 A2
Cook Cl ME5 ..... 32 C2
Cookham Hill ME1 .... 21 A2
Cookham Wood Rd
ME1 ..... 30 B4
Cooks La ME10 ..... 104 B4
Cooks Wharf ME1 .... 22 B4
Cooling Cl ME14 ..... 65 C2
Cooling Comm ME3 .... 3 A4
Cooling Rd ME2 ..... 8 B2
Coombe Cl
Chatham ME5 ..... 40 B3
Snodland ME6 ..... 45 B3
Coombe Dr ME10 .... 105 B2
Coombe Rd
Hoo St Werburgh
ME3 ..... 5 B1
Maidstone ME15 ..... 72 B2
Cooper Rd
Chatham ME5 ..... 40 B3
Snodland ME6 ..... 45 A2
Copenhagen Rd ME7 .. 23 C4
Copland Ave ME12 .... 99 A2
Copperfield Cres ME3 .. 6 C2
Copperfield Dr ME17 .. 93 A4
Copperfield Ho [6]
ME4 ..... 22 C4
Copperfield Rd ME1 .. 21 C2
Copperfields The
ME1 ..... 21 B4
Coppergate ME7 ..... 33 C1
Copperhouse La ME7 . 18 B2
Copperhouse Rd ME2 12 C3
Copperpenny Dr ME7 . 42 B3
Copper Tree Ct ME15 .. 80 B1
Copper Tree Wlk
ME5 ..... 40 C1
Coppice Ct ME7 ..... 42 B4
Coppice Rd ME5 ..... 40 C2
Coppice The ME20 .... 52 C1
Coppice View ME14 ... 66 B2
Copse Cl ME1 ..... 22 B1
Copsehill ME19 ..... 50 C2
Copse The ME3 ..... 11 B3
Copsewood Way
ME15 ..... 74 C3
Corben Cl ME16 ..... 63 B2
Cordelia Cres
Rochester ME1 ..... 20 C2
Rochester ME1 ..... 21 A2
Cork St ME20 ..... 46 A2
Corkwell St ME4 ..... 22 B3
Cormorant Cl ME2 .... 12 C3
Cornflower Cl ME14 .. 74 A4
Cornwall Cl ME15 ..... 81 C3
Cornwallis Ave
Chatham ME4 ..... 22 B1
Gillingham ME8 ..... 25 A4
Cornwallis Cotts
ME17 ..... 89 A2
Cornwallis Rd ME16 .. 71 C4
Cornwallis Rdbt ME8 . 25 A4
Cornwallis Sch The
ME15 ..... 89 B2
Cornwall Rd
Gillingham ME7 ..... 17 A2
Rochester ME1 ..... 21 C3
Corona Terr ME6 ..... 45 A2
Coronation Cres
ME11 ..... 96 A2
Coronation Flats [5]
ME4 ..... 22 C3
Coronation Rd
Chatham ME5 ..... 23 C2
Sheerness ME12 ..... 95 B2
Corporation Rd ME7 .. 17 A3
Corporation St ME1 ... 14 C2
Corral Cl ME5 ..... 24 A2
Corrall Almshouses [5]
ME15 ..... 72 C3
Corrance Gn ME15 .... 80 B4
Cortanore ME10 ..... 106 B4
Cortland Cl ME10 .... 104 A4
Cortland Mews
ME10 ..... 104 A4
Cory's Rd ME1 ..... 15 A2
Cossack St ME1 ..... 22 A3
Cossington Rd ME5 ... 40 B1
Cotswold Gdns ME15 . 74 C2
Cottage Rd ME4 ..... 15 C2
Cottall Ave ME4 ..... 22 C2
Cottenham Cl ME19 ... 60 C3
Coulman St ME7 ..... 17 A1
Coulters Cl ME14 ..... 66 A1
County Gr ME19 ..... 59 B4
County Rd ME14 ..... 65 A1
Court Dr ME16 ..... 71 C4
Courtenay Rd ME15 ... 72 B2
Courteney Rd ME8 .... 34 B4
Courtfield Ave ME5 ... 40 B3
Court Hall ME11 ..... 96 A2
Court Hall Mus★
ME10 ..... 104 A4
Courtlands ME18 ..... 79 B4
Courtlands Cl ME18 ... 79 B4
Court Lodge Farm
ME18 ..... 79 C3
Court Lodge Rd ME7 .. 17 C2
Court Meadow ME8 ... 25 B2
Court Rd
Burham ME1 ..... 46 A4
Burham ME1 ..... 46 B4
Sittingbourne ME10 ... 101 A1
Courtyard The ME8 ... 34 A4
Coventry Cl ME2 ..... 13 A2
Coverdale Ave ME15 .. 81 B2
Coverdale Cl ME5 ..... 32 B3
Covert The ME5 ..... 40 B1
Covey Hall Rd ME6 .... 37 A1
Cowbeck Cl ME8 ..... 35 A2
Cowden Rd ME14 ..... 65 C1
Cowdrey Cl
Maidstone ME16 ..... 71 A2
Rochester ME1 ..... 21 B2
Cowper Rd
Gillingham ME7 ..... 24 A3
Sittingbourne ME10 ... 105 A2
Cox Gdns ME8 ..... 25 A2
COXHEATH 88 B2
Coxheath Prim Sch
ME17 ..... 88 B3
Cox's Cl ME6 ..... 45 A4
Cozenton Cl ME8 ..... 26 B1
Crabtree Cl ME19 ..... 68 C2
Crabtree Rd ME8 ..... 35 A4
Crabtree Rdbt ME14 .. 54 C2
Craddock Way ME8 ... 35 A1
Cragie Wlk ME8 ..... 43 B4
Craig Ho ME1 ..... 22 B1
Cranborne Ave ME15 .. 73 B1
Cranbourne Ave
ME15 ..... 80 C4
Cranbrook Cl
Gillingham ME8 ..... 25 C3
Maidstone ME15 ..... 82 A3
Cranbrook Dr ME10 . 106 A3
Cranford Cl ME8 ..... 26 A1
Cranleigh Gdns
Chatham ME4 ..... 22 A3
Maidstone ME16 ..... 63 C3
Cranmer Ct ME15 ..... 80 C4
Cranmere Ct ME2 ..... 14 C4
Crayford Cl ME14 ..... 65 C2
Cremers Rd ME10 .... 105 A3
Crescent Ho ME2 ..... 14 C3
Crescent St [1] ME10 . 104 B2
Crescent The
Halfway Houses
ME12 ..... 97 C3
Maidstone ME14 ..... 64 C4
Sheerness ME12 ..... 95 A3
Sittingbourne ME10 ... 101 B3
St Mary's Island ME4 ... 10 B1
Crescent Way ME5 .... 31 A1
Cressey Ct [7] ME4 .... 22 B4
Crest Rd ME1 ..... 21 C1
Crestway ME5 ..... 32 B4
Creve Coeur Cl ME14 . 67 A1
Crevequer Chambers [1]
ME8 ..... 26 C1
Cricketers Cl
Harrietsham ME17 ..... 87 B2
Sittingbourne ME10 ... 101 A2
Cripple St ME15 ..... 80 B3
Crismill La ME14 ..... 76 B4
Crismill Rd ME14,
ME17 ..... 76 B3
Crispe Cl ME8 ..... 43 A4
Crispin Ct ME17 ..... 88 B3
Crispin Rd ME2 ..... 13 B4
Crispin Way ME19 .... 68 C3
Croft Cl ME5 ..... 40 C1
Crofters The ME8 ..... 35 C3
Croft The ME19 ..... 50 C2
Croidene Ct ME12 .... 98 B2
Cromer Rd
Rochester ME2 ..... 14 B4
Sittingbourne ME9,
ME10 ..... 106 C2
Crompton Gdns
ME15 ..... 73 A3
Cromwell Rd
Maidstone ME14 ..... 65 B1
West Minster ME11 .... 96 A4
Cromwell Terr ME4 ... 23 A3
Cronin Cl [2] ME20 .... 51 A4
Crosley Rd ME7 ..... 24 A3
Cross Keys ME14 ..... 75 B4
Cross La ME10 ..... 104 A4
Cross St
Chatham ME4 ..... 23 A4
Gillingham ME7 ..... 16 C2
Maidstone ME14 ..... 65 A2
Rochester ME2 ..... 14 B4
Crossway ME5 ..... 31 B2
Cross Way ME1 ..... 21 C3
Crossways
Chart Sutton ME17 ..... 92 A1
Sittingbourne ME10 ... 106 C3
Crow Cnr ME1 ..... 14 C1
Crow La ME1 ..... 14 C1
Crownfields ME14 .... 74 B4
Crown Ho ME1 ..... 21 B4
Crown Quay La [5]
ME10 ..... 104 C2
Crown Rd ME10 ..... 104 A4
Crown St ME7 ..... 17 A2
Croydon Cl ME5 ..... 40 C4
Crundale [2] ME14 .... 65 A1
Crundale Rd ME8 ..... 25 C3
Crusader Cl ME8 ..... 34 B4
Crutches La ME3, ME2 .. 6 B1
Cryalls Bsns Est
ME10 ..... 103 B2
Cryalls La ME10, ME9 . 103 B1
Cuckoowood Ave
ME14 ..... 55 A1
Cudham Cl ME14 ..... 65 C2
Culpeper Cl ME2 ..... 15 B2
Culpepper Rd
Coxheath ME17 ..... 88 A3
Gillingham ME8 ..... 43 A4
Cumberland Ave
ME15 ..... 81 B4
Cumberland Rd
Chatham ME4, ME7 .... 16 B3
Gillingham ME7 ..... 16 C3
Cunningham Cres
ME5 ..... 32 A4
Cunningham Ho ME1 . 21 B4
Curlew Cres ME2 ..... 12 C2
Curtis Way ME1 ..... 31 A3
Curzon Rd
Chatham ME4 ..... 22 C3
Maidstone ME14 ..... 65 A2
Cutbush Almshouses
[3] Maidstone ME14 .... 72 C4
[1] Maidstone ME15 .... 72 C3
Cutbush and Corrall Ct
[1] ME14 ..... 73 A4
Cutbush Cl ME17 ..... 87 B2
Cutbush Ho [2] ME15 .. 72 C3
Cutter Cl ME2 ..... 9 C3
CUXTON 19 B2
Cuxton Com Inf Sch
ME2 ..... 19 B2
Cuxton Com Jun Sch
ME2 ..... 19 B2
Cuxton Ind Est ME2 ... 19 C2
Cuxton Rd
Maidstone ME15 ..... 82 A1
Rochester ME2 ..... 13 C1
Rochester ME2 ..... 14 A3
Cuxton Sta ME2 ..... 19 C2
Cygnet Cl ME20 ..... 51 B2
Cygnet Rd ME5 ..... 40 C2
Cypress Ave ME3 ..... 11 B3
Cypress Ct ME7 ..... 17 C2
Cypress Rd ME2 ..... 8 C1

D

D2 Trad Est ME10....105 A4
Daffodil Rd ME2......13 B3
Dagmar Rd ME4......23 B2
Dajen Bsns Pk ME4....23 C1
Dale Ct ME5..........40 A2
Dale Rd ME1.........21 C3
Dale St ME4..........22 B2
Dalewood ME10.....107 A4
Dalison Ct ME2.......37 B4
Dalton St ME7........16 C2
Damiem Cl ME4......23 A2
Damson Dr ME3......11 B3
Dane Cl ME5.........40 C2
Danecourt Com Sch
 ME8.................25 A2
Dane Ct ME17........88 B2
Danefield Ct ME14....75 A4
Danes Hill ME7.......18 A2
Danes Mead ME10...101 A3
Daniel Ho 5 ME16....64 B1
Danley Mid Sch ME12 97 C4
Danley Rd ME12......97 C4
Danns La ME18, ME19..68 C1
Danson Way ME8.....26 A2
Darby Gdns ME3.......6 B3
Darenth Rise ME5....40 B3
Dargate Cl ME16.....64 A3
Dargets Rd ME5......40 A3
DARLAND...........33 B4
Darland Ave ME7.....24 B1
Darlington Dr ME12...98 B2
Darnley Cl ME2.......13 A2
Darnley Rd
 Rochester ME2........13 B2
 Rochester ME2........14 A2
Dart Cl ME2..........13 C3
Darwin Ct ME1.......15 A1
Dashmonden Cl ME2...8 C2
Davenport Ave ME7...17 B3
Davey Ct ME1.........14 C1
Davie Cl ME12........94 C1
Davie Ct ME12........94 C1
Dawes St ME7........16 C1
Dawn La ME18........69 C3
Dawson Ct 7 ME7....16 A2
Day Ho 2 ME14......73 A4
Deacon Cl ME2.......13 B4
Deacon Est The ME20 53 B2
Deacon Trad Ctr ME2 .14 A2
Deal Ho ME15........81 C4
Deane Ct 8 ME7.....16 C2
Dean Rd
 Rochester ME2........13 C4
 Sittingbourne ME10...104 A4
Deanwood Cl ME8....35 A2
Deanwood Dr ME8....43 B4
Deanwood Prim
 Education Tech Sch
 ME8.................43 A3
Deerhurst Gdns
 ME16................71 C4
Deering Cl ME4.......10 B2
Defiant Cl ME5.......32 B2
Defoe Cl ME5.........32 B2
Deham Ho ME10.....103 C3
Delamark Rd ME12...95 A3
Delamere Gdns 3
 ME6.................45 B4
Delamere Rd ME6....45 B4
Delce Jun & Inf Schs
 ME1.................22 A2
Delce Rd ME1........22 A4
Demelza Cl ME2......19 A2
De Mere Cl ME8......35 A2
Denbigh Ave ME8.....26 A1
Denbigh Cl ME10....100 C1
Denham Rd ME9.....102 B4
Denning Cl ME16.....71 A4
Dennis Cadman Ho
 ME20................53 A1
Dennis Wilcocks Cl
 ME9................102 B3
Denstead Wlk 11
 ME15................82 A2
Denton Cl ME15......81 C4
Denton Gn ME8.......25 B4
Derby Cl ME10.......103 C4
Derby Rd
 Gillingham ME5........24 B2
 Maidstone ME15.......81 A4
Deringwood Dr ME15 .74 B1
Derwent Ho 3 ME15..81 C3
Derwent Way ME8....35 A4
DETLING............57 C1
Detling CE Prim Sch
 ME14................57 B1
Detling Cl
 Gillingham ME8........25 C2
 West Minster ME12....96 C4
Detling Hill ME14.....57 C2
Devon Cl
 Chatham ME5.........32 C3
 Gillingham ME8........26 C1
Devon Rd ME15.......81 A4
Devonshire Rd ME7...17 A3
Dewberry Cl ME4.....10 B1
Dhekelia Cl ME14.....65 A3
Dial Cl ME7...........17 C2
Dial Rd ME7..........17 C2
Diana Rd ME4........23 A2
Dickens Cl ME17......93 A4
Dickens Ct
 Higham ME3...........6 C4
 Rochester ME2........15 A4
Dickens Dr ME19.....51 A1
Dickens Rd
 Maidstone ME14.......64 B4
 Rochester ME1........21 C2
Dickens World★ ME4 16 A4
Dickson Ct 7 ME10..105 A2
Diggerland★ ME2....20 C4
Dignals Cl ME8.......26 C2
Diligent Dr ME10....101 A1
Dillywood Cotts ME3...7 C2
Dilly Wood Fields ME3 .8 A3
Dillywood La ME3.....7 C2
Discovery Dr ME19....69 A3
Discovery Rd ME15...75 A2
Discovery Sch The
 ME18................69 C3
Disraeli Cl ME15......81 C1
DITTON.............52 A1
Ditton CE Jun Sch
 ME20................52 A1
Ditton Court Cl ME20 .51 C1
Ditton Inf Sch ME20..52 A1
Ditton Pl ME20.......51 C1
Dixon Cl ME15........72 B2
Dixwell Cl ME8.......35 A1
Dobbie Cl ME10.....104 A4
Dock Head Rd
 Chatham ME4.........16 A4
 St Mary's Island ME4...10 A1
Dock Rd ME4.........15 C2
Dockside Outlet Ctr
 ME4.................16 A4
Doddington Ct ME16..64 B1
Doddington Rd ME8..26 A3
Does Alley 4 ME10..104 B2
Dogwood Cl ME5.....41 A1
Dolphin Dr ME8......35 B1
Dolphin Ho ME1......15 B1
Dolphin Pk ME10....105 A3
Dolphin Rd ME10....105 A3
Dombey Cl
 Higham ME3...........6 C3
 Rochester ME1........21 C3
Donald Troup Ho
 ME1.................21 C4
Doncaster Cl 7
 ME15................82 A2
Donemowe Dr ME10 .101 A2
Donet Cl ME8.........34 C1
Dongola Rd
 Rochester ME2.........8 B1
 Rochester ME2........14 B4
Dorchester Cl ME3.....2 B3
Dornden Gdns ME5...40 B2
Dorrit Way ME1.......22 A2
Dorset Rd ME12......94 B1
Dorset Sq ME8.......26 A1
Dorset Way ME15.....81 A4
Dotterel Cl ME5......41 A2
Douglas Rd ME16.....72 A3
Doust Way ME1.......15 A1
Dove Cl ME5..........32 B2
Dover Ho
 2 Maidstone ME15....81 C4
 Rochester ME2.........8 C1
Dover St
 Maidstone ME16.......71 B2
Dover St *continued*
 1 Sittingbourne
 ME10...............104 A2
Dowling Cl ME6......44 C3
Downderry Way
 ME20................51 C1
Downer Ct ME1.......31 B4
Downs Cl
 Maidstone ME14.......65 B4
 Sittingbourne ME10...106 A4
Downside ME2.......14 A3
Downsland Ho ME2...19 C2
Downs Rd ME14......65 B4
Downs The ME5......39 A1
Downsview ME5......32 C4
Downs View ME19....59 B4
Downs View Rd ME14 .65 B4
Drake Ave ME12......99 B1
Drake's Ave ME2......13 C4
Drawbridge Cl ME15..81 C4
Dreadnought Ave
 ME12................98 B2
Drewery Dr ME8......34 C1
Drove Rd ME12.......97 C4
Dry End Rd ME20.....52 A3
Dryland Rd ME6......45 A4
Drywall Ind Est
 ME10...............105 A4
Dublin Ho 16 ME15....81 C3
Duchess Cl ME2......13 B4
Duchess of Kent Ct The
 ME20................53 A1
Duchess Of Kent Dr
 ME5.................40 B3
Duke of Clarence Trad
 Est The ME12........94 B4
Dukes Meadow Dr
 ME7.................33 C2
Dukes Wlk 7 ME15...72 C4
Dumergue Ave ME11..96 C2
Duncan Rd ME7......17 A1
Dunedin Cl ME10....103 B1
Dunedin Ho 9 ME15..81 C1
Dunera Dr ME14......65 A3
Dunkeld Ho 6 ME15..81 C3
Dunkirk Dr ME5......31 C2
Dunlin Dr ME4........10 C2
Dunning's La ME1....21 C4
Dunnings The ME16...70 C2
Dunster Terr 3
 ME15................81 C4
Durban Ho 7 ME15...81 C1
Durham Cl ME15......74 A1
Durham Rd ME8......34 C3
Durling Ct ME8.......27 A1
Durrell Gdns ME5.....23 C1
Duval Dr ME1.........31 B4
Dyngley Cl ME10.....104 A4

E

Eadred Way ME10....101 B3
Eagle Cl ME20........51 B2
Eagles Cl ME10......105 B2
Ealing Cl ME5........40 C4
Earl Cl ME5...........40 B4
Earl St ME14..........72 B4
EAST BARMING......70 B1
East Borough Prim Sch
 ME14................65 B1
Eastcourt Gn ME8....25 B4
Eastcourt La
 Gillingham, Lwr Twydal
 ME7 & ME8..........18 C1
 Gillingham ME8........25 B3
East Ct 4 ME15......72 C1
East End Rd ME4, ME7 .17 A4
Easterfields ME19....61 C1
Eastern Ave
 Halfway Houses
 ME12................97 B3
 Queenborough ME11...96 C1
Eastern Rd ME7......17 C2
Eastfield Ho ME16....71 A2
Eastgate ME1.........14 C1
Eastgate Ct ME1......14 C1
Eastgate Terr ME1....14 C1
East Gn ME10........101 B3
East Hall La ME10....105 B3
East La ME12.........94 B3
Eastling Cl ME8.......26 A3
EAST MALLING......61 A3
East Malling Research
 Sta (Horticultural)
 ME19................61 C2
East Malling Sta
 ME19................61 A2
East Park Rd ME20....63 A4
East Rd ME4..........16 A3
East Row ME1........14 C1
Eastry Cl ME16.......63 C3
East St
 Chatham ME4.........23 A3
 Gillingham ME7........17 A2
 Harrietsham ME17.....87 C1
 Sittingbourne ME10...104 C2
 Snodland ME6.........45 C4
Eastwell Cl ME14.....65 C1
Eastwood Rd ME10..103 C3
Eaves Ct ME10.......105 A3
Ebony Wlk ME16......71 A3
ECCLES.............46 A2
Eccles Row ME20.....46 A2
Eccleston Rd ME15...72 B2
Echo Cl ME15.........82 A2
Echo Ho ME10.......105 A1
Echo Wlk ME12.......99 B2
Eclipse Dr ME10.....100 C2
Eddington Cl ME15...80 C2
Eden Ave ME5........32 A3
Edenbridge Dr ME12..94 C1
Eden Farm La ME19...60 A4
Edgeler Ct ME6.......45 A3
Edger Pl 5 ME15.....72 C4
Edgeway ME4........10 B2
Edinburgh Rd
 Chatham ME4.........23 C2
 Gillingham ME7........17 A1
Edinburgh Sq ME15...81 A3
Edisbury Wlk ME8....35 A1
Edmund Cl ME16.....70 C3
Edna Rd ME14........64 C4
Edward Ct ME5.......23 C1
Edward Rd ME11......96 C2
Edwards Cl ME8......34 C1
Edward St
 Chatham ME4.........23 A3
 Rochester ME2........14 B3
 Sheerness ME12.......94 B4
Edward Wlk ME19....61 C4
Edwina Ave ME12.....98 B3
Edwin Rd ME8........34 C4
Edwins Pl ME9.......102 C4
Edyngham Cl ME10..101 B2
Egerton Rd ME14.....64 B3
Egremont Rd ME15...74 B2
Egret Cl ME4.........10 B2
Elaine Ave ME2.......13 B3
Elaine Ct ME2........13 B2
Elaine Prim Sch ME2 .13 B2
Elder Ct ME8.........34 B2
Eldon St ME4.........23 A4
Eleanor Dr ME10....100 C2
Elgin Gdns ME2.......13 A1
Elham Cl ME8........25 B3
Eling Ct ME15........80 B4
Elizabeth Ct
 Chatham ME5.........32 A3
 Gillingham ME8........25 C1
Elizabeth Ho
 Maidstone ME14.......65 A2
 Rochester ME1........21 C4
Elizabeth Smith's Ct
 ME19................60 C3
Ellen's Pl ME9.......102 C3
Ellenswood Cl ME15..74 C1
Ellingham Leas ME15 .81 A3
Elliott Park Sch ME12 98 B3
Ellis Ho 7 ME14......73 A4
Ellison Way ME8......27 A2
Elm Ave
 Chatham ME4.........22 B1
 Chattenden ME3.......10 A4
Elm Cl ME3............6 C3
Elm Court Ind Est
 ME7.................41 B3
Elm Cres ME19.......61 C4
Elmfield ME8.........25 A3
Elmfield Ct ME17.....88 B3
Elm Gr
 Maidstone ME15.......73 A3
 Sittingbourne ME10...105 A2
Elmhurst Gdns ME4...22 B3
Elm La ME12..........99 C1
Elm Rd
 Gillingham ME7........17 B2
 Hoo St Werburgh ME3...11 B3
Elmstone Cl ME16....71 A2
Elmstone La ME16....71 A2
Elmstone Rd ME8.....35 A3
Elm Tree Dr ME1.....21 A2
Elm Wlk ME20........52 C1
Elmwood Rd ME3......3 C2
Elster Pl ME19........69 A3
Elvington Cl ME16....64 A1
Ely Cl ME8............26 B2
Embassy Cl ME7......24 C1
Emerald Cl ME1......31 A3
Emerald Cres ME10..103 C4
Emily Rd ME5.........32 B2
Emsworth Gr ME14...66 A2
Endeavour Foyer The 8
 ME4.................23 B2
Englefield Cres ME3...2 B3
English Martyrs' RC
 Prim Sch ME2.......14 B4
Ennerdale Ho ME15...81 C3
Enterprise Bsns Est
 ME2.................15 B3
Enterprise Cl ME2....15 A4
Enterprise Ctr The
 ME5.................49 A4
Enterprise Rd ME15...72 C1
Epaul La ME1.........14 C2
Eppe Cl 2 ME2.......14 B4
Epps Rd ME10.......104 A1
Epsom Cl
 Maidstone ME15.......82 A2
 West Malling ME19....59 B4
Erith Cl ME14.........65 A4
Ernest Dr ME16.......63 B1
Ernest Rd ME4........23 A3
Esmonde Ho 15 ME7..16 A2
Esplanade ME1.......14 B1
Essex Rd
 Halling ME2...........28 C2
 Maidstone ME15.......81 C2
Estelle Cl ME1.......31 A3
Esther Ct ME10......100 C2
Ethelbert Rd ME1.....21 C4
Ethel-Maud Ct ME7...17 A3
Eton Cl ME5..........39 C4
Eurolink Bsns Pk
 ME10...............105 A3
Eurolink Way ME10..104 B2
Euroway ME20........62 B4
Eva Rd ME7..........24 A3
Evelyn Cl ME2........14 C4
Evelyn Ho 5 ME2.....14 C4
Evelyn Rd ME16......72 A3
Everest Dr ME3.......11 B4
Everest La ME2........8 B1
Everest Mews ME3....11 B4
Everglades The ME7..33 C2
Evergreen Cl
 Gillingham ME7........34 A1
 Higham ME3...........6 B3
 Leybourne ME19.......50 C2
Eversley Cl ME16.....63 C2
Evorg Ho 6 ME4......23 B2
Ewart Rd ME4........22 B1
Ewell Ave ME19.......59 A4
Exeter Wlk ME1......30 C3
Exmouth Rd ME7.....16 C3
Exton Cl ME5.........40 C2
Exton Gdns ME14.....66 C1
Eye The ME4..........15 C1
Eyhorne St ME17.....77 C2
EYHORNE STREET...77 B2
Eynsford Rd ME16....64 A3

F

Fagus Cl ME5.........40 B1
Fairfax Bsns Ctr
 ME15................91 B4
Fairfax Cl ME8........35 A1
Fairfax Ho ME15......82 A1
Fairhurst Dr ME15....88 A4
Fairlawn Cl ME18.....79 B4
Fairlead Rd ME1......22 A1
Fairleas ME10.......107 B4
Fairmeadow ME14....72 B4

Fairservice Cl ME10. . 105 B3
Fairview Ave ME8. . . . . 34 B1
Fair View Com Inf Sch ME8. . . . . 34 C1
Fair View Com Jun Sch ME8. . . . . 34 C1
Fairview Cotts ME15 . . 80 A1
Fairview Dr ME3. . . . . . . 6 B4
Fairview Rd ME10. . . . 104 C1
Fairway Cl ME1. . . . . . . 21 C1
Fairway The
Rochester ME1. . . . . 21 C1
Sittingbourne ME10 . . . 106 B3
Falcon Ct ME10. . . . . . 107 A4
Falcon Gdns ME12 . . . . 99 B3
Falcon Gn ME20 . . . . . . 51 A1
Falcon Ho 3 ME10 . . 104 C2
Falkland Pl ME5 . . . . . . 39 B1
Fallowfield
Chatham ME5 . . . . 32 B4
Sittingbourne ME10 . . . 107 A4
Fallowfield Cl ME14. . . 74 A4
Fanconi Rd ME5 . . . . . . 40 B3
Fancy Row ME14. . . . . . 67 C1
Fane Way ME8. . . . . 43 A4
Fant La ME16 . . . . 71 A2
Faraday Ho ME1 . . . . . . 15 A1
Faraday Rd ME14 . . . . . 65 C3
Fareham Wlk 10 ME15. . . . . 82 A2
Farington Cl ME16 . . . . 71 A4
Farleigh Ct ME16 . . . . . 70 C2
Farleigh Hill ME15 . . . . 72 A1
Farleigh Hill Ret Pk ME15. . . . . 72 A1
Farleigh La ME16 . . . . . 70 C1
Farleigh Trad Est ME15. . . . . 72 A1
Farley Cl ME5. . . . . 41 A2
Farm Cres ME10 . . . . . 107 A4
Farmdale Ave ME1. . . . 20 C2
Farmer Cl ME17 . . . . . . 84 B2
Farm Hill Ave ME2 . . . . . 7 C1
Farm Rd ME5. . . . . 39 B3
Farnborough Cl ME16. 71 B2
Farne Cl ME15. . . . . 80 B2
Farnham Cl ME8. . . . . . 27 B1
Farningham Cl ME14. . 65 C2
Farraday Cl ME1. . . . . . 31 A4
Farrier Cl ME14. . . . . . . 66 B1
Farriers Ct ME8. . . . . . . 36 C4
Fartherwell Ave ME19. . . . . 59 A4
Fartherwell Rd ME19. . 59 A4
Farthing Cnr ME9. . . . . 43 B3
Farthings Cotts ME14 . 55 A1
Fauchon's Cl ME14 . . . 74 B3
Fauchon's La ME14 . . . 74 B4
Fawley Cl ME14. . . . . . . 64 B3
Fay Cl ME1 . . . . 21 B3
Featherbed La ME9 . . 100 C4
Featherby Cotts ME7. . 17 C2
Featherby Inf Sch ME8. . . . . 25 A3
Featherby Jun Sch ME8. . . . . 25 A3
Featherby Rd
Gillingham, Grange ME7. . . . . 18 A1
Gillingham ME8. . . . . 25 A3
Felderland Cl ME17 . . . 81 C1
Felderland Dr ME17. . . 81 C1
Felderland Rd ME17 . . 81 C1
Feldspar Cl
Chatham ME5 . . . . 40 A1
Sittingbourne ME10 . . . 103 C4
Fellows Cl ME8 . . . . 34 B2
Fennel Cl ME16. . . . . . . 71 A3
Fennell Cl ME1 . . . . 21 B3
Fernbank Cl ME5 . . . . . 39 C2
Ferndale Cl ME12. . . . . 97 B3
Ferndale Rd ME7 . . . . . 17 B1
Ferndown Cl ME7. . . . . 34 A1
Fernhill Rd ME16 . . . . . 70 C2
Fernleigh Rise ME20. . 51 C2
Ferns The ME20. . . . . . . 51 C1
Fern Wlk ME10 . . . . . . 105 B3
Ferrier Cl ME8. . . . . 43 B4
Ferry La ME1 . . . . 37 C4
Ferry Rd ME2. . . . . 37 B4
Ffinch Cl ME20 . . . . 62 A4
Field Cl ME5. . . . . 31 B2
Fielder Cl ME10. . . . . . 105 B3
Fielding Dr ME20 . . . . . 51 B3
Fieldings The ME10 . . 106 B4
Fields La ME18 . . . . 78 C3
Fieldview Cl ME12 . . . . 97 A3
Fieldworks Rd ME7 . . . 16 A3
Fiji Terr ME14. . . . . 65 A3
Filer Rd ME12 . . . . 97 C4
Finch Ct ME14 . . . . 64 B3
Finches The ME10 . . . 104 B1
Findlay Cl ME8 . . . . 35 A2
Finglesham Ct ME15 . . 81 A4
Fintonagh Dr ME14 . . . 65 B2
Finwell Rd ME8. . . . . . . 27 A2
Firethorn Cl ME7 . . . . . 17 B2
Firmin Ave ME17. . . . . . 81 B1
Firs Cl ME20. . . . . 52 C1
First Ave
Chatham ME4 . . . . 23 C2
Gillingham ME7. . . . . 24 B3
Sheerness ME12 . . . . . . 95 A2
First La ME17 . . . . 76 A2
Fir Tree Gr
Bredhurst ME7 . . . . 42 B1
Chatham ME5 . . . . 41 A1
Fisher Rd ME5. . . . . 32 B3
Fisher St ME14 . . . . 65 A2
Fitzthorold Ho ME7 . . . 17 B3
Fitzwilliam Rd ME14 . . 66 C1
Five Acre Wood Sch ME15. . . . . 80 C3
Five Bells La 5 ME1 . . 22 A4
Five Ways Ct ME4. . . . . 23 A4
Fiveways L Ctr ME4. . . 23 A4
FIVE WENTS. 92 C2
Flack Gdns ME3 . . . . 5 B1
Flamingo Cl ME5 . . . . . 32 A3
Flanders Cl ME10 . . . . 101 A3
Flaxman Ct 13 ME7. . . 16 A2
Flaxman Dr ME16 . . . . . 63 C2
Fleet Rd ME1 . . . . 22 A1
Fleetwood Cl ME12 . . . 98 C2
Flint Cl ME10 . . . . 100 C2
Flint Gn ME5 . . . . 40 C3
Flood Hatch ME15 . . . . 71 C2
Florence Rd ME16 . . . . 72 A3
Florence St 3 ME2 . . . 14 B4
Florin Dr ME1 . . . . 21 B4
Flower Rise ME14. . . . . 64 C3
Flume End ME15. . . . . . 71 C2
Foley St ME14 . . . . 65 A1
Folkstone Ho 4 ME15. . . . . 82 A2
Fonblanque Rd ME12 . 95 A3
Fontwell Cl ME15 . . . . . 82 A2
Foord Almshouses ME1. . . . . 21 B3
Foord St ME1. . . . . 22 A4
Fordcombe Cl ME15 . . 82 A3
Fordingbridge Cl ME16. . . . . 63 B1
Fordwich Cl ME16 . . . . 63 B3
Fordwich Dr ME2. . . . . . 8 A2
Fordwich Gn ME8. . . . . 25 C3
Forestdale Rd ME5 . . . 48 B4
Forest Dr ME5 . . . . 39 C2
Foresters Cl ME5 . . . . . 39 C2
Forest Hill ME15 . . . . . . 72 B1
Forest Way ME19 . . . . . 68 C3
Forge La
Boxley ME14. . . . . 56 A2
Bredhurst ME7 . . . . 42 A1
Gillingham ME7. . . . . 17 B3
Higham ME3. . . . . 6 C3
Leeds ME17 . . . . 84 A3
Maidstone ME14. . . . . . . 75 B4
Forge Mdw ME17 . . . . . 87 B2
Forge Rd ME10 . . . . . . 104 A4
Formby Rd ME2 . . . . . . 28 C3
Formby Terr ME2 . . . . . 28 C2
FORSTAL 53 C2
Forstal Cotts ME20. . . . 53 C2
Forstal La ME17 . . . . . . 88 C4
Forstal Rd ME20 . . . . . . 54 A2
Forsters ME17 . . . . 93 A4
Forsyth Cl ME19 . . . . . . 51 B1
Forsyth Ct 7 ME7 . . . . 16 C3
Fort Amherst Heritage Pk & Caverns★ ME4. . . . . 15 C1
Fort Luton (Mus)★ ME4. . . . . 23 A1
Fort Pitt Gram Sch ME4. . . . . 22 B4
Fort Pitt Hill ME1, ME4. . . . . 22 B4
Fort Pitt St ME4 . . . . . . 22 B3
Fort St ME1 . . . . 22 A4
Fortune Way ME18. . . . 69 A3
Forum The 2 ME10 . . 104 B2
Forward Way ME1 . . . . 30 C2
Foster Clarke Dr ME17. . . . . 81 B1
Foster Clark Est ME15. . . . . 73 A2
Foster St ME15 . . . . 72 C3
Fostington Way ME5. . 39 C1
Foulds Cl ME8 . . . . 34 B1
Foundry Wharf ME1 . . 22 B4
Fountain La
Maidstone ME16. . . . . . . 70 C2
Sheerness ME12 . . . . . . 94 B3
Fountain Rd ME2 . . . . . . 7 B1
Fountain St 2 ME10. . . . . 104 A2
Four Acres ME19 . . . . . 61 B1
Four Elms Hill ME3 . . . . 9 B4
Four Elms Rdbt ME3 . . . 9 B3
Fourth Ave ME7 . . . . . . 24 B4
Four Wents
Langley Heath ME17 . . . 93 A3
Maidstone ME17. . . . . . . 91 B2
Fourwents Rd ME3 . . . . 5 A3
Fowey Cl ME5 . . . . 32 C1
Fowler Cl ME8. . . . . 42 C3
Foxburrow Cl ME8 . . . . 35 A1
Foxden Dr ME15 . . . . . . 74 B1
Foxglove Cres ME5 . . . 39 B4
Foxglove Rise ME14. . . 64 B3
Foxgrove ME10 . . . . . . 100 C1
Fox Hill ME10, ME9 . . . 105 C1
Foxley Rd ME11. . . . . . . 96 B2
Fox St ME7 . . . . 16 C2
Foxtail Cl ME4 . . . . 10 B2
Francis Dr ME5 . . . . 40 A2
Francis La ME15 . . . . . . 82 A1
Frankapps Cl ME9 . . . 102 B3
Franklin Dr ME14 . . . . . 73 C4
Franklin Rd ME7. . . . . . 17 A1
Franks Ct ME8. . . . . 25 B2
Frederick Rd ME7 . . . . 23 C4
Frederick St ME10 . . . 104 A2
Freelands Rd ME6 . . . . 45 A4
Freeman Ct 3 ME10. . . . . 104 A2
Freeman Gdns ME4. . . 22 C2
Freeman Way ME15. . . 81 C3
Freesia Cl ME7 . . . . 17 C2
Fremlins Rd ME14 . . . . 75 B4
Frensham Cl ME10. . . 105 A2
Frensham Wlk ME5 . . . 39 C1
Freshland Rd ME16 . . . 71 A4
Freshwater Rd ME5. . . 32 B3
Friars Ave ME5 . . . . 39 C2
Friars Pk ME20 . . . . 52 C2
Friars The★ ME20 . . . . 52 C2
Friary Pl 3 ME2 . . . . . . 14 B3
Friary Prec ME2 . . . . . . 14 B3
FRINDSBURY 14 C4
Frindsbury Hill ME2. . . . 8 C1
Frindsbury Rd ME2 . . . 14 B4
Frinstead Wlk ME16 . . 63 B3
Frinsted Cl ME8 . . . . . . 25 C3
Friston Way ME1 . . . . . 31 A4
Frithwood Cl ME15 . . . 74 B1
Frittenden Rd ME2. . . . . 9 A2
Frobisher Cl ME10 . . . 100 C1
Frobisher Gdns ME1 . . 21 C2
Frog La ME19. . . . . 59 C4
Frost Cres ME5 . . . . 32 A3
Froyle Cl ME16 . . . . 63 C2
Fruiterer's Cl ME9 . . . 107 B1
Fulbert Dr ME14 . . . . . . 66 C1
Fullers Cl ME14. . . . . . . 74 C4
Fulmar Rd ME2 . . . . 13 A2
Fulston Manor Sch ME10. . . . . 106 C4
Fulston Pl ME10 . . . . . 104 C1
Furfield Cl ME17. . . . . . 81 C1
Furrell's Rd ME1. . . . . . 15 A1
Furze Hill Cres ME12. . 97 C3

G

Gabriel's Hill ME15 . . . 72 C4
Gadby Rd ME10. . . . . . 103 B3
Gads Hill ME7 . . . . 17 C2
Gads Hill Sch ME3. . . . . 6 C2
Gagetown Terr 1 ME14. . . . . 64 C3
Gainsborough Cl
Gillingham ME8. . . . . 35 A2
Sittingbourne ME10 . . . 103 A3
Gainsborough Dr ME16. . . . . 71 A4
Gainsborough Ho ME1. . . . . 15 A1
Galahad Ave ME2 . . . . . 13 B2
Galena Cl
Chatham ME5 . . . . 40 A1
Sittingbourne ME10 . . . 103 B4
Galleon Cl ME1 . . . . 30 C4
Galleon Way ME2 . . . . . . 9 C3
Galway Rd ME12. . . . . . 95 A2
Gandy's La ME17 . . . . . 90 B2
Garden Cl ME15 . . . . . . 81 C3
Garden Ct ME1 . . . . 29 B1
Gardenia Cl ME2. . . . . . . 8 B2
Garden of England Pk (Mobile Home Pk) ME17. . . . . 86 C3
Garden St ME7 . . . . 16 A2
Gardens The ME17 . . . . 88 B3
Garden Way ME19 . . . . 68 B2
Gardiner St ME7. . . . . . 16 C2
Garfield Rd ME7 . . . . . . 17 A2
Garner Dr ME19 . . . . . . 51 B1
Garrington Cl ME14. . . 65 C2
Garrison Rd ME12 . . . . 94 B4
Gascoyne Cl ME15 . . . . 75 A2
Gas House Rd ME1. . . . 14 C2
Gas Rd
Sittingbourne ME10. . . . . 104 B3
Sittingbourne, Murston ME10. . . . . 105 A4
Gassons Rd ME6 . . . . . . 44 C4
Gatcombe Cl
Chatham ME5 . . . . 32 A1
Maidstone ME16. . . . . . . 63 B1
Gatekeeper Chase ME8. . . . . 35 C4
Gatland La ME16. . . . . . 71 A2
Gault Cl ME15 . . . . 74 C2
Gayhurst Cl ME8. . . . . . 35 A2
Gayhurst Dr ME10 . . . 103 B3
Gaze Hill Ave ME10 . . 104 C1
Gean Cl ME5 . . . . 48 B4
Genesta Cl ME10. . . . . 100 C1
Geneva Ave ME8. . . . . . 25 A2
Gentian Cl
4 Chatham ME5 . . . . . . 39 B4
Maidstone ME14. . . . . . . 66 B1
George La
Leeds ME17 . . . . 84 C3
Rochester ME1. . . . . 14 C2
George Marsham Ho ME15. . . . . 89 B3
George Parris Ct ME12. . . . . 99 A2
George St
Maidstone ME15. . . . . . . 72 C3
Sittingbourne ME10 . . . 105 A2
George Summers Cl ME2. . . . . 15 B4
Georgian Dr ME17 . . . . 88 C3
Georgian Way ME8 . . . 42 C4
Gerald Ave ME4 . . . . . . 22 C2
Gerrard Ave ME1 . . . . . 31 B4
Gerrards Dr ME10. . . . 106 C4
Gibbons Rd ME10. . . . 103 A3
Gibraltar Ave ME7 . . . . 16 B3
Gibraltar Hill ME4 . . . . 22 C4
Gibraltar La ME14 . . . . 64 C4
Gibson Dr ME19 . . . . . . 68 B4
Gibson Ho ME3. . . . . 3 C2
Gibson St ME10. . . . . . 104 A2
Gidd's Pond Cotts ME14. . . . . 66 B2
Giddyhorn La ME16 . . . 63 C1
Gifford Cl ME8. . . . . 25 C3
Gighill Rd ME20 . . . . . . 51 A4
Gilbert Cl ME7. . . . . 34 A1
Gilbert Terr 2 ME14 . . 64 C3
Giles Young Ct 7 ME10. . . . . 104 A3
Gill Ave ME2. . . . . 9 A2
Gilletts La ME19 . . . . . . 61 A2
GILLINGHAM 24 A3
Gillingham Coll The ME7. . . . . 24 C4
Gillingham Gate ME7 . 16 C4
Gillingham Gate Rd ME7. . . . . 16 C4
Gillingham Gn ME7 . . . 17 B2
Gillingham Rd ME7 . . . 17 A1
Gillingham Sta ME7 . . 17 A1
Gills Terr ME8 . . . . 27 C3
Ginsbury Cl ME2. . . . . . 15 B2
Glade The ME5 . . . . 40 A2
Gladstone Dr ME10 . . 105 B2
Gladstone Rd
Chatham ME4 . . . . 22 B2
Maidstone ME14. . . . . . . 65 A2
Gladwyn Cl ME8 . . . . . . 43 A4
Glamford Rd ME2. . . . . 13 A1
Glamis Cl ME5. . . . . 32 A1
Glanville Rd
Gillingham ME7. . . . . 17 A1
Rochester ME2. . . . . 14 A4
Glasgow Ho 8 ME15. . 81 C3
Gleaming Wood Dr ME5. . . . . 49 B4
Gleaners Cl ME14. . . . . 74 A4
Gleanings Mews ME1 . 14 C1
Glebe La
Maidstone ME16. . . . . . . 70 C1
Sittingbourne ME10 . . . 107 B4
Glebe Mdw ME18 . . . . . 78 C3
Glebe Rd ME7 . . . . 24 B3
Glebe The ME2 . . . . 19 C2
Glenbrook Gr ME10 . . 100 C1
Glencoe Jun Sch ME4. . . . . 23 A2
Glencoe Rd ME4. . . . . . 23 A2
Glendale Rd ME12 . . . . 98 C3
Gleneagles Ct ME5 . . . 39 C2
Gleneagles Dr ME15 . . 72 C1
Glenleigh Rd ME18 . . . 78 B2
Glen The ME12. . . . . 98 C3
Glenwood Cl
Chatham ME5 . . . . 23 C1
Gillingham ME7. . . . . 34 A3
Maidstone ME16. . . . . . . 63 C1
Glenwood Dr ME12 . . . 99 A2
Glistening Glade ME8. 35 B2
Globe La ME4 . . . . 15 C1
Gloucester Cl ME8. . . . 36 A4
Gloucester Rd ME15 . . 81 B4
Glover Cl ME10 . . . . . . 101 A3
Glovers Cres ME10. . . 104 B1
Glovers Mill ME4 . . . . . 22 A3
Glynne Cl ME8. . . . . 35 A2
Goad Ave ME5 . . . . 40 B3
Godden Rd ME6 . . . . . . 45 A4
Godden Way ME8. . . . . 25 A4
Goddings Dr ME1. . . . . 21 A3
Goddington La ME17. . 86 C2
Goddington Rd ME2 . . 14 B4
Godfrey Cl ME2. . . . . 7 C1
Godwin Cl ME10 . . . . . 101 A3
Goldcrest Dr ME4. . . . . 10 C2
Golden Wood Cl ME5 . 49 B4
Goldfinch Cl ME20 . . . . 51 B2
Golding Cl
Ditton ME20 . . . . 52 A1
Rochester ME1. . . . . 22 B1
Goldings Cl ME19. . . . . 68 C3
Goldings The ME8 . . . . 34 C4
Goldsmith Rd ME8. . . . 35 B1
Goldstone Wlk ME5. . . 40 A1
Goldsworth Dr ME2. . . . 8 A1
Goldthorne Cl ME14 . . 65 C1
Gooch Cl ME16 . . . . 64 A4
Goodall Cl ME8. . . . . . . 35 B1
Goodnestone Rd ME10. . . . . 105 A2
Goodwin Dr ME14 . . . . 65 B4
Goodwin Rd ME3 . . . . . . 2 B3
Goodwood Cl ME15 . . . 82 A2
Goose Cl ME5 . . . . 32 A3
Gordon Ave ME11. . . . . 96 B1
Gordon Cl ME10 . . . . . 105 B2

Gordon Ct ME17 ......89 A3
Gordon Inf Sch ME2 ..14 A4
Gordon Jun Sch ME2 .14 A4
Gordon Rd
Chatham, Luton ME4 ...23 B2
Chatham ME4 ....16 A3
Gillingham ME7........17 B1
Hoo St Werburgh ME3 ...5 A1
Rochester ME2........14 A4
Gordon Terr ME1......21 C4
Gore Court Rd
Maidstone ME15.......82 A1
Sittingbourne ME10 ...106 B4
Gorham Cl ME6.......45 A3
Gorham Dr ME15 .....74 C1
Gorse Ave ME5 ....31 C1
Gorse Cres ME20 .....62 A4
Gorse Rd
Rochester ME2........13 C4
Sittingbourne ME10 ...105 B3
Gorst St ME7 ....16 C1
Goshawk Ho 1 ME10...............104 C2
Goudhurst Cl ME16 ...72 A4
Goudhurst Rd ME8....25 B3
Gould Rd ME5 ....40 B3
Gower Ho ME14 ......65 A2
Grace Ave ME16 ......64 A2
Grace Rd ME12 ....94 B2
Grafton Ave ME1......31 B4
Grafton Rd ME10 ....104 B2
Graham Cl ME4.......15 C2
Grain Rd ME8.........42 C3
Grampian Way ME15..74 C1
Granada Ho 8 ME15..72 C4
Granada St 9 ME15 ..72 C4
Granary Cl
Gillingham ME8........26 C1
Maidstone ME14.......66 B1
Grand Ct 7 ME7......16 C2
Grandsire Gdns ME3 ...5 B2
GRANGE.............18 B2
Grange Cl ME19 ......50 A2
Grange Hill ME5......23 B3
Grange Ho ME16......70 C2
Grange La ME14 ......55 B1
Grange Rd
Gillingham ME7........18 A2
Rochester ME2........14 B3
Grange Rdbt ME7.....18 A2
Grange The ME19.....61 A3
Grange Way ME1 .....21 C3
Grant Cl ME7 ....25 B1
Grant Dr ME15........81 B2
Grant Rd ME3 ....8 C3
Granville Ct ME14.....65 A2
Granville Pl ME12.....95 A3
Granville Rd
Gillingham ME7........17 B1
Maidstone ME14.......65 A2
Sheerness ME12 ....95 A3
Grapple Rd ME14 .....65 A3
Grasmere Gr ME2......8 C2
Grasslands ME17 .....93 A4
Grassmere ME19 .....51 A2
Grassy Glade ME7 ....34 B2
Gravel Wlk ME1 ......15 A1
Graveney Cl ME3 ......2 C3
Graveney Rd ME15....82 A3
Gravesend Rd
Higham ME2, ME3, DA12................6 C2
Rochester ME2........13 C4
Graylings The ME1....21 B3
Grayshott Cl ME10 ...104 B1
Great Basin Rd ME12..94 A3
Great Ivy Mill Cotts ME15................80 A3
Great Lines ME7 ......16 B1
Great South Ave ME4 .23 A1
Grebe Apartments 15 ME15.................81 C1
Grebe Ct ME20.........51 A1
Grecian St ME14......65 A2
Greenacre Cl ME5 ....32 A1
Greenacre Sch ME5 ..31 C1
Greenbank ME5 ......32 B4
Green Bank Cl ME7 ...34 A1
Greenborough Cl ME15.................81 C2
Green Cl ME1.........22 A2
Greenfield Cl ME20 ...46 B2
Greenfield Cotts ME14................56 A3
Greenfield Rd ME7....17 A2
Greenfields ME15......81 C4
Greenfields Cl ME3 ....9 A3
Greenfinches ME7 ....33 C2
Green Hill ME15 ......75 A1
Greenhithe 3 ME15 ..72 C3
Green La
Langley Heath ME17 ...93 A3
Maidstone ME17.......90 B3
Rodmersham ME9 ....107 B1
Green Lane Cotts ME17................93 A3
Greenlees Cl ME10...103 A3
Green Porch Cl ME10...............101 A1
Greensand Rd ME15 ..74 C2
Green Sands ME5.....49 A4
Greenside ME15 ......73 A3
Greensleeves Way ME18................69 B3
Green St ME7.........16 C1
Greenvale Gdns ME8..25 B2
Greenvale Inf Sch ME4.................23 A2
Greenview Wlk ME8 ..25 A4
Greenway ME5 ....31 A2
Green Way ME16......71 A3
Greenway La ME17....86 B3
Greenways
Maidstone ME14.......66 C1
Sittingbourne ME10 ...105 A1
Greenwich Cl
Chatham ME5.........40 B4
Maidstone ME16.......71 C4
Gregory Cl
Gillingham ME8........43 B4
Sittingbourne ME10 ...101 B2
Grenadier Cl
Gillingham ME8........27 B2
Maidstone ME15.......74 B2
Gresham Cl 3 ME8 ...26 C1
Gresham Rd ME17 ....88 C3
Greyfriars Cl ME16....64 A1
Greystones Rd ME15 ..74 C2
Grey Wethers ME14 ...54 C4
Grieveson Ho ME4....23 A4
Grizedale Cl ME1 .....31 A4
Groombridge Sq 13 ME15.................82 A2
Grosvenor Ave ME4...22 B3
Grosvenor Ho 5 ME15.................82 A1
Grosvenor Rd ME7....25 A1
Grove Ct 4 ME2......14 B3
GROVE GREEN.......66 B1
Grove Green La ME14 .66 B1
Grove Green Rd ME14.................66 C1
Grovehurst Ave ME10...............101 A3
Grovehurst Rd ME10, ME9................100 C4
Grove Park Ave ME10...............103 A3
Grove Park Prim Sch ME10...............103 A4
Grove Rd
Chatham ME4.........23 B2
Gillingham ME7........18 A2
Maidstone ME15.......81 A3
Rochester ME2........14 B4
Upper Halling ME2.....28 A1
Groves The ME6 ......45 A3
Grove The ME14 ......74 C3
Grovewood Ct ME14 ..74 A4
Grovewood Dr ME14 ..74 A4
Guardian Ct ME8 .....25 C1
Guildford Gdns ME2 ..12 C2
Guildhall Mus★ ME11................96 A2
Guildhall Mus The★ ME1.................14 C2
Guiness Dr ME2 ....8 B2
Gulland Ho 4 ME14 ..73 A4
Gullands ME17 ....93 A4
Gundulph Rd ME1 ....22 B4
Gundulph Sq ME1 ....14 C2
Gun La ME2 ....14 B3
Gunnis Cl ME8........43 A4
Gun Tower Mews ME1.................21 B4
Guston Rd ME14......65 C2

H

Hackney Rd ME16.....71 B2
Hadleigh Ct ME7......42 A3
Hadlow Rd ME14......65 C1
Haig Ave
Chatham, Luton ME4................23 A2
Chatham ME1.........22 A1
Gillingham ME7........24 B4
Haig Villas ME3 ....4 A1
Halden Cl ME15.......82 A2
HALE................33 A4
Hale Rd ME3 ....2 C3
Hales Rd ME10 ......106 A3
Haleys Pl ME1 ....46 B4
Halfpenny Cl ME16....70 C2
HALFWAY HOUSES...97 C4
Halfway Houses Prim Sch ME12 ....97 B3
Halfway Rd ME12 .....95 B1
Halifax Cl ME5........32 B2
Hall Cl ME10.........104 A4
HALLING 29 A1
Halling Prim Sch ME2.................37 B3
Halling Sta ME2 ......28 C1
Hall Rd
Aylesford ME20 ....53 A1
Chatham ME5.........40 C3
Wouldham ME1 ....37 C3
Hallsfield Rd ME5.....39 A2
Hallwood Cl ME8 .....35 A1
Hallwood Ho ME5.....40 C2
Halstead Wlk ME16 ...63 C3
Halstow Cl ME15......80 C2
Hambledon Ct ME16 ..71 A3
Hambrook Wlk ME10...............101 A2
Hamelin Rd ME7......33 C4
Hamilton Cres ME10 .103 B1
Hamilton Ct
Chatham ME5.........23 C1
Rochester ME1........21 B4
Hamilton Ho
Coxheath ME17 ....88 B3
Maidstone ME15.......82 A1
Hamilton Rd ME7.....17 A3
Ham La ME7..........41 B3
Hammonds Sq ME6...45 B4
Hamond Hill 6 ME4 ..22 B4
Hampden Way ME19 ..68 B3
Hampshire Cl ME5....32 C3
Hampshire Dr ME15 ..81 A4
Hampshires The ME17.................87 A2
Hampson Way ME14 ..74 C4
Hampton Cl ME5......32 A1
Hampton Rd ME14....65 C2
Ham River Hill ME3 ....2 A2
Hamwick Gn ME5.....40 C1
Hanbury Cl ME18 .....78 C3
Hancock Cl ME3 ....8 B1
Hanes Dene ME2 .....28 B1
Hanover Cl ME10 ....106 B4
Hanover Ct ME14 .....65 B1
Hanover Dr ME8......42 C4
Hanover Gn ME20.....51 A3
Hanover Rd ME17.....88 B3
Hanson Dr ME15......89 B3
Hanway ME8 ....25 A2
Harbledown Ho ME16 71 A2
Harbledown Manor ME8.................25 B3
HARBOURLAND......65 B4
Harbourland Cl ME14 .65 B4
Harcourt Gdns ME8...43 B4
Hardie Cl ME19.......51 A1
Hardinge Cl ME8 .....43 A4
Hards Town ME4......23 A4
Hardwick Ho ME15 ...81 C4
Hardy Cl ME5.........32 B2
Hardy Lodge ME1.....21 B4
Hardy St ME14........65 A2
Harebell Cl
3 Chatham ME5 ......39 C4
Maidstone ME14.......66 B1
Harebell Cl *continued*
Minster (Sheppey) ME12...............98 B1
Haredale Cl ME1......31 A3
Hare St 2 ME4 ....23 B3
Harkness Ct 6 ME10...............105 A2
Harlech Cl ME2........7 C1
Harling Cl ME17 ......81 B1
Harman Ct ME5.......40 B3
Harold Ave ME7 ......24 B4
Harold Rd
Cuxton ME2 ....19 C3
Sittingbourne ME10 ...105 A2
Harold St ME11 ....96 B1
Harp Farm Rd ME14...49 A2
Harple La ME14.......57 A1
Harps Ave ME12 ......99 A2
Harptree Dr ME5 .....31 C1
Harrier Dr ME10.....107 A4
Harrietsham Sta ME17.................87 B2
Harriet Dr ME1 ....21 B3
HARRIETSHAM 87 B1
Harrietsham Ho 13 ME16.................70 C3
Harrietsham Prim Sch ME17.................87 C2
Harris Gdns ME10....105 B3
Harris Ho ME2........37 B4
Harrison Ct 4 ME8 ...26 C1
Harrison Dr ME17.....87 C2
Harris Rd ME12.......95 A3
Harrow Ct ME5 ....40 C4
Harrow Rd ME7.......33 C2
Harrow Way ME14 ....66 B1
Hartington St ME4....23 A3
Hartley Cl ME15 ......82 A2
Hartley Mews ME8....25 B3
Hartlip Cl ME12.......96 C4
Hartnup St ME16 .....71 B2
Hartpiece Cl ME8.....26 C2
Hart St ME16 ....72 B3
Hart Street Bsns Ctr ME16.................72 B3
Harty Ave ME8........42 B3
Harvel Ave ME2.......13 C3
Harvesters Cl ME8....35 B3
Harvesters Way ME14 73 C4
Harvest Ridge ME19 ..50 B2
Harvey Dr ME10 .....107 A4
Harvey Rd ME8 ....35 B4
Harwood Rd ME8 .....27 B1
Haslemere Est ME15..82 A1
Hasted Rd ME9 ......102 B4
Hasteds ME17 ....77 C2
Haste Hill Cl ME17 ....90 A3
Haste Hill Rd ME17 ....90 A3
Hastings Rd ME15 ....73 A3
Hatfield Rd ME2 ......14 A4
Hathaway Ct
Gillingham ME8........35 A4
Rochester ME1........14 B1
Hatherall Rd ME14....65 B2
Hatton Rd ME5 ....40 C3
Havant Wlk 8 ME15 ..82 A2
Haven Cl ME1 ....21 C2
Haven St ME3 ....2 C1
Haven Way ME4 ......10 B1
Havisham Cl ME1.....22 A2
Hawbeck Rd ME8.....42 C3
Hawkenbury Rise ME2 . 8 B2
Hawkes Rd ME20 .....46 A1
Hawkhurst Rd ME8 ...25 B3
Hawkins Cl
Chatham ME7.........16 A2
Sittingbourne ME10 ...100 C1
Hawkridge Gr ME18...68 C3
Hawkwood ME16 .....63 B1
Hawkwood Cl ME1....15 A1
Hawley Ct ME16 ......72 A4
Hawser Rd ME1.......21 C1
Hawthorn Ave ME12 ..94 B1
Hawthornden Cl ME18................69 B3
Hawthorne Ave ME8 ..25 C2
Hawthorne Ho 4 ME16.................70 C3
Hawthorn Ho
5 Chatham ME5 ......31 C1
10 Sittingbourne ME10.............104 A2
Hawthorn Rd
Rochester ME2........13 B2
Sittingbourne ME10 ...104 A2
Hawthorns ME5 ......39 C1
Hawthorns The
Aylesford ME20 ....52 C1
Chatham ME5.........31 C2
Haydon Cl ME16 ......71 A4
Hayes Cl ME3..........6 C3
Hayes Cotts ME19.....58 A3
Hayes Wlk ME19 .....68 C2
Hayfield ME19 ....50 C2
Hayfields ME5 ....41 A2
Haygate Ho ME1......21 C4
Hayle Mill Cotts ME15.................80 A4
Hayle Mill Rd ME15 ...80 A4
Hayle Rd ME15 ....72 C3
Hayley Cl ME2 ....19 C2
Hayman Wlk ME20....46 A2
Haymen St ME4.......22 B3
Haynes Ho 3 ME14...73 A4
Hayrick Cl ME14 ......66 B1
Haysel ME10.........107 A4
Hays Rd ME6 ....45 A2
Haywain Cl ME14 .....74 B4
Hayward Ave ME2 ....14 B4
Hayward's Ho ME1....14 C2
Hazel Ave
Hoo St Werburgh ME3.................11 B3
Maidstone ME16.......63 C1
Hazel Gr ME5.........32 B4
Hazels The ME8.......34 B1
Hazelwood Dr ME16 ..71 A4
Hazen Rd ME18.......69 A3
Hazlemere Dr ME7....18 A1
Hazlitt Dr ME16.......64 A1
Headcorn Rd ME8 ....25 B4
Headingley Rd ME16 ..63 B2
Head Race The ME15..71 C2
Heard Way ME10.....105 A3
Hearne Cl ME10 .....105 A3
Heathcote Cl ME20 ...53 A2
Heather Cl
Chatham ME5.........39 C4
Sittingbourne ME10 ...104 C1
Heather Dr ME15 .....73 A2
Heathfield ME17......93 A4
Heathfield Ave ME14..65 C3
Heathfield Cl
Chatham ME5.........32 B3
Maidstone ME14.......65 B3
Heathfield Rd ME14...65 C3
Heath Gr ME16 ....70 C2
Heathorn St ME14 ....65 B1
Heath Rd
Coxheath ME17 ....88 B3
Langley Heath ME17 ...93 A4
Maidstone, Cock Street ME17................90 B2
Maidstone, East Barming ME16................70 B3
Maidstone ME16.......70 C2
Heathside Ave ME17 ..88 B4
Heath The ME19 ......60 C1
Hedgerow The ME14 ..66 B1
Hedges The ME14.....65 A3
Hedley St ME14.......65 A1
Hellyar Ct ME1 ....21 C4
HEMPSTEAD 34 A1
Hempstead Inf Sch ME7.................34 A1
Hempstead Jun Sch ME7.................34 A1
Hempstead Rd ME7, ME8.................34 A1
Hempstead Valley Dr ME7.................42 A4
Hempstead Valley Sh Ctr ME7.................42 A3
Henbane Cl ME14.....66 B1
Hendry Ho ME3........3 C2
Hendy Rd ME6........45 C4
Henley Bsns Pk ME2..15 A3
Henley Cl
Chatham ME5.........32 A2
Gillingham ME8........35 A4
Henley Fields ME14...66 B2

Henrys Cl ME18....... 78 B2
Henry St
Chatham ME4......... 23 B3
Gillingham ME8........ 27 A1
Herbert Rd
Chatham ME4......... 23 A3
Gillingham ME8........ 35 B4
Herdsdown ME3....... 5 A1
Hereford Cl ME8...... 26 A2
Hereford Rd ME15.... 81 B3
Heritage Dr ME7...... 24 C1
Heritage Rd ME5..... 32 A2
Herman Terr ME4..... 23 A3
Hermitage Ct ME16... 62 C1
Hermitage Farm
ME19................ 59 C4
Hermitage La
Detling ME14......... 57 C4
Maidstone ME16....... 70 C4
Maidstone ME16,
ME20............... 62 C2
Hermitage Rd ME3..... 7 B4
Hermitage The ME19.. 60 A4
Herne Rd ME8........ 25 C2
Hero Ho ME12........ 94 C2
Heron Apartments 3
ME15................ 82 A1
Heronden Rd ME15... 91 B4
Heron Dr ME12....... 98 C1
Heron Rd ME20....... 51 A1
Heron Way ME5...... 32 B3
Hero Wlk ME1........ 30 C3
Herts Cres ME15...... 89 B3
Hertsfield Ave ME2.... 8 A2
Herying Cl ME2....... 37 B4
Hever Cl ME15........ 82 A2
Hever Croft ME2....... 13 C1
Hever Gdns ME16..... 72 A3
Hever Ho ME2......... 8 C1
Hever Pl ME10....... 103 C1
Hewitt Cl
Gillingham ME7........ 17 C2
Maidstone ME16....... 64 A3
Hextable Cl ME16..... 64 A3
Hickory Dell ME7..... 34 A1
Higgins' La ME4...... 15 C1
HIGHAM.............. 6 B4
Higham Cl ME15...... 72 A2
Higham Rd ME3....... 8 C3
Higham View ME14.... 54 C4
High Bank ME1....... 22 A2
High Banks ME15..... 80 A1
Highberry ME19...... 50 C2
Highcroft Gn ME15... 91 B4
High Dewar Rd ME8.. 36 A4
High Elms ME8....... 26 B1
Highfield Cl ME8...... 35 A3
Highfield Rd
Gillingham ME8........ 35 A3
Halfway Houses ME12.. 97 C3
Highgrove Rd ME5.... 32 A1
Highland Rd ME15.... 81 C2
Highlands Cl ME2..... 13 A1
Highridge ME7....... 24 C1
Highridge Cl ME14.... 66 C1
High St
Aylesford ME20....... 53 A3
Chatham, Brompton
ME7................ 16 A2
Chatham ME4......... 23 A4
East Malling ME19..... 61 A2
Forstal ME20......... 53 B3
Gillingham ME7........ 16 C1
Gillingham, Rainham
ME8................ 35 C4
Halling ME2.......... 37 A4
Maidstone ME14....... 72 B4
Minster (Sheppey)
ME12............... 99 B2
Newington ME9...... 102 C3
Queenborough ME11... 96 A2
Rochester ME1........ 14 C2
Rochester, Strood
ME2................ 14 B3
Rochester, Upper Upnor
ME2................. 9 C1
Sheerness, Blue Town
ME12............... 94 B4
Sheerness ME12...... 95 A3
High St *continued*
Sittingbourne ME10... 104 B2
Sittingbourne, Milton Regis
ME10.............. 104 A4
Snodland ME6......... 45 B4
West Malling ME19.... 59 C4
Wouldham ME1....... 29 B1
HIGHSTED.......... 106 C1
Highsted Gram Sch
ME10.............. 106 C4
Highsted Rd ME9,
ME10.............. 106 C3
High View ME3........ 6 C4
Highview Cl ME15.... 80 B4
Highview Dr ME5..... 31 A1
Highview Rd ME12.... 99 A3
Highwoods Cl ME3..... 6 C4
Hilary Gdns ME1...... 20 C1
Hilda Rd
Chatham ME4......... 23 A3
Halfway Houses ME12.. 97 B3
Hildenborough Cres
ME16................ 63 C3
Hillary Rd ME14...... 65 A3
Hillborough Gr ME5.. 40 A3
Hill Brow
Maidstone ME14....... 67 A1
Sittingbourne ME10... 106 A4
Hill Chase ME5....... 39 B3
Hillcrest Dr ME2...... 19 C2
Hillcrest Rd ME4...... 22 C2
Hill Ct ME3............ 9 C4
Hillden Shaw ME15... 80 B4
Hill Rd
Burham ME5.......... 38 A3
Rochester ME1........ 21 A2
Hillshaw Cres ME2.... 13 A1
Hillside ME1.......... 21 A2
Hillside Ave ME2...... 14 B4
Hillside Ct
2 Rochester ME2..... 14 A3
Wateringbury ME18.... 78 C3
Hillside Rd
Chatham ME4......... 23 A4
Minster (Sheppey)
ME12............... 98 C3
Hill's Terr ME4....... 22 C3
Hill Top Cotts ME17... 89 A2
Hilltop Prim Sch ME2.. 8 C1
Hilltop Rd
Minster (Sheppey)
ME12............... 98 B1
Rochester ME2......... 8 C1
Hill View Way ME5.... 31 B1
Hillyfield Cl ME2....... 7 C1
Hilton Dr ME10...... 103 A4
Hilton Rd ME3......... 2 B3
Hinde Cl ME10....... 101 A1
Hinde Ho ME10...... 104 A4
Hines Terr ME5....... 23 C1
Hinton Cres ME7...... 34 A2
Historic Dockyard The★
ME4................ 16 A4
Hoath Cl ME8......... 34 B3
Hoath La ME8........ 34 B3
Hoath Way ME7, ME8.. 34 B1
Hobart Gdns ME10... 103 B2
Hockers Cl ME14...... 67 A4
Hockers La ME14..... 67 A4
Hodgson Cres ME6... 37 A1
Hogarth Ho ME11..... 96 A2
Hog Hill ME14........ 67 B1
Holborn La ME4...... 15 C1
HOLBOROUGH....... 37 A2
Holborough Rd ME6.. 37 A1
Holcombe Rd
Chatham ME4......... 22 C2
Rochester ME1........ 21 C3
Holder Cl ME5........ 32 C2
Holding St ME8....... 26 C1
Hollandbury Pk ME18. 69 B2
Holland Ho ME1...... 15 A1
Holland Rd
Chatham ME5......... 39 B4
Maidstone ME14....... 65 B1
Hollingbourne Rd
ME8................ 25 C2
Hollingbourne Sta
ME17............... 77 B3
Hollingworth Ct
ME14............... 73 B3
Hollingworth Rd
ME15............... 82 A1
Hollow La ME6....... 45 A2
Hollybank Hill ME10. 103 C2
Holly Cl
Chatham ME5......... 32 C4
Gillingham ME7........ 17 B2
Hollycroft ME2....... 19 C2
Holly Farm Rd ME15.. 83 A2
Holly Gdns ME14...... 65 B3
Holly Rd
Rochester ME2......... 9 A2
Rochester, Strood
ME2................ 13 B1
Hollytree Dr ME3...... 6 B3
Hollywood La ME2..... 8 C2
Holmesdale Cl ME15.. 89 B3
Holmesdale Tech Coll
ME6................ 45 A3
Holm Mill La ME17.... 86 C2
Holmoaks
Gillingham ME8........ 26 B2
Maidstone ME14....... 65 C1
Holmside ME7........ 24 B3
Holmside Ave ME12... 97 B3
Holt Wood Ave ME20.. 62 B4
Holtwood Cl ME8..... 35 A2
Holtye Cres ME15..... 73 A2
Holy Family RC Prim
Sch ME15........... 91 B4
Holyrood Dr ME12.... 98 B1
Homefarm Est ME20.. 53 A1
Homefield Dr ME8.... 27 B2
Homeview 3 ME10.. 105 A2
Homeview Terr 2
ME10.............. 105 A2
Homewood Ave
ME10.............. 103 C1
Homewood Inf Sch
ME10.............. 103 C2
Honduras Terr 8
ME14............... 65 A3
Hone St ME2......... 14 B4
Honey Bee Glade
ME8................ 35 B2
Honey Cl ME7........ 34 A1
Honey La ME15....... 82 C2
Honeypot Cl ME2..... 14 B4
Honeysuckle Cl
3 Chatham ME5...... 39 B4
Gillingham ME7........ 41 C4
Honeysuckle Ct
ME10.............. 105 A3
Hoo Comm ME3...... 10 A4
Hook Cl ME5......... 31 B1
Hook La ME17........ 87 A2
Hook Rd ME6......... 45 A4
Hooper's Pl ME1...... 21 C4
Hooper's Rd ME1..... 21 C4
Hoo Rd ME2, ME3...... 9 A3
HOO ST WERBURGH.. 5 C1
Hoo St Werburgh Prim
Sch ME3............. 5 A1
Hope St
Chatham ME4......... 23 A3
Maidstone ME14....... 64 C2
Sheerness ME12...... 94 C2
Hopewell Bsns Ctr
ME5................ 32 C4
Hopewell Dr ME5..... 32 C4
Hopsons Pl ME12..... 99 A1
Horatio Pl ME1....... 21 B4
Hornbeam Ave ME5... 40 B2
Hornbeam Cl ME20... 51 C2
HORN STREET....... 44 B2
Horseshoe Cl
Gillingham ME7........ 33 C1
Maidstone ME14....... 66 B1
Horseshoes La ME17.. 93 A4
Horse Wash La ME1... 14 C2
Horsley Rd ME1...... 21 B4
Horsted Ave ME4..... 22 B1
Horsted Inf Sch ME4.. 31 A1
Horsted Jun Sch ME5 31 A1
Horsted Ret Pk ME5.. 31 A1
Horsted Way ME1..... 31 A3
Horton Downs ME15.. 74 B1
Horwood Cl ME1...... 30 B4
Hospital La 3 ME1... 22 B4
Hospital Rd ME17..... 85 C4
Hostier Cl ME2....... 37 B4
Hotel Rd ME8......... 25 A2
Hothfield Rd ME8..... 26 C1
Houghton Ave ME7... 42 B3
Howard Ave
Rochester ME1........ 22 A3
Sittingbourne ME10... 103 C4
Howard Cl ME12...... 99 A3
Howard Dr ME16...... 63 B1
Howard Rd ME19..... 61 C4
Howard Sch The ME8 35 A4
Howbury Wlk ME8.... 43 A4
Howick Cl ME20...... 62 C4
Howlsmere Cl ME2... 37 B3
Hubbards Cotts ME8.. 27 C2
Hubbard's La ME15... 89 C3
Hubble Dr ME15...... 81 C3
Huckleberry Cl ME5.. 40 B3
Hudson Cl ME8....... 25 C1
Hughes Dr ME2........ 9 A2
Hugh Price Cl ME10.. 105 B3
Hulkes La ME1........ 22 B4
Humber Cres ME2.... 13 C3
Hundred of Hoo Comp
Sch The ME3......... 4 C1
Hunstanton Cl ME8... 43 B3
Hunters Ct 5 ME7.... 16 C3
Huntersfield Cl ME5.. 40 C1
Hunters Way ME7..... 24 B1
Hunters Way W ME5.. 24 B1
Huntingdon Wlk 2
ME15............... 81 C3
Huntington Rd ME17.. 88 A3
Huntsman La ME14... 73 A4
Huntsmans Cl ME1.... 22 B1
Huntsman's Cnr ME4. 31 B4
Hunt St
Nettlestead ME15,
ME18............... 79 A1
West Farleigh ME15.... 79 C1
Hurricane Rd ME19... 68 B3
Hurst Cl ME5......... 31 B2
Hurst Hill ME5........ 39 B2
Hurstings The ME15... 71 C2
Hurst La ME10....... 101 A3
Hurst Pl ME8......... 35 C4
Hurst Way ME16...... 70 B2
Hurstwood ME5....... 39 B4
Hurstwood Rd ME7... 42 B1
Hussar Ho ME1....... 21 C3
Hutchings Cl ME10... 105 B3
Hutsford Cl ME8...... 35 A1
Huxley Ct 3 ME1..... 22 A4
Hyacinth Rd ME2..... 13 B2
Hybrid Cl ME1....... 22 A1
Hyde Rd ME16........ 64 A2
Hyperion Dr ME2...... 7 C1
Hythe Rd ME10...... 103 C3

I

Ice Bowl The★ ME8... 25 A1
Iden Rd ME2........... 8 C1
Idenwood Cl ME8..... 35 A2
Ifield Cl ME15......... 82 A3
Illustrious Cl ME5..... 32 A2
Imperial Ave ME12.... 99 B3
Imperial Rd ME7...... 23 C3
Impton La ME5....... 40 A1
Ingleden Cl ME10.... 101 A2
Ingle Pl ME18......... 68 C2
Ingle Rd ME4......... 22 C2
Ingram Rd ME7....... 17 B2
Inner Lines ME7...... 16 A2
Institute Rd ME4...... 23 A4
Inverness Ho 7
ME15............... 81 C3
Invicta Ct ME10...... 101 A1
Invicta Gram Sch
ME14............... 73 B4
Invicta Rd ME12...... 95 A3
Invicta Villas ME14.... 75 B4
Iona Cl ME5.......... 41 A1
Iona Rd ME15........ 80 B3
Iris Cl ME5........... 48 B4
Ironside Cl ME5....... 32 A4
Irvine Rd ME3......... 6 B3
Island Way E ME4..... 10 C1
Island Way W ME4.... 10 B2
Islingham Farm Rd
ME3................. 9 A4
Ito Way ME8.......... 25 A3
Ivens Way ME17...... 87 B2
Iversgate Cl ME8..... 26 C2
Ivy Pl ME1............ 21 A2
Ivy St ME8............ 35 C4

J

Jacinth Dr ME10..... 103 B4
Jacklin Cl ME5....... 39 C2
Jackson Ave ME1..... 31 B4
Jackson Cl ME8...... 25 C1
Jacobs Ho ME12...... 95 A3
Jade Cl ME10........ 100 A1
Jade Hill ME2........ 28 C2
Jamaica Terr ME14.... 65 A3
James Rd ME2........ 19 C2
James St
5 Chatham ME4...... 22 C4
Gillingham ME7........ 16 C2
Maidstone ME14....... 65 A1
Rochester ME1........ 21 C4
Sheerness ME12...... 95 B3
James Whath an Way
ME14............... 64 C1
Japonica Cl ME5..... 40 C2
Jarrett Ave ME2....... 8 C2
Jarrett's Ct 1 ME10. 105 A2
Jasmine Cl
2 Chatham ME5...... 39 C4
East Malling ME19..... 61 C4
Jasmine Rd ME19..... 61 C4
Jasper Ave ME1...... 22 A2
Javelin Rd ME19...... 68 B3
Jefferson Dr ME8..... 25 C1
Jefferson Rd ME12.... 95 B3
Jeffery St ME7........ 16 C2
Jeffrey St ME14....... 65 A1
Jenkins' Dale ME4.... 22 C3
Jenkins Dr ME15...... 81 C1
Jenner Rd ME1....... 21 C4
Jenner Way ME20..... 46 A2
Jennifer Ct ME3....... 5 C1
Jerome Rd ME20..... 51 A4
Jersey Rd ME2........ 14 A4
Jessica Mews ME10.. 100 C1
Jetty Rd ME12........ 94 B4
Jeyes Rd ME7........ 23 C4
Jezreels Rd ME7...... 24 A3
Jiniwin Rd ME1....... 31 A3
Johannesburg Ho 2
ME15............... 82 A1
Johnson Ave ME7..... 16 C3
Johnson Ho ME10... 103 C2
Johnson Rd ME10... 103 C2
Johnson Way ME12... 98 B3
John St
Maidstone ME14....... 65 A2
Rochester ME1........ 21 C4
Joiners Ct ME4....... 23 B2
Jordan Cl ME15....... 81 C1
Joy Wood ME17...... 81 B1
Jubilee Cres ME11.... 96 A2
Jubilee St ME10..... 104 A3
Jubilee Terr ME7...... 16 C2
Judkins Cl ME5....... 32 C2
Junction Rd ME7..... 24 A4
Juniper Cl
Chatham ME5......... 40 A4
Maidstone ME16....... 63 B2

K

Karloff Way ME2....... 8 B2
Katherine Ct ME5..... 40 B2
Keating Cl ME1....... 21 A3
Keats Rd ME20........ 51 A3
Keefe Cl ME5......... 39 A1
Keel Ct ME2.......... 15 A4
Keeley Mews ME7.... 24 B3
Kellaway Rd ME5..... 40 A2
Kelly Dr ME7......... 16 C3
Kelly Ho ME1......... 30 C3
Kemp Cl ME5......... 39 B4
Kempton Cl ME5...... 40 C2
KEMSLEY........... 100 C3
Kemsley Sta ME10... 100 C3
KEMSLEY STREET... 42 C2
Kemsley Street Rd
ME7................ 42 C1
Kendall Ave ME18.... 69 B3
Kendall Pl 1 ME15... 81 B4
Kendal Way ME8...... 35 A4
Kendon Bsns Pk ME2. 15 A4
Kenilworth Ct ME10.. 103 B3

Kenilworth Dr ME8 . . . 35 A2
Kenilworth Gdns
ME8. . . . . 35 A3
Kenilworth Ho ME16 . . 71 A2
Kennard Cl ME1 . . . . . . 20 C2
Kennington Cl
Gillingham ME8. . . . . 25 B4
Maidstone ME15. . . . . . . 82 A3
Kensington Ho ME16. . 70 C2
Kent Ave
Maidstone ME15. . . . . . . 73 B1
Minster (Sheppey)
ME12. . . . . 98 C2
Sittingbourne ME10 . . . 103 C1
Kent Cl ME1 . . . . 30 C4
Kent County Optholmic & Aural Hospl
ME14. . . . . 72 C4
Kent Inst of Art & Design
Maidstone ME16. . . . . . . 71 B3
Rochester ME1. . . . . 22 B4
Kentish Ct 8 ME16 . . . 72 A4
Kent Rd
Halling ME2 . . . . 28 C2
Snodland ME6. . . . . 45 B2
Kent St ME18 . . . . 68 A2
Kentstone Ct ME4 . . . . 23 A4
KENT STREET 68 A2
Kent Terr ME8 . . . . 27 C2
Kenward Rd ME16 . . . . 63 C1
Kenwood Ave ME5 . . . . 40 A4
Kenya Terr 7 ME14 . . . 65 A3
Kenyon Wlk ME8 . . . . . 42 B3
Kerry Hill Way ME14 . . 64 B2
Kesteven Cl ME2. . . . . . 29 A1
Keston Ct ME8. . . . . 25 A2
Kestrel Cl ME10. . . . . . 107 A4
Kestrel Ct 4 ME10. . . 104 C2
Kestrel Ho ME7. . . . . . . 16 B2
Kestrel Rd ME5 . . . . 40 C2
Keswick Ave ME10 . . . 105 B1
Keswick Ct ME7 . . . . . . 18 A1
Keswick Dr ME16 . . . . . 63 B1
Ketridge La ME18. . . . . 69 C2
Kewlands ME14. . . . . . . 65 C2
Keyes Ave ME4 . . . . 22 C2
Khartoum Rd ME7 . . . . 16 A2
Khyber Rd ME4, ME7. . . 16 B3
Kilburn Ho 6 ME14. . . 65 A1
Killick Rd ME3. . . . . 5 A1
Kiln Barn Rd ME19, ME 20 . . . . 61 C3
Kiln Cl ME10. . . . . 104 C1
Kilndown Cl ME16 . . . . 63 C3
Kimberley Rd ME7 . . . . 24 A3
King Arthur Ct
ME10. . . . . 104 A1
King Arthur's Dr ME2 . . 8 A1
King Edward Rd
Chatham ME4 . . . . 22 C2
Gillingham ME7. . . . . 17 C2
Maidstone ME15. . . . . . . 72 B2
Rochester ME1. . . . . 14 C1
Kingfisher Apartments
13 ME15. . . . . 81 C1
Kingfisher Com Prim Sch ME5 . . . . 32 B3
Kingfisher Ct 11
ME15. . . . . 73 A4
Kingfisher Dr ME5 . . . . 32 C3
Kingfisher Rd ME20. . . . 51 B2
King George Rd ME5. . 39 B4
King George V Memorial Houses ME8 . . . . 25 C2
King Hill ME19. . . . . 59 A1
Kings Acre ME15. . . . . . 74 C1
King's Ave ME1 . . . . 21 C3
King's Bastion ME7 . . . 16 A1
Kings Cotts ME17 . . . . . 84 A2
King's Cotts ME18 . . . . 78 B2
Kingsdale Ct ME5. . . . . 23 C1
Kingsdown Cl
Gillingham ME7. . . . . 42 B4
Maidstone ME16. . . . . . . 72 A4
Kingsdown Ind Est
ME20. . . . . 61 B4
Kingsgate Cl ME16. . . . 71 B4
King's Head Alley
ME12. . . . . 94 B4
KINGS HILL. 68 C2
Kings Hill Ave ME19. . . 68 C4
Kingshill Dr ME3. . . . . . . 5 A2
Kings Hill Sch ME19 . . 68 C3
Kingsley Rd ME15. . . . . 72 C3
Kings Mill Cl ME10. . . 104 A3
Kingsnorth Cl ME3. . . . . 5 B2
Kingsnorth Rd ME8 . . . 25 C4
Kings Oak Mews ME5 . 39 C4
King's Orch ME1. . . . . . . 14 C1
Kings Rd ME12 . . . . 99 B3
King's Rd ME5. . . . . 24 A1
Kings Reach ME15 . . . . 81 B4
Kings Row
1 Maidstone ME15. . . . 72 C1
Rochester ME1. . . . . 21 B4
King's Sch ME1. . . . . . . 14 C1
King St
Chatham ME4 . . . . 23 A4
Gillingham ME7. . . . . 16 C2
Maidstone ME14. . . . . . . 72 C4
Rochester ME1. . . . . 21 C4
Sheerness ME12 . . . . . . 94 B3
Sittingbourne ME10 . . . 104 A3
West Malling ME19 . . . . 59 C4
Kingston Cres ME5 . . . 40 C4
Kingston Dr ME15 . . . . 80 B4
Kingsway
Chatham ME5 . . . . 24 A1
Gillingham ME7. . . . . 24 B1
Kingswear Gdns ME2 . 14 C3
Kings Wlk ME14 . . . . . . 65 B1
Kingswood Ave ME4 . . 22 C2
Kingswood Ho 12
ME16. . . . . 70 C3
Kingswood Rd
Gillingham ME7. . . . . 17 A2
Kit's Coty ME20 . . . . 47 B4
King William Rd 6
ME7. . . . . 16 C3
Kinross Cl ME5 . . . . 32 B3
Kipling Dr ME20 . . . . . . 51 A4
Kirby Rd ME3. . . . . 3 C1
Kirkdale ME15. . . . . 80 A1
Kirkdale Cl ME5 . . . . . . 41 A1
Kirkdale Cotts ME15 . . 80 A1
Kirkdale Rd ME15. . . . . 80 A2
Kitchener Ave ME4 . . . 23 A1
Kitchener Rd
Chattenden ME3. . . . . 9 C4
Rochester ME2. . . . . 14 A4
Kit Hill Ave ME5 . . . . . . 39 B3
KIT'S COTY. 47 A3
Kit's Coty House★
ME20. . . . . 47 A2
Klondyke Ind Est
ME11. . . . . 96 A1
Knavesacre Ct ME8 . . . 35 A1
Knight Ave ME7. . . . . . . 17 A3
Knight Rd ME2 . . . . 14 A2
Knightrider Ct ME15 . . 72 C3
Knightrider St ME15 . . 72 C3
Knights Cl ME3 . . . . 5 B1
Knights Ct ME10 . . . . . 104 A1
Knightsfield Rd
ME10. . . . . 100 B1
Knights Pk ME2 . . . . . . 14 A2
Knights Rd ME3 . . . . 5 A1
Knole Rd ME5 . . . . 40 C3
Knott Ct ME14 . . . . 64 C2
Knowle Rd ME14. . . . . . 65 B2
Knowlton Gdns ME16 . 71 A2
Kyetop Wlk ME8 . . . . . . 35 A2

L

Laburnum Dr ME20 . . . 51 B2
Laburnum Ho ME12. . . 94 C2
Laburnum Pl ME10. . . 104 A2
Laburnum Rd ME2. . . . 13 B1
Labworth Cl ME12 . . . . 97 C3
Lacey Cl ME17 . . . . 93 A4
Lacock Gdns
Loose ME15 . . . . 80 B4
Maidstone ME15. . . . . . . 72 C1
Lacy Cl ME16 . . . . 64 A3
Ladbrooke Ho 7
ME14. . . . . 65 A1
Ladds Cnr ME7 . . . . 18 B1
Ladds La ME6 . . . . 37 A2
Ladyclose Ave ME3 . . . . 2 A3
Ladyfields ME5 . . . . 41 A2
Ladywood Rd ME2. . . . 19 B2
Lakelands
Harrietsham ME17. . . . . 87 C2
Loose ME15 . . . . 80 B3
Lake Rd ME20 . . . . 62 B4
Laker Ho ME14 . . . . 65 A2
Laker Rd ME1. . . . . 30 C2
Lakeside ME6 . . . . 45 A2
Lakeside Pk ME2 . . . . . 15 B3
Lakes The ME20. . . . . . . 51 B4
Lakeview Cl ME6. . . . . . 45 B2
Lake Wlk ME20 . . . . 45 B1
Lakewood Dr ME8 . . . . 34 C2
Lambarde Cl ME2. . . . . 37 A4
Lambard Ho 8 ME14 . 65 A1
Lamberhurst Gn ME8 . 25 B3
Lamberhurst Rd
ME16. . . . . 63 B3
Lambert Mews 4
ME6. . . . . 45 B4
Lambes Ct ME8 . . . . 35 A1
Lambeth Cl ME5 . . . . . . 40 B4
Lambourn Dr ME19 . . . 68 C2
Lambourne Pl ME8 . . . 27 A2
Lambourne Rd ME15. . 74 B2
Lambourn Way ME5 . . . 40 C2
Lambsfrith Gr ME7. . . . 42 B3
Lammas Dr ME10 . . . . 104 A4
Lamplighters Cl ME7. . 33 C1
Lancashire Rd ME15 . . 81 C3
Lancaster Ct ME8. . . . . 34 C3
Lancaster Way ME19. . 68 B3
Lance Cl ME10. . . . . . . 101 A2
Lancelot Ave ME2. . . . . 13 B3
Lancelot Cl ME2 . . . . . . 13 B2
Lancer Ho ME1 . . . . 21 C3
Lancet La ME15. . . . . . . 80 B2
Landor Ct ME7. . . . . 42 A3
Landway The ME14. . . . 74 C4
Langdale Cl ME8. . . . . . 26 A1
Langdale Rise ME16 . . 63 C1
Langdon Rd ME1 . . . . . 21 C4
Langham Gr ME16 . . . . 71 B4
LANGLEY. 92 B4
LANGLEY HEATH. 93 B4
Langley Ho 11 ME16 . . 70 C3
Langley Rd ME10 . . . . 101 A1
Langton Cl ME14. . . . . . 65 C1
Lankester Parker Rd
ME1. . . . . 30 C2
Lansdowne Ave ME15 81 A2
Lansdowne Ct 9
ME4. . . . . 22 C4
Lansdowne Prim Sch
ME10. . . . . 105 B1
Lansdowne Rd ME4. . . 22 B2
Lansdown Rd ME10 . . 105 B2
Lapins La ME19. . . . . . . 68 B2
La Providence ME1 . . . 14 C1
Lapwing Cl ME12 . . . . . 98 C1
Larch Cl ME20 . . . . 51 C2
Larch Cres ME3. . . . . . . 11 B3
Larchcroft ME5 . . . . 40 A4
Larches The ME3 . . . . . . 6 C3
Larch Terr ME12 . . . . . . 94 B1
Larch Wood Cl ME5 . . . 41 A1
LARKFIELD 51 B2
Larkfield Ave
Gillingham ME7. . . . . 24 B4
Sittingbourne ME10 . . . 104 A4
Larkfield Cl ME20. . . . . 51 B1
Larkfield Rd ME20 . . . . 51 C1
Larkfield Trad Est
ME20. . . . . 45 C1
Larkin Cl ME2 . . . . 8 B2
Larking Dr ME16. . . . . . 64 A3
Larkspur Cl 2 ME19 . . 51 B1
Larkspur Rd
Chatham ME5 . . . . 39 B4
West Malling ME19 . . . . 51 A1
Laser Quay ME2 . . . . . . 15 A2
Latimer Pl 4 ME7 . . . . 16 C3
Launder Way ME15 . . . 72 A2
Laura Pl ME1 . . . . 21 A2
Laurel Ho ME12. . . . . . . 94 C2
Laurel Rd ME7. . . . . 16 C3
Laurels The ME16 . . . . . 71 B2
Laurel Wlk ME8. . . . . . . 35 B2
Laurie Gray Ave ME5. . 39 A1
Lavenda Cl ME7 . . . . . . 42 A4
Lavender Cl
1 Chatham ME5 . . . . . . 39 B4
East Malling ME19 . . . . . 61 C4
Lavender Ct ME10 . . . 104 C1
Lavender Ho 3 ME15 . 81 B4
Lavender Rd ME19. . . . 61 C4
Lavenders Rd ME19. . . 59 C2
Lavender Wlk ME19. . . 61 C4
Laverstoke Rd ME16 . . 63 C4
Lawn Cl ME4 . . . . 23 B2
Lawrence Cl ME15 . . . . 80 B3
Lawrence St ME7 . . . . . 16 C1
Laxey The ME15. . . . . . . 72 A1
Laxton Cl ME15 . . . . 74 B3
Laxton Dr ME17. . . . . . . 91 C1
Laxton Way ME10 . . . . 103 C4
Laxton Wk ME18. . . . . . 69 A3
Layfield Cotts ME9. . . 100 B3
Layfield Rd ME7 . . . . . . 17 C3
Lea Ct ME4. . . . . 22 B1
Leafy Glade ME8. . . . . . 34 B2
Leake Ho 2 ME1 . . . . . 21 C1
Leamington Dr ME16 . 71 A4
Leander Rd ME1. . . . . . 30 C3
Leas The ME12. . . . . 99 A4
Leech Ct ME1. . . . . 15 A1
LEEDS. 84 B3
Leeds & Broomfield CE Prim Sch ME17. . . . . . 84 B3
Leeds Castle★ ME17. . 85 B3
Leeds Ho ME2 . . . . 8 C1
Leeds Rd ME17 . . . . 93 A3
Leeds Sq ME8 . . . . 25 B3
Lee Green Rd ME3 . . . . . 2 B2
Lee Rd ME6 . . . . 45 B4
Leet Cl ME7 . . . . 17 B2
Leeward Rd ME1. . . . . . 21 C1
Legge La ME19 . . . . 44 B2
Leicester Rd ME15 . . . . 81 B3
Leigh Ave ME15. . . . . . . 80 C2
Leigh Ct ME12 . . . . 98 A1
Leigh Rd ME3 . . . . 8 C3
Leitch Row ME7 . . . . . . 16 A3
Lendrim Cl 11 ME7. . . . 16 A2
Leney Rd ME18 . . . . 78 C3
Lenfield Ave ME14 . . . . 73 A4
Lenham Ct 10 ME15. . . 73 A4
Lenham Way ME8. . . . . 25 A3
Lenside Dr ME15. . . . . . 74 C2
Len Valley Wlk ME15 . . 74 B1
Leonard Cl ME16. . . . . . 63 B2
Leonard Rd 7 ME4 . . . 23 B3
Leopold Rd 2 ME4 . . . 23 A3
Lesley Pl ME16 . . . . 64 B1
Leslie Rd ME7 . . . . 17 A3
Lested La ME17. . . . . . . 92 A1
Lester Rd ME4. . . . . 23 A3
Letchworth Ave ME4. . 22 C1
Leviathan Way
Chatham ME4 . . . . 16 A4
St Mary's Island ME4. . . 10 A1
Lewis Ave ME8 . . . . 25 B2
Lewis Court Dr ME17. . 90 B3
Lewis Mews ME6 . . . . . 45 A2
LEYBOURNE. 50 B2
Leybourne Cl ME5 . . . . 40 A2
Leybourne Rd ME2. . . . 13 C4
Leybourne, St Peter & St Paul CE Prim Sch
ME19. . . . . 50 C2
Leybourne Way ME20 . 51 A4
Leyton Ave ME7. . . . . . . 24 B1
Libya Terr 6 ME14. . . . 65 A3
Lichfield Cl ME8 . . . . . . 26 A2
Lichfield Ho 12 ME15. . 81 C3
LIDSING. 41 C1
Lidsing Rd ME14. . . . . . 49 C2
Liege Cl ME10 . . . . 101 A3
Lilac Cres ME2. . . . . 13 B2
Lilac Gn 4 ME19 . . . . . 51 B1
Lilac Rd ME2 . . . . 13 B1
Lilk Hill ME14. . . . . 75 B3
Lillieburn ME19. . . . . . . 50 B2
Lime Cres ME19 . . . . . . 61 A3
Lime Ct ME8. . . . . 42 C3
Lime Gr
Halfway Houses
ME12. . . . . 97 B2
Sittingbourne ME10 . . . 104 C2
Lime Kiln Wharf
ME11. . . . . 96 B2
Limetree Cl ME5. . . . . . 32 B4
Lincoln Cl ME2 . . . . 13 A2
Lincoln Rd ME15. . . . . . 81 B4
Lincol n Rd ME7 . . . . . . 17 A3
Lindel Ct ME18 . . . . 69 A3
Linden Cl ME10. . . . . . 103 C1
Linden Dr ME12 . . . . . . 96 B4
Linden Ho 5 ME5 . . . . 39 C4
Linden Rd
Coxheath ME17 . . . . 88 B4
Gillingham ME7. . . . . 17 B1
Lindens The ME20 . . . . 52 C1
Lindisfarne Gdns
ME16. . . . . 72 A3
Lineacre Cl ME8 . . . . . . 35 A2
Lines Terr ME4. . . . . 23 A4
Lingley Dr ME2 . . . . 8 C2
LINK 20 Bsns Pk
ME20. . . . . 51 C3
Links The ME5 . . . . 32 B4
Linkway ME20 . . . . 52 A1
LINTON. 89 B1
Linton Dann Cl ME3. . . . 5 A2
Linton Gore ME17. . . . . 88 C3
Linton Rd ME15. . . . . . . 89 B4
Lintorn Symonds Rd
ME3. . . . . 3 C1
Linwood Ave ME2. . . . . 13 B4
Lion Yd 3 ME10 . . . . . 104 B2
Liphook Way ME16. . . . 63 C4
Lismore Cl ME15. . . . . . 80 B3
Lister Cl ME19 . . . . 61 C4
Listmas Rd ME4 . . . . . . 23 B3
Littlebourne Ave ME8 . 25 B4
Littlebourne Rd ME14 65 C2
Little Buckland Ave
ME16. . . . . 64 A2
Little Ct ME16 . . . . 71 C2
Littlefield Rd ME8 . . . . 27 B2
Little Glovers ME10 . . 104 B1
Little John Ave ME5. . . 39 C2
Little Kit's Coty House★
ME20. . . . . 47 A1
Little Market Row
ME19. . . . . 50 C2
Little Orch ME17. . . . . . 88 C3
Little Oxley ME19 . . . . . 50 C2
Little York Mdws
ME7. . . . . 25 C4
Livingstone Bldgs
ME7. . . . . 17 A1
Livingstone Circ ME7 . 17 A1
Livingstone Rd ME7. . . 17 B1
Livingstone Wlk 6
ME15. . . . . 82 A1
Loaland Bsns Ctr
ME2. . . . . 15 A4
Lobelia Cl ME7 . . . . 17 B2
Locarno Ave ME8 . . . . . 25 A2
Lochat Rd ME3 . . . . 3 B2
Lockham Farm Ave
ME17. . . . . 81 B1
Lockington Gr ME1 . . . 14 C1
Lock La ME14. . . . . 54 B1
Locksley Cl ME5 . . . . . . 39 B2
Lock St ME7 . . . . 16 C1
Lockswood ME16 . . . . . 64 A3
Loddington La ME17 . . 89 C1
Lodge Cl ME18 . . . . 78 B4
Lodge Farmhouse
ME20. . . . . 52 C3
Lodge Hill La ME3 . . . . . 3 C3
Lodge Rd ME14. . . . . . . 66 A1
Lomas Rd ME10,
ME9. . . . . 105 C2
Lombardy Cl ME7. . . . . 34 A2
Lombardy Dr ME14 . . . 65 C1
Londonderry Ho 15
ME15. . . . . 81 C3
London Rd
Ditton ME20 . . . . 52 A1
Gillingham ME8. . . . . 25 C1
Maidstone ME16. . . . . . . 63 C2
Newington ME9 . . . . . . 102 A3
Rochester ME2. . . . . 14 A3
Sittingbourne ME10 . . . 103 B2
London Rd E ME20. . . . 62 C4
London Road Trad Est
ME10. . . . . 103 C2
Long Catlis Rd ME8 . . . 43 A4
Longdown Ho ME5. . . . 31 C2
Longfellow Rd ME7 . . . 23 C3
Longfield Pl ME15 . . . . 81 A4

Longfields Dr ME14 . . . 67 A1
Longford Cl ME8 . . . . . . 36 A4
Longford Ct ME8 . . . . . . 36 A4
Longham Copse
ME15 . . . . 74 B1
Longhill Ave ME5 . . . . . 23 B3
Longhurst Dr ME5 . . . . 39 C2
Longley Rd
Gillingham ME8 . . . . 26 C1
Rochester ME1 . . . . 21 C4
Longparish Cl ME15 . . . 82 A2
Long Rede La ME16 . . . 70 B3
Longridge ME10 . . . . . 107 B4
Longshaw Rd ME15 . . . 82 A1
Longwood ME5 . . . . 40 B1
Lonsdale Dr
Gillingham ME8 . . . . 35 B3
Sittingbourne ME10 . . . 103 B3
LOOSE 89 B4
LOOSE HILL 80 A1
Loose Inf & Jun Schs
ME15 . . . . 80 B2
Loose Rd ME15 . . . . 80 B3
Lord Romney's Hill
ME14 . . . . 74 B3
LORDS WOOD 40 C1
Lords Wood Cl ME5 . . . 40 B2
Lordswood Ind Est
ME5 . . . . 49 A4
Lordswood Inf & Jun
Sch ME5 . . . . 40 B3
Lords Wood La ME5 . . . 40 B3
Lorimar Ct ME10 . . . . . 100 A1
Louisville Ave ME7 . . . . 24 A4
Love La
Minster (Sheppey)
ME12 . . . . 99 B3
Rochester ME1 . . . . 14 C1
Wateringbury ME18 . . . . 78 B3
Lovelace Cl ME8 . . . . . . 43 A4
Lovell Rd ME12 . . . . 98 B1
Lower Bell La ME20 . . . 51 C2
Lower Bloors La ME8 . 26 B3
Lower Boxley Rd 10
ME14 . . . . 65 A1
Lower Fant Rd ME16 . . 71 C2
LOWER RAINHAM 26 C3
Lower Rainham Rd
ME8 . . . . 27 A3
Lower Rd
Maidstone ME15 . . . . 73 A3
Minster (Sheppey)
ME12 . . . . 97 C1
Lower St ME17 . . . . 84 B3
Lower Stone St ME15 . 72 C3
Lower Tovil ME15 . . . . . 72 A2
LOWER TWYDALL 18 C1
Lower Twydall La ME7 &
ME8 . . . . 25 C4
LOWER UPNOR 10 A3
Lower Warren Rd
ME20 . . . . 47 C2
Lower Woodlands Rd
ME7 . . . . 18 A2
Lowfield Rd ME12 . . . . . 97 C3
Low Meadow ME2 . . . . 29 A1
Lubbock Cl ME15 . . . . . 81 C1
Lubbock Wlk ME8 . . . . 35 A1
Lucas Rd ME6 . . . . 44 C3
Lucerne St ME14 . . . . . . 65 A1
Lucks Hill ME19 . . . . 60 A4
Luddenham Cl ME14 . . 65 C2
Lullingstone Cl ME7 . . 42 B3
Lullingstone Rd
ME16 . . . . 63 C3
Lumsden Terr 8
ME4 . . . . 22 B4
LUNSFORD 50 C4
Lunsford District Ctr
ME20 . . . . 51 B4
Lunsford La ME20 . . . . . 51 A2
Lunsford Prim Sch
ME20 . . . . 51 B2
Lushington Rd ME14 . . 64 B3
LUTON 23 B2
Luton High St ME5 . . . . 23 C2
Luton Inf Sch ME5 . . . . 23 C2
Luton Jun Sch ME4 . . . 23 C2
Luton Rd ME4, ME5 . . . . 23 B2
Lyall Way ME8 . . . . 43 B4
Lychfield Dr ME2 . . . . . 14 A4
Lydbrook Cl ME10 . . . 103 C2
Lydd Rd ME5 . . . . 32 B1
Lyle Cl ME2 . . . . 14 B4
Lyle Ct ME16 . . . . 63 C1
Lyminge Cl ME8 . . . . . . 25 C2
Lymington Ct ME15 . . . 91 B4
Lyndhurst Ave ME8 . . . 34 C3
Lyndhurst Gr ME10 . . 106 B4
Lyndhurst Rd ME15 . . . 81 A4
Lynette Ave ME2 . . . . 8 A1
Lynmouth Dr ME12 . . . 99 A3
Lynors Ave ME2 . . . . 8 A1
Lynstead Ho ME16 . . . . 70 C1
Lynsted Rd
Gillingham ME8 . . . . 25 B3
Halfway Houses ME12 . . 97 C4
Lynton Dr ME5 . . . . 40 B3
Lysander Rd ME19 . . . . 68 B3

M

McAlpine Cres ME15 . . 89 B3
MacAulay Cl ME20 . . . . 51 B4
McCudden Row 8
ME7 . . . . 16 A2
MacDonald Rd ME7 . . . 17 A2
Mackenders Cl ME20 . . 46 B2
Mackenders Gn ME20 . 46 B2
Mackenders La ME20 . 46 B2
McKenzie Cl ME20 . . . . 62 C4
Mc Kenzie Rd ME5 . . . . 40 A3
MACKLANDS 27 A2
Macklands Ho ME8 . . . 27 A2
Macklands Way ME8 . . 27 A2
Madden Ave ME5 . . . . . 31 B1
Madginford Cl ME15 . . 74 C2
Madginford Park Inf Sch
ME15 . . . . 74 C2
Madginford Park Jun
Sch ME15 . . . . 74 C2
Madginford Rd ME15 . 74 B2
Madras Ho 2 ME15 . . . 81 C1
Mafeking Rd ME5 . . . . . 39 C3
Magdalen Cl ME7 . . . . . 42 A4
Magnolia Ave ME8 . . . . 34 B1
Magnolia Ho 3
ME16 . . . . 70 C3
Magpie Cl ME20 . . . . . . 51 B1
Magpie Ct ME12 . . . . . . 98 B2
Magpie Hall Rd ME4 . . 23 A2
Magpie La ME9, ME14 . 43 C1
Magwitch Cl ME1 . . . . . 21 B4
Maida Rd ME4 . . . . 23 B2
MAIDSTONE 73 B3
Maidstone Barracks Sta
ME16 . . . . 64 B1
Maidstone East Sta
ME14 . . . . 64 C1
Maidstone Gram Sch
ME15 . . . . 73 A2
Maidstone Gram Sch for
Girls ME16 . . . . 64 B1
Maidstone Hospl The
ME16 . . . . 70 C4
Maidstone Ind Ctr
ME14 . . . . 64 C1
Maidstone L Ctr
ME15 . . . . 73 B2
Maidstone Mus & Bentlif
Art Gallery* ME14 . . . 64 C1
Maidstone Rd
Bredhurst ME7, ME8 . . . 42 B2
Chatham ME4 . . . . 22 C2
Chatham, Walderslade
ME5 . . . . 39 A4
Five Wents ME17 . . . . . . 93 A2
Gillingham ME8 . . . . 34 C2
Rochester ME1 . . . . 21 C3
Maidstone St Michaels
CE Jun Sch ME16 . . . . 72 A3
Maidstone West Sta
ME16 . . . . 72 B3
Mailyns The ME8 . . . . . . 35 A3
Main Gate Rd ME4 . . . . 15 C3
Main Rd
Chattenden ME3 . . . . 9 C4
Hoo St Werburgh ME3 . . . 4 C1
Queenborough ME11,
ME12 . . . . 96 C2
Sheerness ME12 . . . . . . 94 B4
Main St ME4 . . . . 10 B2
Maison Des Fleurs
ME16 . . . . 71 B2
Malden Dr ME14 . . . . . . 65 A4
Mallard Apartments 14
ME15 . . . . 81 C1
Mallard Ct ME12 . . . . . . 98 B2
Mallards Way ME15 . . . 74 C1
Mallard Wlk ME20 . . . . 51 A2
Malling Ct ME19 . . . . . . 60 C3
Mallingdene Cl ME3 . . . 2 B4
Malling Rd
Kings Hill M18,
ME19 . . . . 68 B2
Lunsford ME6, ME20 . . . 45 A1
Snodland ME6 . . . . 45 B3
Malling Sch The
ME19 . . . . 60 C3
Mallings Dr ME14 . . . . . 75 B4
Mallings La ME14 . . . . . 75 B4
Malling Terr ME16 . . . . 71 B4
Mallows The ME14 . . . . 64 B3
Mallow Way 1 ME5 . . . 39 C4
Malta Ave ME5 . . . . 32 A3
Malta Terr 5 ME14 . . . 65 A3
Malthouse Hill ME15 . . 89 B4
Maltings The
Gillingham ME8 . . . . 36 A4
Loose ME17 . . . . 90 A4
Maidstone, Grove Green
ME14 . . . . 66 B1
Malt Mews ME1 . . . . . . 14 C1
Malus Cl ME5 . . . . 40 B1
Malvern Rd ME7 . . . . . . 24 B3
Mamignot Cl ME14 . . . . 67 A1
Manchester Cl ME5 . . . 32 C2
Mandeville Ct 1
ME14 . . . . 65 A1
Mangravet Ave ME15 . . 81 A3
Manningham Ho
ME19 . . . . 61 A2
Manor Cl ME14 . . . . 75 A3
Manor Cotts ME17 . . . . 83 A1
Manor Ct
Gillingham ME7 . . . . 25 C4
Maidstone ME14 . . . . 75 A3
Manor Gdns ME5 . . . . . 39 C4
Manor Gr ME10 . . . . . . 103 C1
Manor Ho 14 ME7 . . . . . 16 A2
Manor House Dr
ME16 . . . . 71 C3
Manor La
Rochester ME1 . . . . 20 C3
Rochester ME1 . . . . 21 A2
Manor Park Ctry Pk*
ME19 . . . . 59 B3
Manor Rd ME4 . . . . 22 C4
Manor Rise ME14 . . . . . 75 A3
Manor St ME7 . . . . 16 A2
Mansel Dr ME1 . . . . 21 A2
Mansfield Wlk ME16 . . 72 A2
Mansion Row ME7 . . . . 16 A2
Manwood Cl ME10 . . . 106 C4
Maple Ave
Gillingham ME7 . . . . 17 B2
Maidstone ME16 . . . . 63 C2
Maple Cl ME20 . . . . 51 B2
Maple Rd
Hoo St Werburgh
ME3 . . . . 11 B3
Rochester ME2 . . . . 13 C2
Maplesden Cl ME16 . . . 70 B3
Maplesden Noakes Sch
The ME16 . . . . 64 B2
Maple St ME12 . . . . 95 A2
Maples The ME12 . . . . . 98 C2
Maplins Cl 5 ME8 . . . . 26 C1
Mara Ct ME4 . . . . 22 C1
Marathon Paddock
ME7 . . . . 24 A4
Marc Brunel Way
ME4 . . . . 16 A3
Marconi Way ME1 . . . . 31 A3
Mardale Cl ME8 . . . . . . 27 A1
Marden Rd ME2 . . . . 8 C1
Margate Cl ME7 . . . . . . 17 B2
Margetts Pl ME2 . . . . . . 10 A3
Marian Ave ME12 . . . . . 98 B3
Marigold Way ME16 . . . 70 C3
Marina Dr ME12 . . . . . . 98 B3
Marine Dr ME3 . . . . 11 B3
Marine Par ME12 . . . . . 95 C3
Mariners The ME1 . . . . 21 B4
Mariners View ME7 . . . 17 C3
MARINE TOWN 95 C3
Marine View ME4 . . . . . 10 B1
Marion Cl ME5 . . . . 40 A2
Marion Cres ME15 . . . . 80 C4
Maritime Cl ME2 . . . . . . 15 A4
Maritime Est ME2 . . . . 15 A4
Maritime Way ME4 . . . 16 A4
Market Bldgs 4
ME14 . . . . 72 B4
Market Colonnade 3
ME14 . . . . 72 B4
Mark St ME4 . . . . 23 A2
Marlborough Ho 4
ME8 . . . . 35 C4
Marlborough Par
ME16 . . . . 70 B2
Marlborough Rd ME7 . 16 B1
Marley Rd ME3 . . . . 5 A2
Marley Way ME1 . . . . . . 21 C2
Marlow Copse ME5 . . . 39 C1
Marlowe Rd ME20 . . . . 51 B3
MARLPIT 91 A2
Marlpit Cotts ME17 . . . 91 A2
Marquis Dr ME7 . . . . . . 42 B3
Marr Cl ME12 . . . . 98 A3
Marrians View 1
ME5 . . . . 23 C2
Marshall Rd ME8 . . . . . 34 C4
Marsham Cres ME17 . . 92 A1
Marsham St ME14 . . . . 72 C4
Marsham Way ME2 . . . 28 C1
Marsh Rd ME2 . . . . 29 A1
Marsh Rise ME10 . . . . 101 B3
Marsh St ME2 . . . . 14 B3
Marsh Way ME20 . . . . . 51 B4
Marston Cl ME5 . . . . . . 39 B3
Marston Dr ME14 . . . . . 65 C1
Marston Wlk ME5 . . . . . 39 B3
Martin Ct ME7 . . . . 42 A3
Martin Rd ME2 . . . . 14 B4
Martin Sq ME20 . . . . . . 51 B2
Mary Ct ME4 . . . . 23 A2
Maryland Ct ME8 . . . . . 35 B1
Maryland Dr ME16 . . . . 70 B2
Mary Last Cl ME6 . . . . . 44 C3
Masefield Dr ME3 . . . . . . 2 B4
Masefield Rd ME20 . . . 51 A4
Mason Way ME2 . . . . 8 B2
Matfield Cres ME14 . . . 65 C1
Matilda Cl ME8 . . . . 34 B4
Matterdale Gdns
ME16 . . . . 70 A2
Matts Hill Rd ME9 . . . . . 43 B2
Maundene Sch ME5 . . 32 B1
Maunders Cl ME5 . . . . . 32 C4
Maximilian Dr ME2 . . . 37 B4
Maxton Cl ME14 . . . . . . 66 C1
Maxwell Dr ME16 . . . . . 63 B2
Maxwell Rd ME7 . . . . . . 16 A2
Mayfair 2 ME2 . . . . 14 C4
Mayfair Ave ME15 . . . . . 80 B4
Mayfield Cl
Chatham ME5 . . . . 40 A1
Gillingham ME8 . . . . 26 B2
Mayflower Ho ME1 . . . 21 B4
Mayford Rd ME5 . . . . . . 41 A2
Maylam Gdns ME10 . . 103 A2
Maynard Pl ME5 . . . . . . 24 A2
Maypole Dr ME18 . . . . . 69 B3
May Rd
Gillingham ME7 . . . . 23 C4
Rochester ME1 . . . . 21 C3
May St
Cuxton ME2 . . . . 19 B2
Snodland ME6 . . . . 45 C4
May Terr ME7 . . . . 16 A3
Mayweed Ave ME5 . . . . 39 B4
Mead Gn ME5 . . . . 40 C3
Meadow Bank ME19 . . 59 C4
Meadowbank Ct
ME19 . . . . 59 C4
Meadow Bank Mews
ME19 . . . . 59 C4
Meadowbank Rd
ME4 . . . . 23 A4
Meadow Cl ME5 . . . . . . 31 C1
Meadowdown ME14 . . 74 A4
Meadowdown Cl ME7 42 A4
Meadows The
3 Maidstone ME15 . . . 72 A2
Meadows The continued
Sittingbourne ME10 . . . 106 C4
Meadowsweet View
ME4 . . . . 10 B2
Meadow View Rd
ME17 . . . . 90 A3
Meadow Way ME1 . . . . 29 B1
Meadow Wlk
Maidstone ME15 . . . . 73 A3
Snodland ME6 . . . . 45 A3
Meads Ave The
ME10 . . . . 100 B1
Meadside Wlk ME5 . . . 31 C2
Mead The ME19 . . . . . . 50 C2
Medina Rd ME20 . . . . . 52 A1
Medlar Gr ME7 . . . . 42 A4
Medlars The ME14 . . . . 66 A2
Medway City Est ME2 15 A3
Medway Cl ME10 . . . . 103 C2
Medway Com Coll
ME4 . . . . 23 A1
Medway Ct ME20 . . . . . 53 A2
Medway Ent Ctr ME2 . 15 A4
Medway Gdns ME4 . . . 15 C3
Medway Heights 5
ME4 . . . . 22 B4
Medway Ho 7 ME14 . . 72 B4
Medway Maritime Hospl
ME7 . . . . 23 B4
Medway Rd ME7 . . . . . . 16 C3
Medway St
Chatham ME4 . . . . 15 C1
Maidstone ME14 . . . . 72 B4
Medway Trad Est
ME16 . . . . 72 B3
Meeres Court La
ME10 . . . . 105 B3
Meeting House La 2
ME4 . . . . 22 C4
Megby Cl ME8 . . . . 35 A2
Meirs Court Rd ME8 . . 35 B2
Melbourne Rd ME4 . . . 23 A3
Melford Dr ME16 . . . . . 71 B4
Mellor Row ME10 . . . . 101 A3
Melody Cl ME8 . . . . 42 C4
Melrose Ave ME19 . . . . 69 B3
Melrose Cl ME15 . . . . . . 80 B3
Melville Ct ME4 . . . . 15 C2
Melville Rd ME15 . . . . . 72 C3
Memorial (General)
Hospl ME10 . . . . 104 B1
Menin Rd ME10 . . . . . . 101 A3
Menzies Ct ME12 . . . . . 98 B1
Mercer Cl ME20 . . . . . . 51 C4
Mercers Pl ME19 . . . . . 68 C2
Mercer Way ME17 . . . . 92 A1
Mercury Cl ME1 . . . . . . 21 A3
Meredale Sch ME8 . . . 27 A1
Meredith Cl ME17 . . . . . 84 A3
MERESBOROUGH 36 A1
Meresborough Cotts
ME8 . . . . 35 C1
Meresborough La ME8,
ME9 . . . . 36 B1
Meresborough Rd
ME8 . . . . 36 A3
Mereworth Cl ME8 . . . . 25 A3
Mereworth Ho ME2 . . . . 8 C1
Meridian Ct ME16 . . . . . 72 A4
Meridian Pk ME2 . . . . . 15 B2
Merivale Gr ME5 . . . . . . 40 B4
Merleburgh Dr
ME10 . . . . 101 A2
Merlin Ave ME20 . . . . . . 51 A2
Merlin Cl ME10 . . . . . . 104 C1
Merlin Ho
Chatham ME4 . . . . 16 B4
2 Sittingbourne
ME10 . . . . 104 C2
Mermaid Cl ME5 . . . . . . 32 A2
Merrals Wood Rd
ME2 . . . . 13 A1
Merriman Ho ME3 . . . . . 3 C2
Merry Boys Rd ME3 . . . . 2 B4
Merryfields ME2 . . . . 8 A1
MERRYMAN'S HILL . . 99 A4
Merston Ct ME3 . . . . 6 C4
Merton Cl ME5 . . . . 32 C1
Merton Rd ME15 . . . . . . 74 B2
Meteor Cl ME10 . . . . . 100 C2
Meteor Rd ME19 . . . . . . 68 B3

Mews The
[1] Maidstone ME16. . . . 64 B1
Rochester ME2. . . . . 13 C3
Sittingbourne ME10 . . . 106 C4
Meyrick Rd ME12 . . . . . 95 A3
Micawber Cl ME5. . . . . 40 A1
Micketts Gdns ME10 . 103 A2
Middlefields ME8. . . . . 36 A4
Middle Mill Rd ME19. . 60 C3
Middle Row [6] ME14. . 72 B4
Middlesex Rd ME15 . . . 81 B3
Middle St [4] ME7 . . . . . 16 A2
Middleton Cl ME8 . . . . 43 B4
Middleton Ct [9]
ME10. . . . . 104 A2
Middletune Ave
ME10. . . . . 100 C1
Middle Way ME10. . . . 105 A1
Midhurst Ct ME15. . . . . 72 C3
Mid Kent Bsns Pk
ME6. . . . . 45 C3
Mid Kent Coll (City Way
Ctr) ME1 . . . . 22 A4
Mid Kent Coll of H & F
Ed ME16. . . . . 71 B3
Mid Kent Coll of Higher
& F Ed ME5. . . . . 31 B2
Mid Kent Sh Ctr The
ME16. . . . . 63 C3
Midley Cl ME16 . . . . 63 C3
Midsummer Rd ME6 . . 44 C4
Mierscourt Cl ME8. . . . 36 A4
Miers Court Prim Sch
ME8. . . . . 35 C3
Mierscourt Rd ME8 . . . 35 B2
Milbourne Gr ME10 . . 100 C1
Milburn Rd ME7 . . . . . . 16 C3
Miles Pl ME1 . . . . 22 A3
Milford Cl ME16 . . . . . . 64 A1
Military Rd ME4 . . . . . . 15 C1
Millbrook ME19. . . . . . . 50 B1
Millbrook Cl ME15 . . . . 72 B1
Mill Cl ME2. . . . . 8 B1
Mill Cotts
Queenborough
ME11. . . . . 96 B2
West Farleigh ME15. . . . 79 C2
Mill Ct ME10. . . . . 104 C1
Millennium Way
ME12. . . . . 94 C2
Millen Rd ME10. . . . . . 104 A3
Miller Cl ME10. . . . . . . 101 B2
Miller Ct ME12. . . . . 98 B1
Millers Wharf [1]
ME15. . . . . 72 A2
Miller Way ME2. . . . . 9 A2
Millfield ME10. . . . . . . 104 C1
Millfields ME5 . . . . 41 A2
Millfordhope Rd ME2 . 12 C3
Millhall ME20. . . . . 52 C2
Mill Hall Bsns Est The
ME20. . . . . 52 B2
Mill Hall Rd ME20. . . . . 52 A3
Mill La
Chatham, Bluebell Hill
ME5. . . . . 39 A1
Chatham, Luton ME5 . . . 23 C1
Coxheath ME17 . . . . 88 C4
Maidstone ME14. . . . . . . 64 C2
Snodland ME6. . . . . 45 C4
Wateringbury ME18 . . . . 78 B3
Millpond Cl ME2. . . . . . 14 B4
Mill Rd
Gillingham ME7. . . . . 16 C2
Rochester ME2. . . . . 14 B4
Mills Cl ME12. . . . . 98 A2
Mills Rd ME20 . . . . 62 B3
Mill St
East Malling ME19 . . . . . 60 C3
Maidstone, Loose
ME15. . . . . 80 A1
Maidstone ME15. . . . . . . 72 B4
Sittingbourne ME10 . . . 104 A3
Snodland ME6. . . . . 45 C4
Mills Terr ME4 . . . . 23 A3
Millstock Terr [2]
ME15. . . . . 72 A2
Mill Stream Jun Sch
ME19. . . . . 60 C3
MILL STREET 60 B3
Mill Way ME10. . . . . . . 104 B4
Mill Wlk ME16 . . . . 70 C3
Millwood Ct [4] ME4. . . 22 C4
Milner Rd ME7 . . . . 17 A3
Milners ME17. . . . . 84 A2
Milstead Cl
Maidstone ME14. . . . . . . 65 C1
West Minster ME12 . . . . 96 C4
Milsted Rd ME8. . . . . . . 25 C3
Milton Ave ME3. . . . . 2 B4
Milton Court Prim Sch
ME10. . . . . 104 A4
Milton Ct ME18 . . . . 68 C3
Milton La ME18 . . . . 69 A3
Milton Rd
Gillingham ME7. . . . . 23 C3
Sittingbourne ME10 . . . 104 A2
MILTON REGIS 103 B4
Milton Regis Halt
ME10. . . . . 104 C4
Milton St ME16 . . . . 71 B2
Mincers Cl ME5. . . . . . . 40 C2
Minerva Rd ME2 . . . . . . 14 A4
MINSTER. 98 C3
Minster Abbey*
ME12. . . . . 99 B2
Minster Coll ME12. . . . 98 A2
Minster Dr ME12. . . . . . 98 C4
Minster Gatehouse
Mus* ME12 . . . . 99 B2
Minster-in-Sheppey
Prim Sch ME12 . . . . . . 99 A3
Minster Rd
Gillingham ME8. . . . . 25 C3
Minster (Sheppey)
ME12. . . . . 98 C2
Minterne Ave ME10 . . 106 A4
Minterne Com Jun Sch
ME10. . . . . 106 A4
Miskin Rd ME3 . . . . 5 B1
Mitchell Ave ME4 . . . . . 22 C2
Mitchell Rd ME19 . . . . . 68 B2
Mitre Rd ME1. . . . . 21 B4
Moat Way ME11 . . . . . . 96 B2
Mockett Ct [4] ME10. . 104 A2
Molehill Copse Prim Sch
ME15. . . . . 81 B3
Monarch Cl ME5 . . . . . . 32 A2
Monarch Terr ME18 . . . 69 B3
Monckton's Ave
ME14. . . . . 64 C3
Monckton's Dr ME14. . 64 B3
Monckton's La ME14. . 64 C3
Moncrif Cl ME14. . . . . . 75 A4
Monkdown ME15 . . . . . 74 C1
Monkwood Cl ME1. . . . 30 B4
Monmouth Cl ME8. . . . 26 A2
Mons Ct ME10 . . . . 101 A3
Montfort Dr ME19 . . . . 68 C2
Montfort Rd
Chatham ME5 . . . . 39 C2
Rochester ME2. . . . . 14 A4
Montgomery Ave
ME5. . . . . 32 A3
Montgomery Rd ME7 . 23 C3
Montpelier Gate
ME16. . . . . 63 B1
Montrose Ave ME5. . . . 24 B2
Moonfleet Cl ME10 . . 101 B3
Moonstone Dr ME5 . . . 40 B2
Moonstone Sq
ME10. . . . . 103 C4
Moore St ME2 . . . . 14 A4
Mooring Rd ME1. . . . . . 22 A1
Moor Park Cl ME8 . . . . 36 A4
Moor St ME8 . . . . 36 B4
MOOR STREET. 36 B3
Morden St ME1 . . . . 21 C4
Morement Rd ME3. . . . . 5 A2
More Park RC Prim Sch
ME19. . . . . 60 A4
Morgan Rd ME2 . . . . . . 14 A4
Morhen Cl ME6 . . . . 44 C3
Morland Dr ME2. . . . . . . 8 A1
Morris Cl
Maidstone ME17. . . . . . . 81 B1
West Malling ME19 . . . . 51 A1
Mortimers Ave ME3. . . . 2 A4
Morton Cl ME15 . . . . . . 81 B2
Mosquito Rd ME19. . . . 68 B3
Mossbank ME5 . . . . 40 A3
Mossy Glade ME8. . . . . 35 B2
Mostyn Rd ME14. . . . . . 73 B4
Mote Ave ME15 . . . . 73 A3
Mote Hall Villas
ME14. . . . . 75 B4
Mote Pk ME15. . . . . 73 C2
Mote Rd ME15 . . . . 72 C3
Motney Hill Rd ME8 . . . 27 A4
Mouat Ct ME5 . . . . 40 A3
Mountbatten Ave
Chatham ME5 . . . . 32 A3
Higham ME3. . . . . 6 C4
Mount Dr ME14. . . . . . . 75 A4
Mount Field ME11 . . . . 96 B2
Mount La ME14 . . . . 75 A4
Mount Lodge ME1 . . . . 21 B2
Mount Pleasant
Chatham ME5 . . . . 23 B3
Forstal ME20 . . . . 53 B3
Mount Pleasant Dr
ME14. . . . . 67 A1
Mount Rd
Chatham ME4 . . . . 22 C3
Rochester ME1. . . . . 21 B2
Mountsfield Cl ME16. . 64 A1
Mount View Ct [3]
ME4. . . . . 22 C3
Moyle Cl ME8. . . . . 43 A4
Mozart Ct ME4. . . . . 22 B3
Muddy La ME10. . . . . . 107 B4
Muir Rd ME15 . . . . 72 C2
Mulberry Cl ME7. . . . . . 42 A4
Mulberry Ct ME14 . . . . 65 B1
Mungeam Ho ME1 . . . . 21 C4
Murrain Dr ME15 . . . . . 74 C1
Murray Rd ME2 . . . . 14 C4
MURSTON. 105 A3
Murston Inf Sch
ME10. . . . . 105 A2
Murston Jun Sch
ME10. . . . . 105 A3
Murston Rd ME10. . . . 105 A2
Murthwaite Ct ME12 . . 98 B1
Museum of Kent Rural
Life* ME14. . . . . 54 B1
Musgrave Rd ME10 . . 104 B4
Musket La
Eyhorne Street
ME17. . . . . 77 B2
Leeds ME17 . . . . 76 C2
Mustang Rd ME19 . . . . 68 B3
Mynn Cres ME14. . . . . . 74 C4
Myrtle Cres ME5. . . . . . 31 C1

N

Nagpur Ho [4] ME15. . . 81 C1
Nag's Head La ME1 . . . 22 A4
Napier Cl ME10 . . . . . . 103 B2
Napier Com Sch ME7 24 A4
Napier Ct ME14. . . . . . . 64 C3
Napier Rd ME7 . . . . 24 A4
Napwood Cl ME8 . . . . . 35 A2
Nares Rd ME8 . . . . 43 A4
Nash Cl ME5. . . . . 40 C2
Nashenden Farm La
ME1. . . . . 30 A4
Nashenden La
Rochester ME1. . . . . 20 C1
Rochester ME1. . . . . 21 A2
Natal Rd ME4. . . . . 23 A3
Nativity Cl ME10 . . . . . 104 A2
Nautilus Cl ME12 . . . . . 98 B2
Nautilus Dr ME12. . . . . 98 B2
Naval Terr ME12 . . . . . . 94 B4
Naylor's Cotts ME7 . . . 42 B1
Neale St ME4. . . . . 22 C2
Neatscourt Cotts
ME12. . . . . 97 A1
Nelson Ave ME12 . . . . . 99 B1
Nelson Cl ME12. . . . . . . 94 B1
Nelson Ct ME5. . . . . 23 C1
Nelson Ho [8] ME15 . . . 82 A1
Nelson Rd
Gillingham ME7. . . . . 24 A4
Wouldham ME1 . . . . 29 B1
Nelson Terr ME5 . . . . . . 23 C1
Nelson Wlk ME10. . . . 103 A3
Neptune Bsns Pk
ME2. . . . . 15 B3
Neptune Cl ME2 . . . . . . 15 B3
Neptune Terr ME12 . . . 95 B3
Neptune Way ME2 . . . . 15 B2
Nestor Ct ME18. . . . . . . 79 B4
Netley Cl ME14 . . . . 66 A2
NETTLESTEAD. 78 B2
Nettlestead Ct ME18 . . 78 A1
Nevill Ct ME19. . . . . 50 A1
Neville Cl ME14. . . . . . . 65 B4
Neville Rd ME4 . . . . 22 B2
Nevill Pl ME6 . . . . 45 B3
Nevill Rd ME6 . . . . 45 B3
Newark Ct [1] ME2 . . . . 14 B3
Newark Yd ME2. . . . . . . 14 B3
New Barns Rd ME14 . . 65 A4
Newbridge Ave
ME10. . . . . 100 C1
Newbury Ave ME16 . . . 63 C2
Newbury Cl ME3. . . . . . . 2 B4
Newchurch Rd ME15. . 72 C1
Newcomen Rd ME12. . 95 A3
New Covenant Pl [4]
ME1. . . . . 22 A4
New Cut ME4. . . . . 22 C4
New Cut Rd ME14. . . . . 66 A1
New Delhi Ho [5]
ME15. . . . . 81 C1
Newenden Cl ME14 . . . 66 A2
Newenden Rd ME2 . . . . 8 C2
NEW HYTHE. 51 C4
New Hythe La ME20. . . 51 C3
New Hythe Sta ME20 . 52 A4
NEWINGTON 102 A3
Newington CE Prim Sch
ME9. . . . . 102 B4
Newington Sta ME9 . 102 B3
Newington Wlk ME14 . 65 C2
Newitt Rd ME3 . . . . 5 B1
Newland Rd ME12 . . . . 96 A4
Newlands Ave ME10 . 103 A3
Newlyn Ct [1] ME14 . . . 72 C4
Newman Dr ME10. . . . 101 B2
Newnham Cl ME8. . . . . 25 C2
Newnham St ME4. . . . . 23 B3
New Rd
Chatham ME4 . . . . 22 C4
Ditton ME20 . . . . 52 A1
East Malling ME19 . . . . . 61 A4
Langley ME17 . . . . 83 A1
Minster (Sheppey)
ME12. . . . . 99 A2
Rochester ME1. . . . . 22 A4
Sheerness ME12 . . . . . . 94 B2
New Road Ave ME4 . . . 22 B4
New Road Ind Est
ME12. . . . . 94 B2
New Road Sch ME4. . . 23 A3
New St ME4 . . . . 22 B3
New Stairs ME4. . . . . . . 15 C2
Newton Cl
Chatham ME5 . . . . 40 C2
[1] Maidstone ME16. . . . 72 A3
NEW TOWN
Halling 28 C2
West Malling 59 A4
Niagara Cl ME18 . . . . . . 69 A3
Nicholas Cl ME16 . . . . . 70 C3
Nicklaus Dr ME5. . . . . . 39 C3
Nickleby Cl ME1 . . . . . . 21 C2
Nightingale Cl
Gillingham ME8. . . . . 35 B2
Larkfield ME20 . . . . 51 A2
Nightingale Ct ME2 . . . 12 C2
Nile Rd ME7 . . . . 23 C4
Nine Acres Rd ME2 . . . 19 B3
Niven Cl ME3. . . . . 8 C3
NOKE STREET 8 B4
Norah La ME3 . . . . 6 B3
Nore Cl
Gillingham ME7. . . . . 24 B1
Sheerness ME12 . . . . . . 95 A2
Noreen Ave ME12 . . . . . 98 B2
Norfolk Cl
Chatham ME5 . . . . 40 C3
Gillingham ME8. . . . . 26 A2
Norfolk Rd ME15. . . . . . 81 A4
Norman Cl
Gillingham ME8. . . . . 34 B1
Maidstone ME14. . . . . . . 65 B2
Rochester ME2. . . . . 20 C4
Norman Rd
Snodland ME6. . . . . 45 B2
West Malling ME19 . . . . 59 B4
Norreys Rd ME8 . . . . . . 35 B3
Norrington Rd ME15 . . 80 C2
North Bank Cl ME2 . . . 13 C1
North Borough Jun Sch
ME14. . . . . 65 A2
Northbourne Rd ME8 . 25 B4
Northcote Rd ME2 . . . . 14 A3
North Cres ME17. . . . . . 88 C4
North Ct [2] ME15. . . . . 72 C1
North Dane Way ME5 . 40 C4
Northdown Cl ME14. . . 65 B3
Northfields ME16 . . . . . 70 B2
Northfleet Cl ME14 . . . 65 C1
Northgate ME1 . . . . 14 C2
NORTH HALLING. 29 A4
Northleigh Cl ME15 . . . 80 B2
North Lockside Rd
ME4. . . . . 17 A4
North Meadow ME19. . 58 A3
North Meadow Cotts
ME19. . . . . 58 A3
Northpoint Bsns Est
ME2. . . . . 15 A4
North Pondside Rd
ME4. . . . . 16 A4
North Rd
Chatham, Brompton ME4,
ME7. . . . . 16 A3
Chatham ME4 . . . . 16 B4
Queenborough ME11 . . . 96 A2
North Side Three Rd
ME4. . . . . 16 C4
North St
Maidstone ME16. . . . . . . 70 B2
Rochester ME2. . . . . 14 B3
Sittingbourne ME10 . . . 101 A1
Warmlake ME17. . . . . . . 93 A1
North Terr ME3 . . . . 3 C2
Northumberland Ave
ME8. . . . . 26 B1
Northumberland Ct
ME15. . . . . 81 B3
Northumberland Rd
ME15. . . . . 81 B4
North View ME15 . . . . . 73 A1
North Way ME14. . . . . . 65 B3
Northwood Dr ME10 . 106 C3
Norton Gr ME5 . . . . 39 B3
Norton Rd ME17 . . . . . . 92 C1
Norway Terr [4] ME14. . 65 A3
Norwich Cl ME2 . . . . . . 13 A2
Norwood Rise ME12 . . 99 A3
Norwood Wlk E
ME10. . . . . 103 B3
Norwood Wlk W
ME10. . . . . 103 A3
Nottingham Ave
ME15. . . . . 81 B3
Nottingham Wlk ME2 . 13 A2
Nursery Ave
Maidstone, Bearsted
ME14. . . . . 75 A3
Maidstone ME16. . . . . . . 63 B2
Nursery Cl ME12. . . . . . 95 B2
Nursery Gdns ME3. . . . . 5 B1
Nursery Rd
Ditton ME20 . . . . 52 A1
Gillingham ME8. . . . . 35 A4
Nutfield Cl ME5. . . . . . . 32 B4
Nutfields ME10 . . . . . . 105 A1
Nutwood Cl ME14. . . . . 74 A4

O

Oakapple Ho [10]
ME16. . . . . 70 C3
Oakapple La ME16 . . . . 70 C3
Oak Ave ME7 . . . . 17 B2
Oak Cl ME3. . . . . 11 B3
Oak Dr
Higham ME3. . . . . 6 B4
Larkfield ME20 . . . . 51 C2
Oakfields ME10 . . . . . . 103 B1
Oak Ho [6] ME5 . . . . 39 C4
Oakhurst Cl ME5. . . . . . 39 C3
Oakland Cl ME5 . . . . . . 39 C3
Oaklands Inf & Jun Sch
ME5. . . . . 39 C4
Oakleigh Cl ME5. . . . . . 39 B2
Oak Rd
Hoo St Werburgh
ME3. . . . . 11 B3

Oak Rd *continued*
Rochester ME2 . . . . 13 B2
Sittingbourne ME10 . . . 105 B3
Oaks Bsns Village The
ME5 . . . . 40 C1
Oaks Com Inf Sch The
ME10 . . . . 106 A4
Oaks Dene ME5 . . . . 39 C1
Oaks The ME20 . . . . 52 C1
Oak Tree Ave ME15 . . . . 81 A3
Oaktree Ho ME10 . . . . 105 A1
Oak Trees Com Sch
ME15 . . . . 81 A3
Oakum Ct ME4 . . . . 23 B2
Oakwood Ct ME16 . . . . 71 C3
Oakwood Park Gram Sch ME16 . . . . 71 B3
Oakwood Rd ME16 . . . . 71 C3
Oakwood Terr ME10 . . 105 B2
Oast Ct ME10 . . . . 106 B4
Oast Ho The [3] ME8 . . . 35 C4
Oasts The ME14 . . . . 75 B4
Oastview ME8 . . . . 36 A4
Ocelot Ct [6] ME4 . . . . . 23 B3
Octavia Ct ME5 . . . . 40 B3
Odiham Dr ME16 . . . . . . 63 C3
OFFHAM 58 A4
Offham Prim Sch
ME19 . . . . 58 A4
Offham Rd ME19 . . . . . . 59 A3
Officers' Rd ME4 . . . . . . 16 B4
Officers Terr ME4 . . . . . 15 C3
Old Bailey The ME17 . . 87 C2
Old Bakery The ME12 . . 98 A1
Old Barn Cl ME7 . . . . . . 33 C2
Old Barn Rd ME19 . . . . 50 C2
Oldborough Manor Com Sch ME15 . . . . 80 C2
Old Carriageway The
ME7 . . . . 41 C4
Old Castle Wlk ME8 . . . 43 A4
Old Chatham Rd
Kit's Coty ME20 . . . . . . 47 B2
Sandling ME14 . . . . 55 A1
Oldchurch Ct [3]
ME16 . . . . 72 A3
Old Church Rd ME1 . . . 37 C1
Old Corn Stores The
ME14 . . . . 75 B4
Old Dr ME15 . . . . 80 A2
Oldfield Cl
Gillingham ME8 . . . . 35 A4
Maidstone ME15 . . . . 74 A1
Oldfield Dr ME1 . . . . . . 29 B1
Old George Ct ME3 . . . . 9 C4
Old Loose Cl ME15 . . . . 80 A1
Old Loose Hill ME15 . . 89 B4
Old Mill La ME20 . . . . . 54 A3
Old Mill Rd ME17 . . . . . 76 B1
Old Oast Bsns Ctr The
ME20 . . . . 53 B1
Old Orchard La ME19 . 50 B1
Old Orch The ME8 . . . . . 36 A4
Old Parsonage Ct
ME19 . . . . 59 C3
Old Pattens La ME4 . . . 22 A2
Old Rd
Chatham ME4 . . . . 22 C4
Wateringbury ME18 . . . . 78 A3
Old School Ct ME3 . . . . . 9 C4
Old School Pl ME14 . . . 65 A1
Old School The ME16 . 70 A1
Old Tovil Rd ME15 . . . . . 72 C2
Old Trafford Cl ME16 . . 63 B2
Old Tree La ME17 . . . . . 90 C3
Old Watling St ME2 . . . 12 B4
Oliver Cl ME4 . . . . 23 B2
Olivers Row ME14 . . . . 75 B4
Oliver Twist Cl ME1 . . . 21 B4
Olivier Dr ME2 . . . . 8 B2
Olivine Cl
Chatham ME5 . . . . 48 B4
Sittingbourne ME10 . . . 100 A1
Olliffe Cl ME5 . . . . 39 C2
Onslow Rd ME1 . . . . 22 A3
Opal Gn ME5 . . . . 40 B2
Orache Dr ME14 . . . . . . 66 B1
Orange Terr ME1 . . . . . . 15 A1
Orbit Cl ME5 . . . . 48 B4
Orchard Ave
Aylesford ME20 . . . . 52 C1
Rochester ME2 . . . . 7 C1
Orchard Bank ME17 . . . 92 A1
Orchard Bsns Ctr
ME16 . . . . 63 C4
Orchard Cl
Coxheath ME17 . . . . 88 B3
Langley Heath ME17 . . . 93 A4
Orchard Cres ME18 . . . 78 B2
Orchard Dr
Maidstone ME14 . . . . 74 A4
Newington ME9 . . . . . . 102 A2
Orchard Gr
Larkfield ME20 . . . . 51 C2
Minster (Sheppey)
ME12 . . . . 99 A2
Orchard Ind Est ME15 91 B3
Orchard Pl
[2] Maidstone ME16 . . . . 72 A3
Sittingbourne ME10 . . . 104 C1
Orchard St
Gillingham ME8 . . . . 35 B4
Maidstone ME15 . . . . 72 C3
Orchard The ME14 . . . . 75 A4
Orchard View ME14 . . . 67 A4
Orchard Villas [1]
ME4 . . . . 22 C3
Orchard Way ME6 . . . . . 45 A3
Orchid Cl
Minster (Sheppey)
ME12 . . . . 98 B1
Rochester ME2 . . . . 12 C2
Ordnance St ME4 . . . . . 22 B3
Ordnance Terr [9]
ME4 . . . . 22 B4
Oriole Way ME20 . . . . . 51 A2
Orion Rd ME1 . . . . 30 C3
Ormsby Gn ME8 . . . . . . 43 B3
Orpines The ME18 . . . . 79 A3
Orwell Cl ME20 . . . . 51 A3
Orwell Spike ME19 . . . . 59 A1
Osborne Rd ME7 . . . . . . 16 C1
Oslin Wlk ME18 . . . . 69 B2
Osprey Ave ME5 . . . . . . 24 B2
Osprey Ct ME10 . . . . . . 104 C1
Osprey Wlk ME20 . . . . . 51 A1
Ostend Ct ME10 . . . . . 101 A3
Ostlers Ct [2] ME6 . . . . . 45 B4
OTHAM 82 C3
OTHAM HOLE 82 C2
Otham La ME15 . . . . 75 B2
Otham St
Maidstone ME15 . . . . 75 B2
Otham ME15 . . . . 82 C3
Otterbourne Pl ME15 . 74 A1
OTTERHAM QUAY 27 C3
Otterham Quay La
ME8 . . . . 27 B2
Otteridge Rd ME14 . . . . 74 C3
Otway St
Chatham ME4 . . . . 23 A3
Gillingham ME7 . . . . 17 A2
Otway Terr [1] ME4 . . . . 23 A3
Overton Ho ME12 . . . . . 95 A3
Owen Cl ME19 . . . . 61 C4
Owens Way ME7 . . . . . . 18 A2
Owletts Cl ME15 . . . . . . 81 B4
Oxford Rd
Gillingham ME7 . . . . 24 A3
Maidstone ME15 . . . . 81 B4
Oxford St ME6 . . . . 45 B4
Oxley Shaw La ME19 . . 50 C2
Oyster Cl ME10 . . . . . . 104 A4

P

Packer Pl ME5 . . . . 32 A4
Paddocks The ME7 . . . . 34 A1
Paddock The ME4 . . . . . 22 C4
Pad's Hill ME15 . . . . 72 C4
Padsole La ME15 . . . . . 72 C4
Padstow Manor [1]
ME7 . . . . 16 C2
Paget Row ME7 . . . . 16 C1
Paget St ME7 . . . . 16 C1
Pagitt St ME4 . . . . 22 B3
Palace Ave ME15 . . . . . 72 C4
Palace Ct ME5 . . . . 24 A2
Palace Ind Est ME15 . . 91 B4
Palace Wood Inf Sch
ME16 . . . . 63 C2
Palace Wood Jun Sch
ME16 . . . . 63 C2
Palmar Rd ME16 . . . . . . 64 A2
Palmerston Rd ME4 . . . 22 C1
Palmerston Wlk
ME10 . . . . 105 B2
Pamela Ct ME7 . . . . 17 A1
Pankhurst Rd ME3 . . . . . 5 A2
Panton Cl ME5 . . . . 40 C4
Papion Gr ME5 . . . . 39 B2
Parade The
Rochester ME2 . . . . 13 B4
Sittingbourne ME10 . . . 106 C4
Parham Rd ME4 . . . . . . 22 C2
Parish Rd ME12 . . . . 98 B1
Park Ave
Gillingham ME7 . . . . 24 A3
Maidstone ME17 . . . . 89 A2
Maidstone, Penenden Heath ME14 . . . . 65 B2
Queenborough ME11 . . . 96 C1
Sittingbourne ME10 . . . 106 B3
Park Barn Rd ME17 . . . 85 A1
Park Cres ME4 . . . . 31 C4
Park Dr ME10 . . . . 106 A3
Parker Cl ME8 . . . . 35 B1
Park Farm Houses
ME20 . . . . 61 B4
Parkfield Rd ME8 . . . . . 26 C1
Parkfields ME2 . . . . 12 C3
Park Ho ME14 . . . . 65 B2
Park La
Maidstone, Cock Stone ME17 . . . . 90 C2
Maidstone, Ringlestone ME14 . . . . 64 C3
Park Manor ME7 . . . . . . 16 B1
Park Rd
Leybourne ME19 . . . . 50 B3
Queenborough ME11 . . . 96 A2
Sheerness ME12 . . . . . . 95 B2
Sittingbourne ME10 . . . 104 A1
Parkside ME3 . . . . 2 B3
Park View Ct ME15 . . . . 74 A1
Park Villas ME14 . . . . . . 74 A4
Park Way
Coxheath ME17 . . . . 88 C3
Maidstone ME15 . . . . 73 A1
Park Way Prim Sch
ME15 . . . . 73 A1
PARK WOOD
Gillingham 43 A4
Maidstone 91 A4
Park Wood Gn ME8 . . . 35 A1
Parkwood Inf Sch
ME8 . . . . 35 B1
Parkwood Jun Sch
ME8 . . . . 35 B1
Park Wood Par ME15 . 82 A1
Park Wood Trad Est
Maidstone ME15 . . . . 91 B4
Otham ME15 . . . . 91 C4
Parr Ave ME7 . . . . 17 A2
Parrs Head Mews
ME1 . . . . 14 C2
Parsonage Chase
ME12 . . . . 98 A1
Parsonage La ME2 . . . . 14 C4
Partridge Ave ME20 . . . 51 A3
Partridge Dr ME4 . . . . . 10 B1
Pasley Rd ME4, ME7 . . . 16 A3
Pasley Rd E ME7 . . . . . . 16 B3
Pasley Rd N ME4 . . . . . . 16 B3
Pasley Rd W ME7 . . . . . 16 A3
Pastime Cl ME10 . . . . . 100 C2
Patrixbourne Ave
ME8 . . . . 25 C2
Pattens Gdns ME1 . . . . 22 B2
Pattens La ME1, ME4 . . 22 B1
Pattens Pl ME1 . . . . 22 A2
Pavilion Dr ME10 . . . . 101 A3
Pavings The ME17 . . . . 77 B2
Payne's La ME15 . . . . . . 80 C3
Peacock Mews [7]
ME16 . . . . 72 A4
Peacock Rise ME5 . . . . 40 A4
Peal Cl ME3 . . . . 5 B1
Pearl Way ME18 . . . . . . 69 B3
Pearman Cl ME8 . . . . . . 27 A1
Pear Tree Alley [2]
ME10 . . . . 104 A3
Pear Tree Ave ME20 . . . 52 A1
Peartree Cotts ME8 . . . 36 B4
Peartree La DA12 . . . . . . 6 A2
Pear Tree La
Gillingham ME7 . . . . 33 B3
Loose ME15 . . . . 80 C2
Pear Tree Pl ME3 . . . . . . 6 B3
Pear Tree Row ME17 . . 82 C1
Pear Tree Wlk ME9 . . . 102 A2
Peckham Cl ME2 . . . . . 14 C4
Peel Dr ME10 . . . . 105 B2
Peel St ME14 . . . . 65 A2
Peggoty Cl ME3 . . . . 6 B3
Pelican Cl ME2 . . . . 12 C2
Pelican Ct ME18 . . . . . . 78 C3
Pemberton Sq [4]
ME2 . . . . 14 C4
Pembroke ME4 . . . . 16 B4
Pembroke Ct ME4 . . . . 23 A4
Pembroke Gdns ME8 . . 43 B4
Pembroke Rd ME17 . . . 88 B3
Pembroke Rise ME4 . . 16 A3
Pembury Ct [6]
ME10 . . . . 104 A2
Pembury Gdns ME16 . . 71 C3
Pembury St ME10 . . . . 104 A2
Pembury Way ME8 . . . . 26 B2
Penenden Ct ME14 . . . 65 B3
PENENDEN HEATH . . . 65 B3
Penenden Heath Rd
ME14 . . . . 65 C3
Penenden St ME14 . . . . 65 A2
Penfold Cl
Chatham ME5 . . . . 32 B3
Maidstone ME15 . . . . 81 C1
Penfold Hill ME17 . . . . . 84 C4
Penfold Way ME15 . . . . 80 A2
Penguin Cl ME2 . . . . . . 13 A2
Penhurst Cl ME14 . . . . . 66 C1
Pennant Rd ME1 . . . . . . 30 C3
Penn Cl ME10 . . . . 107 B4
Pennine Way ME15 . . . 74 C1
Penny Cress Gdns
ME16 . . . . 71 B3
Penny Cress Rd ME12 . 98 B1
Penny Spring Farm (Cvn Pk) ME14 . . . . 57 C2
Penrith Ct ME7 . . . . 18 A1
Penryn Manor [4]
ME7 . . . . 16 C2
Penshurst Cl ME8 . . . . . 26 B2
Penstocks The ME15 . . 71 C2
Pentagon Sh Ctr ME4 22 C4
Pepingstraw Cl ME19 . 58 A3
Pepys Ave ME12 . . . . . . 94 C2
Pepy's Way
Rochester ME2 . . . . 13 C4
Rochester ME2 . . . . 14 A4
Peregrine Dr ME10 . . 107 A4
Peregrine Rd ME19 . . . 68 C2
Peridot Ct ME15 . . . . . . 81 C1
Perie Row [9] ME7 . . . . 16 A2
Perimeter Rd ME20 . . . 52 A3
Periwinkle Cl ME10 . . 104 A3
Periwinkle Ct [3]
ME10 . . . . 104 A3
Perryfield St ME14 . . . . 64 C2
Perry St
Chatham ME4 . . . . 22 B3
Maidstone ME14 . . . . 64 C2
Perth Gdns ME10 . . . . 103 B2
Pested Bars Rd ME17 . 81 B1
Petchart Cl ME2 . . . . . . 19 C3
Peterborough Gdns
ME2 . . . . 12 C2
Petfield Cl ME12 . . . . . . 99 A2
Petham Gn ME8 . . . . . . 25 C2
Petlands ME17 . . . . 81 B1
Peverel Dr ME14 . . . . . . 67 A1
Peverel Gn ME8 . . . . . . 43 A4
Phalarope Way ME4 . . . 10 C2
Pheasant La ME15 . . . . 80 C4
Pheasant Rd ME4 . . . . . 23 C2
Phillippa Ct ME10 . . . . 100 C2
Phillips Ct ME8 . . . . 25 B2
Phoenix Cotts ME18 . . 78 B2
Phoenix Ct [11] ME7 . . . . 16 C2
Phoenix Dr ME18 . . . . . 78 C3
Phoenix Ind Est ME2 . . 15 A3
Phoenix Pk ME15 . . . . . 91 B4
Phoenix Rd ME5 . . . . . . 40 B2
Piccadilly Apartments [4]
ME5 . . . . 23 B3
Pickering St ME15 . . . . 80 C2
Pickwick Cres ME1 . . . 21 C3
Pier Approach Rd
ME7 . . . . 17 A3
Pier Pl ME2 . . . . 10 A3
Pier Rd ME7 . . . . 17 B3
Pier Rd Ind Est ME7 . . 17 A3
Pigtail Cnr ME12 . . . . . . 99 C2
Pike Cl ME20 . . . . 51 B4
Pikefields ME8 . . . . 25 C2
Pikey La ME19 . . . . 60 B1
Pilgrims Lakes ME17 . . 87 C2
Pilgrims Rd ME2 . . . . . . 28 B2
Pilgrims View ME14 . . . 54 C3
Pilgrims Way
Boxley ME14 . . . . 56 C3
Cuxton ME2 . . . . 19 C3
Detling ME14 . . . . 57 C1
Eccles ME20 . . . . 46 C2
Pilot Rd ME1 . . . . 30 C4
Pimpernel Cl ME14 . . . 75 A4
Pimpernel Way ME5 . . 39 B4
Pincus Ho ME10 . . . . . 103 C3
Pine Cl ME20 . . . . 51 B2
Pine Cotts ME14 . . . . . . 64 B4
Pine Gr
Gillingham ME7 . . . . 34 A1
Maidstone ME14 . . . . 65 B2
Pine Ho
[3] Chatham ME5 . . . . . . 31 C1
[5] Maidstone ME14 . . . . 73 A4
Pine Lodge ME16 . . . . . 71 B3
Pine Lodge Touring Pk
ME17 . . . . 76 B2
Pine Pl ME15 . . . . 72 A1
Pine Rd ME2 . . . . 13 C2
Pinewood Dr ME5 . . . . 49 B4
Pinnacles The ME4 . . . . 10 C1
Pintails The ME4 . . . . . . 10 B1
Pippin Cl
Coxheath ME17 . . . . 88 A2
Sittingbourne ME10 . . . 103 C4
Pippin Croft ME7 . . . . . 34 A2
Pippin Way ME19 . . . . . 68 C2
Pirbright Cl ME5 . . . . . . 41 A2
Pitt Rd
Chartway Street
ME17 . . . . 93 C2
Maidstone ME16 . . . . 71 A1
Plains Ave ME15 . . . . . . 73 B1
Plaistow Sq ME14 . . . . . 65 C2
Plantation La ME14 . . . 74 C3
Plantation Rd ME7 . . . . 18 A2
Platters The ME8 . . . . . 34 C3
Playstool Cl ME9 . . . . 102 B3
Playstool Rd ME9 . . . . 102 A3
Plaza Ct [7] ME10 . . . . 104 C2
Pleasant Row [10] ME7 . 16 A2
Pleasant Valley La
ME15 . . . . 88 A4
Pleasent Pl ME12 . . . . . 97 C3
Plewis Ho ME7 . . . . 17 B3
Plomley Cl ME8 . . . . 43 A4
Plough Cotts ME17 . . . 92 C2
Ploughmans Way
Chatham ME5 . . . . 40 A1
Gillingham ME8 . . . . 35 B2
Plough Wents Rd
ME17 . . . . 92 A2
Plover Cl ME5 . . . . 41 A1
Plover Rd
Larkfield ME20 . . . . 51 A2
Minster (Sheppey)
ME12 . . . . 98 B1
Pluckley Cl ME8 . . . . . . 25 C3
Plumpton Wlk [9]
ME15 . . . . 82 A2
Plumtree Gr ME7 . . . . . 42 A4
Plumtrees ME16 . . . . . . 70 C2
Poachers Cl ME5 . . . . . 32 C1
Pochard Cl ME4 . . . . . . 10 B1
Podkin Wood ME5 . . . . 48 A4
Polhill Dr ME5 . . . . 39 C2
Police Station Rd
ME19 . . . . 59 C4
Pollard Ct ME7 . . . . 16 C1
Pond Cotts ME10 . . . . 106 A2
Pond Dr ME10 . . . . 107 A4
Pope St ME16 . . . . 71 B2
Popes Wood ME14 . . . . 66 C2

Poplar Cl
Hoo St Werburgh ME3 11 B3
Rochester ME2 13 C1
Poplar Gr ME16 63 C1
Poplar Rd ME2 13 B1
Poplicans Rd ME2 19 B3
Poppy Cl
Gillingham ME7 17 B1
Maidstone ME16 71 C3
Porchester Cl ME15 80 B2
Port Cl
Chatham ME5 40 B3
Maidstone ME14 67 A1
Porter Cl ME12 98 B2
Porters Wlk ME17 93 A4
Portland Ave ME10 105 B2
Portland Pl 1 ME6 45 B4
Portland Rd
Gillingham ME7 17 B2
Wouldham ME1 37 C4
Portland St 1 ME4 23 B2
Portland Terr ME12 95 A3
Portree Mews ME7 24 B3
Port Rise ME4 22 C3
Portsdown Cl ME16 71 A2
Portsmouth Cl ME2 13 A2
Portway Rd ME3 2 B3
Post Barn Rd ME4 22 C2
Postley Commercial Ctr ME15 72 C2
Postley Rd ME15 72 C1
Postmill Dr ME15 72 B1
Pottery Rd ME3 5 A1
Potyn Ho ME1 21 C4
Poulsen Ct 8 ME10 105 A2
Pout Rd ME6 45 A3
Povey Ave ME2 8 C2
Powell Cl ME20 53 B3
Power Station Rd ME12 97 C4
Powlett Rd ME2 8 C1
Pratling St ME20 54 A4
PRATLING STREET 54 A3
Premier Bsns Ctr ME4 23 C1
Premier Par ME20 52 C1
Prentis Cl ME10 103 B3
Prentis Quay ME10 104 B3
Preston Ave ME7 24 B1
Preston Hall Hospl ME20 53 A1
Preston Way ME8 25 B2
Pretoria Ho 8 ME15 81 C1
Pretoria Rd
Chatham ME4 22 C2
Gillingham ME7 24 A3
Prices Ct 5 ME10 105 A2
Pridmore Rd ME6 45 A4
Priestdale Ct ME4 22 B3
Priestfield Rd ME7 17 B1
Priestfields ME1 21 B3
Priestfield Stad (Gillingham FC) ME7 17 B1
Priestley Dr ME20 51 A4
Primrose Ave ME8 34 B1
Primrose Cl ME4 31 B3
Primrose Dr ME20 52 B1
Primrose Ho 10 ME15 81 C3
Primrose Rd ME2 28 A1
Prince Arthur Rd ME7 16 B2
Prince Charles Ave
Chatham ME5 40 B4
Minster (Sheppey) ME12 99 A2
Sittingbourne ME10 105 B1
Prince Phillip Lodge The ME20 53 A1
Princes Ave
Chatham ME5 32 B1
Minster (Sheppey) ME12 99 B3
PRINCES PARK 32 B2
Princess Mary Ave ME4 16 B3
Princes St ME14 65 A1
Prince's St ME1 21 C4
Princes Way ME14 57 B1
Prinys Dr ME8 42 C4
Priorsdean Cl ME16 70 A1
Priory Ct
Gillingham ME8 25 A2
Rochester ME1 15 A1
Priory Gate 4 ME14 65 A1
Priory Gr ME20 52 B1
Priory Rd
Gillingham ME8 25 A2
Maidstone ME15 72 C3
Rochester ME2 14 A2
Pritchard Ct ME7 23 C3
Progress Est The ME15 91 C4
Prospect Ave ME2 14 B4
Prospect Pl ME16 72 A3
Prospect Row
Chatham, Brompton ME7 16 A2
Chatham ME4 23 A3
Provender Way ME14 66 B1
Providence Cotts ME3 6 B2
Pudding La ME14 72 B4
Pudding Rd ME8 35 C4
Pump Cl ME19 50 B1
Pump La ME7 & ME8 26 A3
Purbeck Rd ME4 22 B2
Purser Way ME7 16 C3
Puttney Dr ME10 101 B2
Pyrus Cl ME5 48 B4

Q

Quarries The ME17 90 B4
Quarry Rd ME15 72 C2
Quarry Sq ME14 65 A1
Quarry Wood Ind Est ME20 62 B4
Quayside ME4 16 B4
Queen Anne Rd ME14 73 A4
QUEENBOROUGH 96 B2
Queenborough Dr ME12 98 C3
Queenborough Fst Sch ME11 96 C2
Queenborough Rd
Halfway Houses ME12 97 A3
Queenborough ME12 97 A1
Queenborough Sta ME11 96 B2
Queendown Ave ME8 35 A1
Queen Elizabeth Sq ME15 81 B2
Queen Mother Ct The ME1 21 B4
Queen's Ave
Maidstone ME16 64 A1
Snodland ME6 45 B4
Queens Ct ME8 36 A4
Queens Ho ME16 71 A3
Queens Rd ME12 99 B3
Queen's Rd
Chatham ME5 24 A1
Gillingham ME7 23 C4
Maidstone ME16 71 B4
Snodland ME6 45 B4
Queen St
Chatham ME4 23 A4
Kings Hill ME18 69 A3
Rochester ME1 21 C4
Queens Way ME14 57 B1
Queen's Way ME12 94 B1
Queenswood Rd ME20 47 B3
Quern The ME15 72 A1
Quested Way ME17 87 A2
Quickstep Cl ME10 101 A2
Quickthorn Cres ME5 31 B1
Quinion Cl ME5 48 B4
Quinnell St ME8 26 B1
Quinton Rd ME10 100 A1
Quixote Cres ME2 8 B1

R

Radleigh Gdns ME1 22 B1
Radnor Cl ME14 64 B3
Raggatt Pl ME15 73 A2
Ragstone Ct ME20 61 C4
Ragstone Rd ME15 74 C2
Railway Rd ME12 94 C2
Railway St Ind Pk ME7 17 A2
Railway St
Chatham ME4 22 C4
Gillingham ME7 17 A2
Railway Terr ME11 96 B2
RAINHAM 35 B4
Rainham Cl ME15 72 C1
Rainham Mark Gram Sch ME8 26 A2
Rainham Rd ME5 23 C3
Rainham Sch for Girls ME8 34 C4
Rainham Sh Ctr 2 ME8 26 C1
Rainham Sta ME8 26 C1
Raleigh Cl ME5 32 A2
Raleigh Way ME12 97 C3
Ramillies Cl ME5 32 A2
Rampion Cl ME14 66 B1
Randall Rd ME4 22 B1
Randalls Row ME15 80 A1
Randall St ME14 64 C2
Randolph Cotts ME2 8 B1
Randolph Ho ME7 16 C1
Randolph Rd ME7 16 C1
Ranelagh Rd ME12 95 A3
Ranscombe Cl ME2 13 A1
Ranscombe Farm Cotts ME2 19 C4
Ratcliffe Highway ME3 4 C2
Ravelin Ho ME12 95 A3
Raven Cl ME20 51 B1
Ravens Dane Cl ME15 74 C1
Ravenswood Ave
Rochester ME2 8 B1
Rochester ME2 14 B4
Rawdon Rd ME15 72 C3
Rayfield Ct ME6 37 B1
Rayleigh Cl ME16 64 A3
Rayleigh Ho 2 ME15 81 B4
Raymer Rd ME14 65 B4
Readers Ct ME18 79 B4
Reading Ho 4 ME15 82 A1
Readscroft Rd ME8 35 A1
Recreation Ave ME6 45 B4
Recreation Cl ME14 65 B2
Recreation Way ME10 101 B3
Rectory Cl
Snodland ME6 45 B4
Wouldham ME1 29 B1
Rectory Grange ME1 21 C2
Rectory La
Harrietsham ME17 87 C1
Maidstone ME16 70 C1
Rectory La N ME19 50 C2
Rectory La S ME19 50 C1
Rectory Rd ME10 105 A1
Reculver Wlk ME15 82 A3
Redan Pl ME12 95 B3
Redbank ME19 50 C2
Redbridge Cl ME5 40 C4
Redcliffe La ME14 65 B3
Rede Court Rd ME2 13 B4
Rede Wood Rd ME16 70 B3
Redfern Ave ME7 17 B1
Redfern Ho ME2 28 B1
Red House Gdns ME18 78 A3
Redland Shaw ME4 22 B1
Red Robin Cotts ME9 102 B3
Redruth Manor 3 ME7 16 C2
Redsells Cl ME15 74 C1
Redshank Rd ME4 10 B1
Redvers Rd ME4 23 A2
Redwell Gr ME18 69 B2
Redwing Cl ME20 51 B2
Redwing Rd ME5 32 B3
Redwood Cl ME5 40 B2
Reed Cl ME20 45 B1
Reedham Cres ME3 2 C3
Reeves Ct ME19 51 B1
Reform Rd ME4 23 B2
Regency Cl
Gillingham ME8 42 C3
Sheerness ME12 94 B4
Regency Ct ME10 103 C2
Regent Dr ME15 80 B4
Regent Rd ME7 23 C4
Regent Way ME18 69 B3
Reginald Ave ME2 19 C3
Reginald Rd ME16 72 A3
Regis Bsns Pk ME12 94 B2
Regis Cres ME10 101 A1
Regis Manor Com Prim Sch ME10 100 C1
Reinden Gr ME15 74 B1
Renown Rd ME5 40 C2
Repton Way ME5 39 C4
Resolution Cl ME5 32 A2
Restharrow Rd ME14 74 A4
Restharrow Way ME4 10 C1
Retreat Cvn Pk The ME18 78 B2
Rettendon Dr ME10 101 A2
Revenge Rd ME5 49 A4
Rhodes Ho 5 ME5 23 C2
Rhode St ME4 23 A4
Rhodewood Cl ME15 74 C1
Richard St
Chatham ME4 22 C4
Rochester ME1 21 C3
Richborough Drive ME2 8 A1
Richmond Cl
Chatham ME5 40 B4
Rochester ME2 9 C1
Richmond Dr ME10 100 C1
Richmond First Sch ME12 95 B3
Richmond Inf Sch ME7 16 C2
Richmond Rd ME7 16 C3
Richmond St ME12 95 B3
Richmond Way ME15 80 B4
Riddles Rd ME10, ME9 103 B1
Ridge Meadow Prim Sch ME5 31 C2
Ridgeway The
Chatham ME4 31 B3
Gillingham ME7 16 C3
Ridgway ME16 71 A2
Ridham Ave ME10 101 B3
Ridley Rd ME1 21 B4
Rigden's Ct 6 ME10 104 A3
Riggall Ct ME2 19 A3
RINGLESTONE 64 B3
Ringlestone Cres ME14 64 C4
Ringlet Rd ME4 10 B2
Ringwood Cl ME8 35 A4
Ringwood Rd ME15 81 A4
Ripon Cl ME8 26 A3
Rise The
Chatham ME4 16 A3
Gillingham ME7 42 A3
Halfway Houses ME12 97 A2
Rochester ME1 22 A3
Ritch Rd ME6 44 C4
River Bank Cl 8 ME15 73 A4
Riverbourne Ct 6 ME10 104 B2
River Dr ME2 13 B3
Riverhead Cl
Maidstone ME16 64 A2
Sittingbourne ME10 103 B1
Rivermead ME4 10 C2
Rivermead Sch ME7 17 B2
Rivers Cl ME18 78 C3
Riverside East Rd ME4 10 C1
Riverside Prim Sch ME8 27 A1
River St 6 ME7 16 A2
River View
Gillingham ME8 26 A3
Maidstone ME15 72 B2
River View Cl 6 ME4 22 C3
River Way ME20 51 C4
Roach St ME2 14 A3
Roan Ct ME2 13 C4
Robert Napier Sch The ME7 24 B3
Roberts Cl ME10 100 B1
Roberts Orchard Rd ME16 70 B3
Roberts Rd
Gillingham ME8 35 B4
Snodland ME6 45 A4
Robin Ct 6 ME1 22 A4
Robin Ho 5 ME16 72 A4
Robin Hood La ME5 39 A1
Robin Hood Lane (Lower) ME5 39 C2
Robin Hood Lane (Upper) ME5 39 B1
Robins Ct ME14 65 B3
Robson Dr
Aylesford ME20 52 B2
Hoo St Werburgh ME3 5 A2
Rocfort Rd ME6 45 B4
ROCHESTER 14 B2
Rochester Airport ME1, ME5 30 C2
Rochester Airport Ind Est ME1 30 C1
Rochester Ave ME1 21 C4
Rochester Castle★ ME1 14 C2
Rochester Cath★ ME1 14 C2
Rochester Cres ME3 5 A2
Rochester Ct ME2 15 B4
Rochester Gate ME1 15 A1
Rochester Gram Sch for Girls The ME1 21 C2
Rochester Ho 1 ME15 81 B3
Rochester Ind Coll ME1 22 A4
Rochester Rd
Burham ME1 46 B4
Chatham ME1, ME5 38 C4
Pratling Street ME20 53 C4
Rochester ME2 20 A4
Rochester St ME4 22 B3
Rochester Sta ME1 15 A1
Rock Ave ME7 23 C3
Rock Farm Oasthouse ME18 78 A2
Rock Rd
Maidstone ME14 65 A2
Sittingbourne ME10 104 A2
Rocks Cl ME19 61 A2
Rocks Rd The ME19 61 B2
Rocky Hill ME16 72 A4
Rocky Hill Terr 2 ME16 72 A4
Rodmer Cl ME12 99 A4
RODMERSHAM 107 C2
Rodmersham Gn ME9 107 B1
RODMERSHAM GREEN 107 B1
Rodmersham Sch ME9 107 B1
Roebuck Ho ME1 15 B1
Roebuck Rd ME1 14 C1
Roentgen Ho ME10 103 C3
Roffen Rd ME1 21 C2
Rolvenden Ave ME8 25 C3
Rolvenden Dr ME10 103 A3
Rolvenden Rd ME2 8 C2
Roman Cl ME5 39 A1
Roman Hts ME14 65 C2
Roman Rd ME6 45 A4
Roman Sq ME10 104 B1
Roman Way ME2 20 C4
Romany Ct ME5 24 A1
Romany Rd ME8 25 C2
Rome Terr ME4 22 C4
Romney Cl ME14 74 C3
Romney Ct ME10 104 A3
Romney Pl ME15 72 C4
Romney Rd ME5 32 B1
Romsey Cl ME2 13 B4
Ronalds Ct 6 ME10 104 C2
Rookery Hill ME6 45 A4
Roonagh Ct ME10 106 B4
Roosevelt Ave ME5 32 A4
Ropemakers Ct ME4 23 A1
Roper Cl ME8 42 C3
Roper's La ME3 5 C4
Rope Wlk ME4 15 C1
ROSEACRE 74 C4
Roseacre Gdns ME14 74 C3
Roseacre Jun Sch ME14 74 C4
Roseacre La ME14 74 C4
Rosebery Cl ME10 105 C2

Rosebery Rd
Chatham ME4 . . . . 22 B2
Gillingham ME7 . . . . 17 A3
Rose Cotts ME2 . . . . 12 B4
Rose Ct ME17 . . . . 88 C1
Roseholme ME16 . . . . . 71 C2
Roseleigh Ave ME16 . . 63 C1
Roseleigh Rd ME10 . . . 106 A4
Rosemary Ave ME12 . . 97 B3
Rosemary Cl 4 ME5 . . 39 C4
Rosemary Ct 1 ME1 . . 22 A4
Rosemary Rd
Maidstone ME15 . . . . 74 C3
West Malling ME19 . . . . 51 A1
Rosemount Cl ME15 . . 89 B4
Rosemount Ct ME2 . . . . 8 A1
Rose St
Rochester ME1 . . . . 22 A3
Sheerness ME12 . . . . . . 94 C2
Rose Street Prim Sch
ME12 . . . . 94 C2
Rose Terr ME19 . . . . 58 A3
Rose Yd ME14 . . . . 72 C4
Rosslyn Gn ME16 . . . . . 63 B1
Ross St ME1 . . . . 22 A4
Rother Vale ME5 . . . . . . 40 C3
Rougemont ME18 . . . . . 69 B2
Roundel The ME10 . . . 106 C4
Roundhay ME19 . . . . . . 50 C1
Roundwell ME14 . . . . . . 75 C3
Round Wood Cl ME5 . . 40 A1
Rover Rd ME5 . . . . 40 B2
Rowan Cl ME20 . . . . 52 C1
Rowan Ho
4 Chatham ME5 . . . . . . 31 C1
7 Maidstone ME16 . . . . 70 C3
Rowan Lea ME5 . . . . . . 23 B1
Rowans The ME12 . . . . 98 C3
Rowan Wlk ME4 . . . . . . 22 B3
Rowbrocke Cl ME8 . . . . 43 A3
Rowe Pl ME20 . . . . 46 A2
Rowland Ave ME7 . . . . . 24 B2
Rowland Cl
Gillingham ME7 . . . . 24 B1
Maidstone ME16 . . . . 72 A3
Royal Eagle Cl ME2 . . . 15 B3
Royal Engineers Mus*
ME7 . . . . 16 B2
Royal Engineers' Rd
ME14 . . . . 64 C3
Royal Fountain Mews
ME12 . . . . 94 B3
Royal Rd ME12 . . . . 95 A3
Royal Sch of Military
Engineering ME3 . . . . . 8 C4
Royal Sovereign Ave
ME4 . . . . 16 B3
Royal Star Arc 5
ME14 . . . . 72 B4
Royston Rd ME15 . . . . . 74 C3
Roystons Cl ME8 . . . . . . 26 C2
Rubin Pl ME19 . . . . 69 A3
Ruckinge Way ME8 . . . 25 C3
Rudge Cl ME5 . . . . 41 A2
Rugby Cl ME5 . . . . 39 C4
Rule Ct ME12 . . . . 94 C1
Rumwood Ct ME17 . . . . 82 C1
Running Horse Rdbt The
ME14 . . . . 54 C1
Runnymede Gdns
ME15 . . . . 80 B4
Rush Cl ME5 . . . . 40 A3
Rushdean Rd ME2 . . . . 13 A1
Rushenden Rd ME11 . . 96 B1
Rushes The ME20 . . . . . 51 C4
Rushmead Dr ME15 . . . 80 B3
Ruskin Cl ME19 . . . . 61 C4
Russell Cl ME10 . . . . . 103 B1
Russell Ct ME4 . . . . 23 B3
Russell Rd ME20 . . . . . . 47 B3
Russells Ave ME8 . . . . . 36 A4
Russell St ME12 . . . . . . 94 C2
Russet Cl ME2 . . . . 13 B4
Russet Ct ME17 . . . . 88 B3
Russets The ME16 . . . . . 63 B1
Russett Cl ME20 . . . . . . 62 B4
Russet Way ME19 . . . . . 68 B2
Ruth Ho 2 ME16 . . . . . 64 B1
Ruth St ME4 . . . . 23 A2
Rutland Pl ME8 . . . . 42 C3
Rutland Way ME15 . . . . 81 C4
Ryan Dr ME15 . . . . 74 C2
Rycault Cl 4 ME16 . . . 72 A3
Rycaut Cl ME8 . . . . 43 A3
Rydal Ho ME15 . . . . 81 C3
Ryde Cl ME5 . . . . 32 B4
Ryegrass Cl ME5 . . . . . . 32 C2

S

Sabre Ct ME7 . . . . 25 A1
Saddlers Cl ME14 . . . . . 66 B1
Sadlers Cl ME5 . . . . 39 A2
Saffron Cl ME16 . . . . . . 71 A3
Saffron Way
1 Chatham ME5 . . . . . . 31 C1
Sittingbourne ME10 . . . 101 A1
Sage Rd ME1 . . . . 21 B3
Sailfield Ct ME4 . . . . . . 15 C3
Sailmakers Ct 5
ME4 . . . . 23 B2
St Agnes Gdns ME12 . . 95 A2
St Albans Cl ME7 . . . . . 17 B3
St Albans Rd ME2 . . . . . 13 A2
St Andrew's Cl ME16 . . 70 C2
St Andrews Pk ME16 . . 70 C3
St Andrews Rd ME7 . . . 17 A3
St Andrew's Rd ME16 . 70 C3
St Andrews Sch ME1 . 21 C4
St Annes Ct ME16 . . . . . 72 A4
St Augustine of
Canterbury RC Prim
Sch ME8 . . . . 43 A3
St Barnabas Cl
Gillingham ME7 . . . . 24 A3
Maidstone ME16 . . . . 63 C4
St Bartholomew's Hospl
ME1 . . . . 22 B4
St Bartholomew's La 4
ME1 . . . . 22 B4
St Bartholomew's Terr
2 ME1 . . . . 22 B4
St Benedict Rd ME6 . . . 44 C4
St Benedicts RC Prim
Sch ME5 . . . . 40 C2
St Catherines Ct ME1 . 15 A1
St Catherine's Hospl
ME1 . . . . 22 A4
St Clement's Ho ME1 . 15 A1
St Davids Gate ME16 . . 70 C2
St Edmunds Way
ME8 . . . . 27 B1
St Edward's RC Prim Sch
ME12 . . . . 94 C2
St Faith's La ME14 . . . . 75 A4
St Faith's St ME14 . . . . 72 B4
St Francis Cl
Maidstone ME14 . . . . 65 B3
Rochester ME2 . . . . 13 B2
St Francis RC Prim Sch
ME15 . . . . 71 B4
St Georges Bsns Pk
ME10 . . . . 105 A2
St George's CE Mid Sch
ME12 . . . . 99 C2
St George's Ct ME12 . . 94 C1
St George's Rd ME7 . . . 16 C2
St George's Sq ME16 . . 72 A3
St Helen's Rd ME12 . . . 95 B2
St Helier's Cl ME16 . . . 71 A2
St James Cl ME19 . . . . . 61 C4
St James' Inf Sch
ME19 . . . . 61 C4
St John Fisher RC Comp
(Lower) Sch ME4 . . . . 22 C2
St John Fisher RC Comp
Sch ME4 . . . . 22 B3
St John's Ave ME10 . . 105 A1
St John's CE Inf Sch
ME4 . . . . 22 B3
St John's CE Prim Sch
ME14 . . . . 74 A4
St John's Cl ME3 . . . . . . 6 C4
St Johns Rd ME3 . . . . . . 5 B2
St John's Rd
Gillingham ME7 . . . . 23 C3
Higham ME3 . . . . 6 C4
St Johns Way ME1 . . . . 21 A2
St Katherine Rd
ME12 . . . . 97 C4
St Katherine's La
ME6 . . . . 45 A3
St Katherine's Sch
ME6 . . . . 45 A3
St Laurence Ave
ME16 . . . . 63 C4
St Leonards Ave ME4 . 22 C2
St Leonards Rd ME16 . 63 C4
St Leonard's St ME19 . 59 B3
ST LEONARD'S
STREET 59 B2
St Leonard's Tower*
ME19 . . . . 59 A3
St Luke's Ave ME14 . . . 65 B1
St Lukes Ct ME14 . . . . . 65 A2
St Luke's Rd ME14 . . . . 65 B1
St Margaret's at Troy
Town CE Prim Sch
ME1 . . . . 21 C4
St Margaret's Banks
ME1 . . . . 15 A1
St Margaret's CE Jun
Sch ME8 . . . . 35 B4
St Margarets Cl ME16 71 A2
St Margaret's Ct 6
ME8 . . . . 35 C4
St Margarets Dr ME8 . . 34 C1
St Margaret's Inf Sch
ME8 . . . . 35 B4
St Margaret's Mews
ME1 . . . . 14 C1
St Margaret's St ME1 . 14 C1
St Marks CE Prim Sch
ME20 . . . . 46 A2
St Marks Ct ME20 . . . . . 46 A2
St Marks Ho ME7 . . . . . 16 C1
St Martins Cl ME9 . . . 102 C4
St Martin's Cl ME14 . . . 57 B1
St Mary's Abbey
ME19 . . . . 59 C4
St Mary's Gdns ME4 . . 16 B3
ST MARY'S ISLAND . . 10 C1
St Mary's Island CE Prim
Sch ME4 . . . . 10 B2
St Mary's Pl ME9 . . . . 102 C4
St Mary's Prim Sch
ME2 . . . . 14 B3
St Mary's RC Prim Sch
ME7 . . . . 17 A2
St Mary's Rd
Gillingham ME7 . . . . 16 C2
Rochester ME2 . . . . 14 B3
St Mary's Row ME12 . . 98 B2
St Mary's View ME9 . . 102 C4
St Matthew's CE Inf Sch
ME1 . . . . 21 A2
St Matthew's Cl
ME9 . . . . 102 C4
St Matthews Dr ME1 . . 21 A2
St Michael's CE Inf Sch
ME16 . . . . 72 A3
St Michaels Cl ME20 . . 54 A3
St Michael's Cl
Chatham ME4 . . . . 22 C3
5 Sittingbourne
ME10 . . . . 104 B2
St Michael's Ct 6
ME2 . . . . 14 B4
St Michael's RC Prim
Sch ME4 . . . . 22 C3
St Michael's Rd
Maidstone ME16 . . . . 71 C3
Sittingbourne ME10 . . . 104 B2
St Nicholas CE Inf Sch
ME2 . . . . 14 A3
St Nicholas Gdns
ME2 . . . . 13 C3
St Patrick's Row
ME9 . . . . 107 B1
St Paul's Cl ME2 . . . . . . 13 A1
St Pauls Inf Sch
ME14 . . . . 65 A3
St Paul's St ME10 . . . . 104 A3
St Peter's Bridge
ME14 . . . . 72 B4
St Peter's CE Prim Sch
ME20 . . . . 53 B3
St Peters Cl ME20 . . . . . 51 C1
St Peter's Cl ME12 . . . . 97 B3
St Peter's Ct ME20 . . . . 52 A1
St Peter's Inf Sch
ME1 . . . . 21 C3
St Peter's Path ME1 . . 15 A1
St Peters Pl ME20 . . . . . 46 A2
St Peter's RC Prim Sch
ME10 . . . . 106 A4
St Peters Rd ME20 . . . . 51 C1
St Peters St ME16 . . . . . 72 B4
St Peter St ME1 . . . . 22 A4
St Philip's Ave ME15 . . 73 A2
St Ronan's Cl ME15 . . . 81 A3
St Simon Stock Sch
ME16 . . . . 71 B4
St Stephen's Cl ME9 . 102 C4
St Stephens Mews
ME1 . . . . 31 B4
St Stephen's Sq ME15 72 A2
St Thomas More Roman
Catholic Prim Sch
ME5 . . . . 32 A1
St Thomas of
Canterbury RC Prim
Sch ME8 . . . . 25 B2
St Welcume's Way
ME17 . . . . 87 C2
St Werburgh Cres ME3 . 5 A1
St Werburgh Ct ME3 . . . 5 A1
St William of Perth RC
Prim Sch ME1 . . . . 21 B2
St William's Way ME1 22 A2
Salem St ME15 . . . . 72 C3
Salisbury Ave ME8 . . . . 35 A4
Salisbury Cl ME10 . . . 105 B2
Salisbury Ho 4 ME15 . 81 B3
Salisbury Rd
Chatham ME4 . . . . 23 A3
Kit's Coty ME20 . . . . 47 B3
Maidstone ME14 . . . . 65 A2
Sallow Cl ME4 . . . . 10 C1
Sally Port ME7 . . . . 16 A2
Sally Port Gdns ME7 . . 16 B2
Salmon Cres ME12 . . . . 98 A2
Saltings Rd ME6 . . . . . . 45 B3
Salt's Ave ME15 . . . . 89 B3
Salts La ME15 . . . . 89 C4
Saltwood Rd ME15 . . . . 72 B1
Samara Cl ME5 . . . . 40 A1
Samphire Cl ME14 . . . . 74 A4
Samphire Way ME4 . . . 10 A2
Sanctuary Rd ME8 . . . . 25 A3
Sandbourne Dr ME14 . 55 A1
Sanders Ct ME12 . . . . . 98 B1
Sandford Rd ME10 . . . 103 A3
Sandgate Ct ME8 . . . . . 43 C4
Sandhurst Cl ME8 . . . . 25 C3
SANDLING 55 A1
Sandling Ct ME14 . . . . . 65 B3
Sandling La ME14 . . . . . 65 A4
Sandling Prim Sch
ME14 . . . . 65 B4
Sandling Rd
Maidstone ME14 . . . . 64 C2
Maidstone, Ringlestone
ME14 . . . . 64 C3
Sandling Way ME4 . . . . 10 B1
Sandown Dr ME8 . . . . . 35 A3
Sandown Rd ME19 . . . . 59 B4
Sandpiper Rd ME5 . . . . 41 A2
Sandra Ct 5 ME2 . . . . . 14 B4
Sandringham Ct
ME19 . . . . 68 C1
Sandringham Ho
ME1 . . . . 21 B4
Sandringham Rd ME8 . 43 B3
Sandstone Dr ME10 . . 100 C2
Sandstone Rise ME5 . . 49 A4
Sandycroft Rd ME2 . . . . 7 C1
Sandy Dell ME7 . . . . 42 A3
Sandy La
Maidstone, Harbourland
ME14 . . . . 65 C4
Maidstone, Penenden
Heath ME14 . . . . 65 C3
Maidstone, Ware Street
ME14 . . . . 67 B1
Snodland ME6, ME19 . . . 44 C2
Sandy Mount ME14 . . . 67 B1
Sanspareil Ave ME12 . . 98 B2
Sappers Wlk ME7 . . . . . 16 C1
Sapphire Cl ME10 . . . . 100 A1
Saracen Cl ME7 . . . . 25 A1
Saracen Fields ME5 . . . 49 A4
Sarafand Ho ME1 . . . . . 21 B4
Sarsen Hts ME5 . . . . 39 C1
Sassoon Cl ME20 . . . . . 51 B4
Satis Ave ME10 . . . . . . 100 C1
Saunders St
7 Chatham ME4 . . . . . . 22 C3
Gillingham ME7 . . . . 16 C2
Savage Rd ME5 . . . . 40 B3
Sawyers Ct ME4 . . . . . . 23 B2
Saxon Ave ME12 . . . . . . 98 C2
Saxon Cl
Kings Hill ME19 . . . . 68 B2
Rochester ME2 . . . . 7 C1
Saxon Pl ME2 . . . . 13 C1
Saxons Dr ME14 . . . . . . 65 B3
Saxon Shore ME10 . . . 101 B3
Saxon Way Prim Sch
ME7 . . . . 17 B2
Saxton St ME7 . . . . 16 C1
Scarborough Dr
ME12 . . . . 99 A4
Scarlett Cl ME5 . . . . 32 C1
Scholars Rise ME2 . . . . 13 A3
Scholey Cl ME2 . . . . 37 B4
School Ave ME7 . . . . . . 24 B4
School Ho ME10 . . . . . 104 A1
School La
Maidstone ME15 . . . . 74 A1
Newington ME9 . . . . . . 102 B4
Wouldham ME1 . . . . 29 C1
School Rd ME10 . . . . . 105 A1
School Villas ME18 . . . . 78 B1
Schooner Wlk ME2 . . . . 9 C3
Schrieber Mews ME7 . 17 A1
Scimitar Cl ME7 . . . . 25 A1
Scocles Cotts ME12 . . . 99 A1
Scocles Rd ME12 . . . . . 99 A1
Scotby Ave ME5 . . . . . . 40 B4
Scotchmen Cl ME12 . . 97 C4
Scotney Ho ME2 . . . . 8 C1
Scott Ave ME8 . . . . 27 A1
Scott Cl ME20 . . . . 61 C4
Scotteswood Ave
ME4 . . . . 22 C2
Scott St ME14 . . . . 64 C2
Scott's Terr ME4 . . . . . . 22 C3
Scragged Oak Cvn Pk
ME14 . . . . 57 C2
Scrapsgate Rd ME12 . . 98 B3
Scrubbs La ME16 . . . . . 71 C4
Seaford Ct ME1 . . . . 14 B1
Seager Rd ME12 . . . . . . 95 C3
Seagull Rd ME2 . . . . 13 A2
Sealand Ct ME1 . . . . 14 B1
Seamew Ct ME2 . . . . . . 12 C3
Seaside Ave ME12 . . . . 99 A4
Seathorpe Ave ME12 . . 99 A4
Seaton Rd ME7 . . . . 24 B3
Seaview Rd ME7 . . . . . . 23 C4
Second Ave
Chatham ME4 . . . . 23 C1
Gillingham ME7 . . . . 24 B3
Secretan Rd ME1 . . . . . 21 B1
Sedge Cres ME5 . . . . . . 39 B4
Sedgemoor Ho ME1 . . 15 B1
Sedley Cl
Aylesford ME20 . . . . 53 A2
Cliffe Woods ME3 . . . . 2 C3
Gillingham ME8 . . . . 42 C3
Selbourne Rd ME7 . . . . 17 A3
Selbourne Wlk ME15 . . 82 A2
Selby Rd ME15 . . . . 91 B4
Sellinge Gn ME8 . . . . . . 25 C3
Selstead Cl ME8 . . . . . . 25 C2
Selwood Cl ME12 . . . . . 97 C3
Semple Gdns ME4 . . . . 22 B3
Senacre La ME15 . . . . . 81 C2
Senacre Sq ME15 . . . . . 82 A3
Senacre Tech Coll
ME15 . . . . 81 B2
Senacre Wood Prim Sch
ME15 . . . . 82 A3
Sessions House Sq
ME14 . . . . 64 C1
Setford Rd ME5 . . . . 32 C2
Settington Ave ME5 . . . 23 C1
Severn Rd ME5 . . . . 32 C1
Sevington Pk ME15 . . . 80 A2
Sexburga Dr ME12 . . . . 98 C4
Sextant Pk ME2 . . . . . . 15 B2
Seymour Rd
1 Chatham ME5 . . . . . . 23 B3
Gillingham ME8 . . . . 27 C1
Shackleton Cl ME5 . . . . 32 B2

Shades The ME2 ...... 12 C3
Shaftesbury Cl ME19 .. 51 A1
Shaftesbury Dr ME16 . 71 B4
Shakespeare Rd
Gillingham ME7 .... 23 C3
Sittingbourne ME10 ... 104 C2
Shalder Ho ME7 ...... 17 A3
Shalfleet Cl 1 ME5 ... 32 A3
Shamel Bsns Ctr ME2 14 C3
Shamley Rd ME5 ..... 41 A2
Shanklin Cl ME5 ...... 32 C4
Sharfleet Dr ME2 ..... 12 B3
Sharnal La ME6 ...... 45 B3
Sharon Cres ME5 ..... 39 C4
Sharsted Way
Gillingham ME7 .... 42 A3
Maidstone ME14 .... 67 B1
Shaw Cl
Cliffe Woods ME3 .... 2 B4
Maidstone ME14 .... 65 C3
Shawstead Rd ME7 &
ME7 .... 33 A1
Shaws Way ME1 ...... 21 C3
Sheal's Cres ME15 .... 72 C2
Sheals Ct ME15 .... 72 C2
Shearers Cl ME14 ..... 74 A4
Shearwater ME16 ..... 63 B1
Shearwater Cl ME2 ... 12 C3
Shearwater Ct ME12 .. 94 C1
SHEERNESS 95 A4
Sheerness Harbour Est
ME12 .... 94 B4
Sheerness Heritage Ctr
(Mus)★ ME12 .... 95 A3
Sheerness-on-Sea Sta
ME12 .... 94 C2
Shelden Dr ME8 ...... 35 C4
Sheldon Bsns Ctr
ME2 .... 15 A4
Sheldon Way ME20 ... 51 C3
Shelley Rd ME16 ...... 71 B2
Shelley Rise ME1 ..... 21 A3
Shenley Gr ME14 ..... 55 A2
Shepherds Gate ME7 . 33 C1
Shepherds Gate Dr
ME14 .... 66 B2
Shepherds Way ME17 93 A4
Shepperton Cl ME5 ... 40 C4
Sheppey Coll ME12 ... 94 C3
Sheppey Com Hospl
ME12 .... 99 A3
Sheppey Community
Hospl ME12 .... 98 B1
Sheppey Cotts ME12 .. 95 B3
Sheppey Rd ME15 .... 80 B3
Sheppey St ME12 ..... 94 B3
SHEPWAY 81 B4
Shepway Ct ME15 ..... 81 A4
Shepway Inf Sch
ME15 .... 81 C4
Shepway Jun Sch
ME15 .... 81 C4
Sheraton Ct ME5 ..... 39 C1
Sherbourne Dr
Maidstone ME16 .... 71 A2
Rochester ME2 .... 8 A1
Sheridale Bsns Ctr
ME2 .... 14 A2
Sheridan Cl
Chatham ME5 .... 32 C3
Maidstone ME14 .... 64 B4
Sheridan Ct ME1 ...... 21 A2
Sheriff Dr ME5 .... 40 A2
Sheringham Cl ME16 .. 64 A3
Sheringham Ho 5
ME15 .... 81 B4
Sherman Cl ME7 ...... 25 B1
Shernolds ME15 ...... 80 C3
Shernold Sch ME16 ... 64 A1
Sherwin Knight Inf Sch
ME2 .... 13 B1
Sherwin Knight Jun Sch
ME2 .... 13 B1
Sherwood Ave ME5 ... 40 A2
Sherwood Ho ME5 .... 40 A3
Shillingheld Cl ME14 .. 66 C1
Ship La ME1 .... 22 B4
Shipley Ct ME14 ...... 72 C4
Shipwrights Ave ME4 . 23 B2
Shirley Ave ME5 ...... 31 A1
Shirley Ct ME15 ...... 81 C1
Shirley Way ME15 ..... 74 C3
Sholden Rd ME2 .... 8 C1
Shorefields ME8 ...... 27 B2
Shoreham Wlk ME15 .. 82 A3
Shorland Ct ME1 ..... 14 B1
Shortlands Gn ME15 .. 82 A1
Shortlands Rd ME10 . 105 A2
Short St
3 Chatham ME4 ...... 23 B3
Sheerness ME12 ...... 94 C2
Shorts Way ME1 ...... 21 A3
Shottenden Rd ME7 ... 17 A3
Shropshire Terr 1
ME15 .... 81 C3
Shrubsole Ave ME12 .. 95 A2
Shrubsole Dr ME14 ... 55 A3
Shurland Ave
Minster (Sheppey)
ME12 .... 98 C2
Sittingbourne ME10 ... 106 C3
Sidney Rd
Gillingham ME7 .... 16 C3
Rochester ME1 .... 21 A2
Sidney St ME16 .... 71 B2
Signal Ct 6 ME8 ..... 26 C1
Silchester Ct ME14 .... 65 C3
Silver Bank ME5 ...... 32 A2
Silver Birches ME5 .... 40 A3
Silver Birch Wlk
ME18 .... 78 B2
Silverdale ME16 ...... 70 C2
Silverdale Ave ME12 .. 98 B2
Silverdale Dr ME8 .... 35 C3
Silverdale Gr ME10 .. 103 C1
Silver Hill
Chatham ME4 .... 22 C3
Rochester ME1 .... 20 C2
Rochester ME1 .... 21 A2
Silver Hill Gdns 4
ME4 .... 22 C3
Silverspot Cl ME8 ..... 35 C3
Silver Tree ME5 ...... 40 B1
Silverweed Rd ME5 ... 39 C4
Simmonds La ME15 ... 82 C2
Simpson Rd
Sittingbourne
ME10 .... 103 B3
Snodland ME6 .... 45 B2
Sinclair Cl ME8 .... 35 B1
Sindal Shaw Ho ME5 .. 39 B4
Singapore Dr ME7 .... 16 B1
Sir Evelyn Rd ME1 .... 21 B1
Sir John Hawkins Hospl
ME4 .... 22 B4
Sir John Hawkins Way
ME4 .... 22 C4
Sir Joseph Williamson's
Mathematical Sch
ME1 .... 21 C1
Sir Thomas Longley Rd
ME2 .... 15 B2
Siskin Wlk ME20 ...... 51 A2
Sissinghurst Dr ME16 . 71 A4
SITTINGBOURNE 104 C4
Sittingbourne Com Coll
ME10 .... 107 C4
Sittingbourne Ind Pk
ME10 .... 104 B3
Sittingbourne &
Kemsley Light Rly★
ME10 .... 101 B1
Sittingbourne Rd
Maidstone, Detling
ME14 .... 66 B4
Maidstone, Penenden
Heath ME14 .... 65 B2
Sittingbourne Retail Pk
ME10 .... 104 B3
Sittingbourne Sta
ME10 .... 104 B2
Skene Cl ME8 .... 27 A1
Skinners Cl ME20 ..... 46 B2
Skinner St
Chatham ME4 .... 22 C3
Gillingham ME7 .... 16 C1
Skinner Street Prim Sch
ME7 .... 16 C2
Skinner's Way ME17 .. 93 A4
Skua Ct ME2 .... 12 C3
Skye Cl ME15 .... 80 B3
Slade Cl ME5 .... 40 B2
Slatin Rd ME2 .... 14 B4
Slicketts Hill ME4 ..... 23 A4
Slipway Rd ME12 ..... 94 A4
Small Hythe Cl ME15 .. 75 A2
Smarden Wlk ME8 .... 27 B1
Smarts Cotts ME14 ... 75 B4
Smeed Cl 4 ME10 ... 105 A2
Smeed-Dean Ctr The
ME10 .... 104 C2
Smetham Gdns ME2 ... 8 B1
Smith Rd ME5 .... 40 B3
Smith St ME2 .... 14 A2
Snipe Ct ME2 .... 12 C3
SNIPESHILL 105 C2
Snodhurst Ave ME5 ... 31 B1
Snodhurst Ho 2 ME5 32 A3
SNODLAND 45 C3
Snodland CE Prim Sch
ME6 .... 45 A4
Snodland Rd ME19 .... 44 B3
Snodland Sta ME6 .... 45 C4
Snowdon Ave ME14 ... 65 B1
Snowdon Cl ME5 ..... 32 B3
Snowdon Par ME14 ... 65 C1
Snow Ho ME7 .... 17 B3
Solent Gdns ME5 ..... 32 B4
Sole Street Farm ME3 .. 8 B3
Solomon Rd ME8 ..... 27 A1
Solomons Rd ME4 .... 22 C4
Somerfield Cl ME16 ... 64 A1
Somerfield Hospl The
ME16 .... 64 B1
Somerfield La ME16 .. 71 C4
Somerfield Rd ME16 .. 71 C4
Somerset Cl
Chatham ME5 .... 32 C4
Sittingbourne ME10 ... 103 B2
Somerset Rd ME15 .... 81 A4
Somner Wlk ME15 .... 91 B4
Sonora Way ME10 ... 100 A1
Sorrell Rd ME5 .... 39 C4
Sortmill Rd ME6 ...... 45 C3
South Ave
Gillingham ME8 .... 25 B2
Sittingbourne ME10 ... 104 C1
South Avenue Jun & Inf
Schs ME10 .... 104 C1
South Aylesford Ret Pk
ME20 .... 62 B4
South Borough Prim Sch
ME15 .... 72 C2
Southbourne Gr ME5 . 40 A4
South Bush La ME8 ... 36 B2
South Cres ME17 ..... 88 B4
Southdown Rd ME12 .. 97 C3
South Eastern Rd
ME2 .... 14 C3
Southey Way 1
ME20 .... 51 A4
Southfields ME1 ...... 21 C3
Southill Rd ME4 ...... 22 C3
South Park Bsns Village
ME15 .... 72 C1
South Park Rd ME15 .. 73 B1
South Pondside Rd
ME4 .... 16 A4
South Rd
Chatham, Brompton ME4,
ME7 .... 16 A3
Chatham ME4 .... 16 B3
Southsea Ave ME12 ... 99 A4
South Side Three Rd
ME4 .... 16 C4
South St
Maidstone ME16 .... 70 A1
Queenborough ME11 ... 96 A2
South Terr ME3 .... 3 C2
South View Gdns
ME12 .... 95 A2
Southwark Rd ME2 ... 13 A2
Southwell Rd ME2 .... 13 A2
Southwood ME16 ..... 70 B2
Sovereign Bvd ME7,
ME8 .... 24 C2
Sovereigns The ME16 . 71 C4
Spade La ME9 .... 36 C2
Spearhead Rd ME14 .. 64 C3
Spectrum Bsns Ctr
ME2 .... 15 B4
Spectrum Bsns Est
ME15 .... 91 B4
Speedwell Ave ME5 ... 39 C4
Speedwell Cl
Gillingham ME7 .... 17 B1
Speedwell Cl *continued*
Maidstone ME14 .... 66 B1
Spekes Rd ME7 .... 34 B2
Speldhurst Ct ME16 ... 71 C4
Spembley Ct ME4 ..... 22 B4
Spencer Cl ME5 ...... 32 A1
Spencer Flats ME5 .... 32 B4
Spencer Way ME15 ... 81 C3
Spenlow Dr ME5 ...... 48 B4
Spicer Homes ME10 . 106 C4
Spiers The ME7 .... 18 C1
Spillway The ME15 .... 71 C2
Spindle Glade ME14 .. 65 C1
Spindlewood Cl ME5 .. 40 B3
Spinnaker Ct 4 ME1 .. 21 C1
Spinnens Acre Com Jun
Sch ME5 .... 40 C1
Spinney The
Chatham ME5 .... 40 B1
Maidstone ME15 .... 73 A2
Spires The
Maidstone ME16 .... 71 C4
Rochester ME2 .... 13 A1
Spitfire Cl ME5 .... 32 B2
Spitfire Rd ME19 ...... 68 B3
Sportsfield ME14 ..... 65 B1
Sportsmans Cotts
ME19 .... 59 B1
Spot La ME15 .... 74 C2
Sprig The ME14 .... 74 C4
Springdale Cotts ME3 .. 8 A3
Springett Cl ME20 .... 46 A2
Springett Way ME17 .. 88 C3
Springfield Ave ME14 . 64 C3
Springfield Rd
Gillingham ME7 .... 17 B2
Lunsford ME20 .... 51 A4
Sittingbourne ME10 ... 103 C3
Springfield Terr 7
ME4 .... 22 C4
Springvale ME8 .... 34 C2
Spring Vale ME16 ..... 72 A4
Springwood Cl 1
ME16 .... 70 C3
Springwood Rd ME16 . 70 C3
Sprotshill Cl ME10 ... 104 A4
Spruce Cl ME20 ...... 51 C2
Spurgeons Cotts
ME17 .... 89 A2
Spurway ME14 .... 74 C4
Square Hill ME15 ..... 73 A4
Square Hill Rd ME15 .. 73 A4
Square The ME10 .... 101 A3
Squires Cl ME2 .... 12 B3
Stable Cl ME5 .... 32 C1
Staceys St ME14 ...... 64 C1
Stadium Way ME10 .. 105 B4
Stadler Cl ME16 ...... 64 A3
Staffa Rd ME15 .... 80 B3
Stafford St ME7 ...... 16 C1
Stag Rd ME5 .... 32 B1
Stagshaw Cl ME15 .... 72 C2
Stake La ME2 .... 28 C2
Stalham Ct ME7 ...... 42 B4
Stalin Ave ME5 .... 32 B4
Stampers The ME15 ... 71 C2
Standen Cl ME8 ...... 43 B4
Stanford Dr ME16 ..... 71 B3
Stanford Way ME2 .... 19 C2
Stangate Rd ME2 ..... 12 C3
Stanhope Ave ME10 .. 104 C1
Stanhope Cl ME14 .... 64 B3
Stanhope Rd ME2 ..... 14 A3
Stanley Ave
Minster (Sheppey)
ME12 .... 99 B3
Queenborough ME11 ... 96 B1
Stanley Rd
Chatham ME5 .... 32 C2
Gillingham ME7 .... 16 C2
Stansted Cl ME16 ..... 64 A3
Staple Cl ME10 ...... 104 A3
Staplehurst Lodge Ind
Est ME10 .... 103 C3
Staplehurst Rd
Gillingham ME8 .... 25 B3
Sittingbourne ME10 ... 103 C3
Staplers Ct ME14 ..... 65 B4
Star Hill ME1 .... 15 A1
Star La ME7 .... 34 A3
Star Mill Ct ME5 ...... 24 A2
Star Mill La ME5 ...... 24 A2
Starnes Ct 5 ME14 ... 65 A1
Station App
Halling ME2 .... 28 C1
Maidstone ME16 .... 72 B3
Station Rd
Aylesford ME20 .... 52 C2
Cuxton ME2 .... 19 C2
Gillingham ME8 .... 27 A2
Harrietsham ME17 ..... 87 B2
Maidstone ME14 .... 64 C1
Newington ME9 ...... 102 B3
Rochester ME2 .... 14 C3
Station St ME10 ..... 104 B2
Steele St ME2 .... 14 A4
Steerforth Cl ME1 .... 21 C2
Step Style ME10 ..... 107 B4
Sterling Ave ME16 .... 63 C1
Sterling Rd
Queenborough
ME11 .... 96 B2
Sittingbourne ME10 ... 106 A3
Sterry Gdns ME15 ..... 81 C3
Steven Cl ME4 .... 23 A3
Stevens Cl ME6 .... 45 B4
Stevenson Cl ME15 ... 72 B3
Stevenson Way ME20 . 51 A4
Stevens Rd ME20 ..... 46 A2
Stewart Ho ME3 .... 3 C2
Stickens La ME19 ..... 60 B3
Stiles Cl ME12 .... 98 B2
Stillwater Mews ME4 . 10 B2
Stirling Cl
Gillingham ME8 .... 43 B4
Rochester ME1 .... 21 A3
Stirling Rd ME19 ...... 68 B3
Stockbury Dr ME16 ... 64 A3
Stockers Brow ME9 .. 107 A1
Stockers Hill ME9 .... 107 A1
Stockton Cl ME14 ..... 65 B4
Stoke Rd ME3 .... 5 C2
Stoneacre★ ME15 .... 82 C3
Stoneacre Cl ME8 ..... 35 A1
Stoneacre Ct 7
ME15 .... 72 C1
Stoneacre La ME15 ... 82 C3
Stonecrop Cl ME4 .... 10 C1
Stonecross Lea ME5 .. 23 C1
Stonehorse Ct ME3 .... 8 A3
Stonehorse La ME2 .... 8 A2
Stones Rdbt ME4 ..... 10 B1
Stoney Bank ME7 ..... 24 C1
Stony La ME1 .... 30 C1
Stopford Rd ME7 ..... 24 A4
Storehouse Wharf
ME12 .... 94 A4
Stour Cl ME2 .... 13 C3
Strand Approach Rd
ME7 .... 17 B3
Strand Rdbt The ME7 . 17 B3
Stratford Ave ME8 .... 35 A4
Stratford Dr ME15 .... 81 B2
Stratford La 2 ME8 ... 35 C4
Stratford Rd ME19 .... 59 A4
Straw Mill Hill ME15 .. 72 A1
Streamside ME20 ..... 51 C1
Stream The ME20 ..... 52 A1
Street End Rd ME5 .... 23 B1
Street Farm Cotts ME3 . 5 C2
Streetfield Rd ME8 .... 26 C1
Street The
Boxley ME14 .... 56 A3
Bredhurst ME7 .... 42 B1
Detling ME14 .... 57 B1
Maidstone ME14 .... 75 B4
Teston ME18 .... 79 B3
Upper Halling ME2 ..... 28 A1
Strode Cres ME12 .... 95 A3
STROOD 13 C3
Strood Ret Pk ME2 ... 14 B3
Strood Sta ME2 .... 14 C3
Strover St ME7 .... 16 C3
St. Saviours Rd ME15 . 81 B2
Stuart Cl ME14 .... 65 C2
Stuart Rd ME7 .... 24 A3
Sturdee Ave ME7 ..... 24 B4
Sturla Rd ME4 .... 23 A3
Sturmer Ct ME19 ..... 68 C2
Sturry Way ME8 ...... 25 C2
Style Cl ME8 .... 43 B4

Styles La ME14 56 A3
Suffolk Ave ME8 26 C1
Suffolk Ct [7] ME8 26 C1
Suffolk Rd ME15 81 B4
Sultan Mews ME5 40 C2
Sultan Rd ME5 40 C2
Summerville Ave ME12 98 B1
Sunderland Cl ME1 21 A3
Sunderland Dr ME8 36 A4
Sunderland Ho [3] ME7 16 C3
Sundridge Dr ME5 40 A4
Sundridge Hill ME2 19 C3
Sunningdale Cl ME8 35 A2
Sunningdale Ct ME15 73 A4
Sunningdale Dr ME8 35 A2
Sunny Bank ME10 105 A3
Sunnyfields Cl ME8 35 B4
Sunnyfields Dr ME12 97 A3
Sunnymead Ave ME7 17 B1
Sunnyside Ave ME12 98 B2
Sunshine Ct [1] ME8 35 C4
Sunstone Dr ME10 100 A1
Sun Terr ME5 40 B4
Superabbey Est ME20 53 C2
Surrey Rd ME15 81 B4
Sussex Dr ME5 40 A4
Sussex Rd ME15 81 B4
Sutherland Gdns ME8 35 B2
Sutton Cl ME8 36 A4
Sutton Rd
Langley ME17 83 A1
Maidstone ME15 81 B2
Sutton St ME14 75 C4
Swain Cl ME2 13 C4
Swain Rd ME8 34 B2
Swale Ho ME11 96 A2
Swale Rd ME2 12 C3
Swallow Ho [4] ME16 72 A4
Swallow Rd ME20 51 A2
Swallow Rise ME5 32 A1
Swan Apartments [12] ME15 81 C1
Swan Cl ME10 105 A2
Swan St ME19 59 C4
Swanstree Ave ME10 107 B4
Sweet Briar Ct ME16 64 A1
Swift Cl ME20 51 B2
Swift Cres ME5 32 C2
Swift Ho [6] ME16 72 A4
Swingate Cl ME5 40 B2
Swingate Inf Sch ME5 40 C1
Swinton Ave ME3 3 C1
Sycamore Cres ME16 63 C1
Sycamore Dr ME20 52 C1
Sycamore Rd ME2 13 B1
Sydney Ave ME10 103 B2
Sydney Rd ME4 23 A3
Sylewood Cl ME1 30 B4
Sylvan Glade ME5 48 B4
Sylvan Rd ME8 34 C4
Sylvestre Cl ME2 37 A4
Symmonds Dr ME10 104 C4
Symons Ave ME4 23 A2

T

Tadburn Gn ME5 40 B4
Taddington Wood La ME5 39 B2
Tadley Ct
Gillingham ME7 17 C2
Rochester ME1 30 C4
Taillour Cl ME10 101 A1
Tail Race The ME15 72 A2
Talbot Rd ME16 63 C2
Tamar Dr ME2 13 C3
Tamarind Cl ME7 42 A4
Tams Gdns ME12 99 B2
Tanglewood Cl ME8 34 C2
Tangmere Cl ME7 17 C1
Tanker Hill ME8 35 A2
Tannery Ct [5] ME10 104 A3
Tappan Dr ME4 10 B2
Target Bsns Ctr ME15 91 B4
Tarragon Rd ME16 71 A3
Tasker Cl ME15 75 A3
Tassell Cl ME19 51 B1
Taswell Rd ME8 27 A1
Tatler Cl ME5 41 A2
Tatsfield Cl ME8 25 A2
Tattershall Rd ME15 72 C1
Taunton Cl ME15 82 A2
Taverners Rd ME8 35 B3
Tavistock Cl
Chatham ME5 39 C1
Gillingham ME8 35 B3
Sittingbourne ME10 103 C2
Tay Cl ME5 32 B1
Taylor Cl ME17 87 B2
Taylor Rd ME6 45 A4
Taylor's La ME2 14 B3
Teapot La ME20 52 C1
Teasaucer Hill ME15 80 A4
Teasel Cl ME14 74 B4
Teasel Rd ME5 39 C4
Tedder Ave ME5 32 A3
Telegraph Hill ME3 6 C3
Telescope Alley ME12 95 B3
Telford Ho [1] ME14 65 A2
Temeraire Manor [2] ME7 16 A2
Tempest Rd ME19 68 B3
Temple Gdns
Rochester ME2 14 A2
Sittingbourne ME10 105 A1
Temple Manor* ME2 14 A2
Temple Mill Prim Sch ME2 8 B1
Temple Sch ME2 8 B2
Temple Way ME19 51 A1
Ten Acre Way ME8 27 B1
Tennyson Ave ME3 2 B3
Tennyson Rd ME7 23 C3
Tenterden Rd ME5 32 B1
Terance Butler Ave ME2 15 B4
Terence Cl ME4 23 A2
Terminus Rd ME16 70 C2
Tern Cres ME2 12 C2
Terrace Rd
Maidstone ME16 72 A3
Sittingbourne ME10 105 A1
Terrace The ME1 14 C1
Terry Wlk ME19 50 C2
TESTON 79 B4
Teston Ho ME18 79 B3
Teston Rd
Kings Hill ME19 59 B1
West Malling ME19 59 A2
Teynham Gn ME8 25 A4
Thackeray Rd ME20 51 A3
Thames Ave ME8 35 B4
Thames View ME3 2 C3
Thames View Cotts ME3 7 A3
Thames View Inf Sch ME8 26 A2
Thames View Jun Sch ME8 26 A2
Thanet Ho [7] ME15 82 A1
Thatchers The ME16 63 B1
Theodore Pl ME7 16 C1
THE QUARRIES 90 B4
Third Ave
Chatham ME5 23 C1
Gillingham ME7 24 C4
Thirlemere Cl ME16 64 A4
Thirlmere Cl
Gillingham ME7 18 A1
Rochester ME2 8 C1
Thirsk Ho [6] ME15 82 A2
Thistlebank ME5 40 A3
Thistledown ME14 74 B4
Thistledown Cl ME7 42 A4
Thistle Hill Way
Minster (Sheppey) ME12 98 B1
Minster (Sheppey) ME12 99 A1
Thistle Wlk ME10 105 A3
Thomas Aveling Sch The ME1 30 C4
Thomas Ct [9] ME10 105 A2
Thomas Rd ME10 105 A2
Thomas St ME1 21 C3
Thompson Cl ME8 36 A4
Thomson Cl ME6 37 A1
Thorn Cl ME5 39 A1
Thorndale Cl ME5 39 A4
Thorndike Cl ME4 31 C4
Thorndike Ho ME4 31 C4
Thornham Rd ME8 25 C3
Thornhill Pl ME14 65 A2
Thorn Wlk ME10 105 B3
Thorold Rd ME5 23 B3
Thorpe Wlk ME8 43 A3
Thrale Way ME8 43 B4
Threshers Dr ME14 66 B1
Thrush Cl ME5 32 B3
Thurnham CE Inf Sch ME14 74 C4
Thurnham La ME14 67 C3
Thurston Dr ME2 13 A3
Thurstone Ct ME14 64 C2
Thyme Wlk ME16 71 A3
Tichborne Cl ME16 63 C2
Tideway The ME1 30 C4
Tilbury Rd ME8 27 A2
Tile Fields ME17 77 C2
Tilghman Way ME6 37 B1
Tilley Cl ME3 5 A1
Timberbank ME5 32 A2
Timber Tops ME5 49 B4
TInker's Alley ME4 15 C3
Tintagel Gdns ME2 13 C3
Tintagel Manor [6] ME7 16 C2
Tintern Rd ME16 64 A3
Titchfield Cl [5] ME15 82 A2
Titchfield Rd ME15 82 A2
Tobruk Way ME5 31 C2
Todd Cres ME10 101 B2
Toddington Cres ME5 39 A1
Tolgate La ME2 14 B3
Tolgate Way ME14 54 C4
Tom Joyce Cl ME6 45 A3
Tomlin Cl ME6 45 B4
Tonbridge Ct ME16 71 C3
Tonbridge Ho ME2 8 C1
Tonbridge Rd
Maidstone, East Barming ME16 70 A1
Maidstone ME16 71 B3
Wateringbury ME18 78 A4
Tonge Rd ME10 105 B2
Topaz Dr ME10 103 B4
Toronto Rd ME7 24 B4
Tourmaline Dr ME10 103 B4
TOVIL 72 A1
Tovil Gn ME15 72 A2
Tovil Green Bsns Pk ME15 72 A1
Tovil Hill ME15 72 A2
Tovil Rd ME15 72 B2
Tovil, St Stephen's CE Inf Sch ME15 72 A2
Tower Gdns ME14 75 A4
Tower Hill ME19 58 A3
Tower La ME14 75 A4
Towers Point ME1 21 B4
Tower View ME19 69 A3
Town Hill ME19 50 A1
Town Hill Cl ME19 50 A1
Town Rd ME3 2 A2
Townsend Rd ME6 45 A4
Townsend Sq ME19 68 C2
Tracies The ME9 102 C3
Trafalgar Par ME12 98 C2
Trafalgar Rd ME1 29 B1
Trafalgar St ME7 16 C1
Tramways ME5 23 C2
Transom Ho [3] ME1 21 C1
Trapfield Cl ME14 75 B4
Trapfield La ME14 75 B4
Trapham Rd ME16 64 A1
Travertine Rd ME5 40 B1
Trelawn Cres ME5 40 B2
Trellyn Cl ME16 70 B2
Trenton Cl ME16 63 B3
Trent Rd ME5 32 B1
Trevale Rd ME1 21 B1
Trevino Dr ME5 39 C2
Trevor Dr ME16 63 C1
Trewin Cl ME20 52 B2
Tribune Ct ME12 94 C1
Tribune Dr ME10 104 B4
Trident Cl ME2 15 B3
Trinity Ct ME20 53 B3
Trinity Rd
Gillingham ME7 16 C2
Sheerness ME12 95 A3
Sittingbourne ME10 101 A1
Trinity Sch ME1 22 A4
Trinity Trad Est ME10 104 B4
Troodos Hill ME14 64 C4
Trotts Hall Gdns ME10 104 B1
Trotwood Cl ME5 48 B4
Troutbeck Ho ME20 52 A1
Troy Mews ME1 21 C4
Troys Mead ME17 77 C2
TROY TOWN 14 C1
Trubridge Rd ME3 5 B1
Truro Cl ME8 26 A3
Tudor Ave ME14 65 B2
Tudor Gr
Chattenden ME3 9 C4
Gillingham ME8 35 C4
Tufa Cl ME5 40 B1
Tufton Rd ME8 26 C1
Tufton St ME14 72 C4
Tunbury Ave ME5 39 C1
Tunbury Ave S ME5 39 C1
Tunbury Prim Sch ME5 39 C1
TUNSTALL 106 A2
Tunstall Rd ME10, ME9 106 A2
Tupman Cl ME1 21 B4
Turgis Cl ME17 93 A4
Turks Hall Pl ME2 28 A1
Turmine Ct ME12 98 B1
Turner Cl ME10 101 B1
Turners Cl ME12 95 A2
Turnstone Rd ME5 40 C1
Turrets The [9] ME10 104 C2
Tuscan Dr ME5 40 C1
Twisden Rd ME19 61 C4
TWYDALL 25 B2
Twydall Ent Ctr ME8 25 C4
Twydall Gn ME8 25 B3
Twydall Inf Sch ME8 25 B2
Twydall Jun Sch ME8 25 B2
Twydall La ME8 25 B2
Twyford Cl ME8 27 A2
Twyford Ct ME14 66 A2
Tydeman Rd ME15 74 B2
Tyland Barn Wildlife Conservation Ctr* ME14 54 C3
Tyland La ME14 55 A3
Tyler Cl ME19 61 C4
Tyler Dr ME8 43 B4
Tyne Cl ME5 32 C1
Typhoon Rd ME19 68 B3
Tyrwhitt-Drake Mus of Carriages* ME15 72 C3
Tysoe Ct ME12 98 B1

U

Ufton Cl ME15 74 A1
Ufton La ME10 104 A1
Ulcombe Rd ME17 93 A3
Ullswater Ho [5] ME15 81 C3
Underdown Ave ME4 22 C1
Underwood ME19 58 A3
Underwood Cl ME15 72 B2
Unicumes La ME16 71 B2
Union Pk ME15 91 B4
Union Pl ME4 23 A4
Union Rd ME12 99 A3
Union St
Chatham ME4 23 A3
Maidstone ME14 65 A1
Rochester ME1 14 C1
Sheerness ME12 94 B3
Unity St
Sheerness ME12 95 B3
Sittingbourne ME10 104 A1
Univ of Greenwich ME4 16 B4
Unwin Cl ME20 53 B3
Upbury Arts Coll ME7 23 B4
Upbury Way ME4 23 A4
Upchat Rd ME2, ME3 9 C3
Uplands Cl ME2 13 A2
Uplands Way ME12 97 A2
Upnor Castle* ME2 9 C2
Upnor Ho ME15 81 C4
Upnor Rd ME2 9 B2
Upper Britton Pl ME7 16 B1
Upper East Rd ME4 16 B4
UPPER FANT 71 C3
Upper Fant Rd ME16 71 C2
Upper Field Rd ME10 105 A3
UPPER HALLING 28 A1
Upper Luton Rd ME5 23 C2
Upper Mill ME18 78 B4
Upper Rd ME15 73 A2
Upper St ME17 84 A1
Upper Stone St ME15 72 C3
UPPER UPNOR 9 C1
Urquhart Cl ME5 32 A1

V

Vale Dr ME5 31 B2
Valence Ho ME15 81 A3
Valenciennes Ho ME4 23 A4
Valenciennes Rd ME10 104 A1
Valentine Cl ME7 25 A1
Valentine Rd ME15 81 C3
Vale Rd ME15 89 A4
Valerian Cl ME5 39 B4
Valetta Way ME1 21 B4
Valiant Rd ME5 40 C2
Valley Dr ME15 80 A2
Valley Park Com Sch ME14 73 B4
Valley Rd ME7 24 B4
Valley Rise ME5 39 C1
Valley The ME17 88 C3
Valley View Rd ME1 21 B1
Vancouver Dr ME8 25 C1
Vange Cottage Mews ME1 21 B4
Vanguard Way ME2 15 B4
Vanity La ME17 88 C1
Varnes St ME20 46 A2
Vaughan Dr ME10 101 A2
Vauxhall Cres ME6 45 B2
Vectis Dr ME10 101 A2
Veles Rd ME6 45 A4
Ventnor Cl ME5 32 C4
Vicarage Cl
Aylesford ME20 53 A3
Halling ME2 28 C1
Vicarage Ct ME9 102 B4
Vicarage La ME3 11 B4
Vicarage Rd
Gillingham ME7 16 C1
Halling ME2 28 B1
Minster (Sheppey) ME12 99 B3
Rochester ME2 14 B4
Sittingbourne ME10 104 A4
Vicarage Row ME3 6 C4
Vicary Way ME16 64 A1
Victoria Cl ME5 39 A2
Victoria Ct [6] ME16 72 A3
Victoria Dr ME19 68 B1
Victoria Orch ME16 71 A3
Victoria Rd
Chatham, Kit Hill ME5 39 B3
Chatham, Luton ME4 23 B2
Sittingbourne ME10 103 C2
Victoria St
Eccles ME20 46 A2
Gillingham ME7 17 A2
Maidstone ME16 72 A3
Rochester ME1 15 A1
Rochester, Strood ME2 14 B3
Sheerness ME12 95 A2
Victoria Terr
Rochester ME1 21 A2
Sittingbourne ME10 103 C2
Victory Manor [1] ME7 16 A2
Victory Pk ME2 15 B3
Victory St ME12 94 C2
Vidal Manor ME7 16 C1
Vidgeon Ave ME3 5 A2

Viewlands ME5 . . . . **23** C3
Viewpoint ME14 . . . . . **65** C4
View Rd ME3 . . . . **2** B3
Viking Cl ME2 . . . . **20** C4
Village View ME5 . . . . . **23** C2
Villa Rd ME3. . . . . **6** B3
Vincent Ct ME12 . . . . . . **95** A2
Vincent Gdns ME12 . . . **95** A2
Vincent Rd
Kit's Coty ME20 . . . . **47** A3
Sittingbourne ME10 . . . **105** B1
Vine Ct ME18 . . . . **78** B4
Vineries The ME7 . . . . . **17** B1
Viners Cl ME10 . . . . . . **106** C3
Vines La ME1 . . . . **14** C1
Vineyard Cres ME8. . . . **27** B1
Vinters Rd ME14 . . . . . . **73** A4
Vintners Way ME14 . . . **74** A4
Violet Cl ME5. . . . . **48** B4
Virginia Rd ME7 . . . . . . **16** C3
Vixen Cl ME5 . . . . **32** C2
Volante Dr ME10. . . . . **100** C1
Vulcan Cl ME5. . . . . **32** B3

W

Wadham Pl ME10 . . . . **107** B4
Waghorn Rd ME6 . . . . . **45** B4
Waghorn St ME4. . . . . . **23** B2
Wagoners Cl ME14. . . . **74** A4
Wain Ct ME12 . . . . **98** B1
WAINSCOTT **9** A3
Wainscott Prim Sch
ME2. . . . . **9** A2
Wainscott Rd ME2 . . . . . **9** A2
Wainscott Wlk ME2 . . . . **9** A3
Wakefield Cl ME2. . . . . **13** A2
Wakehurst Cl ME17 . . . **88** A3
Wakeley Rd ME8. . . . . . **27** A1
Wakeleys Cotts ME8 . . **36** B4
Wake Rd ME1. . . . . **30** C4
WALDERSLADE **39** C1
WALDERSLADE BOTTOM. **40** A2
Walderslade Ctr ME5 . **40** A3
Walderslade Girls Sch
ME5. . . . . **31** C1
Walderslade Prim Sch
ME5. . . . . **40** A3
Walderslade Rd ME5. . **31** C2
Walderslade Woods
ME5. . . . . **39** B2
Waldron Dr ME15 . . . . . **80** A2
Wallace Rd ME1 . . . . . . **31** B4
Wall Cl ME3 . . . . **5** A3
Wallis Ave ME15 . . . . . . **81** C1
Wall The ME10. . . . . . . **104** A3
Walmer Ct [3] ME14 . . . **65** A1
Walmer Gdns ME10 . . **103** C3
Walmer Ho ME2 . . . . **8** C1
Walmers Ave ME3 . . . . . **6** A4
Walnut Cl ME5. . . . . **32** B4
Walnut Tree Ave
ME15. . . . . **80** B1
Walnut Tree Ct ME20 . . **51** C1
Walnut Tree Dr
ME10. . . . . **103** C2
Walnut Tree La ME15 . . **80** B1
Walpole Cl ME19. . . . . . **51** A1
Walsby Dr ME10 . . . . . **101** B2
Walsham Rd ME5 . . . . . **39** C1
Walshaw Ho [2] ME14 . **65** A2
Walsingham Cl ME8 . . **43** A3
Walsingham Ho [3]
ME14. . . . . **65** A2
Walter Burke Ave
ME1. . . . . **29** B1
Walters Rd ME3 . . . . **5** B2
Waltham Rd ME8 . . . . . **25** C3
Warblers Cl [3] ME2 . . . **14** A3
Warden Cl ME16 . . . . . . **71** B4
Warden Mill Cl ME18. . **78** C3
Warden Rd ME1 . . . . . . **21** C2
Wards Hill Rd ME12 . . . **99** A4
Ware St ME14 . . . . **67** A1
WARE STREET **67** B1
Warlingham Cl ME8. . . **27** A1
WARMLAKE **92** C1
Warmlake ME17 . . . . . . **93** B1
Warmlake Bsns Est
ME17. . . . . **93** A1
Warmlake Rd ME17 . . . **92** B1
Warner St ME4 . . . . **22** C3
Warnett Ct ME6. . . . . . . **37** A1
Warnford Gdns ME15 . **80** B4
Warren Cl ME10 . . . . . **107** B4
Warren Rd ME5. . . . . . . **47** B3
Warren Wood Com Prim Sch & Language Unit
ME1. . . . . **30** C4
Warren Wood Rd
ME1. . . . . **30** C3
Warwick Cres
Rochester ME1. . . . . **20** C2
Sittingbourne ME10 . . . **103** B3
Warwick Pl ME16 . . . . . **72** A3
Washington Ho ME15 . **81** C1
Watchmans Terr [6]
ME5. . . . . **23** C2
WATERINGBURY **78** B3
Wateringbury CE Prim Sch ME18 . . . . **78** C2
Wateringbury Sta
ME18. . . . . **78** C2
Water La
Harrietsham ME17 . . . . . **86** C1
[6] Maidstone ME15. . . . **72** C4
West Malling ME19 . . . . **59** C4
Waterloo Hill ME12 . . . **99** B2
Waterloo Rd
Gillingham ME7. . . . . **23** C4
Sittingbourne ME10 . . . **103** C3
Waterloo St ME15. . . . . **72** C3
Waterlow Rd ME14. . . . **65** A2
Watermeadow Cl
ME7. . . . . **33** C2
Watermill Cl
Maidstone ME16. . . . . . . **63** B1
Rochester ME2. . . . . **14** C4
Waters Edge ME15. . . . **72** B2
Waterside ME14 . . . . . . **64** C1
Waterside Ct ME19 . . . **50** C2
Waterside Ct ME2 . . . . **15** B2
Waterside Gate ME16 . **64** C1
Waterside La ME7 . . . . **17** C3
Waterside Mews
ME18. . . . . **78** B2
Watersmeet Cl ME15. . **72** C1
Waters Pl ME7. . . . . **34** A2
Watling Ave ME5 . . . . . **24** A2
Watling Pl ME10 . . . . . **104** C1
Watling St
Gillingham ME5. . . . . **24** A2
Rochester ME2. . . . . **13** A3
Watson Ave ME5. . . . . . . **31** A1
Watsons Hill ME10 . . . **104** A3
Watts' Ave ME1 . . . . **21** C4
Watts Cl ME6 . . . . **45** C4
Watts' St ME4 . . . . **22** B3
Wat Tyler Way ME15. . . **72** C4
Waverley Ave ME12 . . . **98** C3
Waverley Cl
Chatham ME5 . . . . **41** A2
Coxheath ME17 . . . . **88** B3
WAYFIELD. **32** A4
Wayfield Com Prim Sch
ME5. . . . . **32** A3
Wayfield Rd ME5 . . . . . **32** A3
Wayne Ct ME2. . . . . **9** A2
Weald Cl ME15 . . . . **81** A2
Weald Ct ME10 . . . . . . **106** A4
Wealden Ct [5] ME5 . . . **23** B3
Wealden Way ME20 . . . **62** B3
Weatherly Cl ME1. . . . . **21** C4
Weavering Cl ME2 . . . . . **8** B2
Weavering Cotts
ME14. . . . . **74** A3
Weavering St ME14 . . . **74** B4
WEAVERING STREET **66** C1
Weavers The ME16. . . . **63** B1
Webb Cl ME3 . . . . **5** A2
Webster Rd ME8. . . . . . **26** C1
Wedgewood Cl ME16 . **63** B1
Wedgewood Dr ME5 . . **32** A3
WEEDS WOOD. **39** C3
Weeds Wood Rd ME5 . **39** C4
Weekes Ct ME11 . . . . . . **96** B2
Week St ME14 . . . . **72** C4
Weir Mill ME19 . . . . **60** C3
Welcombe Ct ME8 . . . . **35** A4
Weller Ave ME1. . . . . . . **22** A2
Wellesley Rd ME12. . . . **95** B3
Wellington Ho [6]
ME15. . . . . **81** C1
Wellington Pl ME14 . . . **64** C2
Wellington Rd
Gillingham ME7. . . . . **23** C4
Sittingbourne ME10 . . . **103** A4
Wellington Way
ME19. . . . . **68** B3
Well Rd
Maidstone ME14. . . . . . . **65** A1
Queenborough ME11 . . . **96** B2
Wells Ct ME2 . . . . **13** A1
Wells Ho ME10. . . . . . . **105** A2
Wells Rd ME2. . . . . **13** A1
Well St
East Malling ME19 . . . . . **60** B2
Maidstone ME15 & ME17. . . . . **89** A4
WELL STREET **60** B2
Well Winch Rd
ME10. . . . . **103** C3
Wemmick Cl ME1. . . . . **31** A3
Wendover Cl ME2. . . . . **29** A1
Wents Wood ME14. . . . **66** C1
Wentworth Dr
Cliffe Woods ME3 . . . . **2** B4
Gillingham ME8. . . . . **35** B3
Sittingbourne ME10 . . . **103** B3
Wentworth Ho
ME10. . . . . **103** B3
Wesley Cl ME16. . . . . . . **70** B3
West Borough Prim Sch
ME16. . . . . **71** A3
Westbourne St
ME10. . . . . **104** A2
Westbrooke Cl ME4 . . . **23** A2
Westcliff Dr ME12. . . . . **99** B4
Westcourt Rd ME7 . . . . **16** A2
West Ct [3] ME15. . . . . . **72** C1
West Dr ME5 . . . . **31** A1
Westergate Rd ME2. . . . **7** C1
Westerham Cl ME8 . . . **25** B3
Westerham Rd
ME10. . . . . **103** B1
Westerhill Rd ME17 . . . **88** B1
Western Ave
Chatham ME4 . . . . **16** A4
Halfway Houses ME12 . . **97** B3
Western Rd ME16. . . . . **71** B2
Westfield Bsns Ctr
ME2. . . . . **14** C3
WESTFIELD SOLE. . . . **49** A3
Westfield Sole Rd ME5,
ME14. . . . . **49** B4
West Gn ME10 . . . . **101** A3
West La
Sheerness ME12 . . . . . . **94** B3
Sittingbourne ME10 . . . **104** C2
Westlands Ave
ME10. . . . . **103** A2
Westlands Sch The
ME10. . . . . **103** A2
West Lane Trad Est
ME10. . . . . **104** C2
WEST MALLING. **59** C3
West Malling CE Prim Sch ME19 . . . . **59** B4
West Malling Sta
ME19. . . . . **60** A4
Westmarsh Cl ME15. . . **82** A3
Westmead ME20. . . . . . **52** A4
West Mill Rd ME20 . . . . **52** A4
WEST MINSTER. **96** B4
West Minster Prim Sch
ME12. . . . . **94** C1
Westminster Sq
ME16. . . . . **71** A4
Westmorland Cl
ME15. . . . . **81** C3
Westmorland Gn
ME15. . . . . **81** C3
Westmorland Rd
ME15. . . . . **81** C3
West Motney Way
ME8. . . . . **27** A3
Westmount Ave ME4 . . **22** C3
Weston Rd ME2. . . . . . . **14** A4
West Park Rd ME15 . . . **73** A2
West Pas ME12 . . . . **94** B3
West Rd ME4 . . . . **16** A3
Westree Ct [7] ME16. . . **72** A3
Westree Rd ME16 . . . . . **72** A3
West Ridge ME10 . . . . **103** C1
West St
Gillingham ME7. . . . . **17** A2
Harrietsham ME17 . . . . . **87** A2
Queenborough ME11 . . . **96** A2
Rochester ME2. . . . . **8** B1
Sheerness ME12 . . . . . . **94** B3
Sittingbourne ME10 . . . **104** A2
West Malling ME19 . . . . **59** B4
Westview ME4. . . . . **10** B2
Westway ME17 . . . . **88** B3
West Wlk ME16 . . . . **71** A3
Westwood Rd ME15. . . **80** B3
Westwood Wlk ME9. . **102** B4
Wetheral Dr ME5 . . . . . **40** B4
Weybridge Cl ME5 . . . . **40** C4
Wey Cl ME5. . . . . **32** C1
Weyhill Cl ME14 . . . . . . **65** C2
Wharf Rd
Gillingham ME7. . . . . **16** C3
Maidstone ME15. . . . . . . **72** A2
Whatman Cl ME14 . . . . **65** C2
Wheatcroft Cl ME10. . **105** A2
Wheatcroft Gr ME8 . . . **35** C3
Wheatear Way ME5 . . . **32** B3
Wheatfield ME19 . . . . . **50** C1
Wheatfields
Chatham ME5 . . . . **41** A2
Maidstone ME14. . . . . . . **73** C4
Wheatsheaf Cl ME15 . . **80** C4
Wheeler Pl ME18 . . . . . **68** C2
Wheeler St ME14 . . . . . **65** A1
Wheelers The ME8. . . . **34** B2
Wheelwrights The
ME17. . . . . **87** B2
Whiffen's Ave ME4. . . . **15** C1
Whiffen's Ave W ME4 . **15** C1
Whiffen Wlk ME19 . . . . **51** C1
Whimbrel Cl ME10 . . . **101** A2
Whimbrel Gn ME20 . . . **51** A2
Whimbrels The ME4 . . **10** B1
Whimbrel Wlk ME5 . . . **40** C1
Whitchurch Cl ME16 . . **72** A4
Whitcombe Cl ME5 . . . **40** C3
Whitebeam Dr ME17 . . **88** A3
White Gate ME2 . . . . . . **13** C4
Whitegate Ct ME8 . . . . **35** A1
Whitehall Rd ME10 . . **106** B4
Whiteheads La ME14. . **75** A4
White Hill Rd ME9,
ME14. . . . . **43** A1
Whitehorse Hill ME5 . . **23** B3
White Horse La ME15 . **82** B2
White House Cl ME3 . . **11** B4
Whitehouse Cres
ME1. . . . . **46** B4
Whiteleaves Rise
ME2. . . . . **19** B3
White Rd ME4 . . . . **23** A2
White Rock Ct ME16 . . **72** A3
White Rock Pl [5]
ME16. . . . . **72** A3
Whitewall Ctr ME2 . . . **15** A4
Whitewall Rd ME2 . . . . **15** A3
Whitewall Way ME2. . . **15** A3
Whiteway Rd ME11,
ME12. . . . . **96** A3
Whitmore St ME16. . . . **71** C2
Whittaker St ME4. . . . . **23** A4
Whybornes Chase
ME12. . . . . **99** A3
Whyman Ave ME4 . . . . **23** A1
Wicken Ho ME16. . . . . . **72** A4
Wickens Pl ME19 . . . . . **59** C4
Wickham Cl ME9 . . . . **102** B3
Wickham St ME1 . . . . . **22** A3
Wickham Terr ME11. . . **96** A2
Widgeon Rd ME2 . . . . . **13** A2
Wierton La ME17 . . . . . **91** A1
WIGMORE. **42** B4
Wigmore Rd ME8 . . . . . **42** B4
Wilberforce Rd ME17 . **88** C3
Wildfell Cl ME5. . . . . . . **49** A4
Wildman Cl ME8. . . . . . **43** A3
Wildwood Glade ME7 . **42** B4
Wilkinson Pl ME18. . . . **68** C2
Wilks Cl ME8 . . . . **27** B2
Will Adams Ct [9]
ME7. . . . . **16** C2
Will Adams Rdbt ME8 **24** C2
Will Adams Way ME8 . **24** C1
William Baker Ho
ME20. . . . . **62** C4
William Rd ME2 . . . . . . **19** C2
William Rigby Dr
ME12. . . . . **97** C4
William St
Gillingham ME8. . . . . **27** A1
Sittingbourne ME10 . . . **104** A2
WILLINGTON **74** A1
Willington Gn ME15. . . **81** C3
Willington St ME15 . . . **74** B2
Willis Ct ME12 . . . . **98** A1
Willis Ho ME1 . . . . **21** C4
Willow Ave ME3 . . . . . . **11** B3
Willowbank Ct [12]
ME15. . . . . **73** A4
Willowby Gdns ME8. . . **43** B4
Willow Ct ME15. . . . . . . **80** B2
Willowherb Cl ME4 . . . **10** C1
Willow Ho
[2] Chatham ME5 . . . . . . **31** C1
[8] Maidstone ME16. . . . **70** C3
Sheerness ME12 . . . . . . **94** C2
Sittingbourne ME10 . . . **105** A1
Willowmead ME19 . . . . **50** C2
Willow Rd
Larkfield ME20 . . . . **51** A3
Rochester ME2. . . . . **13** B2
Willow Rise ME15. . . . . **74** B1
Willowside ME6 . . . . . . **37** A1
Willows The
Gillingham ME8. . . . . **26** B2
Newington ME9 . . . . . . **102** B3
Sittingbourne ME10 . . . **101** A3
Willow Way ME15. . . . . **73** A3
Wilmecote Ct ME8. . . . **35** A4
Wilmington Way ME8 . **25** B2
Wilson Ave ME1 . . . . . . **31** B3
Wilson Cl ME15. . . . . . . **81** C3
Wilton Dr ME20. . . . . . . **61** B4
Wilton Terr ME10 . . . . **103** A3
Wiltshire Cl ME5. . . . . . **32** C4
Wiltshire Way [4]
ME15. . . . . **81** C4
Wimbourne Dr ME8. . . . **35** A2
Winchelsea Rd ME5. . . **32** B1
Winchester Ave ME5 . . **39** C4
Winchester Ho [3]
ME15. . . . . **81** B3
Winchester Pl [9]
ME14. . . . . **65** A1
Winchester Way ME8 . **36** A4
Windermere Dr ME8 . . **35** A3
Windermere Gr
ME10. . . . . **103** C1
Windermere Ho [4]
ME15. . . . . **81** C3
Windmill Cl ME2. . . . . . . **8** B1
Windmill Ct ME17. . . . . **90** A3
Windmill Hts ME14 . . . **75** A4
Windmill La E ME19. . . **59** C2
Windmill La W ME19 . . **59** A2
Windmill Manor ME7 . **23** C4
Windmill Rd
Gillingham ME7. . . . . **23** C4
Sittingbourne ME10 . . . **103** C4
Windmill Rise ME12. . . **99** C2
Windmill Row ME17 . . **92** C2
Windmill St ME2. . . . . . . **8** B1
Windsor Ave ME4. . . . . **22** C2
Windsor Cl ME14 . . . . . **65** B2
Windsor Ct ME7 . . . . . . **17** A1
Windsor Dr ME10 . . . . **106** A4
Windsor Rd ME7. . . . . . **17** A1
Windward Rd ME1 . . . . **21** C1
Windyridge ME7. . . . . . **24** B1
Winford Mews ME1 . . . **21** A2
Wingate Ct [7] ME10 . **104** A2
Wingham Cl
Gillingham ME8. . . . . **25** C3
Maidstone ME15. . . . . . . **82** A3
Wingrove Dr
Maidstone ME14. . . . . . . **66** B1
Rochester ME2. . . . . **14** C3
Winifred Rd ME15 . . . . **74** B3
Winstanley Rd ME12 . . **95** A3
Winston Ave ME18. . . . **69** A3
Winston Dr ME2 . . . . **9** A2
Winston Rd ME2. . . . . . **13** A1

Winterfield La ME19 . . 60 B4
Wintergreen Cl ME4 . . 10 C1
Wirrals The ME5 . . . . . . 40 A4
Wisteria Ho 11 ME15 . . 81 C3
Witham Way ME2 . . . . . 13 C3
Wittersham Cl ME5 . . . 32 B1
Wivenhoe Cl ME8 . . . . . 27 A2
Wodehouse Cl ME20 . . 51 A4
Wolfe Rd ME16 . . . . 71 A2
Wolf Ho ME4 . . . . 16 B4
Wollaston Cl ME8 . . . . . 43 A3
Woodberry Dr ME10 . 105 B1
Woodbine Cotts ME2 . 28 A1
Woodbridge Dr ME15 . 72 B1
Woodbury Rd ME5 . . . . 39 C1
Woodchurch Cl ME5 . . 32 B1
Woodchurch Cres
ME8. . . . . 25 C2
Woodchurch House
ME8. . . . . 25 C2
Wood Cl ME20 . . . . 62 B4
Woodcourt Cl ME10 . . 106 B4
Woodcut ME14 . . . . 65 A4
Woodfield Way ME3 . . . 9 B4
Woodford Gr ME18 . . . . 69 A3
Woodford Rd ME16 . . . 71 A2
Woodhall Terr ME11 . . 96 B2
Woodhurst ME5 . . . . . . 39 A4
Woodhurst Cl ME2 . . . . 19 B2
Woodland Cl ME19 . . . . 59 A4
Woodland Dr ME12 . . . 98 C3
Woodlands
Chatham ME5 . . . . 40 A2
Woodlands *continued*
Coxheath ME17 . . . . 88 A3
Woodlands Ave ME6 . . 45 A4
Woodlands Cl
Maidstone ME14. . . . . . . 65 B3
Teston ME18. . . . . 79 C4
Woodlands Ct ME5 . . . 39 C3
Woodlands Par ME20 . 62 A4
Woodlands Prim Sch
ME7. . . . . 24 C4
Woodlands Rd
Ditton ME20 . . . . 62 A4
Gillingham ME7. . . . . 24 C4
Sittingbourne ME10 . . . 105 A1
Woodlands Terr ME7 . . 24 C3
Woodland Way ME14 . . 65 B3
Woodlark Rd ME4 . . . . 10 B1
Woodlea ME19 . . . . 51 A2
Woodleas ME16 . . . . . . 70 B2
Woodpecker Glade
ME8. . . . . 35 A2
Woodpecker Rd
ME20. . . . . 51 A1
Woodrush Pl ME4 . . . . . 10 B1
Woodshole Cotts
ME9. . . . . 100 B3
Woodside ME8 . . . . 34 C2
Woodside Gdns
ME10. . . . . 106 A4
Woodside Gn ME3 . . . . . 2 B3
Woodside Rd ME15 . . . 81 A3
Wood St
Chatham ME7 . . . . 16 A2
Cuxton ME2 . . . . 19 B2
Sheerness ME12 . . . . . . 95 A3
Woodstock Rd
Rochester ME2. . . . . 14 A3
Sittingbourne ME10 . . . 106 B3
Woodview Rise ME2 . . . 7 C1
Woodville Rd ME15 . . . 72 C2
Woolaston Cl ME15 . . . 72 B1
Woolbrook Cl ME8 . . . . 27 B2
Wooldeys Rd ME8 . . . . 26 C2
Woolett Rd ME10 . . . . 103 B3
Woollett St ME14 . . . . . 65 A1
Woolley Rd ME15 . . . . . 82 A3
Woolwich Cl ME5 . . . . . 32 A3
Wootton Gn ME8 . . . . . 26 A3
Wopsle Cl ME1 . . . . 31 A3
Worcester Ave ME19 . . 68 C2
Worcester Cl
Minster (Sheppey)
ME12. . . . . 99 A2
Rochester ME2. . . . . 13 B4
Worcester Dr ME10 . . 103 C4
Worcester Rd ME15 . . . 81 B3
Wordsworth Cl ME5 . . . 32 C3
Wordsworth Rd ME14 . 65 B3
Wordsworth Way
ME20. . . . . 51 B4
Workhouse La ME15 . . 88 B4
Workhouse Rd ME17 . . 93 C1
Wormdale Rd ME9 . . . 102 B1
Worsfold Ct 5 ME15 . . 72 C1
Wotton Cl ME15 . . . . . . 81 C1
WOULDHAM. 29 C1
Wouldham All Saints CE
Prim Sch ME1 . . . . 29 B1
Wouldham Rd ME1 . . . 20 B1
Wrangleden Cl ME15 . . 81 C1
Wrangleden Rd ME15 81 C1
Wren Cl ME20 . . . . 51 A1
Wren Ind Est ME15 . . . 91 B4
Wren's Cross ME15 . . . 72 C3
Wren Way ME5 . . . . 32 B2
Wright Cl ME8. . . . . 25 C2
Wyatt Ho 1 ME2 . . . . . 14 A3
Wyatt Pl ME2 . . . . 14 A3
Wyatt St ME14 . . . . 72 C4
Wykeham Cotts ME17 . 89 B2
Wykeham Gr ME17 . . . . 84 B3
Wykeham Rd ME10 . . 105 A2
Wykeham St ME2 . . . . . 14 B4
Wyke Manor Rd
ME14. . . . . 72 C4
Wyles Rd ME4 . . . . 22 B2
Wyles St ME7 . . . . 16 C3
Wylie Ho ME3 . . . . 3 C2
Wylie Rd ME3. . . . . 5 A2
Wyllie Ct ME10 . . . . . . 100 C1
Wyndham Rd ME4 . . . . 22 B2
Wytherling Cl ME14 . . . 66 C1
Wyvern Cl
Sittingbourne
ME10. . . . . 100 C1
Snodland ME6. . . . . 45 B3
Wyvill Cl ME8. . . . . 35 B1

Y

Yalding Cl ME2 . . . . 8 B1
Yantlet Dr ME2 . . . . 12 C3
Yard The ME5. . . . . 40 B3
Yarrow Ct ME14. . . . . . . 66 C1
Yarrow Rd ME5 . . . . 39 C4
Yeates Dr ME10. . . . . . 101 B2
Yelsted La ME14 . . . . . . 49 B3
Yeoman Ct ME14. . . . . . 75 A3
Yeoman Dr ME7 . . . . . . 24 C1
Yeoman Ho ME1 . . . . . . 22 A4
Yeoman La ME14 . . . . . 75 A4
Yeoman Pk ME15 . . . . . 74 C2
Yeoman Way ME15. . . . 74 C2
Yevele Cl ME11 . . . . 96 B2
Yew Rd ME3. . . . . 11 B3
Yew Tree Cl
Aylesford ME20 . . . . 52 C1
Chatham ME5 . . . . 41 A1
Yew Tree Cotts ME14 . . 55 A1
Yewtree Ho 2 ME1 . . . 22 A4
Yewtree Ind Est
ME20. . . . . 52 B2
Yew Tree Pl ME7 . . . . . . 42 B1
Yoke Cl ME2. . . . . 14 B4
Yokosuka Way ME7,
ME8. . . . . 18 A3
York Ave
Chatham ME5 . . . . 39 C3
Gillingham ME7. . . . . 23 C4
York Hill ME5. . . . . 23 C2
York Rd
Maidstone ME15. . . . . . . 73 B2
Rochester ME1. . . . . 21 C3
Youens Pl ME3 . . . . 6 B3
Ypres Dr ME10. . . . . . . 101 A3

Z

Zetland Ave ME7. . . . . . 24 B2
Zillah Gdns ME8 . . . . . . 34 C2

List of numbered locations

In some busy areas of the maps it is not always possible to show the name of every place.

Where not all names will fit, some smaller places are shown by a number. If you wish to find out the name associated with a number, use this listing.

The places in this list are also listed normally in the Index.

10
C1 2 Sunset Square

Page number | Grid square | Location number | Place name

14
A3 1 Wyatt Ho
2 Hillside Ct
3 Warblers Cl
B3 1 Newark Ct
2 Aveling Ct
3 Friary Pl
4 Grove Ct
B4 1 Alexander Ct
2 Eppe Cl
3 Florence St
4 Archway Ct
5 Sandra Ct
6 St Michael's Ct
C4 1 Bill Street Rd
2 Mayfair
3 Christian Ct
4 Pemberton Sq
5 Evelyn Ho

16
A2 1 Victory Manor
2 Temeraire Manor
3 Barfleur Manor
4 Middle St
5 Camperdown Manor
6 River St
7 Dawson Ct
8 McCudden Row
9 Perie Row
10 Pleasant Row
11 Lendrim Cl
13 Flaxman Ct
14 Manor Ho
15 Esmonde Ho
16 Conway Hall
C2 1 Padstow Manor
2 Camborne Manor
3 Redruth Manor
4 Penryn Manor
5 Austell Manor
6 Tintagel Manor
7 Grand Ct
8 Deane Ct
9 Will Adams Ct
10 Chatsworth Rd
11 Phoenix Ct
C3 1 Augusta Cl
2 Annvera Ho
3 Sunderland Ho
4 Latimer Pl
5 Hunters Ct
6 King William Rd
7 Forsyth Ct

21
C1 1 Bakenham Ho
2 Leake Ho
3 Transom Ho
4 Spinnaker Ct

22
A4 1 Rosemary Ct
2 Yewtree Ho
3 Huxley Ct
4 New Covenant Pl
5 Five Bells La
6 Robin Ct
B4 1 Bingley Rd
2 St Bartholomew's Terr
3 Hospital La
4 St Bartholomew's La
5 Medway Heights
6 Hamond Hill
7 Cressey Ct
8 Lumsden Terr
9 Ordnance Terr
C3 1 Orchard Villas
2 Claremont Way
3 Mount View Ct
4 Silver Hill Gdns
5 Coronation Flats
6 River View Cl
7 Saunders St
C4 1 Cambridge Terr
2 Meeting House La
3 Clover St
4 Millwood Ct
5 James St
6 Copperfield Ho
7 Springfield Terr
8 Berkeley Mount
9 Lansdowne Ct

23
A3 1 Otway Terr
2 Leopold Rd
B2 1 Portland St
3 Bright Rd
4 Cobden Rd
5 Sailmakers Ct
6 Evorg Ho
7 Caulkers Ho
8 Endeavour Foyer The
B3 1 Seymour Rd
2 Hare St
3 Short St
4 Piccadilly Apartments
5 Wealden Ct
6 Ocelot Ct
7 Leonard Rd
8 Constitution Hill
C2 1 Marrians View
2 Connaught Mews
3 Christchurch Ct
4 Chickfield Gdns
5 Rhodes Ho
6 Watchmans Terr

26
C1 1 Crevequer Chambers
2 Rainham Sh Ctr
3 Gresham Cl
4 Harrison Ct
5 Maplins Cl
6 Signal Ct
7 Suffolk Ct

31
1 Saffron Way
2 Willow Ho
3 Pine Ho
4 Rowan Ho
5 Hawthorn Ho
6 Bleakwood Rd

32
A3 1 Shalfleet Cl
2 Snodhurst Ho

35
C4 1 Sunshine Ct
2 Stratford La
3 Oast Ho The
4 Marlborough Ho

5 Appletree Ct
6 St Margaret's Ct

39

B4 1 Lavender Cl
2 Aspen Way
3 Honeysuckle Cl
4 Gentian Cl
C4 1 Mallow Way
2 Jasmine Cl
3 Harebell Cl
4 Rosemary Cl
5 Linden Ho
6 Oak Ho

45

B4 1 Portland Pl
2 Ostlers Ct
3 Delamere Gdns
4 Lambert Mews

51

A4 1 Southey Way
2 Cronin Cl
3 Blake Dr
4 Coleridge Cl
5 Chesterton Rd
6 Browning Cl
7 Barrie Dr
8 Christie Dr
B1 1 Carnation Cl
2 Larkspur Cl
4 Lilac Gn

64

B1 1 Mews The
2 Ruth Ho
3 Carrie Ho
4 Claire Ho
5 Daniel Ho
C3 1 Gagetown Terr
2 Gilbert Terr

65

A1 1 Mandeville Ct
2 Crundale
3 Walmer Ct
4 Priory Gate
5 Starnes Ct
6 Kilburn Ho
7 Ladbrooke Ho
8 Lambard Ho
9 Winchester Pl
10 Lower Boxley Rd
A2 1 Telford Ho
2 Walshaw Ho
3 Walsingham Ho
A3 1 Aden Terr
2 Barbados Terr
3 Canada Terr
4 Norway Terr
5 Malta Terr
6 Libya Terr
7 Kenya Terr
8 Honduras Terr

70

C3 1 Springwood Cl
2 Catherine Cl
3 Magnolia Ho
4 Hawthorne Ho
5 Chestnut Ho
6 Birch Ho
7 Rowan Ho
8 Willow Ho
9 Almond Ho
10 Oakapple Ho
11 Langley Ho
12 Kingswood Ho
13 Harrietsham Ho

72

A2 1 Millers Wharf
2 Millstock Terr
3 Meadows The
4 Allnutt Mill Cl
5 Bank View
A3 1 Newton Cl
2 Orchard Pl
3 Oldchurch Ct
4 Rycault Cl
5 White Rock Pl
6 Victoria Ct
7 Westree Ct
A4 1 Birnam Sq
2 Rocky Hill Terr
3 Birkdale Ct
4 Swallow Ho
5 Robin Ho
6 Swift Ho
7 Peacock Mews
8 Kentish Ct
B4 3 Market Colonnade
4 Market Bldgs
5 Royal Star Arc
6 Middle Row
7 Medway Ho
C1 1 Kings Row
2 North Ct
3 West Ct
4 East Ct
5 Worsfold Ct
6 Basil Terr
7 Stoneacre Ct
C3 1 Cutbush Almshouses
2 Cutbush Ho
3 Greenhithe
4 College Wlk
5 Corrall Almshouses
6 College Ct
7 Bychurch Pl
C4 1 Newlyn Ct
2 Bloomsbury Wlk
3 Cutbush Almshouses
4 Colman Ho
5 Edger Pl
6 Water La
7 Dukes Wlk
8 Granada Ho
9 Granada St

73

A4 1 Cutbush and Corrall Ct
2 Day Ho
3 Haynes Ho
4 Gulland Ho
5 Pine Ho
6 Clifford Ho
7 Ellis Ho
8 River Bank Cl
9 Belmont Ct
10 Lenham Ct
11 Kingfisher Ct
12 Willowbank Ct

81

B3 1 Rochester Ho
2 Canterbury Ho
3 Winchester Ho
4 Salisbury Ho
B4 1 Kendall Pl
2 Rayleigh Ho
3 Lavender Ho
4 Clover Terr
5 Sheringham Ho
6 Burdock Ho
C1 1 Bombay Ho
2 Madras Ho
3 Calcutta Ho
4 Nagpur Ho
5 New Delhi Ho
6 Wellington Ho
7 Durban Ho
8 Pretoria Ho
9 Dunedin Ho
10 Auckland Ho
11 Christchurch Ho
12 Swan Apartments
13 Kingfisher Apartments
14 Mallard Apartments
15 Grebe Apartments
C3 1 Shropshire Terr
2 Huntingdon Wlk
3 Derwent Ho
4 Windermere Ho
5 Ullswater Ho
6 Dunkeld Ho
7 Inverness Ho
8 Glasgow Ho
9 Aberdeen Ho
10 Primrose Ho
11 Wisteria Ho
12 Lichfield Ho
13 Chaucer Cl
14 Belfast Ho
15 Londonderry Ho
16 Dublin Ho
C4 1 Chilham Ho
2 Dover Ho
3 Dunster Terr
4 Wiltshire Way

82

A1 1 Capetown Ho
2 Johannesburg Ho
3 Heron Apartments
4 Reading Ho
5 Grosvenor Ho
6 Livingstone Wlk
7 Thanet Ho
8 Nelson Ho
9 Belvedere Ho
10 Balmoral Ho
A2 1 Aintree Ho
2 Ascot Ho
3 Chepstow Ho
4 Folkstone Ho
5 Titchfield Cl
6 Thirsk Ho
7 Doncaster Cl
8 Havant Wlk
9 Plumpton Wlk
10 Fareham Wlk
11 Denstead Wlk
12 Andover Wlk
13 Groombridge Sq

104

A2 1 Dover St
2 Fountain St
3 Freeman Ct
4 Mockett Ct
5 Church St
6 Pembury Ct
7 Wingate Ct
8 Cloisters The
9 Middleton Ct
10 Hawthorn Ho
A3 1 Alexander Ct
2 Pear Tree Alley
3 Periwinkle Ct
4 Bishop Ct
5 Tannery Ct
6 Rigden's Ct
7 Giles Young Ct
B2 1 Crescent St
2 Forum The
3 Lion Yd
4 Does Alley
5 St Michael's Cl
6 Riverbourne Ct
C2 1 Goshawk Ho
2 Merlin Ho
3 Falcon Ho
4 Kestrel Ct
5 Crown Quay La
6 Ronalds Ct
7 Plaza Ct
8 Centre 2000
9 Turrets The

105

A2 1 Jarrett's Ct
2 Homeview Terr
3 Homeview
4 Smeed Cl
5 Prices Ct
6 Harkness Ct
7 Dickson Ct
8 Poulsen Ct
9 Thomas Ct

PHILIP'S MAPS

the Gold Standard for drivers

◆ **Philip's street atlases cover every county in England, Wales, Northern Ireland and much of Scotland**

- ◆ Every named street is shown, including alleys, lanes and walkways
- ◆ Thousands of additional features marked: stations, public buildings, car parks, places of interest
- ◆ Route-planning maps to get you close to your destination
- ◆ Postcodes on the maps and in the index
- ◆ Widely used by the emergency services, transport companies and local authorities

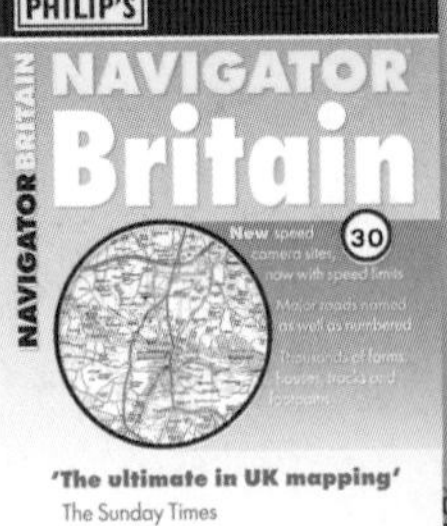

For national mapping, choose **Philip's Navigator Britain** the most detailed road atlas available of England, Wales and Scotland. Hailed by Auto Express as 'the ultimate road atlas', the atlas shows every road and lane in Britain.

Street atlases currently available

England
Bedfordshire
Berkshire
Birmingham and West Midlands
Bristol and Bath
Buckinghamshire
Cambridgeshire
Cheshire
Cornwall
Cumbria
Derbyshire
Devon
Dorset
County Durham and Teesside
Essex
North Essex
South Essex
Gloucestershire
Hampshire
North Hampshire
South Hampshire
Herefordshire Monmouthshire
Hertfordshire
Isle of Wight
Kent
East Kent
West Kent
Lancashire
Leicestershire and Rutland
Lincolnshire
London
Greater Manchester
Merseyside
Norfolk
Northamptonshire
Northumberland
Nottinghamshire
Oxfordshire
Shropshire
Somerset
Staffordshire
Suffolk
Surrey
East Sussex
West Sussex
Tyne and Wear
Warwickshire
Birmingham and West Midlands
Wiltshire and Swindon
Worcestershire
East Yorkshire Northern Lincolnshire
North Yorkshire
South Yorkshire
West Yorkshire

Wales
Anglesey, Conwy and Gwynedd
Cardiff, Swansea and The Valleys
Carmarthenshire, Pembrokeshire and Swansea
Ceredigion and South Gwynedd
Denbighshire, Flintshire, Wrexham
Herefordshire Monmouthshire
Powys

Scotland
Aberdeenshire
Ayrshire
Dumfries and Galloway
Edinburgh and East Central Scotland
Fife and Tayside
Glasgow and West Central Scotland
Inverness and Moray
Lanarkshire
Scottish Borders

Northern Ireland
County Antrim and County Londonderry
County Armagh and County Down
Belfast
County Tyrone and County Fermanagh

How to order Philip's maps and atlases are available from bookshops, motorway services and petrol stations. You can order direct from the publisher by phoning **0190 828503** or online at **www.philips-maps.co.uk**
For bulk orders only, e-mail philips@philips-maps.co.uk